FRAMING CONVERGENCE WITH THE GLOBAL LEGAL ORDER

This interdisciplinary book explores the concept of convergence of the EU with the global legal order. It captures the actions, law-making and practice of the EU as a cutting-edge actor in the world promoting convergence 'against the grain'. In a dynamic 'twist' the book uses methodology to reflect upon some of the most dramatically changing dimensions of current global affairs.

Questions explored include: who and what are the subjects and objects of convergence as to the EU and the world? How do 'court-centric' and less 'court-centric' approaches differ? Can we use political science and international relations as 'service tools'?

Four key themes are probed:

- framing EU convergence;
- global trade against convergence;
- the EU as the exceptional internationalist; and
- positioning convergence through methodology.

Volume 100 in the Series Modern Studies in European Law

Modern Studies in European Law

Recent titles in this series:

Social Legitimacy in the Internal Market: A Dialogue of Mutual Responsiveness
Jotte Mulder

The EU Better Regulation Agenda: A Critical Assessment
Edited by Sacha Garben and Inge Govaere

Administrative Regulation Beyond the Non-Delegation Doctrine:
A Study on EU Agencies
Marta Simoncini

The Interface Between EU and International Law: Contemporary Reflections
Edited by Inge Govaere and Sacha Garben

The Rise and Decline of Fundamental Rights in EU Citizenship
Adrienne Yong

The Court of Justice and European Criminal Law:
Leading Cases in a Contextual Analysis
Edited by Valsamis Mitsilegas, Alberto di Martino and Leandro Mancano

The EU as a Global Regulator for Environmental Protection:
A Legitimacy Perspective
Ioanna Hadjiyianni

Citizenship, Crime and Community in the European Union
Stephen Coutts

Critical Reflections on Constitutional Democracy in the European Union
Edited by Sacha Garben and Inge Govaere

Constitutional Law of the EU's Common Foreign and Security Policy: Competence and Institutions in External Relations
Graham Butler

The Juridification of Individual Sanctions and the Politics of EU Law
Eva Nanopoulos

Sixty Years of European Integration and Global Power Shifts:
Perceptions, Interactions and Lessons
Edited by Julien Chaisse

Fundamental Rights and Mutual Recognition in the Area of Freedom,
Security and Justice: A Role for Proportionality?
Ermioni Xanthopoulou

Law and Judicial Dialogue on the Return of Irregular Migrants
from the European Union
Edited by Madalina Moraru, Galina Cornelisse and Philippe De Bruycker

For the complete list of titles in this series, see 'Modern Studies in European Law' link at www.bloomsburyprofessional.com/uk/series/modern-studies-in-european-law

Framing Convergence with the Global Legal Order

The EU and the World

Edited by
Elaine Fahey

•HART•
OXFORD • LONDON • NEW YORK • NEW DELHI • SYDNEY

HART PUBLISHING

Bloomsbury Publishing Plc

Kemp House, Chawley Park, Cumnor Hill, Oxford, OX2 9PH, UK

1385 Broadway, New York, NY 10018, USA

HART PUBLISHING, the Hart/Stag logo, BLOOMSBURY and the Diana logo are trademarks of Bloomsbury Publishing Plc

First published in Great Britain 2020

A catalogue record for this book is available from the British Library.

Library of Congress Cataloging-in-Publication data

Names: Fahey, Elaine, editor.

Title: Framing convergence with the global legal order : the EU and the world / edited by Elaine Fahey.

Description: Oxford, UK ; New York, NY : Hart Publishing, Bloomsbury Publishing Plc, 2020. | Series: Modern studies in European law ; volume 100 | Includes bibliographical references and index.

Identifiers: LCCN 2020020711 (print) | LCCN 2020020712 (ebook) | ISBN 9781509934379 (hardback) | ISBN 9781509934393 (ePDF) | ISBN 9781509934386 (EPub)

Subjects: LCSH: Foreign trade regulation—European Union countries. | Foreign trade regulation—United States. | Investments, Foreign—Law and legislation—European Union countries. | Free trade—European Union countries. | Law—European Union countries. | Transatlantic Trade and Investment Partnership. | Foreign trade regulation.

Classification: LCC KJE6791 .F73 2020 (print) | LCC KJE6791 (ebook) | DDC 341.242/2—dc23

LC record available at https://lccn.loc.gov/2020020711

LC ebook record available at https://lccn.loc.gov/2020020712

ISBN: HB: 978-1-50993-437-9
ePDF: 978-1-50993-439-3
ePub: 978-1-50993-438-6

Typeset by Compuscript Ltd, Shannon

FOREWORD

At a time of waning multilateralism and retreat in international cooperation, it is important that scholars ask fundamental questions about the global order and the norms that sustain this order. Over the last two decades, a rich global governance literature has emerged to examine various areas of law and policy that have transnational implications or require global solutions. While this literature has discussed many challenges associated with international institutions and supranational governance – whether related to deficiencies in democracy, accountability, or efficiency of these global governance mechanisms – the foundations of this global order have never been questioned to the extent they are today. The threat of the unraveling of the World Trade Organization's (WTO) dispute settlement mechanism or the Paris climate accord; the departure of the United Kingdom from the European Union; and the rise of nativist parties with populist anti-globalisation agendas in several countries are but some examples of the political environment that has become increasingly hostile to global institutions.

The contributions in this volume engage with the challenges underlying the global legal order while revealing forces that continue to drive convergence despite those challenges. The authors offer compelling accounts of the drivers behind, and the implications of, global convergence, by examining cutting-edge economic issues involving trade, investment, public procurement, economic sanctions, export controls, foreign lending and fiscal policy. They engage with important policy questions surrounding labour law, data protection, climate change, human rights, as well as asylum and refugee law. In doing so, they bring together a rich set of examples from multiple areas of law under a unifying theme of global convergence. This collective inquiry is all the more valuable given the authors' deployment of different methodologies and examination of convergence through various channels: multilateralism, regionalism, bilateralism, and unilateralism. The authors further show how convergence can follow both mandatory and voluntary mechanisms and how the main actors driving convergence can be both governments as well as private actors. Finally, the authors acknowledge the many benefits associated with global convergence but also engage with the criticism leveled against the efforts to write uniform rules for the countries with different needs and circumstances.

The focus of this important volume is on the role of the European Union – the champion of global convergence and international institutions – and its efforts to shape the global legal order while navigating the increasingly hostile and uncooperative international environment. Of all the major actors on the world stage, the EU has in the last decades been most committed to the international legal order, seeking to preserve the institutions and pursue treaty-based cooperation.

This raises many important questions, including why the EU has adopted this role, how it seeks to foster global convergence, if it has been successful in this endeavour, and whether the EU's efforts should be applauded or criticised.

There are likely several reasons that explain the EU's central role in the building of a global legal order based on cooperation and convergence. Being itself a construct of multilateralism, the EU can be seen as having an existential interest in preserving multilateralism as a foundation for governing international relations. Beyond this, global convergence has also served the EU's core economic interests as the EU has often been successful in promoting convergence around its own regulatory standards. When the EU successfully exports its own standards – whether through multilateral institutions, bilateral treaties or unilateral actions – the EU can level the playing field and thereby protect the competitiveness of the European industry. This allows the EU to defend its social preferences such as environmental protection without compromising the ability of its domestic industries to compete internationally. The EU also benefits from convergence by obtaining greater legitimacy for its rules. If foreign companies and governments emulate EU standards, those standards are seen as having a wider appeal and thus greater legitimacy. The EU's trade partners are also less likely to challenge the legality of EU standards before institutions such as the WTO if those standards are already replicated globally. Less tangibly, being the global standard-setter serves the EU in expanding its soft power and validating its regulatory agenda, both at home and abroad.

The EU's efforts to promote a global legal order may also be motivated by its desire to replicate its own governance model and regulatory experience abroad. The EU's own successful experience in creating a common market has encouraged it to pursue a global order based on those same rules. More regulation in the EU has meant more integration, predictability, stability, and ultimately, more economic growth. This has fostered a belief that an extensive regulatory convergence is similarly needed to preserve global public goods. In recent years, the challenges surrounding the international order have provided an additional incentive for the EU to assume a greater role in promoting global norms. The US's decision to retreat from multilateral institutions in particular has left a vacuum that the EU has felt compelled to – and has been uniquely positioned to – fill. A scandal such as the Snowden revelations that exposed extensive US government surveillance activities worldwide is just one example of incidents that have further increased the EU's resolve to act as the global guardian of personal data and the right to privacy. Finally, the EU's growing awareness that its relative share in the world economy is declining while Asia's is rising may have similarly contributed to the EU's desire to cement its rules globally at the time when the EU still has the power to do so.

The EU not only has the will but also the means to promote global convergence, and has done so through various channels. It has often entrenched its norms abroad through bilateral or multilateral treaties, most often by negotiating an extensive array of preferential trade agreements that influence the type of regulations that the EU's trade partners must adopt in order to secure access to the single market. The EU has also shaped global norms through its participation in international institutions and standard-setting bodies. It has engaged in transgovernmental networks that provide less formal yet potentially influential settings for transferring EU's regulatory frameworks abroad. Finally, European courts have contributed towards global convergence by issuing judgments that serve as templates for foreign courts. These three mechanisms – politics, bureaucratic dialogues and courts – offer complementary and at times powerful avenues for the EU's norms and regulations to shape the global regulatory environment. Yet all of them also have important limits as they depend on the cooperation by foreign governments as well as effective implementation, both of which are not always readily available.

In addition to these cooperative mechanisms of promoting convergence, the EU has been notably successful in inducing convergence unilaterally. The EU has always seen international cooperation and multilateralism as the preferred path towards global convergence. Yet when those efforts at international cooperation have failed, the EU has increasingly acted as a 'contingent unilateralist' – advancing its preferred norms unilaterally. For example, when global climate change negotiations have faltered, the EU has gone ahead regulating greenhouse gas emissions in the EU, while indicating its readiness to impose a carbon tariff on trading partners that do not follow suit. Similarly, two decades ago, the EU advocated for a WTO agreement on competition policy but its inability to secure such an agreement has not prevented the EU from becoming the world's leading competition enforcer with the power to regulate both domestic and foreign companies with stringent standards and invasive remedies.

Often the EU's unilateral norm-setting takes place quietly under the radar. This passive power that the EU exercises is known as the 'Brussels Effect'. The Brussels Effect refers to the EU's ability to unilaterally regulate global markets. Without the need to resort to international institutions or seek other nations' cooperation, the EU has the unique ability among nations today to promulgate regulations that shape the global business environment, elevating standards worldwide and leading to a notable Europeanisation of many important aspects of global commerce. Different from many other forms of global influence, the Brussels Effect entails that the EU does not need to impose its standards coercively on anyone – market forces alone are often sufficient to convert the EU standard into the global standard as multinational companies voluntarily extend the EU rule to govern their global operations. In this way, the EU wields significant, unique and highly penetrating power to transform global markets, including through its ability to set the standards in diverse areas such as competition regulation, data protection, online hate speech, consumer health and safety or environmental protection.

While it is less commonly disputed that the Brussels Effect is real and effective, its normative implications are more contested. The EU's ability to unilaterally shape the world in its image can be viewed as normatively desirable or undesirable, depending on whom one asks. The EU's critics emphasise how the EU's unilateralism constrains the regulatory space of foreign governments and thus undermines their ability to respond to the needs and preferences of their own citizens to whom they are politically accountable. But the Brussels Effect arguably also generates many benefits abroad. Often those benefits are diffused across a large consumer base that experiences a cleaner environment and enhanced product safety, an enhanced control over their personal data, and less exposure to hateful discourse online, to name a few. Of course, everyone does not share the same preferences and would not trust the government – even that of their own, let alone a foreign government – to make the choices for them in this regard. In the end, whether the Brussels Effect is positive or negative depends on individual preferences that vary across policy areas, individuals' socioeconomic and cultural backgrounds, values and ideologies.

More generally, global convergence of any kind can be viewed as positive or negative. Many global problems require global solutions. There are enormous gains from frictionless trade under uniform rules or from a collective commitment to reduce greenhouse gas emissions to mitigate climate change. Yet all convergence may not be welfare-enhancing. There can be significant costs to convergence if it takes place around a standard that in hindsight proves to be suboptimal. Divergent regulatory regimes allow for experimentation, which can be critical for learning and ultimately provide a pathway towards better policy. A push for global rules can undermine such beneficial experimentation. Global convergence embodied by existing international institutions has also generated a backlash that cannot be dismissed wholesale. Instead, the retreat of multilateral institutions forces us to face serious questions about the uneven benefits of globalisation. The discontent surrounding global institutions today should be viewed as a call to action for politicians, inviting them to think harder on how to re-establish the normative foundations for the global legal order. It should also spur global companies to action, using their private power to drive convergence in issues such as climate change mitigation or a digital environment that safeguards personal privacy. Finally, it is a call for academics to ask new and harder questions about the global legal order, explain why cooperation has failed, and generate new and innovative ideas on how losers from globalisation can be compensated, and how trust in global institutions can be rebuilt.

The chapters that comprise this volume will chart the way for this conversation by engaging with a set of intriguing questions and advancing a debate that is both timely and important. They form a major contribution in their own right, bringing analytical clarity and exciting new perspectives to the pressing legal and policy questions of the day. At the same time, they act as a foundation for an even larger debate and as an invitation for other academics, policy experts and practitioners – across disciplines and subject-matter areas – to join the conversation.

Anu Bradford
Henry L Moses Professor of Law and
International Organisation
Columbia Law School
29 January 2020

CONTENTS

LIST OF CONTRIBUTORS

Aakriti Bhardwaj, University of Nottingham School of Law, Marie Curie Early Stage Researcher and PhD Student in the framework of the Horizon 2020 Marie Curie network on European Union TIP.

Anu Bradford, Henry L Moses Professor of Law and International Organisation, Director, The European Legal Studies Center Columbia Law School.

Paul James Cardwell, Professor of Law, University of Strathclyde.

Michelle Egan, Professor and Jean Monnet Chair *ad personam*, School of International Service, American University.

Elaine Fahey, Jean Monnet Chair of Law & Transatlantic Relations, Professor of Law, Institute for the Study of European Law, City Law School, City University of London and co-PI of EUTIP MSC-ITN.

Magdalena Forowicz, Swiss Ministry of Justice (Federal Office of Justice); Faculty of Law, University of Zurich.

Mauro Gatti, Assistant Professor, University of Bologna.

David Henig, European Centre for International Political Economy, Director of the UK Trade Policy Project.

Frank Hoffmeister, Head of Unit at the European Commission implementing the EU's Trade Defence Policy and Professor of International Economic Law at the Institute for European Studies, Brussels.

Machiko Kanetake, Assistant Professor of Public International Law University of Utrecht.

Jeff Kenner, Chair of European Law at University of Nottingham School of Law and a Vice President of the European Inter-University Centre for Human Rights and Democratisation in Venice and co-PI of EUTIP MSC-ITN.

Isabella Mancini, City Law School, City University of London, Marie Curie Early Stage Researcher with the H2020 EUTIP network and a PhD candidate at City Law School.

Fernanda Nicola, Professor of Law at the Washington College of Law, American University and Director of the Programme on International Organisations Law and Diplomacy.

Jed Odermatt, Lecturer in Law and convenor of Institute of Law and Global Affairs, City Law School, City University of London.

Enrico Partiti, Assistant Professor in Transnational Regulation & Governance at Tilburg Law School, Tilburg University.

Laura Pascual Matellán, Researcher in Criminal Law at the University of Salamanca.

Francesco Pennesi, Erasmus Law School Rotterdam, Marie Curie Early Stage Researcher with the EUTIP network and a PhD Fellow at Erasmus University.

Kornilia Pipidi-Kalogirou, University of Speyer, Marie Curie Early Stage Researcher with the EUTIP network and a PhD candidate at the University of Speyer.

Juan Santos Vara, Associate Professor and Jean Monnet Chair in EU External Action, University of Salamanca.

Gabriel Siles-Brügge, Associate Professor in Public Policy, University of Warwick.

Ramses A Wessel, Chair of European Union Law, University of Groningen.

Introduction: On Framing Convergence of the EU with the Global Legal Order

ELAINE FAHEY

While convergence may not be a political term that captures the state of current global politics of trade wars, disruption of multilateralism and withdrawal from international organisations, it is at the heart of not an inconsiderable scholarship on international law. Convergence may also not yet be at the heart of European law and politics scholarship, but it is arguably one of the most accurate ways of depicting the EU as an actor in the world today – the lone ranger of the global legal order. This book proceeds on the premise that the EU epitomises the concept of convergence and is arguably one of the ultimate convergence actors in contemporary global politics. The EU remains a driving force explicitly behind multilateralism and a rules-based international order.[1] Indeed, as the European Council has recently stated, convergence can also have teeth: 'The EU will promote its own unique model of cooperation as inspiration for others … But to better defend its interests and values and help shape the new global environment, the EU needs to be more assertive and effective'.[2] Emmanuel Macron has called for convergence to be a European 'action': 'Europe is not a second-tier power. Europe in its entirety is a vanguard: it has always defined the standards of progress. In this, it needs to drive forward a project of convergence rather than competition …'.[3]

In this political rhetoric or mantra, EU convergence can be understood as a social ambition in a convergence of policies which has a levelling effect.[4] Yet it is not neutral and may have complex 'teeth'. It is not inhibitive of EU divergence or prohibitive of complex assertions of defence of interests.[5]

[1] European Council, European Council Conclusions EUCO 9/19 (Brussels) 20 June 2019, 10.

[2] *Ibid* 11.

[3] Emmanuel Macron, 'Dear Europe, Brexit Is a Lesson for All of Us: It's Time for Renewal' *The Guardian*, 4 March 2019, www.theguardian.com/commentisfree/2019/mar/04/europe-brexit-uk (last accessed 24 February 2020).

[4] See also K Linos, *Democratic Foundations of Policy Diffusion* (Oxford University Press, 2013).

[5] Simon Evenett, 'We Can also Do Stupid': The EU's Response to American First Protectionism' (2019) Robert Schuman Centre for Advanced Studies Research Paper 2019/52, https://papers.ssrn.com/sol3/papers.cfm?abstract_id=3424862 (last accessed 24 February 2020).

Richard Baldwin, in his masterly work on 'The Great Convergence' as to information technology and the new globalisation, portrays convergence as a 'process' bringing together the world – whilst also obliterating many traditional roles and jobs. It is a form of convergence of means and ends.[6] This *process-oriented* study thereof is arguably less positive in the sense of 'progressive'. Yet it is progressive in its technical and descriptive account thereof and also a metaphor for destruction, renewal and innovation. On the other hand, there is a 'homogeneity' at the heart of the understanding of convergence, particularly in its more scientific forms and it is this element to which this book project turns.

Scholarship, from international economic law,[7] international investment law,[8] international human rights law[9] to sources of Public International Law (PIL),[10] increasingly frames new shifts in sources, practice and jurisprudence, as an explicit narrative of 'convergence'.[11] The previously dominant narrative of *fragmentation* had been conducted within PIL often in a highly court-centric sense, focussing upon sources, their implementation and interpretation thereof.[12] Convergence means many things to many people, but appears to generally capture the direction of the relationship between organisational practices and law-making.[13] Convergence is arguably more broad-brush than fragmentation,[14] depicting coherence and unity between legal regimes from a methodological perspective, through the study of law-making and practice.[15] It depicts everyday actions of convergence, at meta and micro level and can be understood to be a part of any legal system, arguably as a Hegelian dialectic process.[16] Its combination of both

[6] Richard Baldwin, *The Great Convergence: Information Technology and the New Globalization* (Harvard University Press, 2016).

[7] See Jürgen Kurtz, *The WTO and International Investment Law: Converging Systems* (Cambridge University Press, 2016).

[8] Daniel Behn, Szilárd Gáspár-Szilágyi and Malcolm Langford (eds), *Adjudicating Trade and Investment Law: Convergence or Divergence?* (Cambridge University Press, 2020).

[9] Buckley M Carla, Alice Donald and Philip Leach (eds), *Towards Coherence in International Human Rights Law: Approaches of Regional and International Systems* (Brill/ Nijhoff, 2017); Christine Evans, *The Right to Reparation in International Law for Victims of Armed Conflict* (Cambridge University Press, 2014) Ch 12; Magdalena Forowicz, *The Reception of International Law in the European Court of Human Rights* (Oxford University Press, 2010); Meryll Dean 'Bridging the Gap: Humanitarian Protection and the Convergence of Laws in Europe' (2014) 20 *European Law Journal* 34.

[10] Mads Andenæs and Eirik Bjorge (eds), *A Farewell to Fragmentation: Reassertion and Convergence in International Law* (Cambridge University Press, 2015).

[11] *Ibid* (outlining convergence as a response to fragmentation, Ch 1, p 1).

[12] *cf* Mads Andenæs and Eirik Bjorge 'Introduction: From Fragmentation to Convergence in International Law' in Andenas and Bjorge, *ibid.*

[13] *cf* Eirik Bjorge, 'The Convergence of the Methods of Treaty Interpretation' in Andenæs and Bjorge, *ibid* 498 and Philippa Webb, 'Factors Influencing Fragmentation and Convergence in International Courts' in Andenæs and Bjorge *ibid* 146.

[14] See, eg, Kurtz (n 7).

[15] See, eg, Dean (n 9); Graham Cook, 'The Use of Object and Purpose by Trade and Investment Adjudicators: Convergence without Interaction' in Behn, Gáspár-Szilágyi and Langford (n 8).

[16] Andenas and Bjorge (n 10).

organisational practice and law-making appears to provide a flexible narrative of the broadest 'positive' evolution of legal orders.[17] It also enables legal narratives to be articulated focussing upon the direction of their evolution, but also includes cross-fertilisation of fields across disciplines and subjects in its midst. Convergence increasingly appears presented as a factually evident state of affairs. It takes place in law and rule-making procedures, courts and tribunals, for legal, economic, political and even sociological reasons.[18] Its methods span, inter alia, the empirical, histography, comparative law, comparative public law methods with much potential and whilst it can be 'court-centric', it is not necessarily always so.[19]

In an international law context, convergence can be viewed – perhaps pejoratively – as wishful thinking. Many international law scholars would prefer, all else being equal, to find evidence of structural or substance convergence and it is frequently a by-line for a 'progressive' narrative. As Alvarez notes, its complexity often means that legal scholars are loath to define it and instead to seek evidence of its obviousness.[20] Indeed, there are many terms which are synonyms for convergence and it becomes a vast literature of sub-disciplines to seek out commonly used narratives or terms for convergence.[21] Convergence in this context may also mean more holistic views of policies, themes or subjects, eg that trade and human rights or global trade and social justice should converge substantively in their thematic engagement, doctrines and ordering.[22] Convergence here can be commonly defined as a process or state of converging, somewhere between a noun and a verb.[23] This activeness arguably accords well with organisational practice case studies.

[17] *cf* Stephen W Schill, *The Multilateralisation of International Investment Law* (Cambridge University Press, 2009); Joseph HH Weiler (ed), 'Epilogue, Towards a Common Law of International Trade' in *The EU, WTO and the NAFTA: Towards a Common Law of International Trade*? (Oxford University Press, 2001).

[18] For example, Kurtz (n 7) at 1.5; Bjorge (n 13); Webb (n 13).

[19] See Kurtz (n 7) 28–29.

[20] Karl P Sauvant and José Enrique Alvarez, 'International Investment Law in Transition (Introduction)' in Jose Enrique Alvarez and Karl P Sauvant, with Kamil Gerard Ahmed and Gabriela del P Vizcaino (eds), *The Evolving International Investment Regime: Expectations, Realities, Options* (Oxford University Press, 2011) xxxi–xlii, https://ssrn.com/abstract=3167096 (last accessed 24 February 2020).

[21] '… authors take complexity as their byword, even at the risk of alienating readers looking for reassuring evidence of any of the positive-sounding synonyms for convergence, such as "harmonization," "unification," "Europeanization," "internationalization," or "defragmentation".' See Jose Enrique Alvarez, 'Epilogue: "Convergence" is a Many-Splendored Thing' in Daniel Behn, Szilárd Gáspár-Szilágyi and Malcolm Langford (eds), *Adjudicating Trade and Investment Disputes: Convergence or Divergence?* (Cambridge University Press, Forthcoming) iCourts Working Paper Series No 165 6 https://papers.ssrn.com/sol3/papers.cfm?abstract_id=3418891 (last accessed 24 February 2020).

[22] Harlan Grant Cohen, 'What is International Trade Law for?' (2019) 113 *American Journal of International Law* 326.

[23] Oxford English Dictionary, www.oxfordlearnersdictionaries.com/definition/english/convergence (last accessed 24 February 2020).

The EU's place in the global legal order can be understood as arguably a highly dynamic and complex process which is the antithesis of static. Arguably, convergence fits neatly with understandings of EU global actorness and global ambitions. A form of convergence ethic dominates the EU's actions. Convergence has a prevalence to it but yet may be also said not to be well understood in the context of EU studies and political science with respect to its legal peculiarities. Analytical blind spots may not be easily 'taxonomised'.[24] Arguably, today much convergence of EU law and the EU in the world comes from the mimicking/ transfer/ copying or integration of European rules, practices or ideals into other third party contexts, from the formal to the informal, direct to the indirect. Yet who and what should be the form of study of these analytical blindspots of the world? Some argue that the Court of Justice of the European Union (CJEU) is the main agent of *divergence* practices as to internal matters, internal competences and internal views of EU integration. From a legal perspective, placing the Court inside and outside of the narrative can have a dramatic impact on convergence narratives.[25] It also may depend upon a particular moment in (political) space and (political) time(s). For example, the EU's responses to the demise of the World Trade Organization (WTO) have been to formulate divergence therefrom.[26] The most significant dimension of the new political strategy of the European Commission of late 2019 is a 'Green New Deal', predicated ultimately upon *convergence* of all EU policies as to the environment.

This book project seeks to delve into the forms and action component of EU convergence and isolate its meaning and plot its direction in context. All authors subscribe to the notion of the EU as an exceptional convergence actor within the global legal order. The book isolates the *methodology* of this exceptionalism as a normative and descriptive state of affairs. All authors subscribe to the idea that the EU, in its own unique way, increasingly practices and preaches convergence in the global legal order with an explicitness, openness and directness which is sometimes at odds with international law and/ or international politics.

The book has three distinct sections – corresponding to the following themes: framing the EU as a global convergence actor; the global legal order against convergence; and when is EU law and policy more 'inside-out' than 'outside-in'? These are now outlined in the following paragraphs.

[24] Jacco Bamhoff, 'Comparative Dysfunctionalism: How to Study Comparative Global "Legal Failure" in Elaine Fahey, Jed Odermatt and Elizabeth O'Loughlin (eds), *Whose Global Law? Comparative, Regional and Cyber Approaches to Law-Making* (2019) City Law School (CLS) Research Paper No 2019/02, http://openaccess.city.ac.uk/id/eprint/22706/ (last accessed 24 February 2020).

[25] R Bellamy, *A Republican Europe of States* (Cambridge University Press, 2019) 173.

[26] European Commission, 'Statement by Commissioner for Trade Phil Hogan on the Suspension of the Functioning of the WTO's Appellate Body' (Brussels, 10 December 2019), https://trade.ec.europa.eu/doclib/press/index.cfm?id=2089 (last accessed 24 February 2020).

I. Framing the EU as a Global Convergence Actor

Despite the provenance of convergence in PIL and related sub-fields, convergence is argued here to have a powerful resonance with how we understand the EU as an emerging global legal actor, in the post-Lisbon era.[27] The EU increasingly sets new international agendas, standards and rules and is referred to in a vast literature as a 'norm promoter'.[28] The EU also appears as a distinctively consistent internationalist in a world shifting towards populism, and localism, both within and beyond the EU.[29] It even has an express mission to be a 'good' global governance actor, differing from many other international organisations and states. It has done this, in particular, through consistently advocating the creation of *new* international institutions.[30] It is of significance because it shows its highly orchestrated alignment with the international legal order in law-making. Yet, independently there is also a widespread use of external norms now in EU internal law-making in a wide variety of fields of law which will be developed here further,[31] such that it can be argued that this can also be understood as a form of regular practised convergence at the heart of EU law. There is also widespread use of external norms in CJEU jurisprudence, albeit which varies from field to field and according to competence.[32] These organisational practices and law-making techniques may indicate substantial practices of convergence. Nonetheless, the esoteric nature of the EU challenges much about how institutions are understood to act within the global legal order.

As Cremona and Scott outline, there is a significant challenge in formulating EU global action and its effects.[33] This is particularly the case with respect to some of the most complex topics of global governance, eg migration, data, the environment where the EU seeks to have global effects and lead global change despite asymmetric competence and institutional formulations therein. To similar effect, the amount of case studies of Bradford's iconic 'Brussels Effect' work make it a formidable task to go from the descriptive to the normative as a phenomenon – which they purposefully avoid.[34] Convergence, arguably, is not well understood as to EU integration studies, divergence is arguably mainstream in political science,

[27] See Weiler (n 17) for a historical view.

[28] See the iconic Ian Manners, 'Normative Power Europe: A Contradiction in Terms?' (2002) 40 *Journal of Common Market Studies* 235.

[29] John G Ikenberry, 'The End of Liberal International Order?' (2018) 94 *International Affairs* 7; Karen E Smith, 'The European Union in an Illiberal World' (2017) 116 *Current History* 83.

[30] Samuel Issacharoff, 'Democracy's Deficits' (2017) 85 *University of Chicago Law Review* 485.

[31] Elaine Fahey, 'Joining the Dots: External Norms, AFSJ Directives and the EU's Role in Global Legal Order' (2016) 41 *European Law Review* 105.

[32] See, eg, Jan Wouters, Geert De Baere, Jed Odermatt and Thomas Ramopoulos (eds), *Oxford Reports on International Law in EU Courts* (Oxford University Press, 2016).

[33] Marise Cremona and Joanne Scott (eds), *EU Law Beyond EU Borders The Extraterritorial Reach of EU Law* (Oxford University Press, 2019).

[34] Anu Bradford, *The Brussels Effect: How the European Union Rules the World* (Oxford University Press, 2020).

for example as to views on Europe and its status quo, ie as to disintegration. The movement of EU rules beyond borders is not ultimately well understood as an interdisciplinary ideal.[35]

There is a body of literature on 'EU rules beyond its borders' which is influenced by 'Europeanisation' scholarship.[36] Yet, this exact same scholarship is now also immersed in rationalising de-Europeanisation predicated upon Brexit and the challenges of the empirics of evolving Europeanisation here remains to be seen.[37] One of the chief advantages of studying the legal dimension of EU rules beyond their borders is precisely that EU law is underpinned by an internationalist tendency. From an EU law perspective, homogeneity is a problematic outcome of EU global convergence potentially where it is unending, unstructured or there is too much of it in the wrong entities, places or peoples. One of the most controversial aspects of EU law remains its tendency to provoke convergence with entities not seeking, wanting or striving for the active components of convergence. Litigation as to territory often shows the 'worst' side of the global reach of EU law or projected convergence.[38] It is precisely the active component of convergence here as an idea that attracts the most controversy. Naturally, the CJEU has downplayed any understanding of extra-territoriality in this context.[39]

Yet, territory and global reach constitute one of the most murky dimensions of convergence.[40] In the EU's manifold new trade negotiations, the place of convergence is never openly advertised or advanced. As Young states, there is much misconception concerning the scientific contours of convergence and what is envisaged and proposed with third country partners and contrasted with what is agreed as an outcome.[41] To some extent, then, to explore the methodology of convergence as action alone is possibly to denigrate the EU's success or lacks sophistication. After all, convergence is nowadays highly institutionalised, often involving a plethora of actors, agencies, entities and multilateralism. To isolate action here is arguably impossible.

[35] Karina Shyrokykh and Davilė Rimkutė, 'EU Rules Beyond its Borders: The Policy-specific Effects of Transgovernmental Networks and EU Agencies in the European Neighbourhood' (2019) 57 *Journal of Common Market Studies* 4.

[36] *Ibid.*

[37] Frank Schimmelfpennig, 'Brexit: Differentiated Disintegration in the European Union' (2018) 25 *Journal of European Public Policy* 1154; Frank Schimmelfennig and Thomas Winzen, 'Grand Theories, Differentiated Integration' (2019) 26 *Journal of European Public Policy* 1172.

[38] See Jed Odermatt (n 32) Ch 2 and Cardwell and Wessel in chapter 8 of this volume: C-266/16 *Western Sahara Campaign UK v Commissioners for Her Majesty's Revenue and Customs and Secretary of State for Environment, Food and Rural Affairs* (Grand Chamber, 27 February 2018) or Case C-363/18 *Organisation Juivre Europeenne Vignoble Psagot Ltd v Ministre de l'Economie et des Finances* (Grand Chamber, 12 November 2019).

[39] *Western Sahara, ibid.*

[40] Joanne Scott, 'The New EU Extra-territoriality' (2014) 51 *Common Market Law Review* 1343.

[41] Alasdair Young, 'The European Union as a Global Regulator? Context and Comparison' (2015) 22 *Journal of European Public Policy* 9.

II. A Global Legal Order *against* Convergence?

Despite the wording of Art 21 of the Treaty on European Union (TEU) mandating to the EU an entitlement to participate in the global legal order, in general, the external environment is less hospitable to its ambitions.[42] Only the Member States and not the EU have full membership in most international organisations.[43] This renders convergence as an organisational practice of the EU self-evidently complex to unpack as an idea, a practice or a methodology. The path of the EU in the global legal order is not simplified through its newfound legal personality, or consistency and unity as legal goals.[44] The EU has also been confined in its treaties to specific arrangements for the Food and Administration Organization (FAO), the European Bank for Reconstruction and Development (EBRD), the WTO, *Codex Alimentarious* and the Hague Conference of Private International law.[45] It is not a member of the UN, International Labour Organisation (ILO), World Bank, International Monetary Fund (IMF) or Council of Europe for reasons of sovereignty of the Member States as much as the rules of the organisations themselves.[46] While far from coherent, however, the EU and its Member States continue to co-exist and function together, globally. While the EU is often referred to as a 'global actor', its 'actorness' is not always shared across disciplines, vexed by its complex structure.[47] To speak of 'EU convergence' is thus easily contested, challenged and asserted to be incoherent in the world. It demonstrates conceptually the need to reflect more broadly on the specific parameters of 'EU convergence'. There are many examples of the EU seeking to lead organisational practice and engage in evident convergence activities within the global legal order despite its challenges, which are explored next.

[42] See Geert De Baere and Essa Paassivirta, 'Identity and Difference: The EU and the UN as Part of Each Other' in Henri de Waele and Jan-Jaap Kuipers (eds), *The Emergence of the European Union's International Identity – Views from the Global Arena* (Brill, 2013) 21, 26.

[43] Diana Panke, 'The European Union in the United Nations: an Effective External Actor? (2014) 21 *Journal of European Public Policy* 1050.

[44] See Anthony Arnull and Damien Chalmers (eds), *Oxford Handbook of European Union Law* (Oxford University Press, 2015) Parts I, II and VII.

[45] Article 220 TFEU: '1. The Union shall establish all appropriate forms of cooperation with the organs of the United Nations and its specialised agencies, the Council of Europe, the Organisation for Security and Cooperation in Europe and the Organisation for Economic Cooperation and Development. The Union shall also maintain such relations as are appropriate with other international organisations.' Article X1 of the Marrakesh Agreement 1994 (WTO); Constitution of the Food and Agriculture Organization of the United Nations (2017) I-II Article 6. See also Christine Kaddous (ed), *The European Union in International Organisations and Global Governance: Recent Developments* (Hart Publishing, 2015).

[46] Jan Klabbers, 'The Rise of International Organisations' in *An Introduction to International Institutional Law*, 2nd edn (Cambridge University Press, 2009) 16; Frank Hoffmeister, 'Outsider or Frontrunner? Recent Developments under International and European Law: On the Status of the European Union in International Organizations and Treaty Bodies' (2007) 44 *Common Market Law Review* 41.

[47] Elaine Fahey (ed), *The Actors of Postnational Rule-Making: Conceptual Challenges of European and International Law* (Routledge, 2015) Introduction, especially section 2.1; Chad Damro, Sieglinde Gstohl, Simon Schunz (eds), *The European Union's Evolving External Engagement* (Routledge, 2017).

Convergence in organisational practice is arguably well represented through the EU's efforts to create *new* international institutions. The EU is committed in its treaties to being an internationalist as a matter of law and to pursuing multilateral solutions, eg pursuant to Art 21 TEU.[48] Significant entities in the world currently wish to leave or threaten to leave or defund several international organisations (eg African Union from the International Criminal Court (ICC), the UK from the Council of Europe and the EU, the US from the WTO, NATO or UN, amongst others).[49] The EU, by contrast, has and continues to support the development of both existing and new international organisations through institutionalisation. For example, in the European context, the EU has a recent history of promoting and 'nudging' institutional multilateral innovations, from the ICC,[50] a UN Ombudsman[51] to a Multilateral Investment Court[52] in its efforts to promote internationalisation, accountability, legitimacy and the rule of law as a broad global agenda. This committal to internationalisation is expressed through the EU's advancement of institutionalisation.[53] Institutionalisation here is understood as the processes of formalisation and stabilisation of procedures, institutional coordination and the ability of individual actors to influence institutional development, through and by institutions.[54] The EU's newest latest EU Global Strategy on Foreign and Security Policy is also of note here.[55] The central thesis of the Strategy is that the EU will promote a 'rules-based' global order with multilateralism as its key principle and with the United Nations at its core.[56] It seeks to promote a significant amount of unity and consistency across actors and institutions, both inside-out and outside-in, converging around the leading multilateral organisations of the world, in particular the UN.[57] The EU's commitment to the external multilateral legal order explicitly through converging around multilateral institutions and developing new institutions might also be seen to be evidence of concrete convergence. Such processes of institutionalisation may thus be understood as EU convergence *around and into* international norms and institutions. It takes place contrary to the perceived wisdom of renowned international relations

[48] *cf* Bruno De Witte, 'The European Union as an International Legal Experiment' in Grainne de Búrca and Joseph HH Weiler (eds), *The Worlds of European Constitutionalism* (Cambridge University Press, 2012).

[49] Smith (n 29); Ikenberry (n 29).

[50] See International Criminal Court, *The Rome Statute of the International Criminal Court* (1998) 2, United Nations, Treaty Series 2187 No 38544.

[51] See: UN Ombudsman: See United Nations Security Council, UNSC Resolution 2083 (2012).

[52] See Multilateral Investment Court: See Council of the European Union, 'Negotiating Directives for a Convention Establishing a Multilateral Court for the Settlement of Investment Disputes' 12981/17 (Brussels, 20 March 2018).

[53] Elaine Fahey, *Institutionalisation beyond the Nation State: Transatlantic Relations, Data, Privacy and Trade Law* (Springer Law, 2018) 4–8.

[54] *Ibid* 6–8.

[55] 'Shared Vision, Common Action: A Stronger Europe' (Global Strategy for the European Union's Foreign and Security Policy, June 2016).

[56] *Ibid* 3.5.

[57] See 'Shared Vision, Common Action' (n 55).

theorists about post-World War US hegemony, that it is easier to maintain existing international institutions than to create new ones.[58]

The EU treaties and EU law jurisprudence alike reveal a quantifiable panoply of interests, actors, objects and subjects, scattered across them. Convergence may link into these new inquiries and research contexts. It may further the interaction of EU and PIL as an interaction of subjects and objects manifesting.

A. Thematic Reflections for Contributors

Areas of reflection posed to contributors were as follows:

- Does it resonate with shifting debates as to the EU as a norm promoter across fields and sub-disciplines?
- To what extent is the study of the EU as a global actor predominantly qualitative? Is empirical research increasingly data driven or less so?
- How should we understand the EU as an internationalist in this new era?
- How do we understand a broader view of the EU's approach, both now and going forward? Which institutions are most appropriate to study?
- Yet how can we achieve a more nuanced understanding of the widespread vision of the EU as a positive and committed internationalist? Its place within the UN system is often studied autonomously or apart from broader depictions of its role within international organisations, although as a research agenda both are vibrant.
- Can it ever be a veritable 'convergence' actor?
- Is it merely a socialised participant of the global legal order?

Despite the trends outlined in PIL scholarship, it is arguably not an accurate description of the current state of the international political economy. There has never been a more contentious moment in time for the study of convergence in global trade.[59] Many understand the global legal order based upon institutionalised multilateralism and convergence around institutionalised multilateralism in the field of threat to be under threat.[60] Instead, the American isolationism in the era of withdrawal from the Paris Agreement in 2020 and blockages as to the

[58] See generally Robert O Keohane, *After Hegemony Cooperation and Discord in the World Political Economy* (Princeton, 2005).

[59] Sophie Meunier and Jean-Frederic Morin, 'No Agreement is an Island: Negotiating TTIP in a Dense Regime Complex' in Jean-Frederic Morin, Tereza Novotná, Frederik Ponjaert and Mario Telò (eds), *The Politics of Transatlantic Trade Negotiations: TTIP in a Globalized World* (Routledge, 2015) Ch 14.

[60] Anthea Roberts, *Is International Law International?* (Oxford University Press, 2017); Samuel Issacharoff, 'Democracy's Deficits' (2018) 85 *University of Chicago Law Review* 485; Karen Smith, 'The European Union in an Illiberal World' (2017) 116 *Current History* 83.

existence and reform of the WTO form the new status quo. However, the US nonetheless renewed its interest in regionalism in North America, ie through the Agreement between the United States of America, the United Mexican States, and Canada (USMCA). Arguably, different forms of institutional convergence are emerging, perhaps on a significantly less grander or visionary scale beyond the state.

A rare joint appearance by the IMF, the World Bank and the WTO in 2017 saw an unlikely confluence of global institutions seeking to appear jointly to defend global trade against rising anti-global trade sentiments and rising American protectionism.[61] Its exceptionalism has faded fast. Others seek different forms of convergence. In the Namur Declaration, a broad collation of distinguished scholars in political economy, international economic governance, economics and law, sought to change the parameters of how international economic agreements must be negotiated (or renegotiated), moving away from an era where the negotiation of international trade agreements was an esoteric study for a small number of doctrinal lawyers and diplomats.[62] This refashioned interest in the configurations of global trade has occurred for a reason, perhaps beyond mere rising economic nationalism and a backlash against globalisation by ordinary citizens and workers. The role of the 'mega-regionals' as initiatives of change by the Obama-led administration, which amounted to a pivot outside of the WTO, has invited much reflection on its meaning going forward for the future of global trade and multilateralism, which arguably would have seen convergence on a vast scale *outside* of the WTO to a degree. The individual institutional units of the global trading order face uncertain and difficult times, for example, the WTO but predominantly as to non-tariff barriers. The efforts of the Trump administration to derail appointments to the Appellate Body (AB) body, has resulted in an unprecedented dilemma as to the functioning of the body and the rule of law going forward.[63]

The new era of economic nationalism and protectionism is a particularly difficult moment in globalisation for the Nation State and a difficult background tableau for the study of convergence. It is perhaps a longer-term step towards better and even deeper globalisation and arguably progress thereto, when we reflect on the history of globalisation.[64] In this regard, convergence may not be viewed as anything other than downwards and raises the question as to its understanding at global, regional and national levels.[65]

[61] 'Global Institutions Mount Joint Defence of Trade Benefits' *Financial Times*, 2017.

[62] Namur Declaration (5 December 2016), http://declarationdenamur.eu/doc/NamurEN.pdf (last accessed 26 February 2020).

[63] Gregory C Shaffer, 'A Tragedy in the Making? The Decline of Law and the Return of Power in International Trade Relations' (2018) *Yale Journal of International Law*, UC Irvine School of Law Research Paper No 2018-64 at SSRN: https://ssrn.com/abstract=3292361 (last accessed 26 February 2020).

[64] See, eg, Susanne Berger, 'Globalization and Politics' (2000) 3 *Annual Review of Political Science* 43.

[65] See Anu Bradford, 'The Brussels Effect' (2012) 107 *Northwestern University Law Review* 1.

Nonetheless, there has also been an important move to an era of deeper trade agreements in recent times and to address concerns about globalisation, moving towards more sophisticated agreements beyond mere tariff-setting arrangements in a form of grand convergence. The recent movement towards WTO + agreements (ie, adding in data, labour standards, the environment, etc and beyond conventional trade agreements) has put pressure upon the idea of what legitimately can be in an international trade agreement and what forms of additional matters can be subject thereto. However, anti-corruption, data protection, money laundering, statistic harmonisation and tax evasion constitute the issues of this new era. The WTO lacks rules concerning data flows or cyber matters and lacks provisions on a host of matters, for example e-commerce, thereby lacking a clear jurisdictional mandate to deal with many significant contemporary disputes as new actors therein.[66] The new parameters of international engagement in trade on the horizon in these new agreements have been subject to critique, for example, those who deny any legitimacy to such forms of cooperation beyond 'true trade'.

The EU has the convergence of good norms at the centre of its latest trade policies on globalisation, pitching globalisation as a positive force for change, inside and outside of the EU.[67] Here, multilateralism is important, for example, evidenced through EU reform of WTO, Agenda 2030 and the full integration of Sustainable Development Goals into EU policy. An EU Global Adjustment Fund has evolved to assist displaced workers – addressing employment and social consequences of globalisation. EU convergence of good norms is also centre-stage in new generation free trade agreements (FTAs), for example, requiring partner participation in the Paris Agreement or Trade and Sustainable Development chapters. Also, civil society fora and domestic advisory groups are increasingly significant entities in new generation FTAs and in important chapters there, for example EU-Korea FTA, 2011; the Comprehensive Economic and Trade Agreement (CETA) 2016; EU-Mexico FTA.[68] The depth of this convergence still remains to be seen and is under review and evaluation, albeit significant lack of transparency exists as to who forms civil society in EU trade law and how they should be selected.

As indicated above, the EU's responses to the demise of the WTO has been to formulate divergence but also reform from within and without – thus a complex but useful example of how the EU always speaks the language of both convergence and divergence through its own unilateralism.[69]

[66] See Mark Wu, 'The China Inc. Challenge to the Global Trade Governance' (2016) 57 *Harvard Journal of International Law* 261, 263–64.

[67] European Commission, 'Reflection Paper on Harnessing Globalisation' (2017) COM (240) 10 May 2017.

[68] See Bhardwaj and Kenner in chapter 13 of this volume.

[69] See European Commission (n 26).

B. Thematic Reflections for Contributors

Areas of Reflection posed to contributors were as follows:

- How do convergence shifts relate to other fields and branches? Do international relations or political science or political economy mirror this shift? Is convergence more normative than descriptive?
- Is convergence as to trade compatible with debates in other disciplines and subjects? What place is there for convergence in legal and non-legal scholarship going forward?
- What is a useful temporal limit upon convergence if any? How should we frame this limit?
- Does convergence constitute a useful methodological tool of an integration rime within regimes?
- Is convergence a useful methodological device or is it solely normative?
- Does convergence help us/ allow us to avoid getting lost in exceptionalist rhetoric of the EU as a global legal actor?
- Is convergence an enabling 'positive' vision? Is it unduly positive? Does its method overcrowd its normative usefulness?

III. Framing External Effects: Is EU Law more 'Inside-out' than 'Outside-in'?

Contributors to this book project seek to pin down the complexity of external effects and EU law as a methodological challenge. They do this by developing an organic understanding from practice and the methods used by the contributors drawing from a range of case studies in external relations, human rights, the area of freedom, security and justice (AFSJ) and international economic law. Contributors are asked to isolate the phenomena of convergence in their key instructions, by self-selecting their method (historical, empirical, qualitative, quantitative, etc). Most contributors do not proceed from a purely empirical basis or indeed from case studies or case law, but rather attempt to outline narratives of convergence as they arise in the evolution of a subject, eg EU public procurement law or EU trade agreements and labour law. This entails that there are important methodological challenges of external effects tacked here and explicitly. This question of methodology is usually overlooked in the development of global effects.

Contributors will be asked to pinpoint temporal periods. The mapping period is thus normative salient and distinctive. 'Mapping' may ostensibly lack normative ambition. Yet contrariwise, it has the merit of enabling the dynamism of convergence to be identified through temporal isolation in select case studies and is thus essential to capture the zeitgeist of convergence and its application to the EU in the world. It is thus essential that the contours of mapping are more clearly communicated and explicitly in case studies themselves after appropriate direction. Convergence is mainly 'court-centric' by method in most other disciplines: case studies here will chart new unpublished studies of areas and fields of law, more holistically and not explicitly limited to court-centric views of mapping which will accordingly render it novel. Convergence is now a contemporary political ambition of the EU of much topicality. The volume charts the theoretical development thereof and is thus timely. Latest debates about the methods and methodology of EU and PIL are largely data driven[70] or advocate deeper law-in-context methods or historical studies,[71] but are often heavily 'court-centric'.[72] Arguably, the study of the EU as a global actor in law is predominantly institutionally-focussed and is arguably in need of a more diverse methodology to reflect organisational practice and law-making. Isolated studies of the use/ citation of PIL in EU law in legislation or jurisprudence arguably provide a limited snap-shot of practice and need to be pursued in a range of areas and time-periods to have meaning as a methodology. EU legal scholarship has tended to adopt a highly 'court-centric' approach to the EU and the global legal order. This is not to denigrate such an approach – nor is PIL so apart – which should be clearly stated – but rather to emphasise that organisational practice *and* EU law-making look rather different to the isolated study of international law *in* CJEU case law or *in* law-making alone or apart. In other words, a resolutely non-court-centric look at EU action in the global legal order may be considered to be understudied. As a broader study, the EU's attempts at institutional convergence in the global legal order in a systemic sense, beyond its own law-making, are deserving of attention and may be viewed as distinctive and 'apart' in the conventional study of EU international relations law. However, the EU's efforts, effects and intents as to convergence are arguably deserving of being unpacked more carefully, being different to specific organisational practices or the use and citation of PIL in law-making. This enables a systemic view of EU action to be considered, going to the heart of convergence.

To paraphrase seminal work on empirical research, some questions can be answered more easily than others and convergence must be acknowledged to be paradoxically a verb, adverb and noun if legal literature is to be understood correctly.[73] The direction of 'activeness' is problematic here – how time-bound should case studies be? Legal scholarship also has undergone a profound shift in recent times where qualitative empirical research has become far more common and regularised. This shift has the capacity to alter the nature of scholarship and

[70] See, eg, Wolfgang Alschner, Joost Pauwelyn and Sergio Puig, 'The Data-Driven Future of International Economic Law' (2017) 20 *Journal of International Economic Law* 217.

[71] See Rob Van Gestel and Hans-Wolfgang Micklitz, 'Why Methods Matter in European Legal Scholarship' (2014) 20 *European Law Journal* 292, 313–16.

[72] *cf* Michelle Egan, 'Toward a New History in European Law: New Wine in Old Bottles?' (2013) 28 *American University International Law Review* 1223.

[73] See Paul Holland, 'Statistics and Causal Inference' (1986) 81 *Journal American Statics Association* 945.

the direction of its development.[74] Yet how empirical are convergence debates? The tendency of lawyers to rely upon cases, statutes, political debates and other sources in an unsystematic fashion and armed only with doctrinal tolls for analysis is increasingly thought to be highly limiting given how qualitative methods are particularly well suited for analysing evidence and development arguments. Legal scholars may miss, as a result, the ability to answer profound and critical research questions through their more 'limited' methodology. Legal scholars have typically depended rather heavily on doctrinal analysis to conduct research. Such doctrinal tools invariably have lead legal scholars to focus upon cases from, for example, the highest national courts, which introduce a significant ruling that breaks from precedent. To be sure, it is compelling as a technique. However, its utility to make sound generalisations about law and society may be said to be overrated. Moreover, one may state that systematic reviews are not at the core of legal research scholarship, a method typically employed in medical and psychological sciences. While lawyers regularly make claims about law and case law, a minimal number of cases will often satisfy a research question or problem. With this method, a researcher must clearly state the question to be answered, must justify it and be clear about how to define it, must explain any weighting that is to be applied and needs to justify and be transparent about it in a manner which analyses the sample cases to be reviewed, all of which have considerable force and logic to them.[75] Convergence is embedded usually in a narrative and indicates a 'participation' journey. However, its subjects and objects are easily shrouded in the broader narrative. It arguably requires more transparent methodology than ever.

To speak of convergence of legal orders also presupposes a lot about legal ordering beyond the State which this book seeks to explicitly outline. There is also an inherent uncertainty in the depiction of law beyond the Nation State which is challenging from a scientific perspective, and which needs more explicit identification methodologically. More cooperation beyond the Nation State amongst a variety of actors and international organisations may be overwhelmed by discord and betwixt by a need to run faster to stand still. Much of the structure of contemporary legal, political and economic theory is about a concern of the meanings of what may be termed here 'triangulation'. For example, fragmentation, verticalisation and constitutionalisation have been said to 'form the holy tribute of international legal debate in the early 21st century' according to leading public international law theorist Klabbers.[76] Sovereignty, territory and jurisdiction are the greatest challenges to law

[74] Katerina Linos and Melissa Carlson, 'Qualitative Methods for Law Review Writing' (2017) 84 *University of Chicago Law Review* 101; Rob Van Gestel, Hans-Wolfgang Micklitz and Miguel Poiares Maduro, 'Methodology in the New Legal World' (1 May 2012) Working Paper, EUI LAW, 2012/13, http://hdl.handle.net/1814/22016 (last accessed 26 February 2020.

[75] See William Baude, Adam S Chilton and Anup Malani, 'Making Doctrinal Work More Rigorous: Lessons from Systematic Reviews (2017) 84 *University of Chicago Law Review* 37.

[76] See generally Jan Klabbers, Anne Peters and Geir Ulfstein, *The Constitutionalisation of International Law* (Oxford University Press, 2009) Ch 1.

across borders in the global legal age; self-determination, democracy and hyper-globalisation are the 'trilemma', which cannot co-exist in the contemporary legal order.[77] Ordering thus matters for those engaging in accounts of the contemporary legal and political order. Yet does a concern to simplify and engage with a broader audience activate reductionism? At each and every one of the so-called stages of conventional legal theory, ie the semantic, jurisprudential, doctrinal and judicial review stages, convergence invariably poses incredible challenges for 'ordering'.[78]

There is a certain practical and political vulnerability posed by international and transnational law which is arguably at the heart of much EU global convergence. Interactions between two legal orders conventionally focus upon the national reception of formally binding treaties and customary international law. It is far more complex to restate the international reception of national law or the domestic reception of non-binding standards formulated by transnational bodies.[79] The vulnerability posited here specifically lies in the interactions between public and private international law and other private and public standards. Non-binding transnational standards can be very persuasive, for example. As a result, national deference to transnational standards may result in the scientific integrity of transnational standards being contested and invoked so as to avoid domestic political debates. In the case of scientific standards, there can be a fragility to scientific and regulatory standards, subject to contrariwise both defence and contestation. This results in a question of methodological ordering. Where do we begin from? Where do we end our analysis of convergence? Which direction does our analytical prism take us? If we begin from the perspective of the Nation State, we frame the question in one way; to then begin from the perspective of law beyond the State, we take matters another way, and so on.

'Knowledge' is a critical challenge to our understanding of convergence in the global legal order. Many of its prime case studies are not necessarily very transparent or obvious or easy to understand. From the perspective of many scholars, convergence beyond the State is neither fully known nor agreed (especially not as an autonomous agreed data set).[80] Information technology, particularly as to automated decision-making and artificial intelligence, also challenges our views

[77] Hannah Buxbaum, 'Territory, Territoriality and the Resolution of Jurisdictional Conflict' (2009) *American Journal of Comparative Law* 631; Dani Rodrik, *The Globalisation Paradox* (Oxford University Press, 2012) 88.

[78] See Ronald Dworkin, *Justice in Robes* (Harvard University Press, 2006) 9ff.

[79] Yuval Shany, *Regulating Jurisdictional Relations between National and International Courts* (Oxford University Press, 2007); Anthea Roberts, 'Comparative International Law? The Role of National Courts in Creating and Enforcing International Law' (2011) 60 *International and Comparative Law Quarterly* 57; Machiko Kanetake and Andre Nollkaempfer (eds), *The Rule of Law at the National and International Levels: Contestations and Deference* (Hart Publishing, 2016); Dinah Shelton (ed), *International Law and Domestic Legal Systems: Incorporation, Transformation and Persuasion* (Oxford University Press, 2011).

[80] However, many political scientists in particular are currently working on mapping international delegations of authority, international power or are mapping international court and tribunal delegations. This work has the potential to significantly shift legal understandings of the global legal order, eg Eugénia da Conceição-Heldt, ERC Project, DELPOWIO.

on convergence and will require development going forward.[81] Social science scholars are attempting to map borders in the age of globalisation using global satellite technology and attempting to document transnational border crossings. They question whether globalisation stimulates thicker or thinner borders.[82] What is clear is that the shared consensus that legal distinctions between private law and public law (eg between the regulation of persons, things and actions, contract law and property law, family law and inheritance law and constitutional and administrative law) have been significantly eroded in several legal systems because of, inter alia, globalisation and supranationalism. Yet precise agreed data is difficult to pinpoint.[83] In this sense, methodology matters.

IV. Outline of Contributions in this Volume

In Part I, *Framing EU Global Convergence*, Frank Hoffmeister sets out in chapter one that the European Union (EU) is one of the world's major trading powers, accounting for 15 per cent in the world share of global exports and imports. He argues that it has held considerable influence in the WTO and brings a lot of negotiating power to the table when it engages in bilateral FTAs. Since 2006, when Commissioner Mandelson announced the 'Global Europe' strategy, it has indeed concluded numerous new 'Deep and Comprehensive Free Trade Agreements' (DCFTAs) with partners such as Korea, Canada or Singapore. Moreover, between 2013 and 2017 it attempted to bring about Transatlantic Trade and Investment Partnership (TTIP) with the United States. With the election of President Trump in November 2017, however, this project came to an end. Primarily, the EU's DCFTAs embody the joint will of the parties to liberalise trade between them. Against that background, the question whether the EU's practice sets global standards is very pertinent. The chapter focusses upon CETA and considers whether the EU's DCFTA's are the most progressive ones, which other nations would like to imitate? Could they serve as global standards that inspire new multilateral conventions? Or are they more a symbol of European exceptionalism that mainly serve European interests and cannot be regarded as a global blueprint?

In chapter two, Jed Odermatt argues that in recent years, many EU policies have been criticised for being 'unilateral', 'extra-territorial', or even violating international law. In areas such as climate change mitigation, financial market regulation, data protection and human rights, the EU's unilateral approach often stems, not from a disengagement with multilateralism, but from an inability to make progress through multilateral institutions. Its push for greater convergence

[81] Baldwin (n 6).

[82] See Beth Simmons et al, Harvard Institute of Quantitative Social Science project on borders and globalisation (on file).

[83] Ernst-Ulrich Petersmann, *Multilevel Constitutionalism for Multilevel Governance of Public Goods: Methodology Problems in International Law* (Hart Publishing, 2017).

towards its own values and norms can be seen as also weakening the multilateral system. The chapter first discusses the EU's commitment to multilateralism, which is enshrined in the EU Treaties and a part of the EU's foreign policy. It then turns to fields of law where the EU has been challenged and criticised for pursuing a unilateral approach, focusing on climate change policy, data protection and the use of autonomous restrictive measures (sanctions). It argues that 'EU unilateralism' can be understood in terms of divergence and convergence: on the one hand, the EU is seeking to push forward the law and promote greater convergence around its norms, yet by pursuing this policy in a unilateral manner this also leads to greater fragmentation of the very multilateral order it seeks to promote.

Machiko Kanetake in chapter three shows how use of surveillance technology can significantly undermine the rights of individuals not only within the EU but also in its trading partners. In his report of May 2019, the UN's Special Rapporteur on the freedom of opinion and expression raised serious concerns about the status of 'surveillance exports'. The UN Special Rapporteur foremost recommended that states impose an immediate moratorium on the export of surveillance tools and urged the countries to devise appropriate safeguards. 'Dual-use export control' is one of such legal safeguards available to states. Within the EU, the export of dual-use items has been governed foremost by Council Regulation (EC) No 428/2009 of 5 May 2009, which forms an integral part of the EU's Common Commercial Policy. The chapter analyses political initiatives within the EU in the aftermath of the Arab Spring to integrate consideration to human rights risks into the EU's export control. Such initiatives, in a nutshell, oscillate between convergence and divergence at multiple levels. The EU is, in principle, mandated to facilitate convergence of its external action with human rights. The initiatives for human rights convergence are also in line with the UN's Guiding Principles on Business and Human Rights. Yet the integration of human rights into the EU's export control inevitably involves a policy choice which may diverge itself from international human rights law. Furthermore, the attempts to strengthen human rights protection signify divergence from the international regimes on export control, and more fundamentally, from the idea of regulatory harmonisation across participating states. Regardless of the outcomes of the EU's legislative process, the deliberative process itself has unveiled some of the normative and political challenges that underlie the EU's ambition to accommodate human rights in its external action.

In chapter four, Mauro Gatti focuses on international agreements and the decisions of domestic and international tribunals. Recent developments, such as the EU's enlargement and the public outcry about Investor-to-State Dispute Settlement (ISDS), have changed the dynamics of convergence in the external investment policy of the Union. EU institutions and states are reconsidering parts of the international investment protection system, within the EU and at the global level. The new policy of the EU and of its members might suggest a certain divergence of the EU from the paradigm of international investment law, accompanied by greater convergence between the policies of the Union and capital-importing countries.

This is followed by an Epilogue by Michelle Egan, who argues that the EU is at the forefront of setting standards as an internationalist. However, other visions of principled pragmatism, for example as to security, reflects a more nuanced view of Europe's role in the global order.

In Part II, *A Global Order against Convergence?*, Fernanda Nicola in chapter six maps different types of local resistance to global convergence that have worked in tension to the creation of global trading and regulatory regimes by institutional actors such as the WTO, regional international organisations like the EU, and more recently, the Chinese investment and landing regime of the One Belt and One Road Initiative (BRI). Early on, scholars studying these different forms of global convergence explored the dialectics between convergence and local differentiation, by addressing successes or failures of legal transplants, and the philosophies justifying convergence narratives. However, such focus has left in the background the types of resistance and how they operate in tension, by criticising or shaping narratives of global convergence. Nicola outlines four examples of local resistances drawing on theories of economic differentiation and local culture, institutional change and regulatory path dependencies, the Eurocentrism of global convergence and the democratic resistance to an encasement of neoliberalism in global law as a lens for framing global convergence narratives.

In chapter seven, David Henig examines what we can learn about regulatory leadership as exercised by the US and EU from TTIP talks. He argues that it demonstrates how one of the key drivers behind the proposed TTIP between the US and EU was to create a platform to finally make serious progress on tackling their regulatory differences, generating economic growth and responding to the threat from emerging economies to their global regulatory hegemony. TTIP talks stalled after three years with the election of President Trump in 2016, arguably due more to differences on traditional trade issues like procurement and agriculture rather than regulatory differences. Yet progress on regulatory coherence had been slow, reflecting the different approaches of the two parties, which could be characterised as an EU regulator-led process, as against a US private sector-led process. These differences were being discussed, but progress was mostly halted by the end of talks.

Paul James Cardwell and Ramses A Wessel in chapter eight examine primarily divergence rather than convergence. Since EU law was, at the outset at least, a creation of international law then the starting point would be that on such fundamental questions as territory, these definitions should be the same. However, in the context of the EU as a maturing legal system, the aim of the chapter is to consider the extent of *divergence* between EU and international law. First of all – using an *internal* perspective – it will examine the effects of EU norms and rules by looking through a 'territorial' lens and by considering the EU's own definition and understanding of territory in its legal order. Secondly – using an *external* perspective – it will specifically look at the response by one of the EU institutions, the CJEU, in cases where international territorial questions have arisen. Though questions on territorial scope are some of the most politically-charged in international law, they often emerge through seemingly mundane and technical matters of trade.

This part of the chapter explores the extent to which the Court, which was set up to deal with matters of EU law and not to resolve 'general' international law quandaries, has developed its own methods to grapple with such inherently 'political' and thorny questions.

Juan Santos Vara and Laura Pascual Matellán in chapter nine argue that the EU has been strongly and continuously engaged in the process of elaboration of the Global Compact for Migration, delivering EU coordinated statements through the EU delegations in the consultative phase that preceded the adoption of the Compact. Despite the engagement in the process of the elaboration of the Global Compact, several EU Member States decided not to support the final text of the document. The chapter analyses the convergence or divergence between the Global Compact and EU migration policies and the implications arising from the internal division between Member States as regards the implementation process. It seems that the controversies surrounding the adoption of the Global Compact in the last months of 2018 and the lack of consensus among them have probably led EU Member States not to discuss it at EU level since then, avoiding re-opening Pandora's Box.

In chapter 10, Magdalena Forowicz evaluates whether EU and international law converge in the area of solidarity measures and thereby contribute to the development of the principle of solidarity. In its first part, the chapter briefly reviews the development of the principle of solidarity in international law and then evaluates how it has been implemented as part of the newly concluded Global Compact on Refugees. In its second part, the contribution evaluates the evolution of the principle of solidarity and in EU law and then reviews how it was implemented as part of the EU's response to the recent crisis. In both sections, an emphasis is laid on the analysis of resettlement as a key solidarity measure. In its third part, the chapter compares the EU principle of solidarity and cooperation, as well as the corresponding EU burden-sharing measures with the principles and measures contained in international law. The aim is to assess whether there is convergence between the international and EU levels and to evaluate the development of the principle of solidarity and cooperation in general.

Gabriel Siles-Brügge in chapter 11 shows how the EU's external action is not the product of a unitary set of political values or objectives – even if some authors, have pointed out that there has been a move towards more neoliberal (external) policies over time. This runs counter to many of the essentialising arguments expressed by both right-wing Brexiteers and Lexiteers that the EU is – respectively, either an over-regulated Social Democratic space or simply a 'capitalist club'. What approach the EU takes to global convergence is ultimately the product of broader political struggles. We could still see the flagship European Green Deal push the EU in a more environmentally sustainable direction, with the carbon border adjustment mechanism allowing the EU to push global convergence towards lower carbon intensity.

In Part III entitled, *When is EU Law and Policy More 'Inside out' than 'Outside in'?*, Kornilia Pipidi-Kalogirou in chapter 12 considers how FTAs are expanding their utility, turning into governance mechanisms of the EU armoury instead of pure trade-relation regulators. This transformative capacity primarily stems from the inclusion of commitments in FTAs that go beyond pure economic governance, such as the chapters on regulatory cooperation. Although regulatory cooperation does not constitute a new trend in EU trade, under the present state, it represents an original shift. Indeed, the placement of regulatory cooperation within a legally binding treaty is at odds with the past choices of negotiation and commitment. The chapter depicts this 'move to law' by using the concept of 'legalization', an International Relations concept developed to depict the augmenting preference of law for the regulation of international agreements. The findings on the legalisation are later used to examine whether and to what extent regulatory convergence is promoted. In that way, it links legalisation of regulatory cooperation to regulatory convergence.

Aakriti Bhardwaj and Jeff Kenner in chapter 13 outline how until the EU started negotiating new generation FTAs, trade-related obligations on labour standards were implicit under the 'essential elements' clause which underscored their protection as human rights. The coverage of labour standards in EU FTAs now falls under the purview of 'trade and sustainable development' chapters that seek convergence of domestic labour law with ILO standards. Furthermore, through these FTAs, the EU is expanding its normative agenda and addressing regulatory issues such as corruption within national systems and governance issues concerning civil society participation in trade policy. Taking the proposed EU-Mexico FTA as an example, the chapter analyses the potential for vertical and horizontal convergence on labour standards through trade. Vertical convergence refers to the EU's pursuit of international labour standards, whereas horizontal convergence refers to the provisions within the FTA that have an indirect bearing on labour standards and, therefore, are relevant to advancing labour standards in trading countries. The analysis unfolds in the light of the EU's trade policy, external factors that may impact regulatory changes in Mexico such as US-Mexico trade relations and the objective to protect rule of law in economic relations.

In chapter 14, Enrico Partiti demonstrates how private standards and corporations' internal regulatory processes are increasingly used by rule-makers in the EU and its Member States in the transnational discipline of global value chains. The effects of this use could lead to convergence of global production practices with international law through the use of external norms. By harnessing the regulatory capacity of voluntary standards, the EU is capable of fostering compliance with international environmental and social obligation – including by businesses and producers established in extraterritorial jurisdictions. Convergence with international provisions, however, may in fact prove to be shallow. The presence of an additional layer of private regulators, combined with the interplay of private rules with those applicable in the countries of operation, may limit convergence of business conduct with international provisions. To ensure effective convergence, appropriate legal structures are likely to be necessary. Furthermore, convergence with social and environmental domains takes place in the simultaneous divergence with the spirit of international trade obligations. Through a use of private authority which mostly escapes review under WTO provisions, the EU and its Member States are capable of indirectly regulating the conduct of foreign business entities in a manner which would otherwise be constrained, and possibly even sanctioned, by WTO rules.

In chapter 15, Francesco Pennesi outlines how the process of globalisation and the cross-border nature of capital markets are increasingly challenging the ability of domestic jurisdictions to set financial rules in their own jurisdictions. The contribution identifies two determinants of the capacity of equivalence to act as a mechanism of regulatory convergence, particularly in the Brexit context. First, the convergence effects of equivalence are directly dependent upon the capacity of the Commission to preserve its broad discretionary powers and institutional monopoly over the management of EU equivalence policies, in a period when both features are heavily contested, both inside and outside the European Union. Second, the capacity of the EU to employ equivalence as a convergence mechanism will also depend upon the success of recent legislative reforms adopted by the EU to make the equivalence regime a more flexible and proportionate mechanism to extract regulatory alignment in exchange for market access.

In the final chapter, Isabella Mancini explores how a key feature of the latest EU trade negotiations was the pursuance of a 'deep trade agenda' for 'deep integration' with the trade partners. The concept of 'deep' has yet remained unexplored from a fundamental rights perspective. The central question of the chapter asks how a methodological framework of 'convergence' can help the exploration and understanding of 'deepness of fundamental rights' in the new generation of EU trade agreements. Using the Civil Society Forum under CETA as a case study, the chapter argues that while convergence can justify the targeting of certain analytical elements as opposed to others, its usefulness remains limited for more normative explorations.

V. Conclusions

The book project thus wrestles with the framing of the challenges of our times – how can the EU be a global actor? How does it make a difference? What is the nuance of power through law in this context? The book project is unashamedly a methodology project, which seeks to zoom in on the complexity of dynamism and action and also never-ending competence expansions. The breadth of disciplines in the book – lawyers, political scientists, political economy scholars to practitioners hopefully lends some depth to the efforts. To the extent that the development of these themes is at the heart of the European trajectory right now, it also constitutes a vibrant future agenda. This book project thus seeks to delve into the forms and action component of EU convergence and isolate its meaning and plot its direction to depict the EU as an exceptional convergence actor within the global legal order. The book isolates the methodology of this exceptionalism as a normative and descriptive state of affairs. All authors subscribe to the idea that the EU practices and preaches convergence in the global legal order with an increasing explicitness, openness and directness which is sometimes at odds with international law and/or international politics in its own unique way. We hope that the reader enjoys the book and can engage with this agenda.

PART I

Framing EU Global Convergence

1

The EU's Free Trade and Investment Agreements: European Convergence with World Trade Law?

FRANK HOFFMEISTER*

I. Introduction

Accounting for 15 per cent in the world share of global exports and imports (as of July 2019), the European Union (EU) is one of the world's major trading powers.[1] It thus holds considerable influence in the World Trade Organisation (WTO) and brings a lot of negotiating power to the table when it engages in bilateral free trade agreements.[2] Since 2006, when Commissioner Mandelson announced the 'Global Europe' strategy,[3] it has indeed concluded numerous new 'Deep and Comprehensive Free Trade Agreements' (DCFTAs) with partners such as Korea,[4]

* The views expressed herein are those of the author and do not reflect an official position of the European Commission. I would also like to thank Mattijs Kempynck (Bluebook trainee in DG Trade, Unit H3) for his excellent research assistance in preparing this chapter.

[1] Eurostat, 'International Trade in Goods – a Statistical Picture' (3 October 2019) under 1.1, https://ec.europa.eu/eurostat/statistics-explained/index.php?title=International_trade_in_goods__a_statistical_picture (last accessed 26 February 2020.

[2] For an overview of the EUs bilateral trade policy since the Lisbon Treaty, see Frank Hoffmeister, 'Bilateral Developments in EU Trade Policy Seven Years After Lisbon: A Look into the Spaghetti-Bowl à la Bruxelloise' in Marc Bungenberg, Markus Krajewski, Christian J Tams, Joerg Philipp Terhechte and Andreas R Ziegler (eds), *European Yearbook of International Economic Law* (Springer, 2017) 411–36.

[3] European Commission, 'Communication from the Commission to the Council, the European Parliament, the European Economic and Social Committee and the Committee of the Regions on a "Global Europe: Competing in the World – A Contribution to the EU's Growth and Jobs Strategy"' (COM(2006) 567 final, 4 October 2006), https://eur-lex.europa.eu/legal-content/EN/TXT/PDF/?uri=CELEX:52006DC0567&from=EN (last accessed 26 February 2020).

[4] Council Decision (EU) 2011/265/EU of 16 September 2010 on the signing, on behalf of the European Union, and provisional application of the Free Trade Agreement between the European Union and its Member States, of the one part, and the Republic of Korea, of the other part [2011] OJ L127/1. For an official assessment of its implementation see Directorate-General for Trade, 'Evaluation of the Implementation of the Free Trade Agreement between the EU and its Member States and the Republic of Korea' (2018), https://trade.ec.europa.eu/doclib/docs/2019/march/tradoc_157716.pdf (last accessed 26 February 2020.

Canada[5] and Singapore.[6] Moreover, between 2013 and 2017 it attempted to bring about a Transatlantic Trade and Investment Partnership (TTIP) with the United States.[7] With the election of President Trump in November 2017, however, this project came to an end.

Primarily, the EU's DCFTAs embody the joint will of the parties to liberalise trade between them. They ease tariffs, promise tariff-quotas or tackle non-tariff barriers on goods and services. At the same time, they also contain substantive rules, ranging from public procurement over competition to non-economic issues such as sustainable development. A particularly rule-intensive chapter is the one on investment since it stipulates general standards of behaviour for States, which may potentially catch legal and administrative investment barriers from all policy fields.

Against that background, the question whether the EU's practice sets global standards is very pertinent.[8] Are the EU's DCFTA's the most progressive ones, which other nations would like to imitate? Could they serve as global standards that inspire new multilateral conventions? Or are they more a symbol of European exceptionalism that mainly serve European interests and cannot be regarded as a global blueprint?[9] In order to reply to these questions, five distinctive means and ways of the EU's FTA will be analysed: Does the EU reaffirm or build on existing WTO standards, indicating a high level of global convergence, or does it reform or even contract out of international practices, pointing to the opposite direction? In the alternative: Does Europe bring up new topics into the world trade debate, thereby tipping off a new wave of convergence?

Out of the recent DCFTAs, the EU-Canada Comprehensive Economic and Trade Agreement (CETA) is the most advanced text.[10] CETA has been heralded as 'the

[5] Council Decision (EU) 2017/37 of 28 October 2016 on the signing on behalf of the European Union of the Comprehensive Economic and Trade Agreement (CETA) between Canada, of the one part, and the European Union and its Member States, of the other part [2017] OJ L11/1.

[6] Council Decision (EU) 2018/1599 of 15 October 2018 on the signing, on behalf of the European Union, of the Free Trade Agreement between the European Union and the Republic of Singapore [2018] OJ L267/1.

[7] In January 2017, both sides stated that they 'have made considerable progress in negotiating a Transatlantic Trade and Investment Partnership (TTIP) agreement since the negotiations were launched in July 2013', see European Commission and USTR, 'U.S.-EU Joint Report on TTIP Progress to Date' (17 January 2017), http://trade.ec.europa.eu/doclib/docs/2017/january/tradoc_155242.pdf (last accessed on 26 February 2020).

[8] From recent literature see a good overview in Elaine Fahey, *The Global Reach of EU Law* (Routledge, 2016).

[9] On the topic of EU exceptionalism in general international law, see Magdalena Liçková, 'European Exceptionalism in International Law' (2008) 19(3) *European Journal of International Law* 463.

[10] See, eg, European Commission, 'EU – Canada Summit: Newly Signed Trade Agreement Sets High Standards for Global Trade' (Press release, 30 October 2016), <https://europa.eu/rapid/press-release_IP-16-3581_en.htm (last accessed 26 February 2020. See also Kurt Hübner, Anne-Sophie Deman and Tugce Balik, 'EU and Trade Policy-Making: The Contentious Case of CETA' (2017) 39(7) *Journal of European Integration* 843; Stefanie Schacherer, 'TTP, CETA and TTIP: Between Innovation and Consolidation – Resolving Investor-Disputes under Mega-Regionals' (2016) 7(3) *Journal of International Dispute Settlement* 631; Gonzalo Villalata Puig and Eric D Dalke, 'Nature and Enforceability of WTO-plus SPS and TBT Provisions in Canada's PTAs: From NAFTA to CETA' (2016) 15(1) *World Trade Review* 51; or broader Thilo Rensmann (ed), *Mega-Regional Trade Agreements* (Springer/Cham, 2017).

gold standard for future trade deals',[11] with especially high expectations for its investment chapter.[12] It is therefore appropriate to use CETA as a reference point for the usual EU approach in DCFTAs. The EU and its Member States on the one hand and Canada on the other hand signed CETA as a mixed agreement on 30 October 2016.[13] The European Parliament gave its consent on 15 February 2017, and the Canadian Parliament ratified it on 16 May 2017.[14] Lacking full ratification by all EU Member States, the EU parts of CETA are provisionally applied since 21 September 2017.[15]

II. EU Standards on Trade in Goods

A. General Provisions (Chapter 1)

Chapter 1 of CETA contains, next to the usual introductory definitions, a couple of interesting general provisions. Under Article 1.4 CETA, the parties establish a free trade area 'in conformity with Article XXIV of GATT 1994 and Article V of GATS'. This is a reminder of the EU's approach that agreements need to cover at least 90 per cent of all goods and services between the parties to qualify as 'substantially all trade' under these WTO conditions. CETA meets this requirement, as it liberalises 97 per cent of all EU-Canadian trade.[16] For other trading partners, a high

[11] See, eg, EU Commissioner for Trade Cecilia Malmström and the Honourable Chrystia Freeland, Minister of International Trade of Canada, 'Joint Statement on CETA' (29 February 2016), https://ec.europa.eu/commission/presscorner/detail/nl/STATEMENT_16_446 (last accessed 27 February 2020); or lead Member of European Parliament on CETA Mr Atris Pabriks at the occasion of the deal's passing in parliament, www.europarl.europa.eu/news/en/headlines/world/20170219STO63201/ceta-this-deal-is-important-for-europe-geopolitically-as-well-as-economically (last accessed 27 February 2020.

[12] See Luca Pantaleo, 'Investment Disputes under CETA: From Gold Standards to Best Practices?' (2017) 28(2) *European Business Law Review* 163; Gus Van Harten, 'ISDS in the Revised CETA: Positive Steps, But Is It a 'Gold Standard'?' (*Centre for International Governance Innovation*, 2016), https://perma.cc/Y7ZN-MAPK (last accessed 27 February 2020).

[13] Frank Hoffmeister, 'Curse or Blessing? Mixed Agreements in the Recent Practice of the European Union and its Member States' in Christophe Hillion and Panos Koutrakos (eds), *Mixed Agreements Revisited – The EU and its Member States in the world*, (Hart Publishing, 2010) 249–67.

[14] European Parliament, Legislative resolution on the draft Council decision on the conclusion of the Comprehensive Economic and Trade Agreement (CETA) between Canada, of the one part, and the European Union and its Member States, of the other part (10975/2016 – C8-0438/2016 – 2016/0205(NLE) 15 February 2017), www.europarl.europa.eu/doceo/document/TA-8-2017-0030_EN.pdf (last accessed on 27 February 2020); Senate, Royal Assent to An Act to implement the Comprehensive Economic and Trade Agreement between Canada and the European Union and its Member States and to provide for certain other measures (Bill C-30, Chapter 6, 16 May 2017), https://sencanada.ca/en/content/sen/chamber/421/debates/121db_2017-05-16-e?language=e (last accessed 27 February 2020).

[15] Council Decision (EU) 2017/38 of 28 October 2016 on the provisional application of the Comprehensive Economic and Trade Agreement (CETA) between Canada, of the one part, and the European Union and its Member States, of the other part [2017] OJ L11/1080.

[16] WTO Secretariat, 'Factual Presentation on the Comprehensive Economic and Trade Agreement between Canada and the European Union (Goods and Services)' (10 April 2018) paras 3.18 and 3.22, https://docs.wto.org/dol2fe/Pages/FE_Search/FE_S_S009-DP.aspx?language=E&CatalogueIdList=246477,246410,246334,245754,244389,238871&CurrentCatalogueIdIndex=4&FullTextHash=&HasEnglishRecord=True&HasFrenchRecord=True&HasSpanishRecord=True (last accessed 27 February 2020).

threshold may be less relevant. For example, the idea to negotiate an EUUS 'auto-deal',[17] which would only cover the reduction of tariffs for cars between these two blocs, would fly in the face of Article XXIV of the General Agreement on Tariffs and Trade (GATT) 1994, and could thus undermine the WTO. Former EU Trade Commissioner Cecilia Malmström further demonstrated the EU's adherence to the 'substantially all trade' requirement in declining to strike a 'mini trade deal' with the US on lobsters and chemicals. In November 2019, she wrote that 'given the WTO agreement on bilateral preferences, [such a trade deal] should be as part of a wider agreement to liberalise tariffs bilaterally for industrial products, including fisheries'.[18]

Against that background, Article 1.5 CETA is equally important. Under this provision, the parties 'affirm their rights and obligations with respect to each other under the WTO Agreement and other agreements to which they are party'. This means that CETA cannot serve as a shield against WTO litigation, eg by arguing that it would constitute a *lex specialis* or a *lex posterior* between the parties.[19] Rather, under Article 1.5 CETA, parties maintain the possibility to bring WTO cases against each other. It also follows that the subsequent CETA provisions should be regarded as 'WTO plus' and not 'WTO minus'. An example is Article 1.8 (2) CETA, according to which 'each Party *shall ensure* that all necessary measures are taken in order to give effect to the provisions of this Agreement, including their observance at all levels of government'. This formulation is much stricter than Article XXIV (12) of the GATT. Here, the central government only promises to '*take such reasonable measures* as may be available to it' to ensure the observance of WTO commitments by regional and local authorities (emphasis added).

B. National Treatment and Market Access for Goods (Chapter 2)

The cornerstone of Chapter 2 is the national treatment provision in Article 2.3 CETA. To this effect, Article III of GATT 1994 is formally 'incorporated into and made part of the Agreement'. This means that separate tax treatment between domestic and imported goods is forbidden and that the regulatory discrimination affecting

[17] See for reporting on this deal, eg Hans Von Der Burchard, 'EU says it is Willing to Scrap Car Tariffs in US Trade Deal' *Politico*, 19 April 2019, www.politico.eu/article/eu-says-it-is-willing-to-scrap-car-tariffs-in-us-trade-deal/ (last accessed 27 February 2020).

[18] See the Letter of Commissioner Malmström to USTR Robert Lighthizer on 6 November 2019, obtained by Politico's Jacob Hanke, online at www.politico.eu/wp-content/uploads/2019/11/3750_001.pdf?utm_source=POLITICO.EU&utm_campaign=493141980f-EMAIL_CAMPAIGN_2019_11_12_06_00&utm_medium=email&utm_term=0_10959edeb5-493141980f-189531949 (last accessed 27 February 2020).

[19] For background on the use of these principles in WTO dispute settlement, see Graham Cook, *A Digest of WTO Jurisprudence on Public International Law Concepts and Principles* (Cambridge University Press, 2015) 86–95 (under '4.3 Conflict Resolution').

imported goods may fall under scrutiny. Furthermore, Article 2.4 CETA organises the progressive abolition or reduction of customs duties in line with the relevant annexes. Another important WTO plus obligation can be found in Article 2.5 CETA. This provision prohibits duty drawback, duty suspension or duty referral programmes made contingent on the export of a good. Such programmes are allowed under WTO law, but can be countervailed (Annex III to the WTO Agreement on Subsidies and Countervailing Measures). Similarly, the liberal regime on export duties and charges under Article XI of GATT 1994 is tightened by Article 2.6 CETA. The EU and Canada promise not to

> adopt or maintain any duties, taxes or other fees and charges imposed on, or in connection with, the export of a good to the other Party, or any internal taxes or fees and charges on a good exported to the other Party, that is in excess of those that would be imposed on those goods when destined for internal sale.

This will reduce the policy space to enact export taxes or restrictions with the purpose of maintaining certain raw materials within a country to suppress the input prices for domestic industry. Hence, it fits well into the EU's longstanding policy to secure an equal playing field for the access to raw materials around the world by bringing WTO cases[20] or adopting trade defence measures.[21] On import restrictions, Article 2.9 (1) CETA incorporates the standards of Article XI of GATT 1994. Interestingly, the third paragraph of this provision stipulates a new duty to consult the other party when import restrictions on third countries may affect European-Canadian trade.

C. Trade Remedies (Chapter 3)

The trade remedies chapter reaffirms the established rules in the WTO Anti-Dumping Agreement (ADA) and the WTO Agreement on Subsidies and Countervailing Measures (SCM) Agreement. The only WTO plus element can be found in Article 3.3.

[20] See, eg, the EU's WTO litigation against China on certain raw materials. In January 2012, the Appellate Body ruled in favour of the US, the EU and Mexico in the first case (DS 394, 395, 398). Another case brought by the EU, US and Japan on rare earths concluded with positive AB Reports in April 2014 (DS 431, 432 and 433). A third case, brought in October 2016, is currently pending (DS 509).

[21] See Commission Implementing Regulation 2016/387 of 17 March 2016 imposing a definitive countervailing duty on imports of tubes and pipes of ductile cast iron (also known as spheroidal graphite cast iron), originating in India [2016] OJ L73/1, recitals 135–229; Commission Implementing Regulation 2019/244 of 11 February 2019 imposing a definitive countervailing duty on imports of biodiesel originating in Argentina [2019] OJ L40/1, recitals 50–170. Commission Implementing Regulation (EU) 2019/1344 of 12 August 2019 imposing a provisional countervailing duty on imports of biodiesel originating in Indonesia [2019] OJ L212/1, recitals 83–208. The General Court of the European Union has recently ruled in favour of the EU's approach in the first of these regulations (Case T-300/16 *Jindal Saw Ltd* [2019] ECLI:EU:T:2019:235, para 11).

Under the first paragraph, the parties promise to 'consider' applying a public interest test. The background for this provision is the strict Union interest test provided in Article 21 of the EU's basic Anti-Dumping Regulation (ADR) and Article 31 of the basic Anti-Subsidy Regulation (ASR).[22] Under those norms, the Commission shall only adopt trade defence measures if it is convinced that other interests (users, consumers) are not negatively affected in a clearly disproportionate way. This balancing test is a compromise between the more protectionist Member States, which favour strong trade defence action to protect domestic industry and the more liberal Member States, which stress the need not to interrupt established trade flows and keep foreign competition alive.

The second paragraph of Article 3.3 deals with the lesser duty rule. The 'Party's authorities may consider whether the amount of the anti-dumping or countervailing duty to be imposed shall be the full margin of dumping or amount of subsidy or a lesser amount, in accordance with the Party's law'. Again, this provision is inspired by an EU rule laid down in Article 7 (4) of the ADR. The background for this norm is the idea that the purpose of a trade remedy is not to sanction the exporting producers with the full amount of the dumping margin, but to cap the duty at the level of the 'injury margin', ie the level that is sufficient to re-establish a level playing field. While the EU managed to bring this idea into the text of CETA, it does not translate into a hard and binding obligation for Canada. Rather, the Canadian trade defence authorities will only 'consider' the application of the lesser duty rule in accordance with domestic statutes. Moreover, in the meantime, the EU itself has become less adamant about it. In the latest modernisation of the EU's trade defence instruments,[23] the lesser duty rule was abolished for anti-subsidy cases and restricted in anti-dumping cases in the event of significant distortions on raw materials (Articles 7 (2)(a)–(d) of the ADR).

Article 3.4 reaffirms the rights and obligations of the parties under Article XIX of the GATT and the WTO Safeguards Agreement to impose global safeguards. The EU and Canada add to this WTO standard a transparency obligation and a soft exhortation to consider the impact of such safeguards on the trade flows

[22] For further discussion, see Hélène Juramy, 'Anti-Dumping in Europe: What About Us(ers)?' (2018) 11 *Global Trade and Customs Journal* 511. The Union interest-test was applied eg in the PET case (Council Implementing Decision 2013/226/EU of 21 May 2013 [2013] OJ L136/12, recital 23) and the Solar Panels Case (Commission Implementing Regulation (EU) 2017/367 of 1 March 2017 [2017] OJ L56/131, recital 373).

[23] Regulation (EU) 2018/825 of the European Parliament and of the Council of 30 May 2018 amending Regulation (EU) 2016/1036 on protection against dumped imports from countries not members of the European Union and Regulation (EU) 2016/1037 on protection against subsidised imports from countries not members of the European Union [2018] OJ L143/1. For more detail, see Wolfgang Müller, 'The EU's New Trade Defence Laws: A Two Steps Approach' in Marc Bungenberg, Michael Hahn, Christophe Hermann and Till Müller-Ibold (eds), *The Future of Trade Defence Instruments* (Springer, 2018) 45–62 and Frank Hoffmeister, 'The Devil is in the Detail – A First Guide on the EU's New Trade Defence Rules' in Wolfgang Weiss (ed), *The EU's Trade Policy 10 Years after Lisbon* (forthcoming in 2020).

with each other (Articles 3.5–3.6). At first sight, the 'reaffirmation' of the relevant WTO standards is not breathtaking. However, in particular in times where the United States seems to depart from them by applying unilateral safeguards in highly contested situations, the adherence of the EU and Canada to the multilateral rulebook is politically important. They do not only promise to exercise utmost restraint before adopting global safeguards, but also reiterate the prohibition and elimination of other measures, such as voluntary export restraints (VER) (Article 11(1)(b) Safeguards Agreement). Given that the United States has imposed on Canada precisely such a VER on automobiles in the recent exchange of letters at the margin of the revised North American Free Trade Agreement (NAFTA) Treaty,[24] Article 3.4 of CETA seems like an increasingly significant counter-model.

D. Technical Barriers to Trade (Chapter 4)

Chapter 4 on technical barriers to trade starts from the assumption that non-tariff barriers can have a trade-restrictive effect. Accordingly, technical norms should not 'overreach' by being designed to tackle imports specifically. To that effect, the EU and Canada incorporate the relevant disciplines from the WTO Agreement on Technical Barriers to Trade (TBTA) into Article 4.2 of CETA. This covers in particular Article 2.2 TBTA, according to which technical regulations shall not create 'unnecessary obstacles to international trade' and must fulfil a legitimate objective. Moreover, where international standards exist, they shall normally be used (Article 2.4 TBTA). On top of this, the EU and Canada strengthen their cooperation between relevant norm-setting bodies (Article 4.3 CETA) and may discuss such issues in the Trade Committee (Article 4.7 CETA). This is a far cry from an EU-Canada regulatory board, which could harmonise technical standards above the heads of the democratic legislatures on both sides, as sometimes depicted by populist opponents of CETA. Rather, both sides will exchange information about their respective standards and try to find ways to narrow down differences. This idea is fleshed out in Chapter 21 on regulatory cooperation.

E. Sanitary and Phytosanitary Measures (Chapter 5)

Albeit technical on their face, the provisions on animal and plant health can create a lot of political controversy, as eg in the *Hormones* case.[25] Common fears

[24] See the Side Letter Text on 232 CA-US Response from USTR Robert Lighthizer to Canadian Minister of Foreign Affairs Chrystia Freeland (30 November 2018), https://ustr.gov/sites/default/files/files/agreements/FTA/USMCA/Text/Side_Letter_Text_on_232_CA-US_Response.pdf (last accessed 27 February 2020.

[25] Appellate Body Report, *European Communities - Measures Concerning Meat and Meat Products (Hormones)*, WT/DS26/AB/R, WT/DS48/AB/R, adopted 13 February 1998; Panel Reports, *European*

are the lowering of environmental or production requirements to foster trade of 'unhealthy' food. In that respect, both parties are anxious to keep their policy space. Accordingly, the main objective under Article 5.2 (c) is to 'further the implementation' of the Sanitary and Phytosanitary Measures Agreement of the WTO (SPSA). Again, both sides first reaffirm the global standards (Article 5.4), thereby incorporating the important principle that SPS measures must have a scientific basis (Article 2.2 SPSA). The main WTO plus provision is Article 5.6 on 'equivalence'. Under that norm, 'the importing Party shall accept the SPS measure of the exporting Party as equivalent to its own if the exporting Party objectively demonstrates to the importing Party that its measure achieves the importing Party's appropriate level of SPS protection'.

Further details on how to identify an 'appropriate level' of SPS protection are laid down in the relevant Annexes. Importantly, Annex 5-E identifies where the parties have already agreed in which areas such equivalence exists. This constitutes a bilateral push forward, which is encouraged by Article 4 (2) of the SPSA. Another step forward is Article 5.8 on audit and verification. Going beyond Article 8 of the SPSA, which obliges WTO members to respect certain substantive standards in their national control systems, the EU and Canada actually open up their national control systems to audit and verification of the other party.[26] This is designed to strengthen the trust in the proper operation of SPS standards on both sides of the Atlantic. Similar to the Technical Barriers to Trade (TBT) Chapter, the parties also agree on an exchange of information and discussion of SPS matters in a specific Committee established under Article 6.14. It cannot set binding secondary CETA law.

F. Customs and Trade Facilitation (Chapter 6)

While trade rules govern the liberalisation of the applicable requirements to import goods, there is a lot of discretion left to States on how to organise their customs authorities. In order to avoid delays and unnecessary paperwork, modern trade agreements also look at the customs environment. In this regard, the 2013 Bali Ministerial Conference of the WTO adopted the Trade Facilitation Agreement, which established a global standard.[27] In CETA, the parties have also taken up

Communities – Measures Concerning Meat and Meat Products (Hormones), WT/DS48/R/CAN *(Canada)* / WT/DS26/R/USA *(US)*, adopted 13 February 1998.

[26] See also Puig and Dalke (n 10).

[27] General Council Decision on the Protocol Amending the Marrakech Agreement establishing the World Trade Organization (WT/L/940, 27 November 2014). For further reading, see Ben Czapnik, 'Will the Trade Facilitation Agreement's Novel Architecture and Flexibilities Have Unforeseen Consequences? An Analysis in the Context of World Trade Organization Accessions' (2017) 12(1) *Global Trade and Customs Journal* 2; Antonia Eliason, 'The Trade Facilitation Agreement: A New Hope for the World Trade Organization' (2015) 14(4) *World Trade Review* 643; Nora Neufeld, 'The Long and Winding Road: How WTO Members finally reached a Trade Facilitation Agreement' (WTO Staff Working Paper, No. ERSD-2014-06, 7 April 2014).

this theme. However, the most controversial issues cannot be solved in a bilateral context. Therefore, there are no common rules on customs valuation, but only cooperation with a view to reaching common understanding (Article 6.4 (2)). Risk analysis (Article 6.7) and automation (Article 6.8) are encouraged. Advance rulings on tariff classification can only be issued in accordance with domestic law (Article 6.9 (1)). Review and appeal procedures shall be done 'promptly' (Article 6.10). All in all, this chapter will not change the customs implementation on the ground in Europe or Canada, but serves more as a good example of what a modern trade facilitation chapter should look like.

G. Subsidies (Chapter 7)

Subsidies are an increasingly hot topic in international trade. In CETA, the EU and Canada promise increased transparency through mutual notification of subsidies that may distort trade. They use the definition of the WTO Agreement on Subsidies and Countervailing Measures as a basis for this endeavour (Articles 7.1 and 7.2) and reaffirm the global disciplines in full (Article 7.8). A new feature is the consultation mechanism for subsidies concerning trade in services (Article 7.3) and an attempt to curb back agricultural and fisheries subsidies. Article 7.4 even lays down that both sides will strive together for that end in multilateral negotiations. Just how far this will influence the ongoing WTO negotiations on fisheries subsidies remains to be seen.[28] In contrast, Article 7.5 contains a clear-cut prohibition of agricultural export subsidies, thereby mirroring a prohibition reached at the Tenth Ministerial Conference in Nairobi in 2013.[29] At the request of Canada, the EU has also agreed to exclude the audio-visual sector from the chapter, which points to some exceptionalism in international trade on the matter (Article 7.7).

H. Interim Conclusion

In the area of trade in goods, we can identify three main mechanisms on how the EU's bilateral trade policy relates to global standards. First, it reaffirms existing WTO standards, thereby defending these against erosion from other sides. That is visible, for example with respect to Article XXIV GATT and the WTO rules on safeguards. In other areas, such as TBT, SPS and Trade Facilitation, the EU goes into more detail and wishes to bring about more stringent implementing rules that cannot be agreed in a multilateral setting. In the same box we also find 'WTO plus' rules on duty drawback systems or the prohibition of export taxes or duties.

[28] Ministerial Decision on Fisheries Subsidies (WT/MIN(17)/64;WT/L/1031, 13 December 2017).

[29] Ministerial Decision on Export Competition (WT/MIN(15)/45;WT/L/980, 19 December 2015) rec 2.

Finally, there are some rare traits of EU exceptionalism – specific policy space is for example preserved in the audio-visual service area or with respect to certain SPS measures (genetically modified organisms, hormone treated beef), which are not touched by the FTA.

III. EU Standards on Investment

In 2009, a big constitutional shift occurred in EU policy. The Lisbon Treaty integrated 'foreign direct investment' into the EU's common commercial policy under Article 207 of the Treaty on the Functioning of the European Union (TFEU).[30] The Union hence started to develop its own investment policy, building on the previous activities related to the freedom of establishment.

In the first post-Lisbon years, the Union included investment protection clauses into its traditional FTAs, and CETA is the case in point.[31] This approach changed, however, when the Court of Justice held in May 2017 in the Singapore Opinion that the EU's new competence does not extend to 'indirect' investment, ie portfolio investment.[32] While having trade and investment provisions together in one legal text has its economic merits, there was no intention to trigger unanimity in the Council and national ratification for the entire FTA as a 'mixed agreement' by doing so. Accordingly, the EU has split the relevant texts with Singapore and Vietnam into an 'EU only' trade agreement and a mixed investment agreement.[33] It is also possible to negotiate 'stand-alone' investment protection agreements without any parallel trade agreements – examples are the ongoing negotiations with Myanmar[34] and China.

[30] For an overview, see Chien-Huei Wu, 'Foreign Direct Investment as Common Commercial Policy: EU External Economic Competence after Lisbon' in Paul James Cardwell (ed), *EU External Relations Law and Policy in the Post-Lisbon Era* (TMC Asser Press/Springer, 2012) 375–400.

[31] Comprehensive Economic and Trade Agreement (CETA) between Canada, of the one part, and the European Union and its Member States, of the other part [2017] OJ L11/23, Arts 8.9–8.45.

[32] Court of Justice, *Opinion 2/15* [16 May 2017] EU:C:2017:376, para 238.

[33] European Commission, 'Investment Protection Agreement between the European Union and its Member States, of the one part, and the Republic of Singapore, of the other part – Annex 1 to the European Commission Proposal for a Council Decision on the conclusion of the Investment Protection Agreement between the European Union and its Member States, of the one part, and the Republic of Singapore, of the other part' (COM(2018)194 final, 18 April 2018), https://eur-lex.europa.eu/resource.html?uri=cellar:55d54e18-42e0-11e8-b5fe-01aa75ed71a1.0002.02/DOC_2&format=PDF (last accessed 27 February 2020) hereafter 'EU-Singapore IPA'; European Commission, 'Investment Protection Agreement between the European Union and its Member States, of the one part, and the Socialist Republic of Vietnam, of the other part – Annex 1 to the European Commission Proposal for a Council Decision on the conclusion of the Investment Protection Agreement between the European Union and its Member States, of the one part, and the Socialist Republic of Vietnam, of the other part' (COM(2018)693 final, 17 October 2018), https://eur-lex.europa.eu/resource.html?uri=cellar:2d9b97ac-d2e7-11e8-9424-01aa75ed71a1.0001.02/DOC_1&format=PDF (last accessed 27 February 2020).

[34] See Development Solutions (for DG Trade), 'Sustainability Impact Assessment (SIA) in Support of an Investment Protection Agreement between the European Union and the Republic of the Union of Myanmar' (June 2016), https://trade.ec.europa.eu/doclib/docs/2016/december/tradoc_155122.pdf (last accessed 27 February 2020).

A. Establishment of Investment

Turning back to the CETA text, the first noteworthy point is the merger of investment protection provisions ('post-establishment') with market access provisions ('pre-establishment'). Accordingly, Chapter 8 of CETA constitutes quite a novel approach when compared to the traditional bilateral investment treaties (BITs) of Member States.[35]

Article 8.4 lays down a number of market access limitations that are incompatible with CETA. They are inspired by Article XVI (2) of the General Agreement on Trade in Services (GATS) with the difference that the latter norm only applies in specifically designated sectors. Consequently, the scope of Article 8.4 includes a potentially very large amount of sectors.[36] Moreover, Article 8.5 prohibits a number of performance requirements – among which we find local content clauses – which are considered prohibited subsidies in Article 3.1 (b) SCM Agreement. Importantly, lit (f) also prohibits making investment conditional on the transfer of intellectual property, an issue that is currently under scrutiny by the US vis-à-vis China.[37]

B. Non-discriminatory Treatment

Article 8.6 lays down the general principle of national treatment, which is a cornerstone of many BITs. It qualifies that the standard applies 'in like situations' to exclude an overly broad interpretation.[38] A similar approach can only be found in Article 8.7 on most-favoured nation treatment. While both provisions reaffirm that investors from each party should not be treated less favourably than, respectively, investors from the host state and investors from third states, it guards against far-reaching extensions of that principle. The EU and Canada agree in paragraph 4 that procedures and substantive obligations in other investment treaties do not constitute 'treatment' and thus cannot give rise to a breach of this Article. This provision guards against expansive jurisprudence of investment tribunals, like the

[35] See United Nations Conference on Trade and Development (UNCTAD), 'Bilateral Investment Treaties 1995-2006: Trends in Investment Rulemaking' (2007), https://unctad.org/en/Docs/iteiia20065_en.pdf(last accessed 27 February 2020).

[36] For a good description, see WTO Secretariat, Note on CETA (n 16), paras 4.2 to 4.5.

[37] USTR, 'Findings of the Investigation into China's Acts, Policies, and Practices Related to Technology Transfer, Intellectual Property, and Innovation under Section 301 of the Trade Act of 1974' (22 March 2018), https://ustr.gov/sites/default/files/Section%20301%20FINAL.PDF (last accessed 27 February 2020). The US filed a consultation request at the Dispute Settlement Body the day after the report, see Request for consultations by the United States in *China – Certain Measures Concerning the Protection of Intellectual Property Rights*, WT/DS542/1.

[38] See on the 'in like situations' formula in Aikaterina Titi, *The Right to Regulate in International Investment Law* (Nomos, 2014) 139–43.

one in the *Maffezini* case,[39] which had incorporated more favourable procedural provisions from another investment agreement into the Spanish-Argentinian BIT at stake.[40] Finally, Article 8.8 looks at the important issue of indirect discrimination. If the host state's national law stipulates that the managers of a company need to have its nationality, this does not constitute direct discrimination: under such a law, all economic operators must meet the same nationality condition. However, the effect of such a requirement may still be discriminatory. Domestic companies may easily hire managers of their nationality, but finding such managers may hinder the establishment of foreign companies. In order to remove the uncertainty whether or not such discrimination falls under Article 8.6, the EU and Canada have agreed not to require that natural persons in senior management or board of director positions must have any particular nationality. This constitutes a 'TRIMS +' element in the agreement.

C. Investment Protection

Traditionally, BITs enumerate a number of standard protection clauses for the investors operating in the host State,[41] while the legitimate concern of the host State to exercise its regulatory powers may have been mentioned in a preamble. The EU and Canada have departed from this practice since they start their investment protection chapter with a reaffirmation of a right to regulate for legitimate public policy objectives (Article 8.9 (1)). The legal significance becomes clear in paragraph 2, according to which

> the mere fact that a Party regulates, including through a modification to its laws, in a manner which negatively affects an investment or interferes with an investor's expectations, including its expectations of profits, does not amount to a breach of an obligation.

This clause safeguards in particular against an expansive reading of the notion of legitimate expectations or indirect expropriation under classical BIT jurisprudence.[42]

[39] International Centre for Settlement of Investment Disputes (ICSID) Tribunal, *Emilio Augustin Maffezini v Spain* [Decision on Jurisdiction, 25 January 2000] ICSID Case No ARB/97/7.

[40] See Titi (n 28) 136–38 and 417–18 for the further evolution of the issue of non-discrimination and procedural issues.

[41] The Model UK Bilateral Investment Treaty (2005) in Lucy Ferguson, Jan Paulsson and Nigel Blackaby (eds), *Guide to ICSID Arbitration*, 2nd edn (Kluwer, 2010) 289–300, hereafter 'UK Model BIT' serves as a good example of what a 'traditional BIT' looks like.

[42] For more on the concept of 'legitimate expectations', see Anna De Luca, 'Indirect Expropriations and Regulatory Takings: What Role for the "Legitimate Expectations" of Foreign Investors?' in Giorgio Sacerdoti, Pia Acconci, Mara Valenti and Anna De Luca (eds), *General Interests of Host States in International Investment Law* (Cambridge University Press, 2014) 58–75; Michele Potestà, 'Legitimate Expectations in Investment Treaty Law: Understanding the Roots and Limits of a Controversial Concept' [2013] 28(1) *ICSID Review* 88.

In return, Article 8.10 lays down the main standard for the investor's protection. It lumps together 'fair and equitable treatment (FET)' as well as 'full protection and security', but more important is the fact that the EU and Canada define these concepts in a restrictive way.[43] The FET list in Article 8.10 (2) contains the main elements identified in jurisprudence, but qualifies that arbitrariness needs to be 'manifest' and that breaches of due process or transparency must be 'fundamental'. FET also protects the legitimate expectations of an investor, if there was a 'specific representation made to the investor' under paragraph 4. Full protection and security does not extend to legal security, but is confined to 'physical security' only (paragraph 5).[44] In a similar vein, Article 8.10 on expropriation uses existing BIT concepts, including the '"Hull formula" for prompt, adequate and effective compensation' in the case of direct expropriation. At the same time, the EU and Canada interpret the notion of indirect expropriation in a narrow way (Annex 8-A) to keep the regulatory policy space of the host State.

Standards on compensation for losses in emergency or cases of *force majeure* (Article 8.9), the transfer of profits (Article 8.11) and subrogation (Article 8.12) complement the chapter. Interestingly, the EU and Canada have not agreed on a so-called 'umbrella clause' which would lift contract claims to treaty claims, as Canada does not agree with this concept.[45] In other EU investment treaties, however, this concept is present.[46]

The investment chapter does not apply to audio-visual services or the cultural industry (Article 8.2 (3)). Moreover, financial services are regulated by Chapter 13 only (Article 8.3). In addition, Article 8.15 carves out a couple of existing non-conforming measures that the parties have listed in an annex. Articles 8.16 and 8.17 allow the denial of benefits to investors subject to third-party control when that third party is subject to financial sanctions related to the maintenance of peace and security, and the posing of formal reporting obligations to investors.

D. Dispute Settlement

One of the most radical departures from traditional BIT practice[47] is the chapter on dispute settlement. Among the many novelties we can find a commitment to

[43] Frank Hoffmeister, 'The Contribution of EU Trade Agreements to the Development of International Investment Law' in Steffen Hindelang and Markus Krajewski (eds), *Shifting Paradigms in International Investment Law* (Oxford University Press, 2016) 366–67.

[44] August Reinisch, 'The EU and Investor-State Dispute Settlement: WTO Litigators going "Investor-State Arbitration" and Back to a Permanent "Investment Court"' in Marc Bungenberg, Markus Krajewski, Christian J. Tams, Joerg Philipp Terhechte and Andreas R Ziegler (eds), *European Yearbook of International Economic Law* (Springer, 2017) 270–72.

[45] For an empirical account of Canada's reticence to use the umbrella clause, see Katia Yannaca-Small, 'Interpretation of the Umbrella Clause in Investment Agreements' (*OECD Working Papers on International Investment*, 2006) 6, www.oecd.org/daf/inv/investment-policy/WP-2006_3.pdf (last accessed 2 March 2020).

[46] Article 2.4(6) of the EU-Singapore IPA (see n 33).

[47] See, eg, Article 8 of the UK Model BIT.

conduct procedures with full transparency in line with the Mauritius Convention (Article 8.36) and to militate against forum shopping (Article 8.28). Abusive claims can be rejected (Article 8.32–8.33). Most importantly, the current system of ad-hoc nomination of arbitrators by the investor and the defending state (see eg Article 37 of the International Centre for Settlement of Investment Disputes (ICSID) Convention) is put to an end.[48] Instead, the CETA Tribunal is composed of arbitrators that are nominated by the EU and Canada in advance (Article 8.27). Moreover, an appeal is foreseen (Article 8.28), which goes beyond the limited grounds for annulation under the ICSID Convention. All these devices make the enforcement much more akin to a public law system, rather than an international private law mechanism where the will of the parties is decisive. Inspiration has clearly been drawn from the WTO Dispute Settlement Body in this regard.[49]

There is, however, one drawback of the new system: It only applies to disputes between the EU and Canada and is fairly expensive. Reproducing this system for all bilateral FTA partners may hence face practical and financial difficulties. Against that background the EU has launched a parallel initiative, together with Canada, namely to establish a Multilateral Investment Court (MIC) with similar features. The proposal is currently discussed under the auspices of The United Nations Commission on International Trade Law. If successful, it could lead to a situation where all bilateral dispute settlement mechanisms in EU FTAs could be replaced by the MIC. On that road, a couple of legal issues in particular on the relationship between the MIC and the ICSID Convention would have to be solved.[50]

E. Interim Conclusion

In the area of investment, the EU is a leading force in reforming both substantive and institutional investment law. With a stronger emphasis on the right to regulate and more precise investment standards, the rules are less investor-friendly than before. This responds to criticism from civil society, but does not lead to the wrong conclusion that investment protection is a relic of the past. Rather, with the modern formulation of the investment standards, a good balance between legitimate regulatory interests of the host State and legitimate investor interests not to fall victim of arbitrary government action is stuck. At the same time, the commercially inspired investor-to-state dispute settlement system is replaced by a more public law-inspired system of enforcement by an international court system. In this area,

[48] For a brief overview, see Frank Hoffmeister, 'The EU Contribution the Progressive Development of Institutional Aspects in International Investment Law' (2017) 2 *Revue Belge du Droit International* 566, 569–71; UNCTAD (n 35) 99–129.

[49] Hoffmeister, *Ibid*, 576–77.

[50] On the topic of a MIC, see the *European Yearbook of International Economic Law's* special edition: Marc Bungenberg and August Reinisch, *From Bilateral Arbitral Tribunals and Investment Courts to a Multilateral Investment Court – Options Regarding the Institutionalization of Investor-State Dispute Settlement* (Springer, 2018); Hoffmeister (n 48) 574–77.

however, the EU has not yet set a universally accepted blueprint. Rather, it is leading a reform model whose attractiveness is yet to be proven. For the time being, some other important states, including the United States and Japan, are not inclined to make the EU model a global one.[51] This is in stark contrast to certain other third states, which have started to terminate old-style BITS, such as South Africa and India.[52] It may hence become a crucial question for international investment standards whether or not the EU will succeed in building a MIC, which might be at the centre of a reformed international investment protection architecture.

IV. EU Standards on Services

An ever-increasing part of the EU FTAs deal with trade in services. In this area, the EU is aiming high to increase the relatively modest global standards under the GATS.

A. General Principles (Chapter 9)

Under Articles XVI and XVII of the GATS, WTO members make market access commitments listed in an Annex. If there is no entry in that list, States remain free to restrict market access ('positive list'). This organisational principle was adopted in 1994 to allow development countries to accept the GATS as part of the single undertaking. In its bilateral agreements, the EU intends to go further.[53] Reversely, Articles 9.6 and 9.7 CETA start from the opposite assumption that all services are liberalised, unless they are specifically carved out ('negative list'). This is the case for certain sensitive audio-visual and aviation services, for example. Moreover, the Government remains free to provide services in the public interest (Article 9.2 (2) CETA).

B. Temporary Stay of Persons for Business Purposes (Chapter 10)

A particular touchy issue in the services area is the liberalisation of mode 4 services, ie the temporary transfer of natural persons to provide services in the

[51] For the US view, see Stephan Schill, 'The TTIP Negotiations: US versus EU Leadership in Global Investment Governance' (*Kluwer Arbitration Blog*, 4 March 2016), <http://arbitrationblog.kluwerarbitration.com/2016/03/05/the-ttip-negotiations-us-versus-eu-leadership-in-global-investment-governance/ (last accessed 2 March 2020).

[52] For the Indian example, see Prabhash Ranjan, Harsha Vardhana Singh, Kevin James and Ramandeep Sing, 'India's Model Bilateral Investment Treaty: Is India too Risk Averse?' (*Brookings India*, 1 August 2018) 17–36, www.brookings.edu/wp-content/uploads/2018/08/India's-Model-Bilateral-Investment-Treaty-2018.pdf (last accessed 2 March 2020).

[53] For another example, see the Free Trade Agreement between the European Union and its Member States, of the one part, and the Republic of Korea, of the other part [2011] OJ L127/6, Art 7.4.

territory of the other party. The EU and Canada go beyond the thin Point 4 in the GATS Annex on Movement of Natural Persons Supplying Services, according to which visa and immigration rules may not be 'applied in such a manner as to nullify or impair the benefits accruing to any Member under the terms of a specific commitment'. Chapter 10 CETA provides for more transparency, contact points and specific rules for the transfer of 'key personnel' (Article 10. 7 and Annex 10-B). In particular, the parties have agreed on a maximum length of their stay, which provides much more legal certainty than the vague WTO standard quoted above.

C. Mutual Recognition of Qualifications and Domestic Regulation (Chapters 11 and 12)

A frequent barrier for services is the (non-) recognition of diploma for highly qualified self-employed persons. As mentioned in Article VII GATS, a possible resolution is mutual recognition of qualifications. In order to facilitate the process, CETA creates a framework in which the authorities can decide about such recognition. However, an automatic recognition can only occur once the EU and Canada have concluded a Mutual Recognition Agreement, the negotiation of which is encouraged in Article 11.3. If licensing or qualification requirements are kept because of the failure of such negotiations on recognition of qualifications, then the authorities should take speedy and consistent decisions (Article 12.3 and 12.7). Importantly for certain European non-governmental organisations (NGOs), certain water services are excluded from the entire chapter (Article 12.2 (2) (b)(ii)).

D. Specific Services (Chapters 13–15)

On financial services, Chapter 13 increases the market access by both sides with a national treatment clause (Article 13.2). At the same time, CETA cannot undermine the prudential standards on both sides (Article 13.16). The relevant provision gives Parties considerable leeway – as long as prudential measures are 'reasonable', they cannot come into conflict with CETA. This standard is lower than some others used before, which look at proportionality of the prudential measure.[54] Moreover, given the sensitivity of the area, Articles 13.20 and 13.21 enact specific rules for state-to-state and investor-state dispute settlement. Chapter 14 ensures equal access to ports and ports services – a traditionally protected activity in

[54] For more on the so-called 'prudential carve-out', see European Parliament, DG for Internal Policies (Policy Department A: Economic and Scientific Policy), 'Financial Services in EU Trade Agreements' (*IP/A/ECON/2014-08*, November 2018) 17–18, < www.europarl.europa.eu/RegData/etudes/STUD/2014/536300/IPOL_STU(2014)536300_EN.pdf (last accessed 2 March 2020).

Canada – and Chapter 15 strengthens consumers' rights to receive telecommunication services also in remote areas (Article 15.8) and to keep their numbers when switching their provider (Article 15.10). In addition, Chapter 16 on electronic commerce contains the important principle that no tariffs are due on electronic deliveries (Article 16.3). This is another 'WTO plus' commitment seen that there is only a moratorium on new customs duties on electronic transmissions at the WTO level.[55]

E. Interim Conclusion

The services area is increasingly important for international trade flows, but also very sensitive in view of the financial crisis and the possible (too) lax prudential supervision of banks. Against that background, we can see two tendencies. On the one hand, the EU pushes for further liberalisation of services in general by adopting a negative list-approach – that would help the market access of retail services or other services that fulfil basic needs of the consumers, for example. On the other hand, in particular in the financial sector, the EU is anxious not to give away its prudential and regulatory powers. Hence, the modern clauses in this area look more like an attempt to set a global example of tough prudential supervision. At the same time, in the area of professional qualifications, we see that the 'top aim' of mutual recognition is not even possible between two very close economies with a similar political and economic system. This shows that setting global standards for professional qualifications seems like an impossible task.

V. EU Standards on Competition, Procurement, Intellectual Property

A. Competition Policy

The WTO agreements are silent on competition policy, and the 'Working Group on the Interaction between Trade and Competition Policy' (WGTCP)[56] did not produce any tangible result by its last meeting in May 2003 before the Cancun summit of that year.[57]

[55] This moratorium has been in place since the Ministerial Declaration on Global Electronic Commerce (WT/MIN(98)/DEC/2, 20 May 1998).

[56] According to the Singapore Ministerial Declaration (WT/MIN(96)/DEC, 18 December 1996, Point 20) this body was accorded a mandate 'to study issues raised by Members relating to the interaction between trade and competition policy, including anti-competitive practices, in order to identify any areas that might merit further consideration in the WTO framework'.

[57] The WGTCP held its final meeting in May 2003 and had its mandate within the Doha Round revoked in the Cancun negotiations (Chad Damro, 'Destructive Issue Linkages: The Failure of Multilateral Trade-Competition Negotiations' (2012) 57(3) *Antitrust Bulletin* 563, 579–80).

Chapter 17 of CETA fills the vacuum on the WTO level and recalls that both sides will fight against cartels, the abuse of dominant positions by companies and anti-competitive mergers (Article 17.2 and 17.3). These reflect three priorities of the EU's competition policy.[58] However, state aid control, another key feature of the Brussels competition policy, is missing.[59] This topic is often included in EU agreements with neighbouring states, which are encouraged to adopt their own state aid control systems.[60] With Canada, such an approach would not make sense as this country does not aspire to copy the EU's competition policy choices. Instead, the two parties have agreed on important new principles concerning state monopolies or companies with special rights in Chapter 18. Such entities will not discriminate against goods and services from the other party (Article 18.4). This would be a very important breakthrough for the revision of the WTO standards on the matter, where state-owned enterprises often escape the scrutiny of the SCM Agreement.

B. Public Procurement

In general, each WTO member is free to set its own rules on public procurement and to allow the participation of foreign bidders in call for tenders. In the EU, this issue is even left to the Member States. The Commission proposal for an 'International Procurement Instrument' of 2012 (revised in 2016) would create an EU specific instrument, but has not yet been adopted.[61]

In the WTO, procurement rules are only binding on the few Members that have ratified the plurilateral Government Procurement Agreement (GPA). This text is inspired by the EU's procurement regime and contains complicated annexes, which identify the covered sectors and entities. In CETA, the EU and Canada reaffirm and specify the general procurement rules – award decisions must be transparent and impartial (Article 19.14) and public authorities shall not discriminate on the basis of nationality (Article 19.4). The real progress, however, lies in the coverage. The EU obtained a rare commitment from Canada concerning their sub-federal entities (Article 19.2 (4) and Annex 19-2). This may also be seen as a door-opener

[58] Article 101–102 TFEU and Council Regulation (EC) No 139/2004 of 20 January 2004 on the control of concentrations between undertakings (the EC Merger Regulation) [2004] OJ L 24/1.

[59] Article 107 TFEU.

[60] See, eg, the Stabilisation and Association agreement Between the European Communities and their Member States of the one part, and the republic of Serbia, of the other part [2013] OJ L278/14, Art 73. For further reading on competition chapters, see Frank Hoffmeister, 'The Deep and Comprehensive Free Trade Agreements of the European Union – Concept and Challenges' in Marise Cremona and Tamara Takáks (eds), 'Trade Liberalisation and Standardization – New Directions in the "Low Politics" of EU Foreign Policy' (*CLEER Working Paper 2013/6*, 2013) 17–18, www.asser.nl/media/1641/cleer_13-6_web.pdf (last accessed 2 March 2020).

[61] On the original version of this proposal of 2012 (COM (2012) 124), see Frank Hoffmeister, 'The EU Public Procurement Regime on Third Country Bidders – Setting the Cursor between Openness and Reciprocity' in Harri Kalimo and Max S Jansson (eds), *EU Economic Law in a Time of Crisis* (Elgar, 2016) 82–88. The proposal was revised in January 2016 (COM (2016) 34).

in negotiations with other federalist countries. In particular, the US argument that the federal Government cannot legally commit sub-federal entities has lost relative force after CETA.[62] Moreover, the CETA procurement chapter can show China, currently in slow GPA accession negotiations, how many sectoral entities may be open for foreign competition.

C. Intellectual Property

Chapter 20 on Intellectual Property is extremely complex and merits a separate analysis. The red thread is to build on existing Trade-Related Aspects of Intellectual Property Rights (TRIPS) Agreement standards and to enact more disciplines for particular forms of intellectual property (IP) rights. At the same time, the Parties reaffirm in Article 20.3 their attachment to public health and the WTO compromise on compulsory licensing of patents, as laid down in the TRIPS amendment of 2005.[63] The most intricate problem is the relationship between trademarks and geographic indications or GIs (Article 22(1) TRIPS). The latter are a predominantly EU concept, which the Union wishes to promote globally.[64] It argues that certain products cannot bear the name of the geographic region ('Champagne', 'Parma Ham') if they are not produced there. Accordingly, Canada is asked to register key European GIs in a national registry and to prosecute offenders under Canadian law, which are listed in a particular annex (Article 20.18 and Annex 20-A). This is a major exercise in exportation of EU GI standards and runs contrary to the US policy to push for more IP protection through trademarks.[65] Canada's commitment to the GI system is remarkable since it used to align itself with the US's reliance on trademarks.[66] Importantly, in Articles 20.27 and 20.28, the EU asks for

[62] Gary Hufbauer and Tyler Moran argue that the discriminatory 'buy American' practices in sub-federal entities could be regulated under the Commerce Clause of the US Constitution, but that 'the federal government is generally unwilling to "meddle" in the affairs of the states without a strong imperative, so no existing agreements have forced procurement rules on state and local governments'. See Gary Hufbauer and Tyler Moran, 'Government Procurement in US Trade Agreements' (*RSCAS Policy Paper 2015/09*, 2015) 2, https://cadmus.eui.eu/bitstream/handle/1814/37320/RSCAS_PP_2015_09.pdf?sequence=1&isAllowed=y (last accessed 2 March 2020).

[63] General Council Decision on the Amendment of the TRIPS Agreement (WT/L/641, 6 November 2005) 7.

[64] See, eg, the recent agreement with China on Geographical Indications (Joint Press Statement by Commissioner Phil Hogan and Minister Zhong Shan on the End of the Negotiations of an Agreement between the European Union and the Government of the People's Republic of China on Cooperation on, and Protection of, Geographical Indications (6 November 2019), https://ec.europa.eu/info/sites/info/files/food-farming-fisheries/food_safety_and_quality/documents/statement-commissioner-hogan-china-gis_en.pdf (last accessed 2 March 2020).

[65] For an overview of the US position, see Caroline Le Goffic and Andrea Zappalaglio, 'The Role Played by the US Government in Protecting Geographical Indications' (2017) 98 *World Development* 35, 36–37.

[66] Indeed, Canada signed on to the so-called 'Joint Proposal' with the US in the context of the GI negotiations at the WTO level (Article 23.4 TRIPS), see Proposed Draft Trips Council Decision on the Establishment of a Multilateral System of Notification and Registration of Geographical Indications

the *sui generis* protection for pharmaceuticals and relevant patent rules. Finally, there is an extensive set of rules aimed at strengthening the enforcement mechanisms available in the legal order of both sides (Articles 20.32–20.49).

VI. EU Standards on Sustainable Development

A. General Principles (Chapter 22)

Since the EU-CARIFORUM Economic Partnership Agreement,[67] a modern EU trade agreement contains a sustainable development chapter. The underlying idea is to reaffirm that trade and investment standards will not be used to lower social and environmental standards. Rather to the contrary, a trade agreement should provide for a forum to discuss these issues with each other to ensure that competition is not distorted by unduly divergent standards on both sides. To that effect, core International Labour Organisation (ILO) and environmental standards should be observed. Article 22.1 thus recalls the 1992 Rio-Declaration and the 2008 ILO Declaration on Fair Globalisation as the relevant yardsticks.[68] In order to make such issues a legitimate topic of FTA implementation, the EU has proposed to establish a Civil Society Dialogue (Article 22.5). Representatives of trade unions and NGOs can hence discuss their concerns with public officials once a year and recommend remedial action.

B. Labour Standards (Chapter 23)

As Canada has already ratified all major conventions on labour standards,[69] the focus is on their full implementation (Article 23.3). With other trading partners,

for Wines and Spirits (Submission by Argentina, Australia, Canada, Chile, Costa Rica, Dominican Republic, Ecuador, El Salvador, Guatemala, Honduras, Israel, Japan, Korea, Mexico, New Zealand, Nicaragua, Paraguay, the Separate Customs Territory of Taiwan, Penghu, Kinmen and Matsu, South Africa and the United States) (TN/IP/W/10/Rev. 4, 31 March 2011), www.wto.org/english/tratop_e/trips_e/ta_docs_e/5_1_tnipw10rev4_e.pdf (last accessed 2 March 2020).

[67] Economic Partnership Agreement between the CARIFORUM States, of the one part, and the European Community and its Member States, of the other part [2008] OJ L289/3. See on the early sustainable development clauses, Frank Hoffmeister, 'Der Beitrag der EU zur Entwicklung des besonderen Völkerrechts' in W Obwexer (Hrsg), *Der Europaïsche Union im Völkerrecht (Beiheft 2)* (Nomos, 2012) 256–57.

[68] UNCED, 'The Rio Declaration on Environment and Development' (1992, 19), <www.unesco.org/education/pdf/RIO_E.PDF (last accessed 2 March 2020); ILO (97th session), 'ILO Declaration on Social Justice and Fair Globalization' (10 June 2008), <www.ilo.org/wcmsp5/groups/public/---dgreports/---cabinet/documents/genericdocument/wcms_371208.pdf (last accessed 2 March 2020).

[69] The ILO database provides an overview of the ratifications by Canada at www.ilo.org/dyn/normlex/en/f?p=1000:11200:0::NO:11200:P11200_COUNTRY_ID:102582 (last accessed 2 March 2020).

the EU might even insist that a partner country ratifies an additional labour or environmental Convention – as for example in the case of Vietnam.[70] An important point is also the provision of appropriate enforcement mechanisms at national level (Article 23.5).

In case of disagreement, the parties may enter into formal consultation and convene a Panel of Experts (Articles 23.9–23.10). Interestingly, the EU has already triggered such provisions once, namely in the case of the Korean FTA.[71] Here, Korea's lukewarm implementation of trade unionists rights gave rise to a complaint by the EU.

On the other hand, the failure to live up to agreed labour standards is not coupled to the ordinary sanctions system. Hence, trade concessions cannot be unilaterally revoked. This is an outstanding controversial point within the EU, where the left side of the European Parliament asks for a 'hard' enforcement system.[72]

C. Environmental Standards (Chapter 24)

A similar approach can also be witnessed with respect to environmental standards. Existing multilateral conventions are incorporated into CETA and their proper implementation shall be discussed by the Civil Society Forum. In addition, there are new clauses to encourage sustainable measures on forest products (Article 24.10) and a specific chapter on dialogue on science and forestry (Chapter 25). Moreover, parties commit to take effective action against illegal or unreported fishing (Article 24.11).

[70] Proposed FTA between the European Union and the Socialist Republic of Vietnam – Annex 1 to the Proposal for a Council Decision on the conclusion of the Free Trade Agreement between the European Union and the Socialist Republic of Vietnam (COM(2018) 691 final, 17 October 2018) Art 13.4(3), https://eur-lex.europa.eu/resource.html?uri=cellar:cecd32a2-d2e8-11e8-9424-01aa75ed71a1.0001.02/DOC_2&format=PDF (last accessed 2 March 2020).

[71] Request for Consultations by the European Union on 'Republic of Korea – compliance with obligations under Chapter 13 of the EU – Korea Free Trade Agreement' (17 December 2018), <http://trade.ec.europa.eu/doclib/docs/2018/december/tradoc_157586.pdf (last accessed 2 March 2020)) and the subsequent Request for the establishment of a Panel of Experts by the European Union on 'Republic of Korea – compliance with obligations under Chapter 13 of the EU – Korea Free Trade Agreement' (4 July 2019), https://trade.ec.europa.eu/doclib/docs/2019/july/tradoc_157992.pdf (last accessed 2 March 2020).

[72] European Parliament non-legislative resolution on the draft Council decision on the conclusion of the Agreement between the European Union and Japan for an Economic Partnership (*07964/2018 – C8-0382/2018 – 2018/0091M(NLE)*, 12 December 2018) recital 13, www.europarl.europa.eu/doceo/document/TA-8-2018-0505_EN.pdf (last accessed 2 March 2020). Also in favour of an effective enforcement procedure (and specifically a Private Complaint Procedure) are Marco Bronckers and Giovanni Gruni, 'Improving the Enforcement of Labour Standards in the EU's Free Trade Agreements' in Denise Prévost, Iveta Alexovičová and Jens Hillebrand Pohl (eds), *Restoring Trust in Trade: Liber Amicorum in Honour of Peter Van den Bossche* (Hart Publishing, 2018) 157–72.

Finally, another new development has arisen in addition. Pushed by France,[73] the Council is considering whether the reference to the Paris Agreement should become an essential element of any FTA like human rights. Evidently, if such move was taken, the relevant Paris commitments would also become enforceable under the FTA.

VII. Conclusion

This overview of the EU's most advanced FTA has shown that a number of trends need to be distinguished when assessing Europe's role in setting global standards.

First, the EU *reaffirms* many WTO standards and protects them against erosion. This can be observed in the area of goods, where questionable attempts from the US to reintroduce unilateral tariffs or safeguards or illegal voluntary export restraints frustrate the EU's request to abide by the relevant WTO provisions on the matter. Here, the EU does not set new standards, but simply maintains existing ones.

Second, there are a number of instances where the EU *builds on* existing WTO standards and wishes to add new elements of liberalisation. These 'WTO plus' provisions can mostly be found in the area of trade (TBT, SPS, Trade Remedies, Public Procurement). The underlying concept is that those new standards can attract some followers to lead to a new round of liberalisation through a net or critical mass of countries in bilateral relationships willing to go the next step. This can also be seen in the area of services, where the cautious 'positive list' approach is replaced by the more ambitious 'negative list' approach. These WTO 'plus' provisions are considered to constitute a 'blueprint' for new multilateral rules on the matter when the time is ripe. However, some of these additional disciplines are coupled to specific EU economic interests. For example, the protection of European GIs will be less accepted by other trading partners as a necessary rule of global application.

Third, the EU sometimes *reforms* international rules in order to cure perceived weaknesses. This is obvious in the area of international investment law, where EU treaties depart from established BIT practice both in the area of substantive standards and dispute settlement. In this area, the jury is still out on whether it will convince a sufficiently large number of other states to engage in the exercise of formalising the new approach by the establishment of a MIC. Depending on the viewpoint of an observer, this attempt may be qualified as another example of EU exceptionalism rather than setting global standards.

[73] See, eg, the Information from the French, Spanish and Luxembourg delegations on strengthening coherence between the EU Free Trade Agreements and the Paris Agreement on climate change (General Secretariat of the Council 7016/19, 1 March 2019), https://data.consilium.europa.eu/doc/document/ST-7016-2019-INIT/en/pdf (last accessed 2 March 2020).

Fourth, the EU's practice is *restrictive* in protecting a number of specific concerns raised by the European public. Examples of a restrictive approach are related to the precautionary principle in SPS measures, the need to protect audio-visual services and the wish to maintain regulatory space on public health and financial supervision.

Finally, the EU is *progressive* by bringing in related topics into the world of FTAs. A strong chapter on sustainable development is a case in point, where both the ratification and implementation of labour and environmental standards are made a legitimate subject for joint trade committees. In this area, the development is still ongoing as can be seen by the ever-growing importance of such chapters in the EU's practice and the first dispute settlement case against Korea.

In sum, one can say that the EU's practice to reaffirm, to build on, and to reform global standards, while being restrictive and progressive on a number of specific European points is probably not *setting*, but *shaping* global standards. Connecting this finding to the overall research topic of convergence, this means that the EU works as a force in both directions: By reaffirming and building on WTO standards, it stabilises established world trade law, which is based on the fundamental principle of safeguarding free and open markets. Being restrictive on certain issues such as audio-visual services and certain food and safety standards, it also draws limits to further convergence on these issues to preserve policy space in Europe. Finally, the EU's huge reform agenda in the area of substantive and institutional investment law may be triggering a new wave of convergence, which might culminate in the establishment of a new MIC if the initiative finds enough traction in other parts of the world.

2

Convergence through EU Unilateralism

JED ODERMATT

I. Introduction

Much has been made in recent years of the United States' withdrawal from its leadership in multilateral institutions, and its preference to pursue unilateral action. This is often contrasted with the approach of the European Union, which traditionally has been more supportive of international cooperation and multilateral institutions.[1] The EU Treaties commit the Union to respect international law and to seek solutions to international problems through multilateral means, and the EU has sought to influence the development of international law via multilateral institutions, especially through the United Nations and UN bodies. Yet in recent years, many of the EU's policies have been criticised for being 'unilateral', 'extra-territorial', or even violating international law. This points to a certain paradox of the EU as a convergence actor. As the EU becomes more assertive at the international level, as it seeks to play a greater role in a number of fields of global governance, such policies may have the effect of simultaneously undermining that very system of multilateral governance. In areas such as climate change mitigation, financial market regulation, data protection and human rights protection, the EU's unilateral approach often stems, not from disengagement with multilateralism, but from an inability to make progress through multilateral institutions. Its push for greater convergence towards its own values and norms can at the same time have the effect of weakening the general multilateral system. This contribution analyses and discusses this apparent paradox through the lens of EU multilateralism and unilateralism. It discusses how the EU may at the same time be driving forward fields of international law and promoting convergence towards its values and interests, but also risks undermining the integrity of those multilateral institutions.

The first part of the chapter discusses the European Union and its approach to multilateralism. It shows how the EU has a strong commitment to multilateralism,

[1] See Jed Odermatt and Ramses A Wessel, 'The Challenges of Engaging with International Institutions – The EU and Multilateralism Under Strain' in Ramses A Wessel and Jed Odermatt (eds), *Research Handbook on the European Union and International Organizations* (Edward Elgar, 2019) 658.

and that its understanding of what this entails continues to change over time. It argues that multilateralism is about much more than working with a number of actors, but about a commitment to certain values, including the involvement of international institutions, the respect for certain global norms and international law. The second part then discusses fields of law where the EU has been challenged and criticised for pursuing a unilateral approach, focusing on the fields of climate change policy, data protection and the use of autonomous restrictive measures (sanctions). In these areas, it is argued, the EU is pursuing more unilateral measures to promote convergence because it has not been able to find agreement at the international level. The phenomenon of 'EU unilateralism' can be understood in terms of divergence and convergence: on the one hand, the EU is seeking to push forward the law and promote greater convergence around its norms, yet pursuing this policy in a unilateral manner may also lead to greater fragmentation of the very legal order it seeks to promote.

The chapter does not make the argument that unilateral measures and action can never be justified, or that the EU should never pursue certain policies unilaterally. Rather, it argues that in cases where the EU seeks to be a global leader, such action can cause significant friction for non-EU states and other international organisations. This trade-off should be acknowledged. When the EU seeks to promote convergence with EU norms and values via unilateral policies, such policies can have the effect of driving fragmentation of the multilateral order. The argument, moreover, is not only a legal one – states and organisations can and do adopt unilateral acts that are in conformity with international law. As Sands argues, '"Unilateral" acts become especially contentious when they are associated with the *imposition* of one community of its values on another community and where that other community has not consented or acquiesced in the imposition of such values'.[2] The EU is not obligated, under EU law or international law, to pursue such policies solely through multilateral institutions. Yet the EU should acknowledge the drawbacks associated with unilateral approaches. In some instances, EU unilateralism may indeed drive forward and develop international law through convergence with EU norms.

II. The EU and Multilateralism

The EU Treaties commit the Union to multilateralism. Its external action is to be guided by principles including democracy, the rule of law, the universality and indivisibility of human rights and respect for the principles of the UN Charter.[3] Article 21 of the Treaty on European Union (TEU) also sets out that the EU shall

[2] Philippe Sands, '"Unilateralism" Values and International Law' (2000) 11 *European Journal of International Law* 293.

[3] Article 21(1), Consolidated Version of the Treaty on European Union [2008] OJ C115/13 ('TEU').

'promote multilateral solutions to common problems, in particular in the framework of the United Nations'.[4] It shall pursue common strategies and actions to 'promote an international system based on stronger multilateral cooperation and good global governance'.[5] Although Article 3(5) TEU does not explicitly mention multilateralism, it commits the Union to 'strict observance and the development of international law, including respect for the principles of the United Nations Charter'.[6] The EU's commitment to multilateralism is also set out in numerous foreign policy documents and statements (see below).

The EU priorities at the 74th United Nations General Assembly clearly demonstrate the enduring importance of strengthening multilateralism. They set out that '[t]he European Union is an indispensable partner of the United Nations to promote and strengthen multilateralism and the rules-based international order'.[7] The document, moreover, emphasises 'translating multilateralism into action'. This means that the EU is not to pursue multilateralism for its own sake, but in order to address pressing global challenges. EU documents prioritise certain areas of partnership and cooperation in this regard. For instance, in recent years, reform of the UN system, improving partnerships with the UN and regional organisations, conflict prevention and action on climate change, have been some of the EU's key goals in the UN General Assembly. The promotion of human rights and pursuing the UN's sustainable development goals have also been prioritised, as has working on cybersecurity. This appears to recognise that the UN and the EU share some of the most pressing challenges. The issue of migration and forced displacement, which is also set out as a priority area of engagement with the UN, is clearly linked with the issues facing the EU and its own migrant/refugee challenge.

The EU Treaties and other documents highlight the importance of multilateralism. But what does this precisely mean, and what does it require in terms of EU law and policy? There is a debate among International Relations scholars about the precise meaning of multilateralism.[8] According to one view, multilateralism is a form of cooperation between more than two states – it is to be contrasted with unilateralism and bilateralism.[9] This narrow, quantitative definition is concerned with the number of actors involved. This understanding of multilateralism has been broadened to also involve a certain way of doing foreign policy.[10] According to this understanding, multilateralism also involves a commitment to certain

[4] Article 21(1) second para, TEU.

[5] Article 21(2)(h) TEU.

[6] Article 3(5) TEU.

[7] General Secretariat of the Council, 'EU priorities at the United Nations and the 74th United Nations General Assembly, September 2019–September 2020', Brussels, 15 July 2019. Available at http://data.consilium.europa.eu/doc/document/ST-10895-2019-INIT/en/pdf.

[8] Robert O Keohane, 'Multilateralism: An Agenda for Research' (1990) 45 *International Journal* 4, 731–64.

[9] *Ibid.*

[10] De Búrca presents the EU's preference for a 'governance mode' of foreign policy. Gráinne de Búrca, 'The EU as a Legal Power in Global Governance?' in Bart Van Vooren, Steven Blockmans, Jan Wouters (eds), *The EU's Role in Global Governance: The Legal Dimension* (Oxford University Press, 2013) 40.

values: the involvement of international institutions, the respect for certain global norms and a commitment to international law.[11] Multilateralism, then, has both a quantitative and qualitative dimension – it seeks to address international problems through international cooperation of a number of states, but also requires commitment to the principles of this 'rules-based order' to make this system work.

It is understandable then, that the EU's commitment to multilateralism is often equated with its commitment to international institutions. The key institutions in this rules-based order include the World Bank, the International Monetary Fund, the World Trade Organisation and the United Nations and the wider UN system. Yet a commitment to multilateralism, it is argued, involves more than working within institutions, but also a commitment to a set of internationally recognised norms in order for these institutions to function: the sovereign equality of states, the principle of non-intervention and prohibition of the use of force in international relations, as well as a commitment to respect international human rights law. This broader understanding of multilateralism therefore involves a commitment to certain values.

What does a commitment to multilateralism mean for the EU? Multilateralism is usually presented in a positive light. Yet multilateralism should not be viewed as inherently preferable or more desirable than these other foreign policy approaches. The provision of aid is usually a unilateral policy, and EU trade agreements continue to be concluded in a bilateral manner. Moreover, multilateral institutions may be dominated by one or more states, giving the impression of multilateralism, whereas beneath the surface it pursues the goals and policies of a small group of powerful states.[12] There may be instances where the pursuance of objectives has failed at the global level, and unilateral measures seek to fill that gap. This was the argument used to justify the EU's controversial emissions trading scheme applied to aircraft from outside the EU – the policy was justified because negotiations within the International Civil Aviation Organization (ICAO) had failed (see below).

There are a number of advantages to pursuing a multilateral approach. Multilateralism can provide greater certainty and predictability in international relations when other actors agree to certain rules of the game. This rules-based system then has the inherent value of providing stability, since it provides avenues for states to seek to change international rules and develop international law. Multilateralism and multilateral institutions are also closely connected with the provision of global public goods. Multilateralism may also be a more effective

[11] Ruggie discusses three features of multilateralism: indivisibility, generalised organising principles and diffuse reciprocity. John G Ruggie (ed), *Multilateralism Matters: The Theory and Praxis on an International Form* (Columbia University Press, 1993).

[12] This has been described as 'unilateralism with a multilateral cover'. Ruth Wedgwood, 'Unilateral Action in a Multilateral World' in Stewart Patrick and Shepard Forman (eds), *Multilateralism and U.S. Foreign Policy: Ambivalent Engagement* (Lynne Rienner, 2002).

means of pursuing EU objectives, given its nature as a 'normative' power. It has been suggested that the EU has multilateralism and respect for international institutions in its 'DNA'.[13] According to this argument, one should expect the EU to be more open towards multilateralism since it is itself a form of cooperation between states. Established as a form of economic cooperation to respond to the horrors of the Second World War, this argument goes, we should expect the EU to also show a friendly attitude towards other multilateral institutions. However, this is not always the case. The EU has its own strategic and economic interests, and these can be pursued through various methods, of which multilateralism is one form.

Moreover, although the EU Treaties explicitly mention multilateralism as a value and a preferred method of foreign policy, it is by no means a legal obligation. Article 3(5) TEU, which sets out the values and interests the EU is to pursue in its external relations,[14] does not commit the EU to multilateralism, beyond mentioning, 'respect for the principles of the United Nations Charter'. Article 21(1) TEU further provides that the Union's 'action on the international scene' is to be guided by numerous principles, including the 'respect for the principles of the United Nations and international law'.[15] One of the goals of the EU's external action is to 'consolidate and support democracy, the rule of law, human rights and the principles of international law'.[16] This applies not only to 'the Union's external action' but also to 'the external aspects of its other policies'.[17] So while respect for international law and the 'principles' of the United Nations are legal obligations on the EU institutions, there is no similar legal commitment to pursuing multilateralism.

The EU's commitment to multilateralism is also shown in the EU's foreign policy documents. The 2016 EU Global Strategy,[18] for instance, seeks to give effect to the EU's commitment to multilateralism:

> The EU will promote a rules-based global order. We have an interest in promoting agreed rules to provide global public goods and contribute to a peaceful and sustainable world. The EU will promote a rules-based global order with multilateralism as its key principle and the United Nations at its core.[19]
>
> [...]

[13] Stephan Keukeleire and Tom Delreux, *The Foreign Policy of the European Union*, 2nd edn (Palgrave Macmillan, 2014) 301: 'the EU's commitment to a multilateral approach can be seen as part of its DNA'.

[14] Article 3(5) TEU.

[15] Article 21(1) TEU; See Opinion in C-366/10 *Air Transport Association of America and Others v Secretary of State for Energy and Climate Change*, EU:C:2011:637, para 43.

[16] Article 21(2)(b) TEU.

[17] Article 21(3) TEU.

[18] *Shared Vision, Common Action: A Stronger Europe – A Global Strategy for the European Union's Foreign and Security Policy*, European External Action Service, Brussels, June 2016 ('EU Global Strategy 2016').

[19] *Ibid* 8.

> The EU will strive for a strong UN as the bedrock of the multilateral rules-based order, and develop globally coordinated responses with international and regional organisations, states and non-state actors.[20]

Here the EU presents the reasons why it is in the Union's interests to pursue a multilateral approach. As a group of medium-sized states, the Union is more likely to achieve its goals and interests through a rules-based international order, rather than one based on pure power politics.

There are differences in the way the EU presents its commitment to multilateralism in the 2016 EU Global Strategy compared with the 2003 EU Security Strategy. Developed in the wake of the Iraq war, which divided EU Member States, the document puts the EU's commitment to multilateralism front and centre. However, this document views multilateralism as a commitment to multilateral *institutions*, especially the United Nations. The 2016 Global Strategy, on the other hand, does not prioritise the UN and institutions to the same extent. It sees multilateralism as involving other states, other regions, other international organisations, civil society and non-state actors. Moreover, whereas the 2003 Strategy highlighted the role of the United States, the 2016 Strategy sees a diminished importance for the US, demonstrating the importance of other regions, especially Asia. This has recently been expressed in the 2019 Council Conclusions on 'EU action to strengthen rules-based multilateralism'[21] prepared as part of the EU priorities at the United Nations and the 74th United Nations General Assembly.[22] In addition to supporting the UN and existing multilateral agreements, it also prioritises 'extending' multilateralism to new realities. This includes using forums such as the Organisation for Security and Cooperation in Europe (OSCE), the Internet Governance Forum, the Council of Europe and the Organisation for Economic Co-operation and Development (OECD).

Another shift is the importance of ensuring that multilateralism provides results. The emphasis is not on multilateralism for its own sake, but to more effectively address global problems. The 2019 Council Conclusions also stress, therefore, the idea of 'effective multilateralism', or 'translating multilateralism into action': 'An *effective*, relevant and resilient multilateral system must be capable of facing new global realities; remain true to the rules and principles of the UN Charter; and promote the peaceful resolution of disputes among states.'[23] The conclusions set out the EU priorities in order to build 'an *effective* multilateral

[20] *Ibid* 39.

[21] General Secretariat of the Council, 'EU action to strengthen rules-based multilateralism' Brussels, 17 June 2019.

[22] See Press Release, Council of the EU, 'EU Priorities at the United Nations and the 74th United Nations General Assembly adopted' 15 July 2019 ('Council Conclusions'), www.consilium.europa.eu/en/press/press-releases/2019/07/15/eu-priorities-at-the-united-nations-and-the-74th-united-nations-general-assembly-adopted/.

[23] *Ibid* para 1.

system that delivers results in tackling today's and tomorrow's global challenges'.[24] There is an emphasis throughout on effectiveness and providing results. It is not only about making institutions work better, but also broadens multilateralism to include a 'multi-stakeholder approach' that includes human rights defenders, non-governmental organisations, the media, the private sector and social partners, culture and business communities including the tech sector, academia and local governments.[25]

This is why the EU has presented its role in the Iran nuclear deal as an example of its commitment to multilateralism. The 2016 Global Strategy also highlights the need for intersecting multilateralism, that is, cooperation between the Union and other regions. While the Strategy refers to institutions, it also highlights the need for reform of these bodies, including the UN and international financial institutions. There are also a number of policy areas where the Union sees multilateralism as playing a particularly important role. Disarmament, non-proliferation and peace and security are important. The protection of the environment, action against climate change and policy on sustainable development are also given greater prominence. And areas that have not been previously discussed as having a strong multilateral dimension, such as digital governance and cyber-security are also mentioned as key areas that necessitate a multilateral approach.

The EU's support for multilateralism appears to be even more important in a global context in which commitment to multilateral institutions is increasingly challenged. The United States, once viewed as one of the EU's key partners in multilateralism, shows a much more skeptical attitude towards multilateral institutions. The Trump presidency, for example, has shown a clear skepticism (or outright hostility) towards multilateral institutions, seeking to pursue an 'America First' strategy in which the UN and other bodies are given little importance. The Trump foreign policy is driven by 'principled realism', one which prioritises strong sovereign states, and 'deals' between powerful states, rather than through multilateral bodies. The Trump Administration's decision to withdraw the US from the Joint Comprehensive Plan of Action and the Paris Climate Change Agreement – both of key importance for the EU – demonstrates this foreign policy in action. How should the EU and its Member States respond to this shifting global context? Should it also, under certain circumstances, pursue unilateral measures to achieve its aims and objectives? Or should it continue to pursue and support multilateralism, not just in its rhetoric and official statements, but also in its substantive policies? Of course, this is not a binary choice – but as the EU promotes convergence through unilateral measures, this can have the consequence of undermining the multilateral order and rules-based system in more subtle ways.

[24] *Ibid* para 8.
[25] *Ibid* para 9, point 12.

III. EU 'Unilateralism'

The EU's commitment to multilateralism can be contrasted with the trend towards greater unilateralism in EU policy in recent years. As with multilateralism, there is no single (legal) definition of the term, and is used to describe various policies that are adopted by a state or international organisation that have certain external effects, where those policies have not been consented to or agreed upon with other states and organisations. Unilateralism is often associated with powerful states, such as the United States, adopting a self-centred foreign policy, which undermines multilateral values.[26] Unilateralism is therefore not just about a state or organisation adopting a policy alone, but pursuing a policy or taking measures 'that would not fit into existing international norms or rules'.[27]

As with multilateralism, unilateral action is not inherently positive or negative, and much of the EU's 'unilateral' activity ostensibly pursues goals that seek to uphold certain global values, such as human rights or the protection of the environment. Legal scholars have discussed the various ways, for instance, that EU law and policy can have external effects, and in some cases described as a form of EU unilateralism.[28] There has also been a discussion of a trend in EU policy described as the 'global reach' of EU law,[29] encompassing a broad range of policies and actions under which the EU policy has certain effects outside EU territory:

> It includes the extraterritorial application of EU law, the presence of territorial extension, and the so-called 'Brussels Effect', all phenomena concerned with the effects of unilateral legislative instruments and regulatory action beyond the EU's borders. But 'global reach' also refers to the impact of the EU's bilateral relationships in the form of agreements with third countries or third country agencies, and of the EU's engagement with multilateral fora and the negotiation of international legal instruments.[30]

In their study on the topic of *EU Law Beyond EU Borders*, Cremona and Scott discuss the various ways in which the EU has had an effect beyond its own borders in areas such as the regulation of the Internet and data privacy; climate change; EU competition law; financial regulation; and migration. Some of these policies have a clear external element, and are pursued with the intention of protecting 'EU values', such as in the area of human rights or environmental protection.

[26] See Wedgwood (n 12) 17; Gabriella Blum, 'Bilateralism, Multilateralism, and the Architecture of International Law' (2008) 49 *Harvard International Law Journal* 323–79; David M Malone and Yuen Foong Khong (eds), *Unilateralism and U.S. Foreign Policy: International Perspectives* (Lynne Rienner, 2003).

[27] Atsushi Tago, 'Multilateralism, Bilateralism, and Unilateralism in Foreign Policy' in *Oxford Research Encyclopedia, Politics* (Oxford University Press, 2019).

[28] See Joanne Scott and Lavanya Rajamani, 'EU Climate Change Unilateralism' (2012) 23 *European Journal of International Law* 469.

[29] Elaine Fahey, *The Global Reach of EU Law* (Routledge, 2016); Marise Cremona and Joanne Scott (eds), *EU Law Beyond EU Borders: The Extraterritorial Reach of EU Law* (Oxford University Press, 2019).

[30] Marise Cremona and Joanne Scott, 'Introduction' in Cremona and Scott (n 29) 1.

Others are focused more on internal concerns, such as financial stability in the Union.[31] Such policies have been criticised, mostly due to the fact that they – intentionally or otherwise – apply EU law outside of its borders. This argument is sometimes framed in terms of violating principles of public international law regarding extra-territorial jurisdiction. Such policies can also be criticised for pursuing a more unilateral approach. Some of the policies have aggravated other states. It should be pointed out, however, that in many cases the EU has pursued such policies precisely because a multilateral approach did not prove satisfactory. This has been presented as 'contingent multilateralism'.[32] This means that the EU will seek to resolve issues at the global level, but if this fails, it has the prerogative to 'go it alone' and pursue its own agenda and interests. One could argue that the EU's commitment to multilateralism does not prevent it from pursuing its objectives and interests through other measures if and when multilateral processes do not achieve satisfactory outcomes. On the other hand, such an approach to multilateralism can have the effect of undermining the importance of global institutions and lead other states to pursue similar unilateral measures. In order to safeguard and promote certain values and principles, the EU will at times disregard multilateralism to pursue these objectives through various types of unilateral measures.

One may argue that the EU should not be expected to wait for a multilateral solution to emerge before taking action in areas such as climate action, data protection and international security. Yet as discussed above, the argument is not that there is a binary decision between pursuing a multilateral or unilateral course of action, or that unilateral actions are illegal or unjustified. Rather, in the policy fields discussed below, the EU is seeking to uphold and promote certain 'values' at the international level. It should also be acknowledged that by doing so, the EU may also have the effect of undermining values associated with multilateralism, and risks antagonising other states and organisations. The three examples discussed are climate change, data protection and autonomous measures. While these are very different policies in terms of their effects and rationale, they are all areas where the EU has sought to uphold certain values through unilateral action, which at the same time has the consequence of putting strain on multilateral approaches.

A. Climate Change

The first main area where the EU has been criticised for following a unilateral approach has been in the field of climate change.[33] In 2003, the EU adopted

[31] Joanne Scott, 'The Global Reach of EU Law' in Cremona and Scott (n 29): '… it is important to be aware that the vast majority of EU measures that give rise to territorial extension pursue objectives that are internal to the EU and are less prone to causing controversy …'

[32] Scott and Rajamani (n 28).

[33] Scott and Rajamani (n 28).

legislation establishing a scheme for greenhouse gas emission allowance trading,[34] and in 2008 amended this Directive to include emissions from international aviation within the emissions trading system (ETS). The ETS applied to flights that arrive or depart from the territory of an EU Member State. It applied to the entire flight, even in cases where the majority of the flight took place outside the airspace of EU Member States. It was argued that the EU's ETS was in violation of international law due to the 'extra-territorial' scope of the legislation.

The question of whether a certain policy is 'extra-territorial' in nature does not have clear legal criteria. The International Law Commission has defined extra-territorial jurisdiction as 'an attempt to regulate by means of national legislation, adjudication or enforcement the conduct of persons, property or acts beyond its borders which affect the interests of then State in the absence of such regulation under international law'.[35] Yet when the Court of Justice of the European Union (CJEU) was asked to determine the legality of the Directive, it focused on the fact that, although the Directive may have some extra-territorial effects, it was ultimately tied to EU territory.[36] The problem was that, while the Directive applied to EU territory, it applied in a way that took into account activity that occurred outside the EU territory. However, for the CJEU, it was enough that there was at least *some* link to EU territory. While the Court did not explicitly accept the 'effects doctrine' argument, it appears to have been motivated in part by the idea that the EU can legislate with respect to certain activities where it produces effects within the EU.[37]

While this approach to climate change has been criticised for its apparent extra-territorial effect, it has also been presented as a way in which the EU acts as a 'norm entrepreneur', 'using (the threat of) unilateral action to stimulate climate action elsewhere'.[38] Thus, the EU is able to promote convergence towards a EU regulatory regime through the application of its internal law. This policy of using threats may produce certain positive outcomes, but it may not be conducive to fostering the values of mutual respect and cooperation that underpin multilateralism.

[34] Directive 2003/87/EC of the European Parliament and of the Council of 13 October 2003 establishing a scheme for greenhouse gas emission allowance trading within the Community and amending Council Directive 96/61/EC [2003] 25 OJ L275/32, 25 October 2002.

[35] United Nations Report of the International Law Commission Fifty-eighth session (1 May–9 June and 3 July–11 August 2006) General Assembly Official Records, Supplement No 10 (A/61/10), para 2.

[36] Judgment in C-366/10 *Air Transport Association of America* EU:C:2011:864, 21 December 2011.

[37] For a discussion of the 'effects doctrine' and international law, see the discussion of Advocate General Darmon in Joined Cases 89/85, 104/85, 114/85, 116/85, 117/85 and 125/85 to 129/85 *Ahlström Osakeyhtiö and Others v Commission* EU:C:1994:12, 5217–20.

[38] Scott and Rajamani (n 28) 473.

B. Data Protection

Similar problems arise regarding the effort to deal with numerous issues regarding another global phenomenon: the Internet, and the 'extraordinarily complex'[39] issue of the application of EU data protection law. This is a field where the growing importance of privacy as a human right comes into conflict with the commercial interest in data and the increasing 'commodification' of personal information.[40] In addition, the global reach of the Internet, especially the phenomenon of cloud computing, challenges a territorial-based understanding of sovereignty and jurisdiction. This was one of the issues that arose in *Google Spain*.[41] While the main focus of the case has been on the 'right to be forgotten', it also deals with issues of jurisdiction and the extent to which the EU may legislate regarding activity that takes place outside the EU. The impact of such decision may have been limited, however, through recent judgments such as C-507/17 *Google v CNIL* in which the CJEU held that Google and search operators are not required under EU law to remove links on all versions of its search engine.[42]

The EU's legislative efforts in this area still seek to tie EU jurisdiction to nationality or territory, and in this way do not seek to apply EU legislation to non-EU states. The General Data Protection Regulation, for example, ties its scope to EU territory or its relationship to EU citizens or businesses. However, as the ETS discussed above, it does so in a way that makes it possible to apply with respect to activity outside EU territory, since it applies to data controllers and data processers even if they do not carry out those activities within the territory of the Union.[43] It applies when goods and services are offered to data subjects in the EU, and to the monitoring of the behaviour of data subjects as far as their behaviour takes place in the EU. The EU thus bases its jurisdictional basis for such policies on well-recognised international law principles of jurisdiction – nationality and territory – but does so in a way that significantly expands the scope of its Regulation. So while the Regulation may be in conformity with international law, it can also be criticised as a form of EU unilateralism, showing a willingness to legislate outside EU territory. As with climate change policy, the Regulation seeks to protect a global value using internal regulation in a field where there has been an inability to develop rules in multilateral settings. When dealing with such vital

[39] Lokke Moerel, 'Back to Basics: When Does EU Data Protection Law Apply?' (2011) 1 *International Data Privacy Law* 2, 93.

[40] Christopher Kuner, Fred H Cate, Christopher Millard and Dan Jerker B Svantesson, 'The Extraterritoriality of Data Privacy Laws – An Explosive Issue Yet to Detonate' (2013) 3 *International Data Privacy Law* 3, 147.

[41] Judgment in C-131/12 *Google Spain and Google* EU:C:2014:317.

[42] Judgment in Case C-507/17 *Google v CNIL*, EU:C:2019:772, paras 64–65.

[43] Article 3 of Regulation (EU) 2016/679 on the protection of natural persons with regard to the processing of personal data and on the free movement of such data, and repealing Directive 95/46/EC [2016] OJ L119/ (General Data Protection Regulation).

concerns and values, it can be argued that the EU should not wait for rules to be developed on data protection and digital privacy, while the rights of EU citizens are being violated. Yet as with the EU's climate unilateralism, its approach has the effect of antagonising other states that may find themselves caught by this regulatory web.

C. Autonomous Measures (Sanctions)

The two examples above are areas where the EU has sought to expand the reach of its policies in order to protect certain global norms – the protection of the environment and the promotion of data protection rules. Yet the EU has also pursued a more 'unilateral' approach when it comes to its policies regarding restrictive measures. The EU has in the past implemented measures mandated by Chapter VII UN Security Council Resolutions, and in some cases it has even gone further than what was required under these resolutions.[44] Yet the EU has also pursued 'autonomous' sanctions, that is, restrictive measures that do not find their legal basis in UN Security Council resolutions.[45] There is no question that the EU has the competence to impose such measures under EU law, but such unilateral measures may give rise to questions regarding their compliance with international law. As with the policies mentioned above, restrictive measures are internal EU law, and apply within the EU's jurisdiction, but have the effect of promoting convergence with certain EU norms outside its territory – they are a tool of foreign policy.

The EU Guidelines on Restrictive Measures sets out that '[t]he introduction and implementation of restrictive measures must always be in accordance with international law'.[46] They have also raised concerns from some international lawyers – Dupont notes regarding the measures against Iran, '[t]he unprecedented extent of these new EU measures raises various issues regarding their lawfulness under international law'.[47] There has also been debate about whether autonomous restrictive measures taken by the EU should be properly regarded as 'sanctions' in

[44] See in this regard judgment of 14 October 2009, T-390/08 *Bank Melli Iran v Council*, EU:T:2009:401, para 51, where the Court noted that the EU's Common Foreign and Security Policy's legal basis for restrictive measures, now Article 215 of the Treaty on the Functioning of the European Union (TFEU), did not limit the relevant powers of the EU to mere implementation of sanctions imposed by the UN Security Council.

[45] Sanctions against the Central African Republic, the Democratic Republic of Congo, Ivory Coast, Eritrea, Haiti, Iran, Iraq, the Democratic People's Republic of Korea, Lebanon, Liberia, Libya, Somalia and South Sudan have been mandated by UN Security Council resolutions. On the contrary, sanctions against Belarus, Bosnia and Herzegovina, China, Egypt, the Republic of Guinea, Moldova, Myanmar, Syria, Tunisia, the USA, Serbia and Zimbabwe have been autonomously imposed by the EU.

[46] General Secretariat of the Council, Guidelines on Implementation and Evaluation of Restrictive Measures (Sanctions) in the Framework of the EU Common Foreign and Security Policy, Brussels, 4 May 2018, para 9.

[47] Pierre E Dupont, 'Countermeasures and Collective Security: The Case of the EU Sanctions Against Iran' (2012) 17 *Journal Conflict & Security Law* 301, 3.

international law.[48] It has been argued that for measures to be regarded as sanctions, they should meet two criteria: that a competent organ objectively establishes the violation of a rule, and that target measures are imposed to restore legality. Regarding autonomous measures taken by the EU, it has been argued that:

> in the case of the 'autonomous sanctions' both conditions are lacking: a regional international organization lacks any mandate from the international society to ascertain the violation of the international legality and to restore it vis-à-vis a State which is not a member of it.[49]

EU restrictive measures will often set out the legal basis under international law for steps taken. For example, they may be imposed as a response to an illegal act committed by the target state. Sanctions against Russia, Syria and Iran all contain language that sets out that the measures are a response to that state's continued breaches of international law, although this is often couched in very broad terms. Regarding Russia, this includes 'actions which undermine or threaten the territorial integrity, sovereignty and independence of Ukraine'.[50] EU restrictive measures may therefore be seen as countermeasures under international law, as they are a response to a breach of international law by a third state. Countermeasures are dealt with in Article 49 of the International Law Commission's Articles of State Responsibility (ASR),[51] which set out that such measures must be a response to a wrongful act under international law (although the ASR is intended to apply to states, its provisions can be applied by analogy to the practice of an organisation such as the EU).

In order for sanctions to be considered lawful countermeasures, they must meet a number of criteria under international law. One element of countermeasures is that they are to be implemented by the injured party. This gives rise to the question of whether sanctions by the EU should be considered 'injured party' countermeasures or 'third-party' countermeasures.[52] Furthermore, countermeasures must be proportionate to the aim being pursued. They are intended to cease the legal activity of the target state; they therefore must not amount to punishment. They must be non-permanent,[53] allowing the target state to comply with the reach of international law. While sanctions are intended to put pressure on the target state to

[48] 'Either complementary to or substitutive of the UNSC action, the nature of these restrictive measures is open to debate. The question arises whether they fall into the strict legal definition of "sanctions".' Alan Pellet and Alina Miron, 'Sanctions' in *Max Planck Encyclopaedia of Public International Law*, http://opil.ouplaw.com/.

[49] *Ibid.*

[50] Council Regulation (EU) No 269/2014 of 17 March 2014 concerning restrictive measures in respect of actions undermining or threatening the territorial integrity, sovereignty and independence of Ukraine [2014] OJ L78/6.

[51] ILC, 'Draft Articles on Responsibility of States for Internationally Wrongful Acts, with Commentaries' (2001) GAOR 56th Session Supp 10, 43.

[52] See Martin Dawiddowicz, 'Third Party Countermeasures: Observations on a Controversial Topic' in Christine Chinkin and Freya Baetens (eds), *Sovereignty, Statehood and State Responsibility Essays in Honour of James Crawford* (Cambridge University Press, 2015) 340.

[53] *Gabcikovo-Nagymaros Project (Hungary v Slovakia)* Judgment, ICJ Reports 1997, para 87.

comply with international obligations, they are not intended to 'penalise' the state for its actions. EU measures often use a mix of political language disapproving of certain action with legal language setting out the illegality of action by the target state. EU measures could more clearly articulate the internationally wrongful act for which the target state is responsible.

As with the policies discussed above, the EU's practice of imposing unilateral sanctions is subject to criticism for violating international law, especially as they are adopted outside the context of a multilateral institution. Yet as with policy on climate change and data protection, it also shows a greater willingness on the part of the EU to act alone, or outside of multilateral institutions, when it is difficult or impossible to achieve that policy through a multilateral framework. Whereas these other policies deal with the extraterritorial effects of EU regulatory regimes, the sanctions regime comes closer to a breach of international law. Yet the same tension is present – unable to meet its goals through multilateral institutions (in the case of autonomous measures, there is no agreement in the UN Security Council), the EU has sought to uphold its values, and promote convergence, outside of those bodies. Even if this is in conformity with international law, it may have the effect of eroding the effectiveness of multilateral bodies. Such a tension can also be viewed in terms of convergence and divergence. As it seeks to uphold certain values – commitment to climate change action, data privacy, human rights, etc – it produces greater convergence towards those norms, yet by pursuing these policies in a unilateral manner, it may diverge from its aims of strengthening and supporting multilateral institutions.

IV. Conclusion

The EU has begun to develop a new form of unilateralism. In IR debates, unilateralism is usually associated with a hegemon such as the United States pursuing its self-interest. Rather than being founded on narrow self-interest, EU unilateralism is tied with what the EU views as the protection of global norms and values. This has been justified in terms of promoting greater convergence with EU norms and policies – EU unilateralism is presented as more benign because it is used to promote policies that push forward the protection of human rights, data protection and action on climate change. Yet, even if such policies promote convergence and achieve these objectives in the short term, such activity may have the consequence of aggravating the EU's partners, undermining multilateral institutions, and encouraging other states and organisations to follow a similar unilateral path. This may appear somewhat naïve – should we really expect the EU and the Member States to sit on their hands and do nothing, simply because they cannot be achieved through multilateralism? The argument is not that the EU must choose multilateralism in all cases, but that the EU must also take into account the negative effects that this may have for the multilateral order. As discussed above, there is no *legal* obligation in the EU Treaties to pursue multilateralism, but it is clearly set out as a value that it is to be upheld and respected. This should be acknowledged when the EU adopts such unilateral action in the name of promoting convergence with EU law and values. 'Contingent' unilateralism is still unilateralism. At a time when multilateral institutions are under strain, the EU must consider the broader effect that such policies will have, and whether they may promote other actors to pursue similar unilateral approaches. This does not mean that the EU must work through multilateral settings in every policy area, even if there is no hope of progress or consensus, but that the values associated with multilateralism should be kept in mind when adopting such measures.

3

Converging Dual-Use Export Control with Human Rights Norms: The EU's Responses to Digital Surveillance Exports

MACHIKO KANETAKE*

I. Introduction

Demand for digital surveillance technology has created a thriving market on a global scale. In his UN report entitled 'Surveillance and Human Rights' in May 2019, David Kaye, the Human Rights Council's Special Rapporteur on the freedom of opinion and expression, expressed serious concerns about the status of 'surveillance exports'.[1] In the report, the UN's Special Rapporteur made it clear that digital surveillance is 'no longer the preserve of countries' that have the 'in-house' resources to conduct mass and targeted surveillance.[2] The market of surveillance technology has developed globally in order to allow a wide range of governments to make use of advanced digital surveillance. Privacy International, one of the human rights non-governmental organisations and a member of the Coalition Against Unlawful Surveillance Exports, has identified 528 companies as of May 2016 involved in the selling of various types of surveillance technology.[3] It can serve legitimate law enforcement purposes; yet there is no denying that it can readily be turned into a governmental tool to monitor and oppress dissidents. In view of the growing digital surveillance market at the expense of human

* This chapter is based on the following publication by the author: 'The EU's Dual-Use Export Control and Human Rights Risks: The Case of Cyber Surveillance Technology' (2019) 3 *Europe and the World: A Law Review* 1.

[1] UN Human Rights Council and Report of the Special Rapporteur on the promotion and protection of the right to freedom of opinion and expression, 'Surveillance and Human Rights' UN Doc A/HRC/41/35 (28 May 2019) para 2.

[2] *Ibid* para 6.

[3] Privacy International, Submission to the Report of the Special Rapporteur (see n 1) at 1–2, www.ohchr.org/EN/Issues/FreedomOpinion/Pages/SR2019ReporttoHRC.aspx.

rights protection, the UN's Special Rapporteur foremost recommended that states 'impose an immediate moratorium' on the 'export, sale, transfer, use or serving of privately developed surveillance tools' – until 'a human rights-complaint safeguards regime' is in place.[4]

Export control is one of such legal safeguards available to states. More precisely, there is a field of law called 'dual-use' export control which has been applied on a regular basis outside the special frameworks of economic sanctions. Within the EU, the export of dual-use items has been governed foremost by Council Regulation (EC) No 428/2009 of 5 May 2009, which has direct effect in the EU.[5] The scheduled review of the Regulation[6] was caught up by the political controversies in the aftermath of the Arab Spring (2010–2012), which triggered political initiatives within the EU to integrate the assessment of human rights risks into the process of export control. The crux of the matter is that, according to Article 2(1) of Regulation 428/2009, dual-use items have been defined as those which serve 'both civil and military purposes'.[7] A variety of materials, products, facilities, technologies and information that serve civilian purposes could also be employed for building military capacities.[8] As illustrated by the definition of dual-use items, the EU's dual-use Regulation has primarily been justified by the control of 'military' risks. Political resistance has then arisen against the strengthening of the non-military normative pillar in the EU's dual-use export control.

Against this background, this chapter analyses political initiatives within the EU to integrate consideration to human rights risks into the EU's dual-use export control. Such initiatives, in a nutshell, oscillate between *convergence* and *divergence* at multiple levels. On the one hand, given that dual-use export control forms the EU's Common Commercial Policy (CCP), the EU is, in principle, mandated to facilitate convergence of its dual-use export control with human rights and fundamental freedoms (section II). The initiatives for human rights convergence are also in line with the UN's Guiding Principles on Business and Human Rights (UNGPs), which the EU and its Member States have pledged to implement (section III). Yet the integration of human rights into the EU's export control inevitably involves a policy choice which may diverge itself from international human rights law (section IV). Furthermore, the attempts to strengthen human rights protection signify divergence from the international regimes on export control, and more fundamentally, from the idea of regulatory harmonization across participating states (section V). The chapter then concludes (section VI).

[4] UN Human Rights Council and Report of the Special Rapporteur (n 1).

[5] Council Regulation (EC) No 428/2009 of 5 May 2009 setting up a Community regime for the control of exports, transfer, brokering and transit of dual-use items [2009] OJ L134/1.

[6] *Ibid* Art 25(2).

[7] *Ibid* Art 2(1).

[8] For instance, take the use of high-speed photography. It has been used for film productions, electrical discharge and optics, yet certain high-speed photographic technology can also be applied for developing and testing nuclear weapons: Scott Avery Watson and Michael Robert Altherr, 'On the Export Control of High Speed Imaging for Nuclear Weapons Applications' (Los Alamos National Laboratory, 2017) No LA-UR-XYZQ 2017 (2017) 19, 23–24.

II. Convergence with the EU's Commitment in its External Action

A. Political Momentum Following the Arab Spring

The export of digital surveillance technology could be a vehicle for the systematic violation of the right to privacy, freedom of speech and freedom of assembly in the trading partners. For the purpose of this chapter, cyber surveillance technologies are meant to include: mobile telecommunications interception equipment; intrusion software; internet protocol (IP) network surveillance systems; monitoring centres (designed to collect, store and analyse communications data); lawful interception systems and data retention systems (used by service providers to intercept and store data as required by law); and digital forensics (to retrieve and analyse communications data stored in networks, computers and mobile devices).[9]

There are abundant stories of the trade of surveillance technology which has been used to suppress dissidents and human rights activists. During and in the aftermath of the Arab Spring, many incidents came to the surface that revealed the use of exported surveillance technology in those countries which experienced the popular uprising.[10] For example, one of the reported stories pertains to the controversies regarding a software program called FinSpy marketed by Gamma Group, a German-British company. It has been reported that Gamma Group's subsidiary, FinFisher, helped the Government of Bahrain to install the software to monitor pro-democracy activists during the time of the Arab Spring movement.[11] The controversy motivated a group of four pro-democracy activists and politicians to launch legal proceedings in 2018 in the UK against Gamma Group. The claimants argued that the companies involved had sold the spyware to the Government of Bahrain despite the well-documented record of human rights violations.[12] The controversies were also mentioned by the UN Special Rapporteur in his aforementioned May 2019 report.[13]

[9] Mark Bromley, 'Export Controls, Human Security and Cyber-Surveillance Technology: Examining the Proposed Changes to the EU Dual-Use Regulation' (Stockholm International Peace Research Institute, 2017) 6–10; Mark Bromley, et al, 'ICT Surveillance Systems: Trade Policy and the Application of Human Security Concerns' (2016) 2 *Strategic Trade Review* 37.

[10] See, eg, Ben Wagner, 'Exporting Censorship and Surveillance Technology' (Humanist Institute for Co-operation with Developing Countries (Hivos), January 2012); Privacy International, 'Open Season: Building Syria's Surveillance State' (December 2016).

[11] See, eg, Privacy International, 'Six Things we Know from the Latest FinFisher Documents' (*Privacy International*, 15 August 2014), https://privacyinternational.org/blog/1522/six-things-we-know-latest-finfisher-documents; C Currier and M Marquis-Boire, 'Leaked Files: German Spy Company Helped Bahrain Hack Arab Spring Protesters' (*The Intercept*, 7 August 2014), https://theintercept.com/2014/08/07/leaked-files-german-spy-company-helped-bahrain-track-arab-spring-protesters/.

[12] Leigh Day, 'Pro-democracy Activists Launch Legal Action against British Spyware Companies' (*Leigh Day*, 11 October 2018), www.leighday.co.uk/News/News-2018/October-2018/Pro-democracy-activists-launch-legal-action-agains.

[13] UN Human Rights Council and Report of the Special Rapporteur (n 1) paras 42, 44.

In response to the controversies in the aftermath of the Arab Spring, the European Parliament made a series of calls for a revision of the EU's dual-use export control Regulation in order to prevent EU-originated digital technologies from being used against the violations of civil and political rights.[14] The European Parliament adopted the resolution entitled 'human rights and technology' in September 2015, in which the Parliament made explicit reference to the impact of intrusion and surveillance systems on human rights in third countries.[15] What is striking in the resolution of September 2015 is that the European Parliament made it clear that the EU's standards, particularly the EU Charter of Fundamental Rights, 'should prevail' in the assessment of dual-use technologies used in ways that may restrict human rights.[16] The Parliamentary call is ultimately in line with the need for ensuring 'coherence between the EU's external actions and its internal policies' relating to informal and communication technologies (ICTs).[17] The political calls to strengthen the control of ICT exports also came from the Council. In its Action Plan on Human Rights and Democracy 2015–19, the Council catalogued the review of the dual-use regulation 'to mitigate the potential risks' associated with the 'uncontrolled export of ICT products' that 'could be used in a manner that leads to human rights violations'.[18] As evidenced by these remarks, the European Parliament and the Council sent a clear signal, especially in 2015, that the EU would take a proactive step in strengthening the control of ICT exports in order to align its external actions with the EU's own commitment to human rights and fundamental freedoms.

B. The EU's Overall Constitutional Mandate to Foster Human Rights

The integration of human rights risks into export control is particularly pertinent for the EU and its external relations. As noted in the Introduction, the EU's dual-use Regulation forms an integral part of the EU's CCP which includes both trade and investment law and policy. In the EU's external relations, the CCP has been considered as the key field which has also been intertwined with the integration process within the internal market of the Union.[19] As part of the CCP, the EU's

[14] See European Parliament, 'Resolution on the European Defence Union (2016/2052(INI)), P8_TA(2016)0435 (22 November 2016)' para 21.

[15] European Parliament, 'Human Rights and Technology: The Impact of Intrusion and Surveillance Systems on Human Rights in Third Countries (2014/2232(INI))' P8_TA(2015)0288 (8 September 2015).

[16] *Ibid* para 39.

[17] *Ibid* para 2.

[18] Council of the European Union, 'Council Conclusions on the Action Plan on Human Rights and Democracy 2015–2019' 10897/15 (20 July 2015) 24.

[19] Urszula Jaremba, Machiko Kanetake and Ingrid Koning, 'Economic and Non-Economic Values and Objectives in the EU's International Trade: Normative Tensions, Actors and Processes' (2019) 3 *Europe and the World: A Law Review* 1, 2.

law and policies on dual-use export control ought to be carried out 'in the context of the principles and objectives of the Union's external action', as instructed by Article 207 of the Treaty on the Functioning of the European Union (TFEU).[20] One of these principles, referred to in Article 21(1) of the Treaty on European Union (TEU), pertains to 'the universality and indivisibility of human rights and fundamental freedoms'.[21]

Since the mid-1990s, the EU has been taking measures to integrate human rights in its external trade relations. Human rights criteria and clauses have been incorporated in the General System of Preferences and bilateral trade agreements.[22] In the EU Strategic Framework and Action Plan on Human Rights and Democracy, adopted by the Council in 2012, it was pledged that the EU would promote human rights 'in all aspects of its external action without exception'.[23] Within this overall pledge, the Strategic Framework envisaged, as part of the specific action items to promote the protection of the freedom of expression, the inclusion of 'human rights violations' as one of the reasons on the basis of which 'non-listed items may be subject to export restrictions'.[24]

While Article 207 TFEU and Article 21(1) TEU provide an overall mandate, they do not provide concrete guidance regarding the extent to which human rights and fundamental freedoms should and could permeate into the EU's trade and investment policies and law. In practice, much relies on the willingness of EU institutions and Member States, as well as the wider political initiatives that affect the institutional and governmental decision-making. With respect to the regulation of ICT exports, particular political momentum has arrived in response to mass demonstrations and revolt across the Middle East and North Africa from 2010 to 2012.[25] As noted above, the reported incidents regarding the use of EU-originated surveillance technology have motivated a series of Parliamentary calls to revise and rewrite the EU's export control.

C. The Commission's September 2016 Proposal

A watershed moment then came in September 2016 when the European Commission submitted a proposal to recast and replace Council Regulation

[20] Consolidated Version of the Treaty on the Functioning of the European Union [2008] OJ C115/47, Art 207(1).

[21] Consolidated Version of the Treaty on European Union [2008] OJ C115/13, Art 21(1).

[22] Samantha Velluti, 'The Promotion and Integration of Human Rights in EU External Trade Relations' (2016) 32 *Utrecht Journal of International and European Law* 41.

[23] Council of the European Union, 'EU Strategic Framework and Action Plan on Human Rights and Democracy' 11855/12 (25 June 2012) 2.

[24] *Ibid* 19.

[25] See, eg, European Commission, 'Report from the Commission to the Council and the European Parliament on the Implementation of Regulation (EC) No 428/2009 Setting up a Community Regime for the Control of Exports, Transfer, Brokering and Transit of Dual-Use Items' COM(2013) 710 final (16 October 2013) 13.

(EC) 428/2009.[26] In response to the aforementioned Parliamentary requests to strengthen the control of ICT exports,[27] the Commission's proposal placed the protection of human rights as one of the normative pillars of the EU's dual-use export control. The proposal aimed to provide an 'effective response to threats for human rights resulting from their uncontrolled export'.[28] Among a broad catalogue of human rights and fundamental freedoms, particular emphasis was placed, given the context of the most immediately affected rights, on respect for the right to privacy, freedom of expression and freedom of association.[29]

In order to mainstream the human rights pillar of export control, the September 2016 proposal introduced a number of elements which reflected the Parliamentary calls. First, and perhaps most fundamentally, the proposal recognised that it is appropriate to 'revise the definition of dual-use items'.[30] On this basis, the proposal included, within the definition of dual-use items, 'cyber-surveillance technology which can be used for the commission of serious violations of human rights or international humanitarian law'.[31] While the proposal still maintained the basic definition of dual-use items based on 'civil and military' purposes,[32] the proposal's definition effectively went beyond the traditional definition of dual-use items based on military contexts.

Second, one of the most controversial provisions pertained to the human rights due diligence in the context of the so-called 'catch-all' control. It is a residual mechanism to allow authorities to exert export control over items which are not specifically listed by Annex I of the EU's dual-use regulation. According to Article 4(2) of the Commission's proposal:[33]

> If an *exporter*, under his *obligation to exercise due diligence*, is aware that dual-use items which he proposes to export, not listed in Annex I, are intended, in their entirety or in part, for any of the uses referred to in paragraph 1 [including the serious violations of human rights], he must notify the competent authority, which will decide whether or not it is expedient to make the export concerned subject to authorisation.

[26] European Commission, 'Proposal for a Regulation of the European Parliament and of the Council Setting up a Union Regime for the Control of Exports, Transfer, Brokering, Technical Assistance and Transit of Dual-Use Items (recast)' COM(2016) 616 final (28 September 2016) Art 2(1).

[27] See, eg, European Parliament, 'Human Rights and Technology' (n 15) para 36; European Parliament, 'Resolution on the Annual Report on Human Rights and Democracy in the World 2014 and the European Union's Policy on the Matter (2015/2229(INI)' P8_TA(2015)0470 (17 December 2015) para 124.

[28] European Commission Proposal (n 26) 6.

[29] European Commission Proposal (n 26) 6.

[30] European Commission Proposal (n 26) 12, recital para 6.

[31] According to the proposal of September 2016, Art 2(1)(b) reads as follows: '"dual-use items" shall mean items, including software and technology, which can be used for both civil and military purposes, and shall include: … (b) cyber surveillance technology which can be used for the commission of serious violations of human rights or international humanitarian law, or can pose a threat to international security or the essential security interests of the Union and its Member States': European Commission Proposal (n 26) Art 2(1)(b).

[32] European Commission Proposal (n 26) Art 2(1).

[33] European Commission Proposal (n 26) Art 4(2) (emphasis added).

What is striking in this proposed provision was the element of human rights due diligence on the part of *exporters* (ie, not merely on the part of governments). Under Article 4(2) of the Commission's proposal, exporters themselves were under an 'obligation to exercise due diligence'.[34] Exporters must notify the competent authority if the exporters become 'aware' that non-listed dual-use items are intended for the commission of serious violations of human rights or international humanitarian law in situations of armed conflict or internal repression.[35]

Third, on top of these additions, the September 2016 proposal of the Commission mandated Member States' competent authorities to take into account 'respect for human rights in the country for final destination' as well as respect by that country for international humanitarian law in deciding whether or not to grant an export authorisation.[36] Finally, the Commission's proposal introduced the EU's 'autonomous list'[37] subject to export control. Under Regulation 428/2009, dual-use items have been catalogued in Annex I according to ten groups, from 'Category 0' to 'Category 9'. The Commission's September 2016 proposal launched a new group of controlled items concerning 'cyber surveillance technology'.[38] Under this new 'Category 10', the proposal listed items which had not yet been regulated by the Wassenaar Arrangement.[39] It is one of the most comprehensive international regimes. Although the Wassenaar Arrangement is not based on a treaty, its control list serves as the basis for the EU's export control list. Before the proposal, certain surveillance technologies had already been included in the international list; mobile telecommunications interception equipment (or IMSI catchers),[40] IP network communications surveillance systems and intrusion software[41] had already been added to the list within the Wassenaar Arrangement and subsequently to the EU's control list.[42] Yet these additions did not encompass monitoring centres and data retention systems. While Germany introduced

[34] European Commission Proposal (n 26) Art 4(2). See further section V of this chapter below.

[35] European Commission Proposal (n 26). See further section V of this chapter below.

[36] European Commission Proposal (n 26) Art 14(1)(b).

[37] European Commission Proposal (n 26) 9.

[38] European Commission, 'Annexes to the Proposal for a Regulation of the European Parliament and of the Council Setting up a Union Regime for the Control of Exports, Transfer, Brokering, Technical Assistance and Transit of Dual-Use Items (recast)' COM(2016) 616 final, Annexes 1 to 6 (28 September 2016) 243–44, Annex I, Category 10.

[39] *Ibid.*

[40] The Wassenaar Arrangement, *List of Dual-Use Goods and Technologies and Munitions List*, WA-LIST (12) 1 (12 December 2012), Category 5.A.1.f (mobile telecommunications interception).

[41] The Wassenaar Arrangement, *List of Dual-Use Goods and Technologies and Munitions List*, WA-LIST (13) 1 (4 December 2013), Categories 4.A.5 (intrusion software) and 5.A.1.j (IP network communications surveillance systems); Innokenty Pyetranker, 'An Umbrella in a Hurricane: Cyber Technology and the December 2013 Amendment to the Wassenaar Arrangement' (2015) 13 *Northwestern Journal of Technology and Intellectual Property* 153, 162–64.

[42] Commission Delegated Regulation (EU) No 1382/2014 of 22 October 2014 amending council regulation (EC) No 428/2009 setting up a community regime for the control of exports, transfer, brokering, and transit of dual-use items [2014] OJ L371/1. See the Wassenaar Arrangement, *List of Dual-Use Goods and Technologies and Munitions List*, WA-LIST (17) 1 (7 December 2017), Category 4.E.1.

additional national legislation in 2015 in order to control the export of monitoring centres and retention systems,[43] these items were not part of the EU-wide list of dual-use items. On this basis, the European Commission's September 2016 proposal aimed at autonomously regulating the export of lawful interception monitoring centres and event data retention systems and devices.[44]

The Commission's proposal was by no means the first attempt to integrate human rights in the EU's export control regimes. In particular, one must mention that the EU already has its own autonomous export control over torture-related items. In the so-called anti-torture Regulation, the EU promulgated export control on items which could be used for torture and other cruel treatment.[45] Also, 'human rights considerations' are part of the language of Regulation 428/2009. Under Article 8(1) of the Regulation, a Member State may prohibit (or impose an authorisation requirement on) the export of dual-use items 'for reasons of public security or human rights considerations'.[46] That being said, the Commission's proposal marked a significant departure from these precedents. The dual-use Regulation covers a much wider range of items than the torture Regulation. Article 8(1) of Regulation 428/2009 by no means obliges Member States to prohibit (or require authorisation on) any particular exports on the basis of human rights considerations.

III. Convergence with International Standards on Business and Human Rights

A. UNGPs' Human Rights Due Diligence

In this sense, the September 2016 proposal was a noteworthy attempt to situate human rights as one of the normative pillars of the EU's dual-use export control. The proposal's normative ambition can be defended, not only by Article 207 TFEU and Article 21(1) TEU. It should also be understood as being part of the initiatives to converge the EU's dual-use control with its commitment to promote the implementation of the UNGPs.[47] While the EU has taken a wide range of measures to facilitate the implementation of the Guiding Principles,[48] including

[43] Germany, Submission to the Report of the Special Rapporteur (see n 1) (February 2019) at 1, www.ohchr.org/EN/Issues/FreedomOpinion/Pages/SR2019ReporttoHRC.aspx.

[44] European Commission Annexes (n 38) 243–44, Annex I, Category 10.

[45] Council Regulation (EC) No 1236/2005 of 27 June 2005 concerning trade in goods which could be used for capital punishment, torture, or other cruel, inhuman, or degrading treatment or punishment [2005] OJ L200/1.

[46] Regulation 428/2009 (n 5) Art 8(1).

[47] United Nations, 'Guiding Principles on Business and Human Rights: Implementing the UN "Protect, Respect and Remedy" Framework' (2011) HR/PUB/11/04 (2011).

[48] Daniel Augenstein, Mark Dawson and Pierre Thielbörger, 'The UNGPs in the European Union: The Open Coordination of Business and Human Rights?' (2018) 3 *Business and Human Rights Journal* 1.

in its external action,[49] such measures were yet to cover the specific context of ICT exports. In 2013, for instance, the Commission developed the ICT sector-specific guide for the implementation of the UN Guiding Principles.[50] The guide was based on the EU's 2012 Strategic Framework on human rights and democracy, in which the EU pledged that it would encourage and contribute to the implementation of the Guiding Principles.[51] Yet these initiatives did not include any specific reference to the implications of the UNGPs within the context of ICT exports.

The UNGPs, which were endorsed by the UN Human Rights Council in 2011, compiled a set of foundational and operational principles regarding the following three interrelated pillars: the state's duty to protect human rights, the corporate responsibility to respect human rights, and, finally, access to effective remedy. Within the second pillar of corporate responsibility, the UNGPs expect companies to conduct due diligence. According to Operational Principle 17, 'business enterprises' should carry out 'human rights due diligence' for the sake of identifying, preventing, mitigating and accounting for how they address their adverse impacts on human rights.[52] According to the UNGPs, due diligence should cover adverse human rights impacts that the business enterprise 'may cause *or* contribute to'.[53]

The formulation of the UNGPs is broad enough to cover due diligence in the context of business decisions to develop and export their products and technology. The UN's Special Rapporteur on the freedom of expression also made special reference to the UNGPs, which, in the view of the Special Rapporteur, should be used as a precondition for companies to participate in the surveillance market.[54] The Special Rapporteur ultimately recommended that the states participating in the Wassenaar Arrangement develop a framework by which 'the licensing of any technology' would be 'conditional' upon 'companies' compliance with the Guiding Principles'.[55]

B. Resistance from Industry Associations and Member States

Despite the fact that the Commission's 2016 proposal was in line with the UNGPs, the provision regarding exporters' human rights due diligence invited a great

[49] European Commission, 'Communication from the Commission to the European Parliament, the Council, the European Economic and Social Committee and the Committee of the Regions: A Renewed EU Strategy 2011–14 for Corporate Social Responsibility', COM(2011) 681 final (25 October 2011) at 14; European Commission, 'Commission Staff Working Document on Implementing the UN Guiding Principles on Business and Human Rights – State of Play', SWD(2015) 144 final (14 July 2015) at 6–9, 17–21.

[50] European Commission, 'ICT Sector Guide on Implementing the UN Guiding Principles on Business and Human Rights' (2013).

[51] Council of the European Union, EU Strategic Framework and Action Plan on Human Rights and Democracy (n 23) 3.

[52] United Nations Guiding Principles (n 47) 17.

[53] *Ibid* 17 (emphasis added).

[54] UN Human Rights Council and Report of the Special Rapporteur (n 1) para 60.

[55] UN Human Rights Council and Report of the Special Rapporteur (n 1) para 66(f).

deal of controversy. Contestation surrounded the alleged 'political' nature of human rights assessment. The Federation of German Industries (*Bundesverband der Deutschen Industrie*: BDI) had claimed, already before the submission of the Commission's proposal, that companies were 'not in a position to take political decisions'.[56] According to the BDI, a mere reference to 'human rights violations' was found to be too broad to be left in the hands of companies.[57] Instead, the BDI demanded that EU institutions specify human rights violations and list specific countries with the records of systematic human rights violations.[58]

Likewise, DIGITALEUROPE, which represents the digital technology industry in Europe, expressed its concerns regarding uncertainties created by the inclusion of human rights language in relation to the exporters' obligations. A much more preferred option for DIGITALEUROPE was for EU institutions to identify a list of excluded end-users in advance and avoid relying on the broad protection of human rights through a catch-all provision.[59] DIGITALEUROPE regarded that companies were not in the best position to assess human rights risks attached to ICT exports. Instead, in the words of DIGITALEUROPE, '[g]overnments are much better prepared' to identify possible cases of human rights violations as the governments have better access to relevant information.[60]

Despite concerns raised by industry associations, the European Parliament, in its first reading, gave strong support to the Commission's proposal in January 2018; 571 members of the Parliament voted in favour, 29 against and 29 abstained.[61] There were a number of the Parliamentary amendments attached, which have led, for instance, to the exclusion of the critical term 'obligation' under Article 4(2) of the Commission's proposal concerning exporters' due diligence. However, some other amendments appeared to strengthen the catch-all controls under Article 4 even further. The Parliamentary amendments referred to the UNGPs, as well as the Organisation for Economic Co-operation and Development (OECD) Guidelines for Multinational Enterprises and the OECD Due Diligence Guidance for Responsible Business Conduct, in order to provide further normative content to due diligence.[62] According to the Parliament's amendment on Article 4(2), an exporter must notify the competent authority if the exporter becomes aware,

[56] BDI, 'EC Dual-Use: Review of the EC Dual-Use Regulation' (January 2016) at 7, https://bdi.eu/media/topics/global_issues/downloads/201601_FINAL_BDI-Assessment_Reform_EC_Dual-Use.pdf.

[57] *Ibid* at 6.

[58] *Ibid* at 6–7.

[59] DIGITALEUROPE, 'European Commission Proposed Recast of the European Export Control Regime: Making the Rules Fit for the Digital World' (24 February 2017) at 3, www.digitaleurope.org/resources/european-commission-proposed-recast-of-the-european-export-control-regime/.

[60] DIGITALEUROPE, 'Updated DIGITALEUROPE Comments on Proposal for Recast of Export Control Regulation' (30 January 2018) at 2, www.digitaleurope.org/resources/updated-digitaleurope-comments-on-proposal-for-recast-of-export-control-regulation/.

[61] P8_TA-PROV(2018)0006 (17 January 2018).

[62] European Parliament, 'Control of Exports, Transfer, Brokering, Technical Assistance and Transit of Dual-Use Items', First reading, P8_TA-PROV(2018)0006 (17 January 2018), Amendment 11 (Recital 13 a (new)).

while exercising due diligence, that the export 'may be intended' for the commission of human rights violations.[63] The amendment appears to further extend the coverage of catch-all control in comparison to the Commission's 2016 proposal, under which the notification duty arises when the exporter is aware that items 'are intended' (as opposed to 'may') for 'serious' human rights violations.[64]

Among EU Member States, the Dutch Government notably advocated the EU's proactive role in promoting the regulation of ICT exports on the basis of their human rights risks. In her letter addressed to the House of Representatives in August 2018, the Dutch Minister for Foreign Trade and Development noted that the Netherlands see the EU as a 'frontrunner' in overcoming the risks of human rights violations by cyber surveillance technology.[65] While the Dutch Government stressed the need for clarifying the concepts of cyber surveillance technology and related human rights,[66] the Government supported the strengthening of rights-based control. The Netherlands suggested a more explicit reference to corporate social responsibility in a revised dual-use regulation, and favoured the introduction of the 'due diligence' term based on the UNGPs and OECD Guidelines, provided that it remains sufficiently clear what is expected from exporters.[67]

Yet the Netherlands' position stood in stark contrast to that of other EU Member States. The Parliamentary endorsement of January 2018 was followed by dissent from a number of EU Member States against the EU's autonomous approach. Shortly after the conclusion of the first reading by the Parliament, the 11 EU Member States, in their Working Paper of 29 January 2018, listed their fundamental points of disagreement with the Commission's proposal.[68] As elucidated in the Working Paper, which was drafted primarily by Germany and France, the Member States preferred not to alter the catch-all controls under Article 4 of Regulation 428/2009.[69] There is 'no need for additional catch-all controls', as put by the Working Paper.[70] Each Member State can decide whether to introduce additional control, according to Article 8 of the EU's dual-use Regulation.[71] According to the 11 Member States, the term 'due diligence' should be a matter of self-regulation by companies and their internal compliance programmes.[72]

[63] *Ibid* Amendment 34 (Article 4, para 2).

[64] *Ibid.*

[65] De Minister voor Buitenlandse Handel en Ontwikkelingssamenwerking, 'Betreft Stand van zaken herziening dual use-verordening en inzet kabinet', BZDOC-799712230-66 (29 August 2018) at 2.

[66] *Ibid* at 2.

[67] *Ibid* at 3.

[68] Council of the European Union, 'Working Paper: EU Export Control – Recast of Regulation 428/2009', WK 1019/2018 INIT (29 January 2018), available via EURACTIV.com, at www.euractiv.com/wp-content/uploads/sites/2/2018/02/11_member_states_dual-use.pdf. The document was drafted on behalf of the Croatian, Czech, French, German, Italian, Polish, Portuguese, Romanian, Slovak, Slovenian and Spanish delegations.

[69] *Ibid* at 4.

[70] *Ibid.*

[71] *Ibid.*

[72] *Ibid* at 5.

The fundamental disagreements expressed by the 11 Member States are reflected in the Council's negotiating position issued in June 2019.[73] With regard to the residual catch-all control over non-listed items under Article 4 of the EU's dual-use Regulation, the Council's negotiating mandate simply omitted any specific reference to human rights and international humanitarian law.[74] '[H]uman rights considerations' remain part of the grounds on the basis of which each Member State may choose to prohibit or impose an authorisation requirement on additional items.[75] Overall, the Council distanced itself from the Commission's proposal that aimed at strengthening the human rights pillar and the control of cyber surveillance technology.

IV. Divergence from International Human Rights Law

Whether or not the Council's negotiating position can be normatively defended touches upon the heart of the recurring issue of how the EU integrates human rights in its external trade relations. This inevitably involves an autonomous policy choice. The narrative of 'obligations' does not inform the direction of policy revision, given that international human rights law has not imposed an obligation to ensure respect for civil and political rights of those individuals who are affected by exported surveillance technology. In this sense, it is worth remembering that human rights considerations in the Commission's proposal go much further beyond pre-existing international human rights obligations, especially those under the International Covenant on Civil and Political Rights (ICCPR).

This is, in essence, due to the basic jurisdictional hurdle provided in the ICCPR. According to Article 2(1) of the ICCPR, states parties' obligations apply to individuals within its territory and subject to jurisdiction.[76] According to the Human Rights Committee, which monitors the implementation of the ICCPR, the jurisdictional clause of the ICCPR should be interpreted broadly so that the Covenant is applicable to anyone within the effective control of a state party, regardless of whether they are within a state's territory.[77] Even if one accepts the Human Rights Committee's interpretation, it is still difficult to argue that the ICCPR is applicable to the context of dual-use export control. Those individuals who may be affected by exported surveillance technology are outside the exporting state's jurisdiction.

[73] Council of the European Union, 'Proposal for a Regulation of the European Parliament and of the Council Setting up a Union Regime for the Control of Exports, Brokering, Technical Assistance, Transit and Transfer of Dual-Use Items (recast): Mandate for Negotiations with the European Parliament' (5 June 2019) at 4 (recital 5).

[74] *Ibid* at 18 (Art 4(1), (2)).

[75] *Ibid* at 22 (Art 8(1)).

[76] International Covenant on Civil and Political Rights, 16 December 1966, 999 UNTS 171 (1966) Art 2(1).

[77] Human Rights Committee, 'General Comment No. 31: Nature of the General Legal Obligation Imposed on States Parties to the Covenant' UN Doc CCPR/C/21/Rev.1/Add.13 (29 March 2004) para 10.

Despite the ICCPR's hurdle that limits its applicability, the Human Rights Committee has already engaged with the deliberation of human rights risks attached to ICT exports. In the Human Rights Committee's Concluding Observations on Italy in 2017, the Committee rendered its observations regarding the 'right to online and digital privacy'.[78] The Committee expressed its concern about allegations that companies based in Italy have been 'providing online surveillance equipment to Governments with a record of serious human rights violations'.[79] On this basis, the Human Rights Committee further noted its concern about the 'absence of legal safeguards or oversight mechanisms regarding the export of such equipment', referred to in Article 17 of the ICCPR concerning the right to privacy.[80] Having expressed its concerns, the Human Rights Committee noted that Italy should review its regulatory mechanisms to ensure that 'all corporations under its jurisdiction, in particular technology corporations, respect human rights standards when engaging in operations abroad'.[81] These remarks of the Human Rights Committee seem to indicate that the ICCPR is applicable to states parties' licensing decisions for the export of certain ICT products and technical assistance.

Nevertheless, despite the indication from the Conclusion Observation, it is by no means clear how the basic applicability test under Article 2(1) of the ICCPR can be overcome in the context of export control. It is safe to say, overall, that it is still premature to conclude that the ICCPR is *strictu sensu* applicable to a state's decision to authorise exports in general. Furthermore, even if the ICCPR is applicable to a state's licensing decisions, the obligations under the ICCPR pertains to those of states parties. Due diligence envisaged by the European Commission's 2016 proposal was that by *exporters themselves*. Therefore, the Commission's proposal was its proactive attempt to go much beyond the framework of international human rights law and to achieve convergence between the EU's external action and the UNGPs' expectation towards business enterprises.[82]

V. Divergence from International Export Control Regimes

A. Divergence from the International Level-Playing Field

While the Commission's 2016 proposal has normative foundations in Article 21(1) TEU and the EU's commitment to implement the UNGPs, one of the frequently

[78] Human Rights Committee, 'Concluding Observations on the Sixth Periodic Report of Italy' UN Doc CCPR/C/ITA/CO/6 (1 May 2017) paras 36–37.

[79] *Ibid* para 36.

[80] *Ibid.*

[81] *Ibid* para 37.

[82] See section III. A of this chapter.

invoked grounds for resistance against rights-based control pertained to the need for adherence to the international regimes. The EU's dual-use Regulation is indeed based on international treaties and non-treaty export control regimes.[83] At the beginning of Annex I of Regulation 428/2009, which provides the list of dual-use items, it is clearly stated that the list 'implements internationally agreed dual-use controls', including the Wassenaar Arrangement, the Missile Technology Control Regime, the Nuclear Suppliers' Group, the Australia Group, and the Chemical Weapons Convention.[84] In this vein, the Commission's 2016 proposal marked the departure, not merely from the international list of controlled items, but from the assumption that the EU's list reflects an internationally agreed list.

Member States were divided as to whether the EU's export control should diverge itself from the Wassenaar Arrangement and other export control regimes. The Dutch Government was in favour of promoting the EU's leadership role in tightening ICT exports on the basis of human rights risks. According to the letter of August 2018, the Dutch Government, while acknowledging the need to minimise the deviation from the international regimes, expressed the locus of its priority. The Dutch Government took the position that to overcome the risks of human rights violations 'outweighs' the preservation of the international level-playing field.[85]

Yet the Netherlands' stance did not resonate with many other EU Member States. In their working paper of January 2018, the 11 EU Member States, including Germany and France, put forward their strong preference for harmonisation with international regimes. The 11 Member States observed that the 'EU does not work in isolation' in regulating international exports.[86] According to the 11 states, the four international export control regimes (ie, Wassenaar Arrangement, the Missile Technology Control Regime, the Nuclear Suppliers' Group, and the Australia Group) create a 'level-playing field more globally'.[87] The need for adherence to the international or global 'level playing field' was echoed by another working paper, dated 15 May 2018, prepared by nine EU Member States. Expressing their dissent towards the EU's autonomous path, the states observed that the Commission's proposal was a 'fundamental deviation' from the EU's traditional adherence to international regimes.[88] Should the EU take unilateral measures, it could 'seriously undermine the competitiveness of EU-based industry'.[89]

[83] See Machiko Kanetake, 'Balancing Innovation, Development, and Security: Dual-Use Concepts in Export Control Laws' in N Craik, et al (eds), *Global Environmental Change and Innovation in International Law* (Cambridge, Cambridge University Press, 2018) 180.

[84] Regulation 428/2009 (n 5) Annex I.

[85] De Minister voor Buitenlandse Handel en Ontwikkelingssamenwerking (n 65) at 2.

[86] 'Working Paper: EU Export Control' (n 68) 1.

[87] 'Working Paper: EU Export Control' (n 68) 1.

[88] 'Working Paper: Paper for Discussion – For Adoption of an Improved EU Export Control Regulation 428/2009 and for Cyber Surveillance Controls Promoting Human Rights and International Humanitarian Law Globally' WK 5755/2018 INIT (15 May 2018) at 2 (on file with the author). The Working Paper was prepared on behalf of the Czech Republic, Cyprus, Estonia, Finland, Ireland, Italy, Poland, Sweden and the United Kingdom.

[89] *Ibid.*

The repeated emphasis on the international level-playing field then defined the Council's negotiating mandate released in June 2019. The Council put a stronger emphasis on regulatory harmonisation, not just among EU Member States, but between the EU's dual-use export control and international treaties and control regimes. As contrasted with the language of the Commission's 2016 proposal,[90] the Council's negotiating mandate deleted the passage that justified the addition of controlled items on the basis of human rights risks.[91] Based on the assumption that the EU's dual-use export control should be in line with international regimes, the Council also sees the EU's global role – albeit not proactively promoting human rights-based control. The Council's negotiating mandate referred to the need for promoting 'upward convergence'.[92] This means that the Council, the Commission, and Member States should 'promote international adherence' to the rules set out in the EU's dual-use Regulation 'as an international standard' by proactively engaging in international forums and providing assistance to third countries.[93]

B. Divergence from Military Risks

Member States' resistance on the basis of adherence to international regimes was intertwined with the idea that dual-use export control remains, in essence, designed to mitigate military risks. The idea that export control aims at controlling military risks can be seen in the founding document of the Wassenaar Arrangement.[94] As articulated by the founding document, the Wassenaar Arrangement aims to ensure that transfers of conventional arms and dual-use goods and technologies do not contribute to the development of 'military capabilities' which undermine regional and international security and stability.[95] The concept of military risks is multi-faceted and, perhaps more importantly, human rights risks are already intertwined with the control of military items. Yet this does not change the basic fact that dual-use export control has developed essentially to regulate military risks, especially those associated with the development of the weapons of mass destruction. By taking into account this military rationale, the UN Human Rights Council's Special Rapporteur acknowledged that the Wassenaar Arrangement is 'tailored to reduce threats to regional and international security' and thus that the framework is 'ill-suited' to addressing the 'threats that targeted surveillance posed to human rights'.[96]

[90] European Commission Proposal (n 26) 14 (recital 17).
[91] Council's Negotiating Position of June 2019 (n 73) at 7 (recital 18).
[92] Council's Negotiating Position of June 2019 (n 73) at 11 (recital 29).
[93] Council's Negotiating Position of June 2019 (n 73) at 11 (recital 29).
[94] The Wassenaar Arrangement on Export Controls for Conventional Arms and Dual-Use Goods and Technologies, 'Initial Elements', 11–12 July 1996, www.wassenaar.org/docs/IE96.html.
[95] *Ibid* para I.1.
[96] UN Human Rights Council and Report of the Special Rapporteur (n 1) para 34.

In this sense, the Commission's 2016 proposal invited a sense of discomfort among EU Member States. While the proposal maintained the traditional definition of dual-use items, it suggested, in its recital, that it is appropriate to 'revise the definition of dual-use items'.[97] However, according to the negotiating mandate of June 2019, it was clear that the Council intended to preserve the fundamental definition of dual-use items. While the Council's negotiating mandate referred to cyber-surveillance items, they were absorbed into the catalogue of 'dual-use items' based on, to reiterate, the civilian-military dichotomy.[98] On this basis, the Council's negotiating position removed any reference to human rights and humanitarian law from the basic definition of 'dual-use items'.[99]

VI. Conclusion: Between Convergence and Divergence

As of 1 December 2019, the recast process of Regulation 428/2009 has yet to be finalised and it remains to be seen how the negotiation progresses among the European Commission, the Council and the European Parliament. Regardless of the outcomes of the EU's legislative process, it is intriguing, in itself, to unpack the deliberation at the Parliament, Council, and various stakeholders regarding the Commission's proposal. In principle, the EU and Member States pledged to implement the UNGPs, and, the Commission's proposal, despite conceptual incoherence and uncertainties, was an important step forward in bringing the EU's export control more in line with its own advocacy for the UNGPs. Yet the idea of situating some of the civil and political rights as a normative pillar of the EU's dual-use export control has invited resistance. Undoubtedly, concerns over the EU's economic competitiveness underlie political resistance on the part of industry associations, a number of EU Member States, and some members of the European Parliament. Yet the EU's overall promise to integrate human rights 'in all aspects of its external action without exception'[100] made it necessary for EU Member States to invoke some non-economic justifications as part of their narrative to contest the Commission's 2016 proposal. One of these narratives was the need for adherence to the international export control regimes and the traditional definition of dual-use items based on military purposes.

Overall, the legislative process and deliberation surrounding the Commission's proposal highlight some of the challenges that the EU encounters in integrating human rights and fundamental freedoms in its external trade relations. Despite the commitment to 'business and human rights', the insertion of human rights norms in the EU's dual-use export control has met strong resistance. One of the

[97] UN Human Rights Council and Report of the Special Rapporteur (n 1) 12, recital para 6. See section II, C of this chapter.
[98] Council's Negotiating Position of June 2019 (n 73) at 4 (recital 5).
[99] Council's Negotiating Position of June 2019 (n 73) at 12 (Art 2(1)).
[100] EU Strategic Framework and Action Plan (n 23) 2.

bases for contestation even pertained to the characterisation of human rights assessment as political, which was presented as if business enterprises are not suitable for assessing human rights risks. Given that dual-use export control would give rise to criminal penalties at the level of the Member States, it is critical to ensure certainty and foreseeability. Yet the narrative employed in response to the Commission's proposal may have revealed some of the pragmatic difficulties at the epistemic level in permeating human rights norms into the decision-making of business enterprises, including within the ICT sector.

Against the EU's overall mandate to integrate human rights into its external action, the stronger emphasis on human rights within the Commission's proposal was a noteworthy attempt. It asked the EU institutions and related stakeholders the critical question of whether the EU could and should take a more proactive position in the development of export control which has been shaped by a strong need for harmonisation across industrialised countries. As highlighted by the debates, however, the EU has been internally torn between the ambition for convergence and the realities that divergence may bring. On the one hand, the EU has articulated its normative ambition to converge its export control with human rights norms envisaged by the UNGPs. On the other hand, however, this leads to the inevitable divergence from international export control regimes, which may put EU businesses in an economically disadvantaged position. Between these two demands, compromise is inevitable; yet this may come at the expense of the human rights of those individuals within the EU's trading partners.

4

The EU and International Investment Agreements: To Diverge is to Converge

MAURO GATTI*

I. Introduction

The 'convergence ethic' that dominates the understandings of the EU's external action[1] finds a specific manifestation in the area of international investment law. This chapter suggests that, while international investment agreements (IIAs) may function as instruments of convergence, the nature of this convergence is problematic – and so is the EU's relationship with IIAs. For the purpose of this chapter, 'convergence' is defined as the process or state of converging,[2] ie an increasing similarity between different sets of rules. Convergence may concern different rules from a single legal system, rules from two or more domestic legal orders, or rules from a domestic legal system and the international legal order. While convergence is particularly evident when rules are mimicked[3] – something that may be termed as *positive* convergence – convergence may also concern the absence, elimination, or non-application of rules, that is, *negative* convergence.

International investment law constitutes an interesting case study for the investigation of convergence between international law, EU law and the laws of third countries because of its peculiar characteristics. IIAs may indeed promote the convergence of domestic legal orders towards deregulation (or non-regulation) of economic activities – a form of negative convergence. Although Western European countries, with the EC/EU's support, promoted IIAs for several years, the European policy is currently more cautious, as there is the risk that IIAs might involve EU law in the convergence towards deregulation. The extent of the change in the EU's policy, at any rate, remains ambiguous.

* I thank the editor, Giulia Evolvi, Eva Żelazna and the anonymous reviewers for their comments. The usual disclaimer applies.

[1] See the Introduction to this volume by Elaine Fahey.

[2] See *Oxford English Dictionary*.

[3] For instance, it is often argued that European rules are mimicked by third states or regions, see the Introduction to this volume by Elaine Fahey.

Section II shows that EC/EU Member States are among the main promoters of IIAs and the institutionalisation of international investment tribunals, in the form of Investor-to-State Dispute Settlement (ISDS). For years, the global network of IIAs has discouraged capital-importing states from adopting and applying laws in the public interest. IIAs have fostered deregulation (or non-regulation) in several states, thus promoting a form of negative convergence that is in the interest of EC/EU Member States and their investors (section III). Recent developments, such as the EU's enlargement and the public outcry about ISDS, have changed the dynamics of convergence in the external investment policy of the Union. EU institutions and states are reconsidering parts of the international investment protection system, within the EU (section IV) and at the global level (section V). The new policy of the EU and of its members might suggest a certain divergence of the EU from the paradigm of international investment law, accompanied by greater convergence between the policies of the Union and capital-importing countries (section VI).

The chapter focuses on international agreements and the decisions of domestic and international tribunals and does not systematically investigate policy debates, such as the discussion at the United Nations Commission on International Trade Law (UNCITRAL) on the possible reform of ISDS.[4]

II. European Support for Traditional Investment Agreements

The debate about international investment law often focuses on the alleged fragmentation that concerns this sector. States disagree about the content of customary rules regarding investors' rights, with industrialised countries traditionally favourable to broad protection standards and developing countries more critical.[5] Because of the impreciseness of customary law in this area, industrialised states have sought to 'treatify' investment law, through the conclusion of investment agreements, mostly bilateral in character.[6]

The European Community/Union and its Member States have actively supported this 'treatification'. The first country to enter into an IIA was an EEC Member State, Germany, which concluded a bilateral investment agreement with Pakistan in 1959. Other Western European countries soon concluded IIAs with third countries, notably developing or middle-income countries. IIAs became

[4] See UNCITRAL Working Group III (Investor-State Dispute Settlement Reform), Note by the Secretariat, Possible reform of investor-State dispute settlement (ISDS), 18 September 2017, UN Doc A/CN.9/WG.III/WP.142.

[5] Jeswald W Salacuse, *The Law of Investment Treaties* (Oxford University Press, 2015) 56, 75–78, 81 and 85.

[6] *Ibid* 87–88.

increasingly frequent over the subsequent decades, especially since the 1990s, to the extent that there are currently about 2,300 such treaties in force.[7]

Until recently, IIAs were concluded by EU Member States, on the basis of their competences. EU Member States remain among the main users of such agreements: as of 2018, there were about 1,400 IIAs entered into by an EU Member State and a third state,[8] as well as about 200 IIAs between EU Member States.[9] Despite the limitedness of its competences, the European Community included some investment-related provisions in the bilateral agreements with third countries.[10] The European Commission also encouraged the Member States to enter into investment agreements with third countries.[11]

IIAs do not create global standards *stricto sensu* because each IIA is an independent legal instrument, with specific content and wording. Nonetheless, IIAs have similar content, since capital-exporting states seek 'to base investment relations on uniform standards'[12] in order to protect their investors.[13] This is true, in particular, for 'traditional' IIAs, ie all IIAs except for the 'new generation' investment agreements recently negotiated by the EU and some states (discussed below, in section V). Traditional IIAs contain several standard investor rights;[14] for instance, they generally contain prohibitions of expropriation and obligations of 'fair and equitable treatment'. These standards are formulated in a similar, though not identical, manner in the different IIAs.

It is possible that different IIAs – or even the same IIA – might be applied in different ways in different circumstances.[15] Traditional IIAs define investors' rights in a vague manner. For instance, they generally contain provisions such as 'investments of investors of each Contracting Party shall at all times be accorded

[7] See UNCTAD, Investment Policy Hub, https://investmentpolicy.unctad.org/international-investment-agreements/advanced-search (last accessed 4 March 2020).

[8] List of the bilateral investment agreements referred to in Article 4(1) of Council Regulation (EU) No 1219/2012 of the European Parliament and of the Council establishing transitional arrangements for bilateral investment agreements between Member States and third countries [2018] OJ C149/1.

[9] European Commission, 'Commission Provides Guidance on Protection of Cross-Border EU Investment, (19 July 2018), https://europa.eu/rapid/press-release_MEMO-18-4529_en.htm (last accessed 4 March 2020).

[10] Stephen Woolcock, *The EU Approach to International Investment Policy after the Lisbon Treaty* (European Parliament, 2010) 9–10.

[11] See, eg, European Commission Communication, 'Investment Promotion and Protection Clauses in Agreements between the Community and Various Categories of Developing Country: Achievements to Date and Guidelines for Joint Action' COM(1980) 204 (8 May 1980).

[12] Stephan W Schill, *The Multilateralization of International Investment Law* (Cambridge University Press, 2009) 92.

[13] Andrew Newcombe and Lluis Paradell, *Law and Practice of Investment Treaties* (Wolters Kluwer, 2009) 47, 58, 62 and 114.

[14] Schill (n 12) 74; Susan D Frank, 'The Legitimacy Crisis in Investment Treaty Arbitration: Privatizing Public International Law through Inconsistent Decisions' (2005) *Fordham Law Review* 1521, 1529–35.

[15] See, eg, *AES Corporation v The Argentine Republic*, ICSID Case No ARB/02/17, Decision on Jurisdiction, 26 April 2005, paras 24–26.

fair and equitable treatment'[16] but do not define the meaning of either 'fair' and 'equitable'. Given the vagueness of investment protection standards, the actual scope of investor's rights is defined in practice by interpreters, notably arbitral tribunals. Numerous IIAs indeed provide for the creation of *ad hoc* arbitral tribunals that have jurisdiction on cases brought by the investors of one party against the other party (the so-called Investor-to-State Dispute Settlement mechanism). Arbitral tribunals interpret different IIAs with different wording, which apply in different contexts; in addition, arbitral tribunals are not bound by precedents. Consequently, they may adopt different interpretations of similar provisions and do so in practice: on several occasions, arbitral tribunals have reached opposite interpretations of the applicable legal rules, even in the presence of similar facts.[17]

Although international investment law is characterised by a multitude of international agreements, whose interpretation is inconsistent, it may constitute an instrument for the promotion of convergence at the global level, as shown in the next section.

III. Convergence through Traditional Investment Agreements

Traditional IIAs arguably foster convergence between the legal orders of different states by discouraging regulation in the public interest. IIAs might dissuade states from exercising their so-called 'right to regulate', ie their ability to regulate in order to achieve objectives such as the protection of public health, the environment or consumers. In other words, the states bound by IIAs may have an incentive, in some circumstances, not to adopt or apply legislation in the public interest, a phenomenon known as 'regulatory chill'.[18] The existence of regulatory chill is debated in the literature: scholars have identified numerous episodes of regulatory chill but there is no definitive proof of its extent.[19] At any rate, several states – especially developing or middle-income countries – perceive regulatory

[16] Agreement between the Government of the United Kingdom of Great Britain and Northern Ireland and the Government of the Republic of Bulgaria for the Promotion and Reciprocal Protection of Investments, signed on 11 December 1995, Art 2(2).

[17] See UNCITRAL Working Group III (Investor-State Dispute Settlement Reform), Note by the Secretariat, Possible reform of investor-State dispute settlement (ISDS): Consistency and related matters, 28 August 2018, UN Doc A/CN.9/WG.III/WP.150, pp 2–11; *cf*, eg *Enron Corporation & Ponderosa Assets, LP v Argentine Republic*, ICSID Case No ARB/01/3, Award, 22 May 2007, paras 322–345 and *Continental Casualty Co. v. Argentine Republic*, ICSID Case No ARB/03/9, Award, 5 September 2008, paras 189–230.

[18] *cf* Kyla Tienhaara, 'Regulatory Chill and the Threat of Arbitration: A View from Political Science' in Chester Brown and Kate Miles (eds), *Evolution in Investment Treaty Law and Arbitration* (Cambridge University Press, 2011) 610.

[19] *Ibid* 616–18.

chill as a serious issue.[20] Even industrialised countries (and the EU) have adopted solutions to tackle regulatory chill (see below, section V).

Probably, states are concerned about regulatory chill because, once they have ratified a traditional IIA, they cannot exclude *a priori* that an investment tribunal might interpret extensively investors' rights, equating regulatory change with liability under IIAs.[21] For instance, according to the broadest interpretation of fair and equitable treatment, investors have a right to the 'stability of the legal and business framework',[22] implying the protection of their 'legitimate expectations'.[23] Foreign investors may, therefore, expect host states to act 'free from ambiguity and totally transparently' in their relations with the foreign investors, so that the latter may know beforehand 'any and all rules' that will govern their investments.[24] While arbitral tribunals recently seem to favour less expansive interpretations of fair and equitable treatment,[25] it would seem that the 'legitimate expectations' of the investors may still be based on 'implicit' assurances stemming from a law or regulation,[26] which states cannot frustrate by altering their laws 'substantially',[27] 'radically',[28] or in an 'unreasonable' manner.[29]

The unpredictability in the interpretation of investment agreements – and the expectation that arbitral tribunals might exceed their mandate, by interpreting IIAs extensively[30] – is reinforced by the conflicts of interests allegedly affecting

[20] Submission from the Government of Brazil to UNCITRAL Working Group III, 11 June 2019, UN Doc A/CN.9/WG.III/WP.171, para 3; Submission from the Government of South Africa, 17 July 2019, UN Doc A/CN.9/WG.III/WP.176, para 63; Rohan Perera, Legal Advisor to the Ministry of Foreign Affairs of Sri Lanka, 'Technical Assistance and Capacity Building, Lessons Learned from Experiences and the Way Forward', Symposium 'Making the Most of International Investment Agreements: A Common Agenda', Paris, 12 December 2005, www.oecd.org/daf/inv/internationalinvestmentagreements/36055317.pdf (last accessed 4 March 2020).

[21] See further Federico Ortino, 'The Obligation of Regulatory Stability in the Fair and Equitable Treatment Standard: How Far Have We Come?' (2018) *Journal of International Economic Law* 845.

[22] *Occidental Exploration and Production Company v The Republic of Ecuador*, LCIA Case No UN3467, Final Award, 1 July 2004, para 183; see also, inter alia, *LG&E Energy Corp, LG&E Capital Corp, and LG&E International, Inc v Argentine Republic*, ICSID Case No ARB/02/1, Decision on Liability, 3 October 2006, para 125.

[23] See further Michele Potestà, 'Legitimate Expectations in Investment Treaty Law: Understanding the Roots and the Limits of a Controversial Concept' (2013) *ICSID Review – Foreign Investment Law Journal* 88.

[24] *Técnicas Medioambientales Tecmed, SA v The United Mexican States*, ICSID Case No ARB (AF)/00/2, Award, 29 May 2003, para 154.

[25] See, eg, *EDF (Services) Limited v Romania*, ICSID Case No ARB/05/13, Decision in liability, 8 October 2009, para 217.

[26] *9Ren Holding v Spain*, ICSID Case No ARB/15/15, Award, 31 May 2019, para 227; see also *Total SA v Argentine Republic*, ICSID Case No ARB/04/1, Decision on Liability, 27 December 2010, paras 119 and 295.

[27] *Enron Corporation & Ponderosa Assets* (n 17) para 264.

[28] *Eiser Infrastructure and Energía Solar v Spain*, ICSID Case No ARB/13/36, Award, 4 May 2017, para 382.

[29] *Impregilo SpA v Argentine Republic*, ICSID Case No. ARB/07/17, Final Award, 21 June 2011, para. 291.

[30] Submission from the Government of Ecuador to the UNCITRAL Working Group III, 17 July 2019, UN Doc A/CN.9/WG.III/WP.175, para 11.

the members of such tribunals.[31] These conflicts may take the form, in particular, of 'issue conflicts', ie situations where an arbitrator has either a pre-existing view or a conflicting interest in a case they are deciding: arbitrators may indeed work as counsel in other proceedings.[32] This is likely a frequent issue in investor-to-state dispute settlement, given the recurring legal issues under the same or similar legal instruments.[33] Conflicts of interest may also be the consequence of the uni-directionality of ISDS mechanisms. As the existence of arbitral tribunals depends on claims, and claims can be brought only by investors, the interest in system-preservation may lead to undue attention to investors' interests.[34]

States are likely to perceive the threat of legal action by investors as a concrete danger, since arbitral tribunals may impose pecuniary and non-pecuniary remedies through a binding and generally final award. Pecuniary remedies can be highly dissuasive: the average compensation is higher than 500 million dollars.[35] Moreover, awards of arbitral tribunals can be easily enforced. Thanks to the 1958 New York Convention[36] and domestic laws based on international soft law,[37] investors can enforce international arbitral tribunals' in the territories of the parties to the IIAs concerned, as well as in the territories of most other states. Therefore, 'governments might refrain from imposing regulatory measures in the public interest due to the threat of investment arbitration and the high damages it entails'.[38] In other words, IIAs may foster 'regulatory chill' in capital-importing countries by promoting deregulation (the repeal or non-application of domestic laws) or non-regulation (the failure to adopt laws in the public interest) in their legal orders. Regulatory chill is likely to be reinforced by the legal costs entailed by international arbitral proceedings. Legal and arbitration costs for the parties

[31] See UNCITRAL Working Group III, Note by the Secretariat, Possible reform of investor-State dispute settlement (ISDS), Ensuring independence and impartiality on the part of arbitrators and decision makers in ISDS, 30 August 2018, UN Doc A/CN.9/WG.III/WP.151.

[32] David Gaukrodger and Kathryn Gordon, *Investor-State Dispute Settlement: A Scoping Paper for the Investment policy Community* (OECD, 2013) 50; See also Gavan Griffith and Daniel Kalderimis '"Pure" Issue Conflicts in Investment Treaty Arbitration' in David Caron et al (eds), *Practising Virtue: Inside International Arbitration* (Oxford University Press, 2015).

[33] International Council for Commercial Arbitration *Report of the ASIL-ICCA Joint Task Force on Issue Conflicts in Investor-State Arbitration*, 2016, www.arbitration-icca.org/media/6/81372711507986/asil-icca_report_final_5_april_final_for_ridderprint.pdf (last accessed 4 March 2020) para 12.

[34] *cf* Gaukrodger and Gordon (n 32) 48; Hannes Lenk, *The EU Investment Court System. A Viable Reform Initiative?* (University of Gothenburg, 2019) 72.

[35] *Investor-State Dispute Settlement: Review of Developments in 2017* (UNCTAD, 2018) 5, https://unctad.org/en/PublicationsLibrary/diaepcbinf2018d2_en.pdf (last accessed 4 March 2020).

[36] Convention on the Recognition and Enforcement of Foreign Arbitral Awards, New York, 1958. On the status of ratification, see www.uncitral.org/uncitral/en/uncitral_texts/arbitration/NYConvention_status_map.html (last accessed 4 March 2020).

[37] UNCITRAL Model Law on International Commercial Arbitration, 1985, with Amendments as adopted in 2006, www.uncitral.org/pdf/english/texts/arbitration/ml-arb/07-86998_Ebook.pdf (last accessed 4 March 2020).

[38] Submission from the Government of South Africa to UNCITRAL Working Group III, 17 July 2019, UN Doc A/CN.9/WG.III/WP.176, para 63; see also, eg, the submission of Brazil, 11 June 2019, UN Doc A/CN.9/WG.III/WP.171, para 3.

may amount to several millions of dollars.[39] Even when a responding state is successful in defending its measures in front of an arbitral tribunal, it may have to pay substantial amounts to cover its defence. Investors routinely exploit this situation by bringing up cases that have little or no chance of succeeding (so-called 'frivolous claims'), with the apparent purpose of deterring states from implementing certain policies.[40] Dissuading states from acting in the public interest might even constitute the main objective of ISDS proceedings.[41]

Regulatory chill may be described as a form of negative convergence: states parties to different IIAs may have a similar incentive not to adopt legislation in the public interest. This convergence towards deregulation is not the product of a precise set of international rules, but a possible consequence of similar ill-defined commitments set in a vast network of IIAs, interpreted by various arbitral tribunals, whose awards are inconsistent and may have serious financial implications for state parties. To the extent that they promote regulatory chill, the vague standards of IIAs may arguably have 'the potential to shape domestic administrative law, influence the deployment of judicial proceedings', and serve as 'quasi-constitutional' standards that set limits to the activity of national legislators.[42]

The convergence promoted by traditional IIAs is hardly neutral since it fosters the idea that government intervention should be minimised through 'privatization, deregulation and liberalization', consistently with the programme of the neoclassical school of thought.[43] The neoclassical approach, which is the mainstream economic school of thought, apparently inspires, in particular, the policy of the European Commission, notably in the trade and investment area.[44]

The convergence fostered by IIAs is not neutral from the perspective of international relations, either. Traditional IIAs are concluded especially (though not exclusively) in the context of unequal relationships between capital-exporting and capital-importing countries, which often have different levels of economic development and influence on the world stage. Though it is frequently claimed that

[39] *cf* Jeffrey Commission, 'How Much Does an ICSID Arbitration Cost? A Snapshot of the Last Five Years' (*Kluwer Arbitration Blog*, 2016) http://arbitrationblog.kluwerarbitration.com/2016/02/29/how-much-does-an-icsid-arbitration-cost-a-snapshot-of-the-last-five-years/ (last accessed 4 March 2020): '[between 2011 and 2015] average respondent costs were US$4,954,461.27'.

[40] European Commission DG Trade, Public consultation on modalities for investment protection and ISDS in TTIP, https://web.archive.org/web/20181206201955/http://trade.ec.europa.eu/doclib/docs/2014/march/tradoc_152280.pdf (last accessed 4 March 2020).

[41] Krzysztof Pelc, 'What Explains the Low Success Rate of Investor-State Disputes?' (2017) *International Organization* 559, 569.

[42] Schill (n 12) 80; this author, at any rate, does not connect the quasi-constitutional character of investment protection standards to regulatory chill; *cf* Salacuse (n 5) 252–53.

[43] Richard E Werner, *New Paradigm in Macroeconomics: Solving the Riddle of Japanese Macroeconomic Performance* (Palgrave, 2005) 3–4; See also Alberto Ruiz-Villaverde, 'Editor's Introduction: The Growing Failure of the Neoclassical Paradigm in Economics' (2019) *The American Journal of Economics and Sociology* 13, 20; Lenk (n 34) 54.

[44] Gabriel Siles-Brügge, *Constructing European Union Trade Policy: A Global Idea of Europe* (Palgrave, 2014) 77–84.

IIAs reflect the interests of capital-importing countries, as they allegedly promote foreign investments,[45] there is limited evidence in favour of this argument.[46] In any event, the negative effects for developing countries seem evident: since most (though not all) ISDS proceedings are brought by investors from capital-exporting countries against capital-importing countries,[47] IIAs *de facto* protect mostly the investors of one party and do not provide any immediate benefit to the other party. For instance, Dutch companies have initiated more than 100 ISDS proceedings against other states, but no known proceedings have been brought against the Netherlands.[48] In the case of Germany, the ratio is 64 to 3, and for the US it is 178 to 17.[49] Capital-importing countries have very different ratios: while Polish companies initiated such proceedings in only seven cases, Poland was a defendant in 30 proceedings; in Slovakia, the ratio is 1 to 13; in Mexico, it is 4 to 32.[50]

Given the policy and international relations implications of IIAs, it is not surprising that they are opposed by numerous actors, including non-governmental organisations[51] and states. Developing countries, and Latin American states in particular, endorsed a completely different approach for years, for example by supporting the UN General Assembly's Charter of Economic Rights and Duties of States (1974), which recognises, inter alia, each state's right to 'regulate and exercise authority over foreign investment within its national jurisdiction in accordance with its laws'.[52] Brazil never ratified an agreement containing ISDS, while others, such as Bolivia, Ecuador, India, Russia, South Africa and Venezuela recently withdrew from various treaties enabling ISDS.[53] It seems increasingly difficult to speak of an 'isolated opposition of some states' to the IIAs regime.[54]

It seems possible to argue, therefore, that the convergence promoted through IIAs is at least perceived by states as a means to promote – not genuine

[45] eg Schill (n 12) 109, 119.

[46] Jonathan Bonnitcha, *Assessing the Impacts of Investment Treaties: Overview of the Evidence* (IISD, 2017) www.iisd.org/sites/default/files/publications/assessing-impacts-investment-treaties.pdf; UNCTAD, *The Role of International Investment Agreements in Attracting Foreign Direct Investment to Developing Countries* (UN, 2009), https://unctad.org/en/Docs/diaeia20095_en.pdf (last accessed 4 March 2020).

[47] See, eg, UNCTAD, *Investor-State Dispute Settlement: Review of Developments in 2017* (June 2018) https://unctad.org/en/PublicationsLibrary/diaepcbinf2018d2_en.pdf (last accessed 4 March 2020): 'Developed-country investors brought most of the 65 known cases in 2017'; 'As in previous years, the majority of new cases were brought against developing countries and transition economies.'

[48] See UNCTAD, Investment Dispute Settlement Navigator, https://investmentpolicy.unctad.org/investment-dispute-settlement/, updated as of 31 July 2019.

[49] *Ibid.*

[50] *Ibid.*

[51] See, eg, 'Stop ISDS', https://stopisds.org/ (last accessed 4 March 2020).

[52] General Assembly Resolution 3281 (XXIX), Charter of Economic Rights and Duties of States, 12 December 1974, Art 2(1).

[53] Tim R Samples, 'Winning and Losing in Investor–State Dispute Settlement' (2019) *American Business Law Journal* 115.

[54] Charles N Brower and Stephan W Schill, 'Is Arbitration a Threat or a Boon to the Legitimacy of International Investment Law?' (2009) *Chicago Journal of International Law* 471, 496.

multilateralism – but the interests of some states and their investors, as well as the neoclassical economic policy of their governments.[55]

IV. A Rejection of Convergence via Intra-EU Agreements? The *Achmea* Case

Unlike developing countries, Western European states and EU institutions have always been staunch supporters of IIAs (see above, section II) but their position has changed over the last few years. EU institutions adopted a completely new approach to IIAs concluded among EU Member States (hereinafter: intra-EU agreements), as shown in this section. The approach of EU institutions to IIAs with third countries (hereinafter: extra-EU agreements) is more ambiguous and is discussed in the next section.

The EC (and then the EU) promoted IIAs for decades, by suggesting, in particular, that candidate countries from Central and Eastern Europe should conclude bilateral investment agreements with EC/EU Member States in order to prepare for accession to the Community (subsequently, the Union).[56] This approach does not seem unreasonable from the Commission's perspective: if IIAs enhance deregulation, they can foster convergence between formerly socialist systems and the liberal order of the EU.

The completion of the 2004, 2007 and 2013 enlargements, however, brought about a change of perspective. Once candidate countries became Member States, IIAs lost their usefulness as an instrument for convergence between a candidate country's legal order and the legal order of the EU. At the same time, there was a risk of conflict between the plethora of IIAs concluded by former candidates (which are mostly capital-importing countries) with older EU Member States (which are mostly capital-exporting countries). This risk was evidenced in the *Micula* case, where Romania was contemporarily bound, under an intra-EU agreement, to provide compensation to an investor, while it was forbidden to do so under EU competition law, as such compensation amounted to state aid.[57]

It would seem, therefore, that intra-EU agreements might discourage EU institutions and Member States from applying EU rules adopted in the public interest (such as competition law). In other words, regulatory chill is now a risk for the EU itself. These considerations may contribute to explain why the Commission abandoned its traditionally unconditional support for IIAs, to the extent that this institution now argues that intra-EU investment agreements cannot be applied

[55] See above n 43 and n 44.

[56] Case C-284/16 *Slowakische Republik v Achmea BV*, Opinion of AG Wathelet, EU:C:2017:699I–8531, para 40.

[57] See Commission Decision 2015/1470/EU, 30 March 2015 [2015] L232/43.

in the Union, inter alia, because they conflict with EU internal market rules.[58] The Commission's argument did not convince arbitral tribunals[59] but found fertile ground at the Court of Justice.

In the *Achmea* judgment (2018),[60] the Court held that, to be compatible with EU law, an international tribunal set up by two Member States should have at least one of three characteristics: it should belong to the judicial system of the Member States, its awards should be reviewable by the Member States' courts, or – most importantly – it should not resolve disputes 'liable to relate to the interpretation or application of EU law'.[61] Therefore, an investment tribunal created by an intra-EU investment agreement is incompatible with the autonomy of EU law in so far as it may interpret EU law, whether its interpretation of EU law is binding for EU institutions or not.[62]

The Slovakia-Netherlands bilateral investment treaty at stake in *Achmea* expressly enables the arbitral tribunal to take into account the laws of the contracting parties and the agreements between them (including EU law) and is, in this respect, incompatible with EU law.[63] It is expected that many other intra-EU investment agreements might be in a similar situation.[64] Consequently, EU Member States, in the aftermath of the *Achmea* judgment, declared their intention to terminate intra-EU investment agreements[65] and 23 of them most of them signed a plurilateral agreement to terminate almost all such agreements.[66]

In *Achmea*, the Court did not expressly take issue with the convergence to deregulation (and non-regulation) potentially promoted by IIAs, but the judgment seems to reflect the logic of divergence. On the one hand, *Achmea* fostered divergence between EU and international investment law: after *Achmea*, intra-EU agreements do not apply in the Union under EU law, though they apply under international law, as affirmed by arbitral tribunals.[67] On the other hand,

[58] See European Commission's observation in *Achmea BV v The Slovak Republic*, UNCITRAL, PCA Case No 2008–13, Award on Jurisdiction, Arbitrability and Suspension, 26 October 2010, para 177.

[59] *Ibid.*

[60] Case C-284/16 *Slowakische Republik v Achmea BV* [2018] EU:C:2018:158.

[61] *Ibid* paras 39–56.

[62] *Ibid* para 39.

[63] *Ibid* paras 40–42.

[64] See, eg, Luca Pantaleo, 'La mancata esecuzione del lodo arbitrale nel caso Achmea: quale futuro per le controversie in materia di investimento intra-UE?' (2018) *Il diritto dell'Unione europea*; Matthew Happold and Michael De Boeck, 'The European Union and the Energy Charter Treaty: What Next After ACHMEA?' in Mads Andenas, Matthew Happold and Luca Pantaleo (eds), *The EU External Action in International Economic Law – Recent Trends and Developments* (TMC Asser Press, 2020).

[65] The Member States Declarations are available at https://ec.europa.eu/info/sites/info/files/business_economy_euro/banking_and_finance/documents/190117-bilateral-investment-treaties_en.pdf (last accessed 5 March 2020).

[66] The exception being the Energy Charter Treaty; the text of the Plurilateral Agreement is available at http://ec.europa.eu/info/sites/info/files/business_economy_euro/banking_and_finance/documents/200505-bilateral-investment-treaties-agreement_en.pdf (last accessed 11 May 2020).

[67] See, eg, *Magyar Farming Company Ltd, Kintyre Kft and Inicia Zrt v Hungary*, ICSID Case No ARB/17/27, Award of the Tribunal, 13 November 2019, paras 207–10.

Achmea reduced the potential for conflicts between IIAs and EU law, limiting the former's ability to 'chill' the latter. While IIAs might generally lead states to refrain from applying legislation in the public interest – and thus converge towards deregulation – *Achmea* might have given EU institutions and Member States greater leeway to 'diverge' by adopting and applying legislation in the public interest.

It is possible that the Court deliberately sought this outcome: in *Achmea*, the Court adopted a formalist and allegedly 'maximalist' reading of the autonomy of EU,[68] since it focused on the 'abstract possibility' of interference with the EU's autonomy,[69] while there was no substantive incompatibility between the intra-EU agreement in question and EU law.[70] By contrast, the Court adopted a more restrained understanding of autonomy in other cases, such as Opinion 1/00.[71] The 'maximalist' approach that characterises *Achmea* was perhaps motivated by the specificity of its context.[72] It may be hypothesised that the Court acknowledged that intra-EU investment agreements might threaten the EU's right to regulate and, consequently, adopted an extensive interpretation of autonomy, in order to reduce potential conflicts between EU and intra-EU investment agreements.

The Court's concern for the EU's right to regulate seems to be confirmed by Opinion 1/17, where the Court expressly acknowledges that an investment agreement might, at least in principle, interfere with the EU's ability 'to operate autonomously within its unique constitutional framework'.[73]

V. Limitation of Convergence through Extra-EU Agreements: Opinion 1/17

While, after *Achmea*, divergence seems to prevail at the intra-EU level, the EU's relationship to extra-EU investment agreements is more ambiguous.

The Lisbon Treaty granted the EU external competence on foreign direct investment, which allows the Union to directly negotiate IIAs jointly with its Member States.[74] At first, the European Commission seemed to follow the traditional approach of its Member States, as the negotiations for an EU-US Transatlantic

[68] Panos Koutrakos, 'The Autonomy of EU Law and International Investment Arbitration' (2019) *Nordic Journal of International Law* 41, 52.

[69] Sebastian Wuschka, 'Investment Protection and the EU after Achmea' (2018) *Zeitschrift für Europarechtliche Studien* 25, 38.

[70] Koutrakos (n 68) 50.

[71] Koutrakos (n 68) 47; Opinion 1/00 (European Common Aviation Area) [2002] EU:C:2002:231, para 12.

[72] On the influence of context on the interpretation of autonomy in the Court's case law, see Eva Kassoti and Jed Odermatt, 'The Evolution of Autonomy – Some Reflections on Investor-State Dispute Settlement in the Light of Opinion 1/17' (forthcoming).

[73] Opinion 1/17 (EU-Canada CET Agreement) [2019] EU:C:2019:341, para 150.

[74] See Opinion 2/15 (Accord de libre-échange avec Singapour) [2017] EU:C:2017:376.

Trade and Investment Partnership (TTIP) initially aimed at establishing an ISDS mechanism. The TTIP, however, attracted the attention of the public, which vocally rejected the use of traditional ISDS;[75] the Commission, therefore, had to abandon traditional ISDS. This development was probably favoured by other factors, such as an increase in the number of ISDS cases brought against capital-exporting countries, eg *Vattenfall v Germany*.[76]

Over the last two decades, several industrialised countries, ranging from the US to the Netherlands, have reconsidered their policy on IIA, by modifying their model bilateral investment treaties and introducing 'new generation' investment agreements.[77] This practice served as an example for the European Union in the negotiation of its own 'new generation' agreements. The Council authorised the negotiation, and the Commission negotiated, several agreements, including the TTIP (later discontinued) and the trade and investment treaties with Canada (Canada-EU Comprehensive Economic and Trade Agreement, CETA), Singapore, Vietnam and Mexico.[78] The Commission is currently negotiating an investment-related agreement with Chile.[79]

New generation investment agreements are similar to traditional IIAs, since they contain typical obligations regarding, for instance, non-expropriation and fair and equitable treatment. They provide for international tribunals that have jurisdiction on the violation of investors' rights, in the context of investor-to-state disputes. However, new generation agreements also present some innovative aspects. CETA, for instance, replaces ISDS with an Investment Court System (ICS), which should reduce conflicts of interests among arbitrators, notably by ensuring the permanent character of the tribunal.[80] The CETA tribunal nonetheless maintains several of the key elements of traditional international investment arbitration, such as the possibility to adjudicate only claims submitted by investors,[81]

[75] See European Commission Staff Working Document, Online public consultation on investment protection and investor-to-state dispute settlement (ISDS) in the Transatlantic Trade and Investment Partnership Agreement, 13 January 2015, SWD(2015) 3 final, p 14.

[76] See *Vattenfall v Germany (I)*, ICSID Case No ARB/09/6; *Vattenfall v Germany*, ICSID Case No ARB/12/12.

[77] See further Aikaterini Titi, *The Right to Regulate in International Investment Law* (Nomos, 2014) 53–75; Aikaterini Titi, 'Le 'droit de réglementer' et les nouveaux accords de l'Union européenne sur l'investissement' (2015) *Journal du droit international* 39.

[78] Comprehensive Economic and Trade Agreement (CETA) between Canada, of the one part, and the European Union and its Member States, of the other part [2017] OJ L11/34; Investment Protection Agreement between the European Union and its Members, of the one part, and the Republic of Singapore, of the other part (authentic texts as of April 2018), available at http://trade.ec.europa.eu/doclib/press/index.cfm?id=961; EU-Vietnam Investment Protection Agreement (authentic text as of August 2018), available at http://trade.ec.europa.eu/doclib/press/index.cfm?id=1437; EU-Mexico Global Agreement, as agreed in principle in April 2018, available at http://trade.ec.europa.eu/doclib/press/index.cfm?id=1833.

[79] Council, Directives for the negotiation of a Modernised Association Agreement with Chile, 8 November 2017, Council Doc 13553/17 ADD 1.

[80] Additionally, the EU is supporting the establishment of a Multilateral Investment Court, see CETA (n 78) Art 8.29.

[81] CETA (n 78) Art 8.23(1).

or the remuneration of the tribunals' members depending in part on the number of working days devoted to a dispute.[82]

Another innovation of the EU's new generation agreements lies in the 'reaffirmation' of the parties' 'right to regulate' within their territories to achieve legitimate policy objectives, such as the protection of public health, safety, the environment or public morals, social or consumer protection or the promotion and protection of cultural diversity.[83] New generation agreements also specify that investment standards should 'not be interpreted as a commitment from a Party that it will not change the legal and regulatory framework, including in a manner that may negatively affect the operation of covered investments or the investor's expectations of profits'.[84] Furthermore, they specify the content of investment standards. Fair and equitable treatment, for instance, is defined as denial of justice, fundamental breach of due process, abusive treatment (such as coercion), manifest arbitrariness and (with the exception of the EU-Singapore Agreement) targeted discrimination on manifestly wrongful grounds.[85]

The objective of these innovations seems to circumscribe the scope of investors' rights and limit the discretion of investment tribunals in the interpretation of the agreements.[86] The expected result is that the parties should have more leeway to implement public interest policies. In other words, international law and international bodies would have less capability to restrain the conduct of the parties, which may implement more divergent policies in practice – and potentially depart from the neoclassical dogma in terms of economic policy.[87] It would thus seem that the European Union seeks to reduce the degree of convergence towards deregulation ensured by traditional investment agreements.

This reading of recent trade and investment agreements seems to be corroborated by Opinion 1/17 of the Court of Justice, concerning the compatibility between CETA and EU primary law. As the investment-related provisions of CETA are similar to those of the other new generation agreements of the EU, Opinion 1/17 *de facto* concerns these agreements as well.

According to Opinion 1/17, EU legislation is adopted democratically and is deemed, by virtue of the principles of conferral of powers, subsidiarity and

[82] CETA (n 78) Art 8.27(14); see also Opinion 1/17 (n 73) para 61.

[83] CETA (n 78) Art 8.9(1); see also CETA Joint Interpretative Instrument, 27 October 2016, Council Doc 13541/16; EU-Vietnam Agreement (n 78) Chapter 2, Art 2.2(1); EU-Singapore Agreement (n 78) Chapter 2, Art 2.2(1); EU-Mexico Global Agreement (n 78), Investment Chapter, Art 1.

[84] EU-Mexico Global Agreement (n 78) Investment Chapter, Art 14(1). See also EU-Singapore Agreement (n 78) Chapter 2, Art 2.2(2); EU-Vietnam Agreement (n 78) Chapter 2, Art 2.2(2); CETA (n 78) Art 8.9(2).

[85] CETA (n 78) Art 8.10(2); EU-Vietnam Agreement, Chapter 2, Art 2.5(2); EU-Singapore Agreement (n 78), Chapter 2, Art 2.4(2); EU-Mexico Global Agreement (n 78) Investment Chapter, Art 15(2). The parties can in any case introduce additional elements of the fair and equitable treatment obligation at a subsequent stage.

[86] See further Ewa Żelazna, *The EU International Investment Policy after the Treaty of Lisbon 2009: An Institutional Perspective* (PhD thesis, University of Leicester, 2018) 69–71.

[87] On international investment agreements and neoclassical thinking, see Lenk (n 34) 54–56.

proportionality, 'to be both appropriate and necessary to achieve a legitimate objective of the Union'.[88] If the CETA tribunal were to

> have jurisdiction to issue awards finding that the treatment of a Canadian investor is incompatible with the CETA because of the level of protection of a public interest established by the EU institutions, this could create a situation where, in order to avoid being repeatedly compelled by the CETA Tribunal to pay damages to the claimant investor, the achievement of that level of protection needs to be abandoned by the Union.[89]

If CETA had such an effect, it would impossible for the Union 'to operate autonomously within its unique constitutional framework'.[90]

In other words, an investment agreement, such as CETA, might potentially enable an investment tribunal to restrict *de facto* EU institutions' ability to legislate in the public interest. The Court thus seems to recognise the risk of regulatory chill and the consequent possibility of convergence towards deregulation.[91] Opinion 1/17 thus makes explicit the concerns that possibly inspired *Achmea*, too (see above, section IV).

The Court could have followed the *Achmea* precedent further, by adopting a 'maximalist' reading of EU autonomy and concluding that CETA is incompatible with EU primary law, thereby averting the risks for the EU's right to regulate.

There are at least two reasons why CETA might be incompatible with the EU's autonomy. First, the CETA tribunal might interpret EU law, as the tribunal in *Achmea*; consequently, it may be incompatible with the EU's autonomy. It is true that CETA, unlike the treaty at the origin of the *Achmea* case, does not expressly authorise the investment tribunal to interpret EU law: the latter should assess domestic law only 'as a matter of fact' and should follow the 'prevailing interpretation given to the domestic law by the courts or authorities' of the parties.[92] However, the CETA Tribunal will inevitably have to give a 'meaning' to domestic law, as implicitly recognised by CETA itself.[93] While 'municipal laws are merely facts' from the standpoints of international courts,[94] an international tribunal may find it indispensable to interpret and apply municipal law.[95] For instance, the

[88] Opinion 1/17 (n 73) para 151.

[89] Opinion 1/17 (n 73) para 150.

[90] Opinion 1/17 (n 73) para 150.

[91] This argument seems consistent with the case law: the Court had already acknowledged the possibility of regulatory chill at the domestic level, by ruling on the non-contractual liability of EU institutions, see case C-120/06 P *FIAMM and others v Council and Commission* [2008] EU:C:2008:476, paras 171 and 174.

[92] CETA (n 78) Art 8.31(2).

[93] CETA (n 78) Art 8.31(2).

[94] Permanent Court of International Justice, Certain German Interests in Polish Upper Silesia, 25 May 1926, p 19.

[95] Wilfred Jenks, 'The Interpretation and Application of Municipal Law by the Permanent Court of International Justice' (1938) *British Yearbook of International Law* 67, 71; see further Jarrod Hepburn, 'CETA's New Domestic Law Clause' (*EJILTalk!*, 17 March 2016) www.ejiltalk.org/cetas-new-domestic-law-clause/ (last accessed 5 March 2020).

CETA Tribunal might have to interpret EU and national norms on nationality, in order to determine whether an investor might be a 'citizen' of the European Union, ie 'a natural person holding the nationality of a Member State'.[96] While the CETA tribunal should probably follow the interpretation of EU law that the Court of Justice has given,[97] it might be confronted with new interpretative issues, which the Court of Justice has never addressed. However, the Court of Justice took CETA at face value, accepting that the tribunal's examination of domestic law 'cannot be classified as equivalent to an interpretation'.[98]

Second, CETA might be incompatible with the EU's autonomy because it might threaten the EU's right to regulate. While CETA, like other new generation agreements, introduced several innovations in these respects, they might be insufficient to generate legal certainty and prevent regulatory chill. For instance, the recent agreements mention that fair and equitable treatment is breached in case of 'fundamental' breaches of due process and 'manifest' arbitrariness – but do not define either 'fundamental' or 'manifest'.[99] International arbitral tribunals have made use of ample discretion in the past, for instance by introducing concepts such as 'legitimate expectations' that have no explicit anchoring in the text of investment treaties.[100] It would not be entirely surprising if the new agreements negotiated by the Union were interpreted creatively, too.

Nonetheless, the Court found that CETA is compatible with the EU's ability 'to operate autonomously'. The Court approvingly acknowledged, inter alia, the mentioning of the 'right to regulate' in CETA and the specification that a mere change in the law cannot be deemed to negatively affect investors' expectations.[101] The Court also notices that the jurisdiction of the CETA Tribunal to find infringements of the obligation to accord 'fair and equitable treatment' to covered investments is specifically circumscribed to specific situations (eg abusive treatment). This purportedly demonstrates that the CETA Tribunal does not have jurisdiction on 'the required level of protection of a public interest'.[102] Therefore, the Court concludes that the CETA tribunal cannot 'call into question

[96] See CETA (n 78) Arts 1.2 and 8.1; *cf Soufraki v UAE*, Decision of the *Ad Hoc* Committee on the Application for Annulment of Mr Soufraki, ICSID Case No ARB/02/7, 5 June 2007, para 59; Devashish Krishan, 'Nationality of Physical Persons' in Federico Ortino, et al (eds), *Investment Treaty Law: Current Issues II* (BIICL, 2007) 60–61.

[97] Opinion 1/17 (EU-Canada CET Agreement) [2019], Opinion of AG Bot, EU:C:2019:72, para 137.

[98] Opinion 1/17 (n 73) para 131.

[99] The agreement with Mexico specifies, in a footnote, that 'The mere illegality, or a merely inconsistent or questionable application of a policy or procedure, does not in itself constitute manifest arbitrariness', while a 'total' and 'unjustified' 'repudiation' of a law or regulation, or a 'measure without reason' are likely to constitute manifest arbitrariness. Given the uncertain meaning of the words and expressions used in this footnote, one might doubt whether it might be sufficient to orient the interpretation of manifest arbitrariness in practice; see the EU-Mexico Global Agreement (n 78), Investment chapter, fn 16.

[100] Potestà (n 23).

[101] Opinion 1/17 (n 73) para 154. See also paras 152–55.

[102] Opinion 1/17 (n 73) paras 158–59.

the level of protection of public interest determined by the Union following a democratic process'.[103]

It would seem that EU institutions have a different attitude towards intra-EU and extra-EU investment agreements. The former are unacceptable, possibly because they are likely to conflict with EU law, as there is an overlap between intra-EU investment agreements and the internal market provisions of the EU.[104] Extra-EU agreements seem less problematic, in the eyes of EU institutions. The Commission energetically supports extra-EU investment agreements, to the extent that only public opinion's outrage convinced it to exclude the most problematic feature of traditional IIAs, the ISDS mechanism, from new generation treaties. The Court seems slightly more sceptical, as it admits that, in principle, these agreements might interfere with the EU's right to regulate (the EU's ability 'to operate autonomously within its unique constitutional framework'). Nonetheless, the Court seems to accept – quite optimistically – that the CETA Tribunal will not interpret the agreement (and EU law) creatively, and therefore will not bring about regulatory chill in the Union. The innovations introduced with CETA seem sufficient, at least according to the Court, in preventing the EU's involvement in a global convergence towards deregulation.

VI. Concluding Remarks

The current international investment regime may arguably interfere with domestic authorities' ability to regulate in the public interest, at the expense of the protection of health, safety, the environment and labour rights.[105] Traditional IIAs generally contain broad and vague investment protection standards, which are interpreted by arbitral tribunals whose independence is questionable, whose decisions are to a large extent unpredictable, whose proceedings are costly, and whose awards may force states to pay significant sums as compensations for foreign investors.

To avoid the financial risks linked to international investment proceedings, states might decide not to adopt legislation in the public interest or not to enforce it (so-called 'regulatory chill'). Investment agreements may thus promote convergence of domestic laws to deregulation or non-regulation: capital-importing states are incentivised to prioritise the protection of (foreign investors') property over the protection of public goods. This convergence is neutral neither in ideological terms, as it promotes neoclassical economic policy,[106] nor in international relations terms, as it fosters the interests of capital-exporting countries.

[103] Opinion 1/17 (n 73) para 156.
[104] *Achmea* (n 58) para 177.
[105] See, eg, submission from the Government of South Africa, UNCITRAL Working Group III (Investor-State Dispute Settlement Reform), 14–18 October 2019, para 11.
[106] On neoclassical thinking, see the papers cited above in nn 43 and 44.

Faced with such economic and political reality, it is hardly surprising that capital-exporting countries – including Western European states – created and support the current international investment regime.[107] The convergence brought about by IIAs is generally consistent with the economic ideology prevailing in the so-called 'Global North' and negatively affects only the countries that are likely to be defendants in international arbitral proceedings; until recently, these countries belonged almost exclusively to the 'Global South' or the former Soviet space. The European Community's support for traditional IIAs cannot be described as an expression of the quintessential 'convergence ethic'[108] that makes it a 'driving force behind multilateralism and the global rules-based international order',[109] but appears as a manifestation of Western European states' interests and mainstream economic policy.

Over the last two decades, the context changed. It became evident that even capital-exporting countries can be defendants before arbitral tribunals. At the same time, several capital-importing countries became members of the European Union. EU institutions reacted by steering the Union policy in a partially new direction. The EU seems to prioritise the right to regulate over the enforcement of international investment law. The Court of Justice, with the *Achmea* judgment, essentially imposed the termination of most intra-EU investment agreements. The change of policy in respect of extra-EU agreements was less drastic. The Commission, with the benevolent approval of the Court, introduced 'new generation agreements' that intend to limit the discretion of investment tribunals and enhance the policy space of the parties. In principle, new generation investment agreements should enable the Union to implement policies that diverge from the deregulation promoted by traditional IIAs.

This departure from the traditional IIAs regime may be read in two ways. On the one hand, it may be a cosmetic measure introduced to make the regime more palatable to public opinion. The European Commission always supported traditional ISDS and agreed only *obtorto collo* to set up permanent tribunals, which remain, at any rate, partially similar to ISDS mechanisms. New generation agreements contain innovations meant to protect the 'right to regulate' of the parties, but, at the same time, maintain some of the most problematic elements of IIAs, such as vague investment protection standards. It is possible, therefore, that new generation agreements may not allow greater divergence in terms of economic policy but rather enforce, with different means, the usual convergence to deregulation.

On the other hand, the EU's new policy might exemplify a genuinely new balance between domestic authorities' right to regulate and the protection of investors' interests. Western European countries (and the European Commission) supported traditional IIAs for decades, while several capital-importing countries

[107] *cf*, *mutatis mutandis*, AG Wathelet in *Achmea* (n 56) para 36.
[108] See the Introduction to this volume by Elaine Fahey.
[109] European Council meeting of 20 June 2019, conclusions, EUCO 9/19, p 10.

opposed them, as they favoured the right to regulate over the protection of foreign investors. The Union's position remains distant from the policy of countries such as Brazil, which rejects investment tribunals and standard investment clauses.[110] Nonetheless, they all seem to converge around the general idea of 'regulatory autonomy' in the adoption of measures in the public interest.[111] Those measures might diverge, in terms of means, but respond to a necessity that, at least in principle, is shared by the Union and its partners: addressing societal objectives other than protecting investors' rights. Diverging about the means might hopefully become a way to converge about the values.

[110] See, eg, Cooperation and Investment Facilitation Agreement between the Federative Republic of Brazil and the Co-Operative Republic of Guyana, 2018, Art 4(4).

[111] *cf* eg CETA (n 78) Art 8.9(1) and the model Cooperation and Facilitation Investment Agreement of Brazil (2015) Preamble.

5

Epilogue: EU Global and Regional Convergence

MICHELLE EGAN

Studying convergence is one of those research endeavours where substance and methods are tightly interrelated. It is a comparative exercise that is temporal and spatial in its methodological nature and intent. Convergence is thus a multi-dimensional issue in terms of legal and policy analysis. The idea of legal convergence and more generally the idea of internationalism in law have been fuelled by the developments in the European Union. To see if European attempts at legal and regulatory convergence are impacting the global order, we need to ask: When does it occur (or not)? How can it be measured? When does it become irreversible? What are the unintended consequences of such convergence? Convergence can best be studied by means of incrementalism,[1] punctuated equilibrium[2] or through path-dependency to determine its institutional stickiness.[3]

Convergence is the means by which European organisational practices and law-making are seen as shaping the liberal order which ties in with discussions of the EU as a 'normative power' or 'market power' in transferring or adopting the domestic integration of European rules, practices or ideals into other third party contexts.[4] This ideational as well as practical transfer of law and rule-making procedures, courts and tribunals, for legal, economic, political and even sociological reasons, can take place in a multi-level context.[5] As such, it can be driven by economic logic to reduce transaction costs and facilitate commercial

[1] Charles E Lindblom, 'The Science of "Muddling Through"' (1959) 19 *Public Administration Review* 79.

[2] Bryan Jones and Frank Baumgartner, 'Representation and Agenda Setting' (2004) 32 *Policy Studies Journal* 1, 1.

[3] Paul Pierson, 'Increasing Returns, Path Dependence, and the Study of Politics' (2000) 94 *The American Political Science Review* 2, 251.

[4] See Damro Chad, 'Market Power Europe' (2012) 19 *Journal of European Public Policy* 2 682; see also Ian Manners, 'Normative Power Europe' (2002) 40 *Journal of Common Market Studies* 235.

[5] Elaine Fahey, *Introduction to Law and Global Governance* (Elgar Publishing, 2018).

transactions, not least given the emergence of global value chains.[6] Convergence can also foster sociological engagement as legal networks with authoritative and policy-relevant expertise can collaborate and shape common legal principles through benchmarking, best practices and policy learning. Convergence may also arise from overlapping treaty norms and litigation, or from private standards that have been legitimised as a component in EU law-making through delegation to ensure regulatory compliance.[7] As such, legal convergence is seldom a total displacement of the prior legal order but often a set of overlapping nested legal regimes.

Within Europe, we see convergence driven by different modes of governance. As such, convergence may be the product of conditionality where the asymmetrical nature of power in accession negotiations pushes applicant states to adopt the *acquis communitaire* as a precondition for membership. This can promote a legal convergence agenda through rule of law and good governance measures. Convergence may also derive from harmonisation and mutual recognition through reciprocal acceptance of common rules and standards. Europe can promote economic convergence through alignment of macroeconomic indicators. Such convergence has also enabled the EU to leverage its internal cohesion on economic and foreign policy objectives to promote its ideas, norms and interests beyond its borders in a period in which institutionalised multilateralism is under pressure. This is occurring through the efforts to promote a Multilateral Investment Court through The United Nations Commission on International Trade Law (UNCITRAL) or digital tax measures through the Organisation for Economic Co-operation and Development (OECD) for example. The Lisbon Treaty also promotes convergence between the two European courts – the Court of Justice of the European Union and the European Court of Human Rights – in order to foster a fundamental rights discourse.[8] The transmission of rules and practices can also shape other regional organisations, as in the case of international courts in Latin America and Africa, though these are often adapted to specific local contexts.[9] While these examples demonstrate the 'direct effect' of European legal influence, highlighting the unintended effects of convergence is an important caveat to the legal and political scholarship in this field. These include the lack of transparency and accountability when law is delegated to different legal venues, such as the risk of abuse of investor state dispute mechanisms and undue attention to investor interests or the dilemmas in exporting dual-use technologies.[10] Specific choices may also limit subsequent change and adaptation as the constraints posed by choosing one global

[6] See chapter 12 of this volume by Kornilia Pipidi-Kalogirou.

[7] See chapter 14 of this volume by Enrico Partiti.

[8] *cf* Sonia Morano-Foradi and Stelios Andreadakis, 'Reflections on the Architecture of the EU after the Treaty of Lisbon: The European Judicial Approach to Fundamental Rights' (2011) 17 *European Law Journal* 5 595.

[9] Alter Karen, 'The Global Spread of European Courts' (2011) 35 *West European Politics* 1 135, 139.

[10] See chapter 3 of this volume by Machiko Kanetake and chapter 4 by Mauro Gatti.

standard over another may generate lock-in effects that discourage innovation. This may lead to deeper structural issues facilitating polarisation or segregation that may in the long term facilitate divergence rather than convergence.

While policymakers are often seen as drawing lessons from Europe, through both formal and informal channels, the narrative of European convergence has often been viewed as the externalisation of European policies, whether it is single market practices, competition rules, or dispute settlement regimes. The 'reception' of those rules varies in terms of state and administrative capacity, political oversight and market surveillance, and public support in third country markets. It is often tempting for scholarship to include only successful cases of convergence to depict the 'actorness' of the European Union in shaping global rules and norms. However, using cases of concomitant variation, as well as longitudinal comparisons can add a more nuanced approach to whether shifts in sources, practice and jurisprudence have generated deep seated convergence in processes and outcomes. Such convergence requires a period of policy change followed by a period of policy stability so that we can determine if that convergence is institutionalised within the European polity and to understand how it is externalised through domestic reception of European constitutional practices. For example, this may be neighbouring states through regulatory alignment. Or convergence may occur via strategic engagement and lobbying pressures within international institutions to create a coherent and unitary legal framework that generates a 'bandwagon' effect.[11]

Much of the literature on convergence is based on certain suppositions of the EU as consciously promoting its norms, practices, ideas and values beyond its borders. Less attention is given to the effect of international legal norms and practices on European governance and institutions. Yet convergence as a concept also requires us to consider 'solubility', 'complexity' and 'scale', as well as 'accountability' and 'sustainability'. If we want to measure its direction and components, these types of variables across cases may help us understand the EU as an emerging global legal actor, in the post-Lisbon era, in terms of its effectiveness as well as its importance to understand how different interests and preferences lead to internal as well as external contestation. In addition, to the structural determinants of bargaining power, in the European case, the need for coordinated action may provide an advantage in shaping legal outcomes as this 'tied hands strategy' can be used as leverage in shaping demands and concessions.

The chapters in this part of the book highlight the ways in which the global reach of EU law impacts a diversity of policy areas as economies and societies become increasingly more interconnected. The issues in question, however,

[11] Sieglinde Ghstol Gstohl, 'Models of External Differentiation in the EU's Neighbourhood: An Expanding Economic Community?' (2015) 22 *Journal of European Public Policy* 854–70; *cf* Alasdair Young, 'Liberalizing Trade, not Exporting Rules: The Limits to Regulatory Co-Ordination in the EU's "New Generation" Preferential Trade Agreements' (2015) 22 *Journal of European Public Policy* 9, 1253–75; Anu Bradford, 'Exporting Standards: The Externalization of the EU's Regulatory Power via Markets' (2014) 40 *International Review of Law and Economics* 158.

generate a diversity of changes in legal behaviour. There are several themes that emerge from the chapters about the rationale and impact of the EU engaging in convergence activities within the regional and global legal order. First, there are the constraints that make it harder to exercise European legal jurisprudence outside of their community boundaries. This may be due to the lack of access or authority within specific institutional venues so European institutions have not been given conferred powers to shape legal and political outcomes. It may also be due to multiple interests and veto points that make it difficult to exercise their influence, making changes in the status quo significantly more difficult.[12] Decision rules can shape the way in which interests are defined and issues framed as the prevailing institutional conditions and rules will affect the substantive policy outcomes that are likely to be achieved.[13] Second, domestic law may have pre-empted the field so that efforts to promote European social values and regulatory ideals may face resistance due to the embeddedness of existing legal norms and practices. Though in relation to the field of trade and investment, the EU has fostered a form of internal convergence through provisions in the Lisbon Treaty, there are still policy areas where national provisions are paramount. In the case of conflict of interest provisions, monitoring bodies and potential penalties differ across international institutions, as well as states which have far greater regulatory capacity to control and limit the likelihood of conflicts of interest.[14] Third, the institutional venues available for negotiations vary in terms of issues, rules, actors and scope. Though this may allow different interest groups to express their preferences for specific negotiation forums, it can also dissipate scarce resources and lead to inconsistent norms and rules. If trade issues cannot be resolved in specific venues due to gridlock, it may lead governments to focus on alternative options. For Europe, resolving the toughest trade problems focused initially on multilateralism. Consequently, the failure of the Doha Round has led to rules-based plurilateral and multilateral alternatives, with the European Union at the forefront of new updated free trade agreements that explicitly export World Trade Organisation (WTO) plus provisions, including geographical indicators, conformity assessment, and data privacy as well as the development of new institutions, such as the Multilateral Investment Court to respond to transparency and accountability concerns.[15] Fourth, the expansion of rulemaking has moved the locus of authority from national to regional, international and transnational bodies. Beyond courts and tribunals that formulate law as principles, standards and values, the growth

[12] George Tsebelis, 'Decision Making in Political Systems: Veto Players in Presidentialism, Parliamentarism, Multicameralism and Multipartyism' (1995) 25 *British Journal of Political Science* 3, 289.

[13] Fritz W Scharpf, 'Decision Rules, Decision Styles and Policy Choices' (1989) 1 *Journal of Theoretical Politics* 2, 149.

[14] Jean-Pierre Casey and Karel Lanoo, *The MFID Revolution* (Cambridge, Cambridge University Press 2009).

[15] See Frank Hoffmeister in chapter 1 of this volume.

of administrative policies, processes and procedures formulated as guidelines, memoranda, and codes of practice, as well as private rulemaking through regional or transnational standards, creates new forms of cooperation that may not have legal force. While the OECD is one of the most influential actors in the field of conflicts of interest, formulating guidelines to influence its Member States, it has much the same role in pursuing guidelines for digital taxation where voluntary participation and membership to promote legal convergence differs from such activities that, when performed domestically, are bound by specific legal requirements. Fifth, the acceptance of certain legal principles in international law promotes legal convergence. This includes principles of non-discrimination and fidelity which are designed to prevent states from breaching international legal obligations. As commitments must include all levels of government, it promotes legal convergence at both federal and subnational levels.

For some, the extent to which policies are becoming similar is questionable, with some studies suggesting convergence and others highlighting continued divergence.[16] European integration is often seen as a market-oriented project, and a good case can be made that the EU as a whole, has helped shape convergence in various areas of global economic governance. Issues such as internet and data privacy, emissions trading, investment protections and financial regulation have led scholars to document the 'spillover' effects of European regulations on third country markets.[17] Some of the concerns that are generated by such 'global activism' and first mover advantage in shaping rules and norms, may in fact, subvert multilateralism, as the policies are rooted in unilateral action, even if designed to promote public goods, through specific provisions on climate action or animal rights.[18] Yet some European actions could be less about global public goods provisions than providing club goods which are excludable. Club goods often requires a 'membership' payment in order to enjoy the benefits of the goods. This means that efforts to promote institutional convergence through European law, transnational rules, voluntary standards or administrative practices, the so-called California or Brussels effect, may in fact raise problems of excludability.

The assumption that the promotion of European rules and norms is a positive, sum game, is based on the premise that the output legitimacy justifies the EU's attempts at institutional convergence in the global legal order to achieve some designated goals and uphold certain values such as commitments to human rights, data privacy and climate action. While convergence is viewed in a positive sense of 'progressive' promotion of a 'rules-based' global order with multilateralism as its key principle, the European Union has also sought to build coalitions of the

[16] Thomas Plümper and Christina Schneider, 'The Analysis of Policy Convergence or: How to Chase a Black Cat in a Dark Room' (2009) 16 *Journal of European Public Policy* 7, 990.

[17] Alasdair Young, 'Europe's Influence on Foreign Rules: Conditions, Context and Comparison' (2015) *Journal of European Public Policy* 22/9. 1233–52; Anu Bradford, 'The Brussels Effect' (2012) 107 *Northwestern University Law Review* 1, 1.

[18] See Jed Odermatt in chapter 2 of this volume.

willing to advance specific interests in multilateral institutions, as well as sought to foster democratic norms and values when it faces its own internal challenges of democratic backsliding and illiberalism. There are inherent contradictions in European legal mobilisation for democracy and rights, not only for those entities not seeking convergence to European norms, but also because there are new non-western institutions coming up, with competing ideas and norms that are now in play. For example, China with the creation of new multilateral institutions like the Asian Infrastructure Investment Bank (AIIB) or BRICS generally with their New Development Bank (NDB) and China's Belt and Road Strategy do not accept the liberal order as reflected by European economic and legal organisational practices. In choosing to accept that there are a lot of regional orders and regional institutions emerging, which are not always effective, they do matter in affecting regional security and economy in different parts of the world.[19]

In discussing how the European Union is one of the driving forces behind multilateralism and a rules-based international order, convergence may reflect efforts to deal with many of the same concerns as market integration. Convergence may be in response to interdependence, externalities and rent-seeking effects, where there is a need to mitigate transaction costs through collective action. Such promotion of legal norms and rules may have to deal with the actions of their peers, such as US action, including blocks on appointment to the WTO Dispute Resolution Panel or scrutiny of foreign direct investment practices as it pertains to critical infrastructure and security, for example (CFIUS).[20] While some argue that historical conditions have led to distinct normative systems for trade and investment legal regimes, others accept interconnections, and even functional convergence, between the fields, as negotiated trade agreements, legal and arbitration proceedings and common legal treaty norms and litigation tools have generated transnational epistemic communities. Judges and lawyers now regularly communicate on a transnational basis that may lead to a process of mutual recognition or legal borrowing that promotes a selective process of cross-fertilisation of legal ideas. Yet there are also high market entry barriers to promoting rule convergence beyond the state. States may use different approaches and powers to address specific challenges as in the case of whistleblowing or conflict of interest regulations.[21] If the monitoring bodies and punitive measures differ – in areas where there is cross-border jurisdiction or cross-border economic or legal activity – then it raises a host of challenges ranging from forum shopping to inconsistent rulings across different legal 'markets'. Even if the European Union advocates for the legal dimension of rules beyond their borders, signalling its

[19] Amitav Acharya, 'How Ideas Spread: Whose Norms Matter? Norm Localization and Institutional Change in Asian Regionalism' (2004) 58 *International Organization* 239.

[20] The Committee on Foreign Investment in the United States.

[21] Vigiilenca Abazi, The EU Ombudsman, Conflicts of Interest and International Practice (2019); Vigiilenca Abazi, 'Whistleblowing in Europe: A New Era of Legal Protections' in P Czech, L Heschl, K Lukas, M Nowak and G Oberleitner (eds), *European Yearbook on Human Rights* (Intersentia, 2019).

position as a global legal actor, there are differing modes of 'norm promotion' and legal persuasion that are available in its legal 'toolkit'. Pushing for specific standards or organisational practices through dialogue with judges, technical aid and assistance, recommendations or legal guidance is far different than pushing specific legal mandates and verification mechanisms in international agreements where the scope of rights and obligations has particular consequences if signatories default.

If convergence is related to such terms as isomorphism, policy transfer or policy diffusion, how can we parse out the different causal mechanisms that promote such as an explicit narrative of 'convergence' to understand the effects of global and regional convergence? We can focus on common affiliations, negotiations and institutional membership as the European Union is likely to be most successful in working with like-minded actors and institutions.[22] Research could also focus on the asymmetrical bargaining relationship that accrues from the size of the regional bloc as the European Union is able to use its internal coordination to shape global standards, leveraging its market power and regulatory authority to ensure acceptance of its preferred outcomes or ensuring a level-playing field in trade agreements to avoid a 'race to the bottom'.[23] Attention might also focus on the role of different time horizons which may shield courts and tribunals from scrutiny. Rulings may expand jurisdictional principles and legal authority, but may not be applied in specific cases, be subsequently deferred, generate further arbitration, or may lead to exclusions from fully reviewing issues.[24] The changing composition of rule-making is also important in thinking about convergence in the conduct of public authorities as the transfer of regulatory functions to agencies, as well as the shift to managerial government, has changed the nature of administrative governance. Interactions between organisational practices and legal traditions can lead to a 'trading up' in the sense of international reception of European (internal) rules as well as the acceptance of non-binding standards formulated by transnational public and private bodies within Europe. This suggests a rich panoply of administrative and regulatory powers that should be part of the ongoing debate on the rule of law in the global arena. As an internationalist, the EU is at the forefront of such global standard-setting. With global interdependence coming not only just from trade but also from finance, from production networks, from global challenges like environment or pandemics, the withdrawal of the United States from global leadership may generate new opportunity structures for Europe to map legal norms and market practices. However, the European Global Security Strategy (EUGS), with its vision of 'principled pragmatism', reflects a more nuanced view of Europe's role in the global order. Much more circumspect in ambition

[22] Beth Simmons and Zachary Elkins, The Globalization of Liberalization: Policy Diffusion in the International Political Economy (2004) 98 *American Political Science Review* 1, 171.

[23] See Young (n 17).

[24] Karen Alter, 'Who Are the "Masters of the Treaty"?: European Governments and the European Court of Justice' (1998) 52 *International Organisations* 1, 121.

compared to its predecessor, the European Security Strategy, the EUGS has scaled back the transformative ambition of EU foreign policy. Yet the goal is to promote convergence across actors, institutions, policies and instruments, integrating the traditional domains of foreign policy such as diplomacy, defence and development with the external dimension of European internal policies, from research and infrastructure, to energy and trade.[25]

As the chapters in this volume illustrate, focusing on explanatory conditions and diverse methodological approaches can help push the convergence agenda further. But the broader question is whether the EU is a lone ranger – to use Fahey's description[26] – in a way that challenges the distinctive sovereign-based global legal order that was the main normative focus of multilateral institutions in the post war period. We need to also consider how the diffusion of such foundational legal ideas and norms were translated and adopted into a post-colonial setting in which principles of self-determination, non-discrimination, non-intervention or equality meant that norm setting occurred outside of Europe. Such domestic experiences may also explain some of the resistance to European efforts at promoting legal convergence in multilateral institutions as well as the more distinctive 'softer, informal' approaches to regional integration outside of Europe in Latin America, Africa and Asia.[27]

[25] Natalie Tocci, *Framing the EU Global Strategy, A Stronger Europe in a Fragile World* (Palgrave, 2017).

[26] See Elaine Fahey, in the Introduction to this volume.

[27] For the role of informal norms, see Pek Koon Heng, 'The "ASEAN Way" and Regional Security Cooperation in the South China Sea RSCAS 2014/121' (Robert Schuman Centre for Advanced Studies Global Governance Programme) 145; Acharya (n 19) 239–75; for legal adaptation and convergence, see Alter (n 9) 135–54.

PART II

A Global Legal Order *against* Convergence?

6

Resistances to Global Convergence

FERNANDA G NICOLA

I. Introduction: Beyond Global Convergence

A convergentist bias, namely the need to further harmonise the legislation to enhance market transactions, became central in Western legal consciousness with the consolidation of national economies in the nineteenth century. The functional method in comparative law that originated at the beginning of the twentieth century as social-purpose functionalism relied on the organic function of law reflecting the needs of societies.[1] Comparative lawyers as social engineers would find best solutions for the nation and eventually the global community. In this vein, the comparative law masters, Zweigert and Kötz highlighted that the best legal solution to apply among different legal regimes was based on those rules that advanced market efficiency and streamlined legal processes.[2] However, this type of massive legal transfer driven by 'best' outcomes for every legal system has been criticised by lawyers who are well aware of the shortcomings of the 'one size can fit all' formula.[3]

After the Second World War, some of the main institutional players fueling global convergence were primarily the United Nations (UN) through its conventions, the Bretton Woods Institutions with its International Financial Institutions (IFIs), the General Agreement on Tariffs and Trade (GATT), the European Economic Community (EEC), and the Council of Europe (CoE). These International Organisations (IOs), not only created global convergence through international treaties, but also through transnational legal regimes for free trade and investment that regulated directly domestic legal orders through the rulings of the European

[1] See Roscoe Pound, 'The Scope and Purpose of Sociological Jurisprudence' (1912) 25 *Harvard Law Review* 489, 516.

[2] See Konrad Zweigert and Hein Kötz, *An Introduction to Comparative Law*, 3rd edn (Oxford University Press, 1998).

[3] See Ralf Michales, '"One Size Can Fit All" – Some Heretical Thoughts on the Mass Production of Legal Transplants' in Günter Frankenberg (ed) *Order from Transfer: Comparative Constitutional Design and Legal Culture Law* (EEP, 2013).

Court of Justice (ECJ) or the Appellate Body of the WTO.[4] Above all, the bias was that these IOs would be the principal and most powerful actors pushing for regulatory and institutional converge of global markets. At the other end, domestic regimes, expressing diverse social preferences embedded in local contexts, became the primary sites of resistance to global convergence. Due to this increased economic interdependence, the establishment of transnational legal regimes and technological transformations, legal scholarship has focused on grasping the effects of global convergence on the legal profession and among legal regimes.[5] Lawyers have highlighted the tension between harmonising and globalising forces on the one hand, and their emerging critiques on the other, shaping the dialectics of a 'global legal consciousness'.[6]

To reinforce the dialectic between global convergence and local divergences scholars addressing the different philosophies of convergence predicted that: 'behind every universalizing force there are particularizing ones in play'.[7] John H. Merryman described how internal forces were producing at the same time legal convergence and divergence, simultaneously spurred by divergent goals of 'Transnational interest' versus 'Legal parochialism'.[8] Both forces were at work through unification or legal transplants of law on the one hand, and home rule doctrines and decentralisation in local government law on the other.[9] In a chart Merryman showed how, depending on the context, weak or strong forces of convergence and divergence were at work. These would alternate and create regimes with strong transnational convergence in the market and weak domestic resistances in the family and human rights regimes. Despite this seemly natural and humanistic convergence in the West, divergence remained strong over central questions where cultural, moral and religious norms are openly at play, such as the abolition of capital punishment, reproductive rights and same sex marriage.

This false dichotomy between the sphere of the market and the sphere of the family exceptionalised the latter as harder to globalise than commercial transactions.[10] This family law exceptionalism has been challenged by liberal

[4] See Mathias Reimann, 'The Progress and Failure of Comparative Law in the Second Half of the Twentieth Century' (2002) *50 The American Journal of Comparative Law* 671, 679–80.

[5] See Yves Dezelay and Bryant G Garth (eds), *Lawyers and the Rule of Law in an Era of Globalization* (Routledge, 2011); Jan Klabbers and Mortimer Sellers (eds), 'Internationalizing the American Law School Curriculum' (in Light of the Carnegie Foundation's Report), in *The Internalization of Law and Legal Education* (2 Ius Gentium: Comparative Perspectives on Law and Justice, Springer Publishing, 2008) 49–112.

[6] See Duncan Kennedy, 'Three Globalizations in Law and Legal Thought: 1850–2000' in David Trubek and Alvaros Santos (eds), *The New Law and Economic Development: A Critical Appraisal* (Cambridge University Press, 2006).

[7] John Henry Merryman, 'On the Convergence (and Divergence) of the Civil Law and the Common Law' (1981) 17 *Stanford Journal of International Law* 357, 371.

[8] *Ibid* 374.

[9] *Ibid* 361.

[10] See Fernanda Nicola, *Family Law Exceptionalism in Comparative Law* (2010) *American Journal of Comparative Law.*

feminists working through gender equality policies and ideologies even advocated by the World Bank.[11] Gender feminism has powerfully shaped constitutional dialogues on anti-discrimination law and harmonised gender policies driven by market equality ideals rather than moral values.[12] The harmonisation of family law shows how global convergence is possible in all fields of law, but what remains contextual and understudied is why resistances in family law emerge despite convergentist forces. More interestingly, this chapter maps how the different types of resistances embedded in local, cultural or political values, and institutional path dependencies resist social change.

Global convergence of legal regimes happens through what comparative lawyers have called legal transplants or transfers which are the major ways to spread legal rules and regulatory policies.[13] The modes of legal transfer range from imposition through colonisation to soft influences such as prestige, modernisation and economic efficiency as rationales to justify global convergence.[14] In focusing on these tools of convergence, the ability of legal transfer to create uniformity throughout different legal regimes also creates new diversification and balkanisation in their contextual adaptation. For instance, there is high unpredictability of what happens on the ground once legal rules on the books are transferred and contextualised in a new legal culture. Often, what lawyers 'package' as a transferrable piece of legislation to a new local context might lead to more fragmentation rather than greater convergence.[15] Additionally, the role and perception of legal elites involved at home or abroad in the legal transfer,[16] holding conflicting views on the purposes of what the transplant should really achieve, ends up shaping the resistance to or acceptance of the harmonised legislation.[17]

Four false assumptions about global convergence are common among lawyers and politicians alike. The first entails that this convergence happened under the guise of global institutions while local differentiation and cultural norms were prime sites of resistance to legal harmonisation. A second false assumption is the divide

[11] See Catherine Powell, *Gender Indicators as Global Governance: Not Your Father's World Bank* (2016) 17 *Georgetown Journal of Gender & the Law* 777.

[12] See Janet Halley, Prabha Kotiswaran, Rachel Rebouché and Hila Shamir, *Governance Feminism: An Introduction* (University of Minnesota Press, 2018); Stéphanie Hennette Vauchez, 'The Society for the Protection of Unborn Children v. Grogan: Rereading the Case and Retelling the Story of Reproductive Rights in Europe' in Bill Davies and Fernanda Nicola (eds), *EU Law Stories: Contextual and Critical Histories of European Jurisprudence* (Cambridge University Press, 2017).

[13] See William Twining, 'Diffusion and Globalization Discourse' (2006) 47 *Harvard International Law Journal* 507; David Marsh and JC Sharman, 'Policy Diffusion and Policy Transfer' (2009) 30 *Policy Studies* 269, 274 (2009).

[14] Michele Graziadei, 'Comparative Law as the Study of Transplants and Receptions' in Mathias Reimann and Reinhard Zimmerman (eds), *The Oxford Handbook of Comparative Law* (Oxford University Press, 2008) 442–61.

[15] See Gunter Frankenberg (ed), *Order from Transfer: Comparative Constitutional Design and Legal Culture* (Edward Elgar, 2013).

[16] See William Twining, 'Diffusion of Law: A Global Perspective' (2004) 36 *The Journal of Legal Pluralism and Unofficial Law* 49 1, 1–7.

[17] See Jorge L Esquirol, 'The Failed Law of Latin America' (2008) 56 *American Journal of Comparative Law* 75.

between global or transnational versus local or domestic regimes that was not only playing out at institutional level but reproduced false asymmetries in substantive economic and social policies.[18] The entrenchment of the Reagan-Thatcher agenda of the 1980s, coupled with the law and economics movement dominated by the Chicago school, secured the legitimacy of the neoliberal mantra of the Washington Consensus that provided 'one size fits all' recipes of market liberalisation and deregulation with the sole protection of contract and property rights.

A third false assumption among lawyers was that global convergence, driven by IFIs, the World Trade Organisation (WTO) and the EU would lead towards greater harmonisation which meant a regulatory race to the bottom and the dismantling of the welfare state.[19] An equally dominant perception among lawyers was that social and welfare regimes that were embedded in domestic legal orders always offered better social protections while preserving traditional values. This belief led to a strong assumption among lawyers that transnational law, as opposed to social domestic regimes, suffered from a neoliberal bias.[20] Yet some scholars have proven this wrong when for instance, models of regulatory convergences promoted by the EU, through its Brussels effect aim at raising social, privacy and environmental protections.[21] In the same vein there are also neoliberal models of governance at the local or city level advancing efficiency and exclusion through the increasing privatisation of cities.[22]

A final false assumption was that Western standards of democracy through the spreading of free market and rule of law values to the Central and Eastern European countries would diffuse constitutional democracy and capitalism globally. This assumption has also been proven wrong.[23] In fact the spreading of an alternative model to constitutional democracy, which Victor Orbán has called 'illiberal democracies', is diffusing rapidly through Latin America, Asia and the Middle East.[24] Despite local and supranational resistances from activists on the ground to transnational institutions and courts, the spread of illiberalism in East-Central Europe is well entrenched. Due to the failure of the transition process in these countries aspiring to models of capitalism and rule of law which led them to abandon their socialist regimes overnight, the transition appeared more like a form of colonisation from the West rather than an organic transition to democracy.

[18] See Fernanda G Nicola, 'Transatlanticisms: Constitutional Asymmetry and Selective Reception of U.S. Law and Economics in the Formation of European Private Law' (2008) *Cardozo Journal of International and Comparative Law* 87.

[19] See Fritz Scharpf, *Governing in Europe: Effective and Democratic?* (Oxford University Press, 1999); Wolfgang Streeck, Fritz Scharpf, Gary Marks and Phillippe C Schmitter, *Governance in the European Union*, 1st edn (Sage Publications, 1996).

[20] See Wolfgang Streeck, *How Will Capitalism End? Essays on a Failing System* (Verso, 2016).

[21] See Anu Bradford, *The Brussels Effect* (Oxford University Press, 2020).

[22] See Sheila Foster and Fernanda G Nicola, 'Comparative Urban Governance for Lawyers' (2014) 42 *Fordham Urban Law Journal* 1, 1.

[23] See Kim Scheppele, 'Autocratic Legalism' (2018) 85 *Chicago Law Review* 2, 545.

[24] Mark A Graber, Stanford Levinson and Mark Tushnet, *Constitutional Democracy in Crisis?* (Oxford University Press, 2018).

The lack of local institutions and civil society that could drive the transition from socialism to liberal democracy led to weak institutions and the creation of strong oligarchs who became authoritarian leaders.[25]

This chapter addresses four different types of resistance to global convergence rooted in local, institutional, decolonising and democratic critiques. The first critique relies on the literature that has criticised the way global convergence remains disembedded from its economic, societal and cultural context so that it creates greater irritation or fragmentation rather than uniformity.

A second critique is the one put forward by institutionalists and comparative administrative lawyers who emphasise regulatory path dependencies and the slow and non-linear process of institutional change and adaptation.

A third critique is based on a decolonisation perspective that shows the pervasive dominance and superiority of the European white culture depicted as the classical cradle of civilisation.[26] The trauma of the Holocaust towards the Jewish population in Europe partially replaced the trauma created by European colonisers through racial and economic domination especially in Africa. After the Second World War the visionary project of European integration was mostly inward-focused and started on a blank slate that bracketed the colonial past. Today, this allows European lawyers to take no responsibility for the cost of the European single market to the former colonies, nor for the plague of economic migration.

The fourth democratic critique is timely in an age in which scholars talk about economics for inclusive prosperity (EfIP) to address economic and racial disparities throughout the world.[27] The democratic resistance to neoliberal ideology happens at all institutional levels whether in Brussels, Ankara or Basilia. As Quinn Slobodian has explained, the encasement of global neoliberalism was deliberately planned by economists and lawyers belonging to the Geneva school in the early twentieth century who sought to protect global markets and free movement of capitals from domestic redistributive policies.[28] Through new transnational free trade, financial and investment regimes, these lawyers reframed the types of protections for property rights and production modes across borders. Democratic resistance to these transnational regulations reclaims more accountability, transparency and participation in economic governance. Here, while sovereign power has been limited by the WTO or the EU, there is a confused attribution of powers between technocratic and representative governments encasing neoliberal policies from democratic oversight.[29]

[25] See Fernanda Nicola, *Another View of the Cathedral: What does the Rule of Law Crisis Tell us about Democratizing the EU? Maastricht* (2018) *Journal of European and Comparative Law* 1–6; Gabor Halmai, *Illiberalism in East-central Europe*, EUI Department of Law Research Paper No 2019/05 (2019).

[26] See Martin Bernal and David Chioni Moore, *Black Athena Writes Back: Martin Bernal Responds to His Critics* (Duke University Press Books, 2001).

[27] See Suresh Naidu, Dani Rodrik, Gabriel Zuchman and Lenore Palladino, *Economics after Neoliberalism* (edited by Joshua Cohen) (Boston Review Forum, 2019).

[28] See Quinn Slobodian, *Globalists. The End of Empire and the Birth of Neoliberalism* (Harvard University Press, 2018).

[29] See Antoine Vauchez, *Democratizing Europe* (Palgrave Pivot, 2016).

All four modes of resistance show that these are in tension with the forces driving global convergence. At the same time, if more than one mode of resistance to global convergence is at work, these can join forces or create new conflicts among each other. Mapping how multiple forms of resistance to global convergence operate reveals the false assumptions held by lawyers and the need to contextualise narratives of global convergence.

II. Economy, Society and the Embeddedness of Legal Culture as Global Irritants

In Weberian terms human behaviour and its mode of rationality characterises the legal order and how this structures and is in turn structured by economic life.[30] The varieties of capitalism literature uses Max Weber's methodology to show how ethical, professional or religious norms influence the legal order that organises markets and societies. In following this approach scholars have focused on the varieties of modalities of production in capitalist regimes to show internal variations in European markets. To advance the Weberian model, Karl Polanyi showed the embeddedness of economic activity in social, cultural and legal regimes was also constrained by these non-economic institutions.[31]

Legal scholars influenced by economic sociologists and historians such as Weber and Polanyi have pointed to major forms of legal irritants existing in global law that are at work when convergentist and harmonising regulations try to modify existing norms. If global convergence arises from transnational legal regimes such as EU regulations or rulings of the European Court of Human Rights (ECtHR), the transposition of regulations or rulings that require domestic implementation can create forms of irritation rather than unification of the law. In his work on the adaptation of European consumer law in the UK, Gunther Teubner showed vividly how the transplantation of good faith rules in good faith consumer contracts led UK judges to struggle when addressing a relatively vague norm in their legal system.[32] The outcome of transplanting continental good faith rules in consumer contracts was initially ignored by British judges to the extent that this provision created more irritation and deepened old cleavages rather than harmonised European private law. Teubner's article pointed out early on how the divergent political economies of the UK and German legal systems were far from converging and that legal professionals were resistant to the attempts to create a uniform European civil code.[33]

[30] See Max Weber, *On Law in Economy and Society*, 2nd edn (Harvard University Press, 1954).

[31] See Karl Polanyi, *The Great Transformation: The Political and Economic Origins of our Time*, 1st edn (Farrar & Rinhart, 1944).

[32] See Gunther Teubner, 'Legal Irritants: Good Faith in British Law or How Unifying Law Ends Up in New Divergences' (2003) 61 *The Modern Law Review* 1.

[33] See Pierre Legrand, 'European Legal Systems are not Converging' (1996) 45 *International and Comparative Law Quarterly* 1.

Taking a more radical approach founded on the cultural contingency of legal systems, Pierre Legrand argued that European legal systems were not converging. In pushing back against the convergence thesis, Legrand showed that the approximation between civil law and common law in Western Europe, as described by some of the masters of comparative legal scholarship, was based on a merely positivist understanding of law and lacked thick descriptions showing how differentiation of linguistic and mental attitude is a function of the community where we belong. Therefore, rules become a form of cultural identity and behind them also lies a socio-cultural dimension that has to do with its implementation by a complex web of legal and non-legal actors.[34] The notion that European legal systems are not converging is due to what Legrand called the non-transcendence of acculturation as an English legal experience, which cannot be fully grasped by civil lawyers and vice-versa. This 'irreducible epistemological chasm', as Legrand called it, fueled the resistance by national lawyers against a uniform European civil code driven by a humanist rational and legal homogeneity.[35]

This cultural approach to law when transposed to the idea of convergence of Western legal systems, has led scholars such as James Whitman to highlight some of the deep roots of the Atlantic divide, which he shows through an intellectual history that portrays the different *mentalité* behind notions of privacy in the US and in European countries. Whitman explains in hindsight why Europeans, led by the German dignitary vision of individual privacy, were successful in regulating data privacy. This contrasts with to the liberation of the US approach to data privacy, which has led to difficulties and a fragmentation in the regulation of private companies as opposed to the Government.[36]

The scholarship on the forms of resistance to global convergence in corporate governance is also based on institutional history, culture and political economy of different legal regimes has shown a decade after the financial crisis that law and markets evolve jointly yet the most successful industrial economies differ greatly in their organisational characteristics.[37] The most recent globalizing force has been set in motion by the Chinese government through its investment and financial loan regimes since 2013. The Belt and Road (BRI) Initiative has affirmed China's emerging global role as a lending powerhouse building global infrastructures for its markets.[38] Nevertheless, details about the Initiative and its practical effects remain poorly understood and some of its critics show how some of the harsher critiques of the BRI Initiative come from within the continent rather

[34] *Ibid* 58.

[35] *Ibid* 80.

[36] See James Q Whitman, 'The Two Western Cultures of Privacy: *Dignity* Versus Liberty' (2004) 113 *Yale Law Journal.*

[37] Curtis J Milhaupt and Katharina Pistor, *Law and Capitalism: What Corporate Crises Reveal About Legal Systems and Economic Development around the World* (University of Chicago Press, 2018).

[38] Yuen, Yuen Ang, 'Demystifying Belt and Road: The Struggle to Define China's "Project of the Century"', *Foreign Affairs* (*Foreign Affairs*, 22 May 2019), www.foreignaffairs.com/articles/china/2019-05-22/demystifying-belt-and-road (last accessed 6 March 2020).

than outside, ranging from a surplus of economic production to the inability to control the internal immigration regime between urban and rural provinces in China.[39] BRI appears to be more of a clever labeling device rather than a defined legal or commercial regime under which projects are specifically classified. It would seem natural, then, that it is difficult for outside observers and foreign firms to determine precisely if a project is under the umbrella of BRI, whether it is being at least partially funded or facilitated through BRI, or if it merely has the appearance of BRI through Chinese direct investment but is actually something entirely different.

As commentators have pointed out the difficulty of obtaining pertinent information about the progress of the BRI project through its sprawling bilateral investment treaties, its dubious economic performance, and any other metrics one might see fit to monitor, would appear to encumber all parties involved, including the firms contributing to projects, the governments of the countries in which projects are taking place, and Chinese government planners themselves.[40] Finally, within Asia, the Chinese BRI has also experienced new resistances coming from some of the first lenders who took advantage of a repayment budget with less stringent requirements for meeting social and environmental safeguards and flexible payment terms. However, Chinese high risk loans also entailed higher interest rates in repayment, and financial flexibility due to its economic surplus.[41] This was the case in Sri Lanka where China was willing to provide a $1.3 billion loan and when Sri Lanka could not repay the interest on its debt, China took equity in the port. These aggressive lending practices are already beginning to cause friction with other countries, with the Government of the Maldives expressing frustration that the scale of debt owed to China was 20 per cent of the gross domestic product (GDP).[42] This globalising convergence has produced new legal irritants in Asia where a variety of property rights arranged through different entitlement and legal regimes that derive from cultural and legal path dependency often clash with the aggressive BRI investment and property.[43]

[39] See David Dollar, 'China's Rise as a Regional Global Power: The AIIB and "One Belt, One Road"' (*Brookings Institution*, 15 July 2015), www.brookings.edu/research/chinas-rise-as-a-regional-and-global-power-the-aiib-and-the-one-belt-one-road/ (last accessed 6 March 2020).

[40] Jonathan Hillman, *Statement before the U.S.-China Economic and Security Review Commission: 'China's Belt and Road Initiative: Five Years Later'* (A testimony by Jonathan Hillman Fellow Simon Chair in Political Economy and Director of the Reconnecting Asia Project, Center for Strategic and International Studies, 2018).

[41] *Ibid.*

[42] See Iain Marlow and Li Dandan, 'How Asia Fell out of Love with China's Belt and Road Initiative' (New York, BNN Bloomberg, 2018) 2.

[43] See David Kennedy, 'Some Caution About Property Rights as a Recipe for Economic Development' in Joseph E Stiglitz and David Kennedy (eds), *Law and Economics with Chinese Characteristics: Institutions for Promoting Development in the 21st Century* (Oxford University Press, 2013).

III. Institutional Change and Administrative and Regulatory Path Dependencies

The literature on institutional change has shown the persistence of legal institutions throughout regime changes due to path dependencies and their embeddedness in cultural communities where the interpretation and implementation of the law takes place.[44] Take for instance data privacy, a recently new regulatory field where technological innovation puts pressure on the need to carefully balance the regulation of a field full of opportunities and dangers for entrepreneurs and consumers alike. Over the last 30 years however, administrative path dependencies of a more or less decentralised regulatory system have characterised the different types of regulatory regime and institutional changes in both the EU and the US.[45]

For instance, the decentralised administrative structure of the EU with a centralised adjudication in the Court of Justice of the EU (CJEU) has inevitably contributed some implementation features of the new European General Data Protection Regulation (GDPR).[46] This is because even though the GDPR represents a novelty as a first comprehensive regulatory text, focused mostly on protecting individual data privacy, it does not revolutionise the institutional context of EU Law. The complexity of the GDPR architecture is hard, if not impossible to replicate, as this includes an uneven implementation through the Members States' agencies as well as open-ended rules for the domestic legislations to transpose further into national bills. Second, the harmonising and centralising jurisprudence of the CJEU has crafted the fundamental rights and dignitary approach to data privacy embedded in GDPR leading to regulatory choices on the right to be forgotten often in opposition to the right of free speech. This happened in sharp contrast to the US legal regime on individual rights and free speech at the core of the Supreme Court of the United States' jurisprudence.[47] If the dignitary dimension of data privacy as a fundamental right derives from the German constitutional tradition which has then spread within EU law jurisprudence,[48] the much narrower US data privacy approach privileges free liberty values that are compatible with free speech protections in what is mostly a consumer protection approach.[49]

[44] Whitman (n 36) 1151. See James Mahoney and Kathleen Thelen, *Explaining Institutional Change. Ambiguity, Agency and Power* (Cambridge University Press, 2009).

[45] See *ibid.*

[46] Regulation (EU) 2016/679 of the European Parliament and of the Council of 27 April 2016 on the protection of natural persons with regard to the processing of personal data and on the free movement of such data, and repealing Directive 95/46/EC (General Data Protection Regulation or GDPR) [2016] OJ L119/1.

[47] See Carpenter *v United States*, 138 S Ct 2206 (2018).

[48] See Francesca Bignami and Giorgio Resta, 'Transatlantic Privacy Regulation: Conflict and Cooperation' (2015) 78 *Law and Contemporary Problems* 4.

[49] See Jeffrey Rosen, 'The Right to be Forgotten' (2012) 64 *Stanford Law Review*.

Finally, embedded within the political economy regime of the GDPR there are many regulatory choices, which represent the type of social market economy and EU interventionist and producerist regime.[50] For instance, the GDPR adopts an ex-ante regulatory approach with the aggressive right to opt-in,[51] rather than opt-out from sharing one's data. If the EU competence is well entrenched in its commerce clause for the scope of regulating and harmonising the internal market to avoid differences that could create barriers to trade, the US federal regulator has lagged behind. In fact, data privacy regulation in the United States lacks an overarching federal mechanism by which data privacy is standardised. While states are free to craft their own privacy laws, the US lacks a GDPR-like federal law to guide the creation of such state laws. Prompted by the Watergate scandal, the Privacy Act 1974 was one of the first privacy tools crafted to manage the collection, maintenance, use and dissemination of individuals' personal data obtained by federal agencies.[52] However, the Privacy Act solely governs the data stored by federal agencies, not businesses or other entities, which leaves individuals at the mercy of companies like Facebook and Amazon.[53] Similarly, the remaining US privacy regulations are situation-specific, leaving a dearth of legal protection in the data privacy sphere.

The findings of the comparative administrative law literature,[54] together with the theory of institutional change developed by sociologists,[55] shows that despite the fact that GDPR is globally relevant for companies and influential for lawyers concerned with data privacy compliance, its ability to lead to institutional change in the US remains pretty weak. In fact, among US legislators the federal Government had privileged a sectoral and fragmented approach to regulate data privacy siloed in different economic sectors such as health or consumer protection. The current state of data privacy regulation in the US shows more broadly that the reception and transfer of the GDPR to third countries despite its adequacy and its regulatory innovation remains uncertain because of administrative path dependencies and the GDPR's uneven enforcement in the EU. In particular, in the consumer protection field, the California Consumer Protection Act (CCPA) has emerged as a powerful alternative, demonstrating once again that the California Effect described by Vogel in the realm of environmental law is still relevant, yet some of the regulatory differences emerge. The CCPA does not adopt an approach based on human dignity but rather a consumer protection approach to data privacy regulation based on political economic choices entailing ex-post market intervention,

[50] See Jim Whitman, 'Consumerism versus Producerism' (2008) 117 *Yale Law Journal*.

[51] See GDPR (n 46) Art 15(3).

[52] Privacy Act of 1974, 5 United States Code § 552a.

[53] *Ibid.*

[54] See Susan-Rose Ackerman and Peter Lindseth, 'Comparative Administrative Law: Outlining a Field of Study' (2010) 28(2) *Windsor Yearbook of Access to Justice* 435; Francesca Bignami and David Zaring (eds), *Comparative Law and Regulation: Understanding the Global Regulatory Process* (Edward Elgar Publishing, 2016).

[55] Mahoney and Thelen (n 44).

more active consumer litigation and eagerness to balance consumer protections with economic incentives for online platforms in their jurisdictions.

This institutional change and regulatory differentiation approach has led to the non-convergence of administrative practices even inside the EU in the implementation of the GDPR.[56] For instance the differentiated enforcement of the GDPR led to a variety of data privacy regimes in the EU. France is among a group of EU Member States that have decided to adopt a single bill for the implementation and adaptation of the GDPR and the Police Directive.[57] The New Personal Data Protection Act (NDPA) implements the GDPR by creating new rights for the data subject, amends the current Loi No 78-17 du 20 Juin 2018 governing personal data protection, and gives stronger enforcement mechanisms to *La Commission Nationale de l'Informatique et des Libertés* (CNIL), the French Data Protection Authority.[58] In conformity with the GDPR, the CNIL is given the power to create guidelines and standards for data protection, strengthened investigation powers with regards to data centres and data controllers, allows the CNIL to increase administrative fines, and introduces penalties for obstructing the CNIL's operations.[59]

While the CNIL is being afforded greater liberties in enforcing the GDPR and protecting personal data, the Irish Office of the Data Protection Commissioner (IDPC) is taking a more relaxed approach to GDPR compliance. Where the CNIL is given increased inspection powers with regard to data-retention centres, be it in data controller locations or otherwise, the IDPC prefers negotiation to on-site inspections.[60] This is particularly troubling because a majority of the big tech companies that are governed by the GDPR are headquartered in Ireland, attracted by the more lenient regulations and tax incentives. Not only does this risk competition among EU states to have big tech companies headquartered within their jurisdiction, but it also allows those companies to escape stringent applications of the GDPR. Furthermore, Ireland has only recently announced that they intend to initiate a probe against Google for its data privacy practices related to online advertising.[61]

[56] See Bignami and Zaring (n 54).

[57] Transposition of the Directive (EU) 2016/680 of the European Parliament and of the Council of 27 April 2016 on the protection of natural persons with regard to the processing of personal data by competent authorities for the purposes of the prevention, investigation, detection or prosecution of criminal offences or the execution of criminal penalties, and on the free movement of such data [2018] OJ C680/1, http://ec.europa.eu/transparency/regexpert/index.cfm?do=groupDetail.groupMeetingDoc&docid=12946.

[58] Karen Mc Cullagh, Olivia Tambou and Sam Burton (eds), *National Adaptations of the GDPR* (Collection Open Access Book, Blog Droit Europeen, 2019) 52.

[59] *Ibid* 54–55.

[60] Nicholas Vinocur, 'On GDPR Anniversary, French Privacy Watchdog says Penalties are Looming' (*POLITICO*, 25 May 2019) 4.

[61] Ryan Browne, 'EU Regulator Launches Probe into Google over Data Privacy' (*CNBC*, 22 May 2019), www.cnbc.com/2019/05/22/irish-data-privacy-watchdog-to-probe-google-over-potential-gdpr-breach.html (last accessed 6 March 2020).

These administrative and regulatory path dependencies show how institutional change happens through small incremental shifts rather than institutional takeovers or revolutions. Thus, the challenge for global converge is to grasp the resistances presented by the entrenchment of national bureaucracies and attitudes in domestic administrative law. Resistances to institutional change are inevitable as administrations thrive through professionals that protect and reinforce established hierarchies and traditions.

IV. A Decolonisation and Racial Perspective to Eurocentric Convergence

A decolonisation perspective to global convergence shows how forms of resistance are not only based on geographical, legal or political resistance but they are also nested within a hegemonic cultural knowledge that the coloniser attempts to cover with dominant national or international narratives of the civilised and the uncivilised.[62] In the work of Sherally Munshi, comparative lawyers should revamp a decolonising critique in legal scholarship. This approach departs from a Eurocentric approach that since the Second World War focused mostly on the institutional innovations of the global North with the new players constituted at Bretton Woods, the WTO and the EU. It rather focuses on the lessons learnt from the decolonisation movements in the 1960s in Asia, Africa and the Middle East and the Chicano, Feminist and gay liberation movements in the US.[63] Additionally, as Munshi explains, the origins of critical theory cannot only be attributed to the French 1968 movement and its theorists but ought to be revamped from the peripheries and the anticolonial critics. The idea of a minor comparativism aims to add complexity to single national narratives and grasp the history of minorities within one nation to highlight particularities of ethnic groups and diasporas in the creation of transnational networks creating new opportunities in a postcolonial future.[64]

This perspective highlights cultural resistances from within multiple nations taking the form of transnational networks moving from intimate to global scales. The study of these networks can revamp genealogies of resistances that originate in the global South and become new opportunities for economic emancipation in the global North.[65] These stories of minority networks in the EU law are

[62] See Franz Fanon, 'The Colonizer and the Colonized and Antony Anghie, Colonialism and the Birth of International Institutions: Sovereignty, Economy and the Mandate System of the League of Nations' (2002) 34 *New York University Journal of International Law & Politics* 513.

[63] See Sherally Munshi, 'Comparative Law and Decolonizing Critique' (2017) 65 *American Journal of Comparative Law* 226.

[64] See Sherally Munshi, '"You Will See My Family Became So American": Toward a Minor Comparativism' (2015) *63 American Journal of Comparative Law* 3, 655.

[65] See Eleanor M Brown, 'The Blacks Who "Got Their Forty Acres": A Theory of Black West Indian Migrant Asset Acquisition' (2014) 89 *New York University Law Review* 1.

seldom analysed in resistance to Europeaness or Britishness.[66] In fact the legacy of European colonialism is not central to the narratives of European integration where it remains an ancillary project to regulate the EU's relations to the oversea territories.[67] However, some scholars have shown how the project of 'Euafrica' was very much alive during the Treaty of Rome negotiations during 1955–57 and that while ending colonialism the European founding fathers were also 'securing its continuation'.[68] When the decolonising approach travels to EU law it is clear that there is no methodic understanding on how post-colonial ties have influenced the global convergentist model that the EU seeks to offer especially as a benevolent civilizer in its foreign relations. The dark legacy of unjust and racialized jurisprudence of the US Supreme Court is still very much alive in opinions such as *Dred Scott*[69] and *Korematsu*,[70] which still influence contemporary judgments.[71] In particular, racial ideologies in these cases supported the decisions of the Supreme Court, whereas in European law, especially when the cases reach the ECJ, the 'Echoes of Empire'[72] that were openly present in the Schuman declaration have been suppressed.[73]

The dark legacies of European integration have emerged in the current immigration crisis in which, rather than addressing upfront the colonial legacies and the cost of fortress Europe to its former subjects on the African continent,[74] the EU has attempted to outsource migration management outside its borders.[75] While the benevolent EU spreads its values of democracy, rule of law and

[66] See Afua Hirsch, *Brit(ish): On Race, Identity and Belonging* (Jonathan Cape, 2019).

[67] See Dimitry Kochenov, 'The Application of EU Law in the EU's Overseas Regions, Countries, and Territories after the Entry into Force of the Treaty of Lisbon' (2012) 20 *Michigan State Journal of International Law* 2 669, 669–743.

[68] See Peo Hansen and Stefan Jonsson, *Eurafrica: The Untold History of European Integration and Colonialism* (Bloomsbury Publishing, 2014).

[69] See *Dred Scott v Sandford* 60 US 393 (1857) (in an opinion written by Justice Taney, the majority held that 'a negro, whose ancestors were imported into [the U.S.], and sold as slaves', whether enslaved or free, could not be an American citizen and therefore did not have standing to sue in federal court).

[70] See *Korematsu v United States* 323 US 214 (1944) (the Supreme Court ruled that the evacuation order violated by Korematsu was valid. The majority found that the Executive Order did not show racial prejudice but rather responded to the strategic military imperative of the President).

[71] See *Trump v Hawaii* 138 US Supreme Court 2392 (2018) (commonly referred to as the 'Travel Ban case'); Robert Tsai, 'How Activists Resisted – and Ultimately Overturned – an Unjust Supreme Court Decision' *The Washington Post*, 30 January 2018), www.washingtonpost.com/outlook/2019/01/30/how-activists-resisted-ultimately-overturned-an-unjust-supreme-court-decision/?utm_term=.4faf093aa696 (last accessed 6 March 2020).

[72] See Kalypso Nicolaidis, Berny Sebe and Gabrielle Maas (eds), *Echoes of Empire: Memory, Identity and Colonial Legacies* (Bloomsbury Publishing, 2015).

[73] See Peo Hansen and Stefan Jonsson, *Euroafrica Incognita: The Colonial Origins of the European Union, History of the Present* (Bloomsbury Publishing, 2017) 1, 1–32.

[74] See Daniela Caruso and Joanna Geneve, 'Trade and History: The Case of EU-Algeria Relations' (2014) 33 *Boston University International Law Journal* 1.

[75] See E Tendayi Achiume, 'The Postcolonial Case for Rethinking Borders' (*Dissent Magazine*, Summer 2019), www.dissentmagazine.org/article/the-postcolonial-case-for-rethinking-borders (last accessed 6 March 2020).

human rights in its external action,[76] its immigration rationale of the place of first arrival to seek asylum and hot spots outside its jurisdiction is spreading to other jurisdictions like the US which is now implementing similar neo-colonial immigration policies towards Central and Latin America.[77]

V. Democratic Resistance Beyond the 'Encasement' of Neoliberalism in Global Law

The fourth type of resistance responds to the global convergence of neoliberal ideology. In an age of great economic and racial inequalities and declining life expectancy, economists and lawyers have developed new models of 'inclusive prosperity'.[78] Since the 1980s, the pervasiveness of neoliberal economics, combined with the faith in the judicial and property rights protection for markets was endorsed openly and implemented by the Washington consensus. Moved by this mantra, the World Bank and the IMF spread democracy and capitalism through 'shock therapy'.[79] The economic orthodoxy of the Washington consensus called for catching up with the globalised financial and trade regimes through aggressive privatisation reforms and deregulation of markets.[80] This policy has continued in a more subdued tone and through different tools despite the critiques of the shock therapy in Russia and Asia. By at the end of the 1990s, even the US law and development scholars noted that neoliberal policies were never really dismantled through the incorporation of social policies.[81]

Dani Rodrik has addressed this as the 'skewed agenda' of globalisation, in that it privileges excessively the liberalisation of trade and financial markets while totally dismissing the costs to developing countries and restrains their policy space to develop their own economic strategies.[82] Rodrik also suggested that

[76] See Consolidated Version of the Treaty on European Union [2008] OJ C115/13, Art 21; Marise Cremona, 'The Union as a Global Actor: Roles, Models, and Identity' (2004) 41(2) *Common Market Law Review*.

[77] See Max Fisher and Amanda Taub, 'Trump's Immigration Approach Isn't New: Europe and Australia Went First' *The New York Times*, 18 July 2019), www.nytimes.com/2019/07/18/world/trump-migration.html (last accessed 6 March 2020).

[78] See Naidu, Rodrik, Zuchman and Palladino (n 27).

[79] See Jeffrey Sachs, 'Shock Therapy in Poland: Perspectives of Five Years' (The Tanner Lectures on Human Values, University of Utah, 6–7 April 1994).

[80] See *ibid* 4 explaining that such fast reforms were driven by globalisation showing the path to 'borrow technology, capital and management techniques to help catch up economically after decades of falling behind'.

[81] See Kerry Rittich, 'The Future of Law and Development: Second Generation Reforms and the Incorporation of the Social' in A Santos and D Trubek, 'Critical Approaches to Law and Development' (2004) 26 *Michigan Journal of International Law* 1.

[82] See Dani Rodrik, 'After Neoliberalism, What?' (Alternatives to Neoliberalism Conference by the New Rules for Global Finance Coalition, Harvard University, 23–24 May 2002), http://drodrik.scholar.harvard.edu/files/dani-rodrik/files/after-neoliberalism-what.pdf (last accessed 6 March 2020).

global institutions, rather than pushing for global convergence and deep integration, should promote local experimentation in both institutional innovation and goals to achieve more sustainable growth. The strength of Rodrik's vision is to catalyse local resistances rather than ally with the populist backlashes to neoliberal globalisation and provide a new trade agenda that could be implemented by a more balanced national and transnational governance.[83]

The challenge with Rodrik's vision lies in the entrenched ideology promoted by globalist lawyers and economists that has pervaded the narratives at the core of the creation of the Bretton Woods Institutions, the GATT and the EU.

In Quinn Slobodian's *Globalists*,[84] a group of politicians, economists and lawyers in the 1920s shaped neoliberalism as a coherent project challenged by the welfare states in the global North and decolonisation movements in the global South. Their fear was that wealth redistributors would take away their privilege and their property rights so that a strong state was needed to protect global capital. This Slobodian counter move explains the neoliberal paradox for which state power is essential to enforce the smooth running of the free market and protect property entitlements, but to do so it should not rest on democratic politics.[85] To do so the encasement of neoliberal politics occurred through less democratic and transparent regulatory processes put forward by international organisations appearing extremely technical but also allowing national government to implement them.

The shift of power from the national to the supranational was not a one-way trajectory, as once the competition policy was elaborated by EU technocrats implemented by domestic institutions. What has been called the EU incomplete path to integration or the quasi-federal supranational model was exactly the globalists' goal. A confusing mix of national and supranational competences allowed globalists to diminish the ability of Member States to fully regulate and democratise their economic and financial interests. This shift of economic regulatory power from the nations to the EU, WTO and a global Investor-States Dispute Settlement regimes protecting foreign investments also weakened national democracies.

The resistance to the encasement of neoliberalism in the EU is often confused as it appeared in the non-movement of the *gilets jeaunes* protests exposing President Macron's inability to enact equitable climate policies to ameliorate the condition of the French working class. In contrast, a progressive resistance would encourage more democratic representation at the national or supranational level of EU redistributive policies such as the New Deal for Europe[86] or a new Treaty

[83] See Dani Rodrik, *Straight Talk on Trade: Ideas for a Sane World Economy* (Princeton University Press, 2018).

[84] See Quinn Slobodian, *Globalists: The End of Empire and the Birth of Neoliberalism* (Harvard University Press, 2018).

[85] See JM Mason, 'The Market Police' (*Boston Review*, 1 June 2018) http://bostonreview.net/class-inequality/j-w-mason-market-police (last accessed 6 March 2020).

[86] See 'A New Deal for Europe' (*European Spring*), https://europeanspring.net/new-deal-for-europe/ (last accessed 6 March 2020).

addressing European fiscal policy on the Democratization of the Economic and Social Government of the European Union (TDEM).[87]

However, this democratic resistance to global converge when riddled by social policies can split, just like Duncan Kennedy described in his Right or Left Social consciousness, which characterised the fascist and the socialist parties of the 1930s in Europe.[88] This split reemerges today among the Right and Left wing populists, with similar agendas yet different political values. These range from *Podemus* in Spain aiming at a deeply democratic and redistributive agenda, to *Fidesz* in Hungary aiming at creating an illiberal democracy in which a Christian democratic party has created a mafia state around its leadership.[89]

VI. Conclusion

This taxonomy of resistances offers another lens through which to view global convergence. This can be better understood by lawyers through its dialectics with different types of resistance often in conflict or alliance with each other depending on the globalisation context and its underlying politics. For instance, when economic globalisation creates convergence, such as in the case of the BRI attempting to create similar property, lending and financial regimes in Malaysia, resistances against the global agenda of President Xi Jinping were driven by different forms of resistance. On the one hand, there was the legal irritation created by new financial and property regimes imposed on the Malaysian legal system that were at odds with the local practice. On the other, the decolonisation critique revamped, for the Malaysian government, the legacy of the British colonial past and the fear of a new Chinese economic colonisation.[90] In this case, both forms of resistance worked together against the BRI's attempt to spur global convergence.

A different example of two forms of resistance working in opposition to global convergence, but in conflict with each other emerges from Right and Left populist movements displaying a similar anti-European attitude.[91] Not surprisingly, Right and Left wing populists in Italy were allied in the creation of the first Conte government in 2018 sharing a deep skepticism towards the EU but motivated by

[87] See Stephanie Hennette, Thomas Piketty, Guillaume Sacriste and Antoine Vauchez, *How to Democratize Europe* (Harvard University Press, 2019) (based on the Treaty on the Democratization of the Economic and Social Government of the European Union, Manifesto for the Democratization of Europe' http://tdem.eu/en/treaty/ (last accessed 6 March 2020).

[88] See Duncan Kennedy, 'Three Globalizations in Law and Legal Thought: 1850–2000' in D Trubek and A Santos (eds), *The New Law and Economic Development: A Critical Appraisal* (Cambridge University Press, 2006) 19–73.

[89] See Balint Magyar, *Post-Communist Mafia State: The Case of Hungary* (CEU Press, 2016).

[90] See Syed Aljunied, *Radicals: Resistance and Protest in Colonial Malaya* (Northern Illinois University Press, 2015).

[91] See Bojan Bugaric, 'The Two Faces of Populism: Between Authoritarian and Democratic Populism' (2019) 20 *German Law Journal*.

two different critiques. Left wing populists worried about democratic accountability in what they deemed a technocratic European regime in Brussels, while Right wing populists worried mainly about immigration due to their nativist, islamophobic and white supremacist values. The conflict between these two populist movements, both resisting global governance, resulted in a split and the creation of a second government, also Conte-bis, supported this time by centre left and Left populist parties. However, part of this split has also been attributed to the Right wing populists openly supporting the first BRI initiative in Italy, a symbolic victory of President Xi Jin Ping now also penetrating a G8 Member country. In contrast to the Right wing populists, the Left wing populists were more lukewarm on this front due to the dangerous shift in Italy's geopolitical alliance towards the East rather than its traditional US Western partner.[92] A taxonomy of resistances is crucial for lawyers to grapple with the underlying politics of resistances to the global legal order.

[92] See Federiga Bindi, 'Italy's Long Standing Friendship with China' (*Carnegie Endowment for International Peace*, 2019), https://carnegieendowment.org/2019/05/20/why-did-italy-embrace-belt-and-road-initiative-pub-79149 (last accessed 6 March 2020).

7

EU and US Regulatory Coherence in TTIP – Similarities and Differences

DAVID HENIG

I. Introduction

The heart of the Transatlantic Trade and Investment Partnership (TTIP) trade deal between the European Union and United States of America was to be an ambitious agreement intended over time to dramatically reduce non-tariff barriers (NTBs) to trade through differing regulations.[1] For example, a report by the Centre for Economic Policy Research for the UK Government in March 2013 stated that

> Looking at the gains attributable to removing tariffs as opposed to lowering NTBs, it is obvious that the majority of the increase is attributable to the lowering of NTBs. For the UK and US, this is particularly true. Here, the reduction of NTBs is accountable for up to 90 per cent of the increase in GDP.[2]

Outside of regional agreements such as the creation of the EU Single Market or that between Australia and New Zealand,[3] such ambition is unprecedented.

The TTIP talks lasted from June 2013 to November 2016 but ultimately failed to reach an agreement. Talk were suspended after the election of President Trump, with EU Trade Commissioner Cecilia Malmstrom saying that

[1] This was variously known as regulatory coherence, regulatory cooperation, regulatory alignment and living agreement. Here we use the term regulatory coherence. A good overview is provided at Elizabeth Golberg, 'Regulatory Cooperation – a Reality Check' (Mossavar-Rahmani Center for Business and Government at Harvard Kennedy School, April 2019) 115, www.hks.harvard.edu/sites/default/files/centers/mrcbg/img/115_final.pdf (last accessed 9 March 2020).

[2] Centre for Economic Policy Research, 'Estimating the Economic Impact on the UK of a Transatlantic Trade and Investment Partnership (TTIP) Agreement between the European Union and the United States – Final Report' (Final Project Report Reference P2BIS120020, Centre for Economic Policy Research, March 2013), https://assets.publishing.service.gov.uk/government/uploads/system/uploads/attachment_data/file/198115/bis-13-869-economic-impact-on-uk-of-tranatlantic-trade-and-investment-partnership-between-eu-and-us.pdf (last accessed 9 March 2020).

[3] Australia New Zealand Closer Economic Relations Trade Agreement, and Exchange of Letters (entered into force 1 January 1983) Australian Treaty Series No 2 (1983), https://dfat.gov.au/trade/agreements/in-force/anzcerta/Pages/australia-new-zealand-closer-economic-relations-trade-agreement.aspx (last accessed 9 March 2020).

> For quite some time TTIP will probably be in the freezer and then what happens when it is defrosted, we will have to wait and see. I think we should be realistic. I don't see the resumption of any TTIP negotiation for quite a long time.[4]

Subsequent talks between the two led to agreement in one of the areas of TTIP regulatory coherence, the mutual recognition of Good Manufacturing Practice inspections in the pharmaceuticals sector.[5] However, the ambitious goals of the TTIP agreement in regulatory coherence, to gradually align regulations between EU and US, fell with the end of the TTIP talks.

TTIP negotiations did not fail because of regulatory coherence. Public opposition within the EU typically focused on the issue of Investor State Dispute Settlement, the right of inward investors to take governments to a tribunal, on which subject 150,000 responses were received to a 2014 consultation.[6] For negotiators, the failure to tackle some of the traditional market access issues, such as US protection of their public procurement markets through various Buy America and Buy American schemes, and EU protection of their agriculture sector were more significant.

Equally the regulatory coherence chapters of TTIP were not completed, and we have no publicly available joint text that can be analysed. What we can however see is the different approaches to the subject that the two parties took and compare the US text as agreed in the Trans Pacific Partnership[7] or updated US-Mexico-Canada Agreement (USMCA),[8] with the proposed EU text that was published.[9]

[4] Philip Blenkinsop, 'U.S. Trade Talks in Deep Freeze after Trump Win, says EU' *Reuters* (Brussels, 11 November 2016), www.reuters.com/article/us-usa-election-eu-trade-idUSKBN1361UN (last accessed 9 March 2020).

[5] European Medicines Agency, 'EU and US Reach a Milestone in Mutual Recognition of Inspections of Medicine Manufacturers' (European Medicines Agency, 2019), www.ema.europa.eu/en/news/eu-us-reach-milestone-mutual-recognition-inspections-medicines-manufacturers (last accessed 9 March 2020).

[6] European Commission, 'Online Public Consultation on Investment Protection and Investor-to-State Dispute Settlement (ISDS) in the Transatlantic Trade and Investment Partnership Agreement' Commission Staff Working Document Report SWD(2015) 3 final, https://trade.ec.europa.eu/doclib/docs/2015/january/tradoc_153044.pdf (last accessed 9 March 2020).

[7] The agreement now known as the Comprehensive and Progressive Trans Pacific Partnership (CPTPP) and signed by 11 countries was negotiated as the Trans Pacific Partnership (TPP) involving these 11 countries plus the USA. The USA withdrew from the TPP after the election of President Trump, and the remaining members made some changes to this before agreeing to proceed with a rebranded CPTPP. This chapter uses the final CPTPP text as an example of US thinking on the subject of regulatory coherence, as it was widely understood that the US approach in TTIP was similar to that taken in TPP negotiations. Comprehensive and Progressive Agreement for Trans-Pacific Partnership (signed 8 March 2018), https://dfat.gov.au/trade/agreements/in-force/cptpp/official-documents/Pages/official-documents.aspx (last accessed 9 March 2020).

[8] Agreement between the United States of America, the United Mexican States, and Canada (signed 30 November 2018), https://ustr.gov/trade-agreements/free-trade-agreements/united-states-mexico-canada-agreement/agreement-between (last accessed 9 March 2020).

[9] The EU published significant amounts of material on TTIP, which is still present at the time of writing at the European Commission, 'EU Negotiating Texts in TTIP' (European Commission News Archive, Brussels, 14 July 2016), http://trade.ec.europa.eu/doclib/press/index.cfm?id=1230 (last accessed 9 March 2020).

This chapter examines these contrasting approaches, based on the text and also contemporaneous discussions involving the author[10] with US and EU negotiators. It outlines the general issue of regulatory coherence that the two sides wished to solve, and had indeed worked on together for many years. It also discusses the progress of negotiations, analyses the available texts, and from this draws some conclusions about the way the two sides approached this task.

TTIP, and particularly the regulatory coherence discussions, were a practical implementation of the principle of convergence. They were launched at a point where US and EU desires to seek to export their regulatory systems seemed compatible, and the proposals made say much about the role of trade agreements in EU and US global ambitions. Ultimately both the EU and US wanted to export what they saw as their core regulatory approaches through TTIP but ran out of time to reconcile texts which differed considerably in detail.

II. Why was Regulatory Coherence so Important in TTIP?

There has been a steady growth in regulations governing products and services in developed countries for many years. There is no particularly good measure of this, but in the EU Jacques Pelkmans[11] has commented that 'In the vast domain of the internal market, "regulation" is EU's core business.'[12] In the USA the Mercatus Centre at George Mason University has made attempts at measuring regulation, showing the dramatic rise since 1970, and calculating that 'By 2016, there were 104.6 million words of federal regulation.'[13] Both in the USA and EU there is also relevant regulation at lower levels, in other words US states and EU Member States.

The rise in regulations means that virtually all products in the USA and EU are subject to regulations, on the final product, the way it must be tested, and often the way it is produced. This in turn means that virtually all goods trade between

[10] At the time working for the UK Government on TTIP, including on regulatory cooperation.

[11] Pelkmans has worked on EU trade and investment issues for many years with the Centre for European Policy Studies and others: Jacques Pelkmans, 'The Economics of Single Market Regulation', Bruges European Economic Policy Briefings (Department of European Economics Studies, 2012) 25, <www.google.com/url?sa=t&rct=j&q=&esrc=s&source=web&cd=16&ved=2ahUKEwiBgN7L38HkAhUFZMAKHSXTCrsQFjAPegQICRAC&url=https%3A%2F%2Fwww.coleurope.eu%2Fsystem%2Ffiles_force%2Fresearch-paper%2Fbeep25.pdf%3Fdownload%3D1&usg=AOvVaw2zV_mIPptutRosByAUrZ9O (last accessed 9 March 2020).

[12] *Ibid.*

[13] See, eg, Patrick McLaughlin, Jonathan Nelson, Jim Pagels and Oliver Sherouse, 'The Impossibility of Comprehending, or Even Reading, all Federal Regulations' (*Mercatus Center at George Mason University*, 2017), www.mercatus.org/publications/regulation/impossibility-comprehending-or-even-reading-all-federal-regulations (last accessed 9 March 2020).

countries must take place in line with these regulations. Where these regulations differ between countries this must add cost to trade, whether this is in terms of designing one product to meet differing regulations, different products with essentially the same function, or the same product tested in different markets. Typically, these regulations do differ between countries.[14]

The disciplines of the World Trade Organisation (WTO) provide little assistance in reducing regulatory differences causing trade barriers. The Agreement on Technical Barriers to Trade[15] states that 'products imported from the territory of any Member shall be accorded treatment no less favourable than that accorded to like products of national origin' and 'Members shall ensure that technical regulations are not prepared, adopted or applied with a view to or with the effect of creating unnecessary obstacles to international trade'. More positively the Agreement states that 'Members shall give positive consideration to accepting as equivalent technical regulations of other Members' but the only compulsion is to notify other members of proposed technical regulations. There is little evidence this has reduced regulatory differences.

The economic impact of regulatory differences is thought to be significant but has never been satisfactorily calculated. A major Organisation for Economic Cooperation and Development (OECD) study published in 2017 was summarised by saying:

> The analysis shows that trade costs may arise from unintended regulatory heterogeneity across jurisdictions, including information, specification and conformity assessment costs. Evidence on the magnitude of these trade costs remain largely unknown, although they are likely to vary significantly by sectors.[16]

Given that the EU Single Market removed most regulatory barriers, another way to look at the economics of this is to measure the likely benefits there. One of the most recent studies of this summarises the result that 'a total estimate of the economic benefits of the Single Market of between 8% and 9% higher GDP on average for the EU' however this includes the impact of both tariffs and regulatory barriers having been removed.[17]

[14] See, eg, Caroline Freund and Sarah Oliver, 'Table 1 Differences in Regulations between EU and US Side Turn-Signal Lamps' in 'Gains from Harmonizing US and EU Auto Regulations under the Transatlantic Trade and Investment Partnership' Peterson Institute for International Economic Policy Brief (2015) Number PB15-10, < www.piie.com/publications/pb/pb15-10.pdf (last accessed 9 March 2020).

[15] World Trade Organisation, Agreement on Technical Barriers to Trade (Uruguay Round), www.wto.org/english/docs_e/legal_e/17-tbt_e.htm (last accessed 9 March 2020).

[16] Organisation of Economic Cooperation and Development, 'International Regulatory Co-operation and Trade: Understanding the Trade Costs of Regulatory Divergence and the Remedies' (24 May 2017) summary recovered from www.oecd.org/gov/international-regulatory-co-operation-and-trade-9789264275942-en.htm (last accessed 9 March 2020).

[17] Jan in 't Veld, 'Quantifying the Economic Effects of the Single Market in a Structural Macromodel' (2019) European Commission Discussion Paper ISSN 2443-8022, https://ec.europa.eu/info/sites/info/files/economy-finance/dp094_en.pdf (last accessed 9 March 2020).

More specific work was however carried out on US-EU barriers in advance of the launch of the TTIP talks. In December 2009, a major sector-by-sector study by Ecorys concluded that an 'ambitious scenario could push EU GDP to be 0.7% higher in 2018 compared to the baseline scenario (i.e. do nothing).'[18] This ambitious scenario did not assume that all regulations would be aligned, or in the authors' terminology, actionable, rather that: 'in an ambitious scenario Ecorys has assessed that roughly 50% of NTMs and regulatory divergence can be eliminated' with others unlikely due to being 'driven by geography, language, preferences, culture or history'.

This Ecorys study was used as an input by other models predicting TTIP impact, most notably a Centre for Economic Policy Research (CEPR) study for the UK Government showing the impact of tackling such barriers (here included in the broader category of NTBs or Non-Tariff Barriers) being significantly higher than for tariffs. As the study noted:

> Looking at the gains attributable to removing tariffs as opposed to lowering NTBs, it is obvious that the majority of the increase is attributable to the lowering of NTBs. For the UK and US, this is particularly true. Here, the reduction of NTBs is accountable for up to 90 per cent of the increase in GDP. The lower share of gains from the removal of tariffs for the UK and US, as well as the lower aggregated effect is due to the lower a priori levels of tariffs between the US and UK, than between the US and EU.[19]

Given the context of the 2008 financial crisis and the slow global recovery, the promise of economic growth provided by tackling regulatory differences in TTIP was welcome, not least as it seemed relatively painless to achieve. Launching talks at the G8 summit in Northern Ireland in 2013, the then President of the Commission, José Manuel Barroso, said:

> Huge economic benefits are expected from reducing red tape, avoiding divergent regulations for the future. I would rather have our companies invest in new, innovative products and services and job creation than in double-testing, our multiple inspections, or even separate manufacturing lines.[20]

As well as the broad positive economic impact, tackling regulatory differences was thought to be of particular benefit to small and medium enterprises struggling to

[18] Dr Koen G Berden, Prof Dr Joseph Francois, Mr Martin Thelle, Mr Paul Wymenga, Ms Saara Tamminen, 'Non-Tariff Measures in EU-US Trade and Investment – An Economic Analysis' (11 December 2009) Ecorys OJ 2007/S 180-219493 Final Report, www.gtap.agecon.purdue.edu/resources/download/5177.pdf (last accessed 9 March 2020).

[19] Centre for Economic Policy Research, 'Estimating the Economic Impact on the UK of a Transatlantic Trade and Investment Partnership (TTIP) Agreement between the European Union and the United States' (March 2013) P2BIS120020, https://assets.publishing.service.gov.uk/government/uploads/system/uploads/attachment_data/file/198115/bis-13-869-economic-impact-on-uk-of-tranatlantic-trade-and-investment-partnership-between-eu-and-us.pdf (last accessed 9 March 2020).

[20] Cabinet Office, Prime Minister's Office, 10 Downing Street, 'G8 Summit: US & EU Trade Statement' (June 2013), www.gov.uk/government/speeches/g8-summit-us-eu-trade-statement (last accessed 9 March 2020).

cope with differing regulations. A 2014 study for the European Commission of barriers to market for companies of this size concluded that 'The challenge of complying with technical rules and regulations for all goods is the most frequently cited issue'.[21]

Some non-governmental organisations (NGOs) saw the overall intent of TTIP as being deregulatory,[22] and threatening to the precautionary principle.[23] But this was rarely raised by government or business in my own experiences, rather the often unstated additional motive for regulatory cooperation in TTIP was the fear that this was the last chance for the US and EU to join together to set global rules before the rise of China and other emerging economies made this impossible. A senior figure in one large transatlantic manufacturer commented in a 2014 meeting that 'next year for the first time we will sell more product in China than in the US and EU combined. And that will mean increasingly setting the rules that suit China as much as the EU and US'.[24] Writing from a Chinese point of view in a chapter entitled 'TTIP and its implications for China', Sun Zhenyu and Tu Xinquan commented that

> In order to face the challenges posed by the rise of the emerging economies (especially that of China), to respond to the attendant global power shift, and to continue to maintain its position in the world, the US needs to develop new world trade rules that reflect its own interests and revitalise its own economy. Combined with the North American Free Trade Agreement (NAFTA) and TPP, TTIP has been put on the table as part of the US strategic response to the changes in the current global political and economic situation.[25]

This motivation was also evident from the EU as to why TTIP talks on regulatory coherence were so significant.

III. Progress of Negotiations

TTIP negotiations formally commenced at the G8 summit in June 2013.[26] The decision to commence talks was based substantially on a positive report produced

[21] European Commission, Report: 'Small and Medium Sized Enterprises and the Transatlantic Trade and Investment Partnership' (European Union, 2015) ISBN: 978-92-79-46618-2, https://trade.ec.europa.eu/doclib/docs/2015/april/tradoc_153348.pdf (last accessed 9 March 2020).

[22] Corporate Europe Observatory, 'Cooperating to Deregulate: TTIP Fits Neatly with the Domestic Deregulation Agenda of the EU' (2015), https://corporateeurope.org/en/international-trade/2015/11/cooperating-deregulate (last accessed 9 March 2020).

[23] There is a narrative that TTIP regulatory coherence failed because of differing US and EU views of the precautionary principle. This however was not a significant subject given both sides take precautionary approaches in different areas, see Elvire Fabry and Georgio Garbasso, 'The Reality of Precaution: Comparing Risk Regulation in the US and Europe' (Notre Europe Jacques Delors Institute, 18 July 2014), https://institutdelors.eu/wp-content/uploads/2018/01/precautionprincipleuseu-fabry-garbasso-ne-jdi-july14.pdf (last accessed 9 March 2020).

[24] Author recollection.

[25] M Sait Akman, Simon J Evenett and Patrick Low (eds), *Catalyst? TTIP's Impact on the Rest* (CEPR Press, 2015), www.tepav.org.tr/upload/files/1432112973-6.Catalyst_TTIP_s_Impact_on_the_Rest.pdf (last accessed 9 March 2020).

[26] See www.gov.uk/government/speeches/g8-summit-us-eu-trade-statement.

by a high level joint working group, which included a substantial section on regulatory coherence.[27] This section started by saying:

> A significant portion of the benefit of a potential transatlantic agreement turns on the ability of the United States and EU to pursue new and innovative approaches to reduce the adverse impact on trade and investment of non-tariff barriers, with the aim of moving progressively toward a more integrated transatlantic marketplace. The HLWG recommends that the two sides explore new means of addressing these 'behind-the-border' obstacles to trade, including, where possible, through provisions that serve to reduce unnecessary costs and administrative delays stemming from regulation, while achieving the levels of health, safety, and environmental protection that each side deems appropriate, or otherwise meeting legitimate regulatory objectives.

In delivering these benefits from regulatory coherence, the EU and US did not start from scratch. As recounted by Peter Chase, who was US Chamber of Commerce Vice President for Europe between 2010–16, there had already been joint statements in 2002 and 2011, which provided an outline framework. As he writes,[28]

> Further, the 2011 Common Understanding says explicitly that 'regulatory measures should aim to avoid unnecessarily divergent or duplicative requirements between the US and the EU, when appropriate.' Moreover, the US and the EU 'should also explore a process to exchange regulatory information of the Unified Agenda and Work Programme, respectively, … and have a fixed agenda item at the High Level Regulatory Cooperation Forum' with a view to seeing whether the two parties can work together on areas both are considering. The Understanding also encourages new regulatory cooperation measures, and obliges both to flag upcoming regulatory proposals likely to have international trade and investment effects, and/or publishing an Annual Notice to solicit public comments.

Drawing on these precedents, the EU presented Member States with their early thoughts on TTIP areas, including regulatory cooperation, soon after the formal launch of talks. A non-paper envisaged enhanced consultation, greater impact assessment, sector specific initiatives, and an overall institutional mechanism. It also noted that nothing agreed could or should prevent parties from regulating as they saw fit, which could be reasonably interpreted as there being no intention to create a secondary law-making function to cover both the EU and US through TTIP.

According to Commission negotiators, the discussion of regulatory coherence at the first round of TTIP talks, in July 2013, was insubstantial,[29] with the US having prepared little. The next full round of negotiations did not take place until

[27] See https://ustr.gov/about-us/policy-offices/press-office/reports-and-publications/2013/final-report-us-eu-hlwg.

[28] See http://aei.pitt.edu/64584/1/SR110_Regulatory_Cooperation_in_TTIP.pdf.

[29] Accounts of early TTIP negotiating rounds and papers were not publicly shared as later ones were; these are therefore reflections from those involved in the process.

November, where discussion was described as positive, but the EU were starting to be concerned that the US approach was to build on consultation provisions within the Technical Barriers to Trade chapter, which seemed to be of limited ambition. It is worth noting that while there was a lively debate within the EU about the content of TTIP, this was not at this stage shared in the US, and there was little public signalling of a position. A third round of talks took place in December 2013.

In early 2014 negotiators and regulators from both sides, along with various stakeholders, met for an informal discussion of regulatory cooperation at Wilton Park in the UK. The report from this event, while not specifying who had said what, notes that 'As both the EU and US offer transparency at different stages, the challenge is how to align and structure the two systems. Both sides will have to adapt and find common procedures for regulatory co-operation on rules relating to trade'.[30] A further clue as to the differing approaches of the US and EU came in a *Financial Times* story in February 2014, in which it was reported that the US was making a priority of improving the transparency of EU regulatory processes[31] (also known as Good Regulatory Practices or GRP). It appears that by this time there was a clear gap emerging between the parties on how regulatory coherence would be addressed, with the EU favouring institutional mechanisms involving regulators, and the US transparency for public comment.

A major report on regulatory cooperation was issued by the Swedish Board of Trade in March 2014,[32] which concluded that

> As regards more comprehensive regulatory cooperation in various sectors, the Board assesses that such work will demand explicit channels for bilateral dialogue, forums where specific regulatory interests may find expression, and a process that enables an objective assessment of existing and future rules, with equal representation from both parties.

This reflected received EU wisdom by this stage that a horizontal regulatory approach was needed.

Both the Wilton Park event and Swedish Board of Trade report are indicative of the significant amount of effort expended in 2013 and 2014 to define the regulatory elements of TTIP. Those involved recall a significant TTIP conference circuit and numerous academic discussions, at this stage very much with the aim of making a breakthrough which could be supported by both sides. However there is no doubt this activity continued to be more apparent in the EU than the US, where the 'Asian pivot' saw Trans Pacific Partnership being considered the more

[30] See www.wiltonpark.org.uk/wp-content/uploads/Report-WP1307.pdf.

[31] See www.ft.com/content/6e9b7190-9a65-11e3-8e06-00144feab7de.

[32] The report was updated in 2015 and is available from www.kommers.se/Documents/dokumentarkiv/publikationer/2015/Publ-Regulatory-Co-operation-and-Technical-Barriers-to-Trade-within-TTIP.pdf.

important negotiation.[33] The gap between the sides, in terms of both substance and importance, led to slow progress.

The US presented formal negotiating text to the sixth round of TTIP talks in July 2014, focusing on GRP, which the EU believed to be inadequate in meeting the promise of regulatory cooperation. By the seventh round, starting at the end of September 2014, there was a public report which commented that 'Further clarifications on the US proposal on regulatory coherence were made'.[34] In December 2014 the EU finally presented draft text to incorporate both US and EU issues, and after discussion with Member States this was made public in February 2015.[35] This text emphasised the EU's direction of travel that each side would publish their planned regulatory asks, identifying to the other side those likely to have a major impact on trade and investment, and then regulators could request consultations. A regulatory coherence body would oversee this work, and an annual meeting with stakeholders would allow them to provide input. At the press conference of the ninth round of negotiations in April 2015, EU Chief Negotiator, Ignacio Garcia-Bercero, said: 'On horizontal regulatory issues, detailed proposals have already been tabled from both sides in previous rounds. The teams have now started the work of trying step by step to identifying common ground, bringing our proposals closer together'.[36]

Some further progress was made in bringing the two sides together in May 2015 when Commission Vice President Timmermans launched a better regulation package which in part aimed to meet US requests for greater transparency, which were also shared by a number of EU Member States. For example, one US request had been for EU public consultation on secondary legislation, and the EU committed to this:

> For the first time, the draft texts of delegated acts – measures which amend or supplement nonessential elements of EU legislation – will be open for public comments on the Commission's website for four weeks. This is in parallel to the existing consultation of Member State experts.[37]

Then perhaps due to a coordinated timetable, the US administration in June 2015 published guidelines on implementing International Regulatory Cooperation, encouraging US regulators to cooperate with counterparts including in the EU.[38]

However the pace of progress on this chapter continued to be slow, as the US continued to resist elements of the EU text on institutional provisions.

[33] See, eg, https://foreignpolicy.com/2016/09/06/the-unfinished-legacy-of-obamas-pivot-to-asia/. TPP was agreed in October 2015, but thereafter US efforts switched from negotiation to ratification.

[34] Recovered from www.sice.oas.org/TPD/USA_EU/Negotiations/7th_round_to_ends_e.pdf.

[35] See https://trade.ec.europa.eu/doclib/docs/2015/february/tradoc_153120.pdf.

[36] Recovered from www.sice.oas.org/TPD/USA_EU/Negotiations/9th_round_press_conference_e.pdf.

[37] See https://ec.europa.eu/commission/presscorner/detail/en/IP_15_4988.

[38] See www.reginfo.gov/public/jsp/Utilities/eo13609-working-group-guidelines.pdf.

The EU revised the text in February 2016, and progress was reported at the 12th round in February 2016, as the public report said 'Both sides agreed to intensify inter-sessional work in the run up to the next negotiating round with a view to clarifying outstanding issues, and to consolidate the respective texts'.[39] The 13th and 14th rounds saw further discussions on creating a joint text on regulatory cooperation, but it is not clear that such a text was ever agreed, even with the square brackets which would signify areas of disagreement, by the time TTIP talks came to an end in late 2016.

IV. Comparing US and EU Approaches to Regulatory Cooperation

The last version of the EU draft text on TTIP regulatory cooperation available on their website is dated March 2016.[40] It is notable that in this version the text was separated from that of GRP, where there was a separate textual proposal,[41] whereas in earlier drafts the two had been combined. The US did not publish its proposals, however at the time of TTIP negotiations were also involved with the Trans Pacific Partnership (TPP) talks, and suggested that the text in that agreement reflected its own views. The US subsequently withdrew from TPP, and the agreement was rechristened the Comprehensive and Progressive Trans Pacific Partnership (CPTPP). The relevant part of CPTPP[42] is Chapter 25, which is entitled Regulatory Coherence, but mostly focuses on GRP. The US appears to have refined their approach further in the US-Mexico-Canada (USMCA) agreement intended as a NAFTA (North American Free Trade Agreement) replacement, where Chapter 28 is entitled Good Regulatory Practices.[43]

The most significant difference between EU and US texts is clearly then the way in which the US focuses on GRP, to great detail in USMCA, with 20 clauses compared to 11 in USMCA and the EU TTIP GRP proposal. There is no place in the US text for discussions between regulators from different countries, except for some rather vague words on cooperation on implementing GRP. Their text is rather concerned with domestic regulatory processes. The US belief outlined at the time of TTIP was that this should be covered by the Technical Barrier to Trade chapter, and Chapter 8 of CPTPP does include a small reference in clause 10, that 'A Party may request another Party to provide information on any matter arising under this Chapter. A Party receiving a request under this paragraph shall

[39] Recovered from www.sice.oas.org/TPD/USA_EU/Negotiations/12th_round_EU_report_e.pdf.

[40] See https://trade.ec.europa.eu/doclib/docs/2016/march/tradoc_154377.pdf.

[41] See https://trade.ec.europa.eu/doclib/docs/2016/march/tradoc_154380.pdf.

[42] CPTPP text can be found in various places, for example www.mfat.govt.nz/assets/CPTPP/Comprehensive-and-Progressive-Agreement-for-Trans-Pacific-Partnership-CPTPP-English.pdf.

[43] See https://usmca.com/good-regulatory-practices-usmca-chapter-28/.

provide that information within a reasonable period of time, and if possible, by electronic means'. However this is some way short of a formal process of regulatory cooperation. The US was clearly reluctant to involve its regulatory agencies within international agreements.

There are significant common elements in the Good Regulatory Practice texts prepared by the EU and US, namely advanced warning of regulations, consultation on the content, and preparation of an impact assessment. The provisions on providing an annual summary of upcoming regulations are similar in EU TTIP text and CPTPP, and neither goes into much detail. Article 28.6 of USMCA only expands this slightly. Impact assessment text is also similar, but that on consultation has been expanded significantly in USMCA.

In CPTPP and EU TTIP proposals, dispute settlement would not apply to the chapters covering GRP. USMCA provides an opportunity however, in stating that

> No Party shall have recourse for dispute settlement under Chapter 31 (Dispute Settlement) for a matter arising under this Chapter except to address a sustained and recurring course of action or inaction that is inconsistent with a provision of this Chapter.

As was described above, the US emphasised GRP in regulatory coherence discussions during TTIP. The text they suggested as a guide in CPTPP has marked similarities to that put forward by the EU in TTIP, suggesting the two parties could have come to a conclusion there, though the significant expansion of this text in USMCA suggests the US has greater ambitions in this area. The US reasoning for this priority has never been adequately explained in public however. The US already has strong domestic consultation mechanisms in terms of the Administrative Procedures Act[44] but it does not seem like it is motivated by a sense that this provides other countries with an unfair advantage. In discussions, its concern rather seemed to be that large US companies were not allowed a fair say on regulations made in other countries, and that if this was allowed it would be more likely to lead to coherence between the US and other regulations.

By contrast there is no equivalent US text to that put forward by the EU on regulatory cooperation, which includes strong regulator involvement, supported by a public process. Although US trade negotiators were somewhat resistant to the ideas contained within this during talks, by 2016 they had started to engage seriously, and it is reasonable to suggest the text could have been concluded. The reasons for US reticence were not always clear but seemed to centre around its power to negotiate commitments that largely independent regulators would have to deliver. In this the guidance on International Regulatory Cooperation and the work of the Administrative Conference of the US (ACUS) was helpful in at least

[44] See United States Environmental Protection Agency, 'Summary of the Administrative Procedure Act' 5 USC §551 et seq (1946), www.epa.gov/laws-regulations/summary-administrative-procedure-act (last accessed 9 March 2020).

proving that it was not illegal for US regulators to cooperate in such a way.[45] The United States Trade Representative (USTR) also regularly convened meetings of regulator representatives during the TTIP process, and may have sought to persuade them over time to take commitments as required by the EU.[46]

The EU approach and text on regulatory cooperation was debated extensively by the Commission and Member States for three years, clearly also drawing on conversations involving EU and US negotiators, Member States and their domestic teams, NGOs with suspicion of regulatory cooperation[47] and academics.[48] The concerns to assuage public opinion are clear with the first two pages of the text expressing the rights to regulate and how this chapter can help good regulation, culminating with text stating: 'The provisions of this Chapter shall not oblige the Parties to achieve any particular regulatory outcome'.

The core of the EU's proposal comes in Article x.4, with the text:

> The Parties shall pursue and keep under periodic review ongoing regulatory cooperation and, in this context, shall periodically update each other on any developments related to their upcoming regulatory measures. They agree to collaborate bilaterally and at international level with a view to identifying opportunities for cooperation and, where appropriate, aim at achieving common or compatible regulatory measures. To this end, regulatory authorities of either side will have the opportunity to propose to the regulatory authorities of the other side particular steps to deepen existing cooperation or to start new cooperation and will receive timely feed-back on their proposals.

This then is very much envisaged as a regulator-to-regulator conversation.

Going further, the text then in x.4.2.b goes on to say 'each Party shall take account of approaches by the other party, when the other Party has adopted or is planning to adopt regulatory measures on the same or a related matter'. This then is a practical proposal for deepening regulatory alignment. Article x.5.1 describes some specific examples, before introducing in the next paragraph the possibility of proposals coming from stakeholders, to which a response must be given. The public element was partly a further way to assuage NGO concerns, but in large

[45] See Jonathan B Wiener and Alberto Alemanno, 'The Future of International Regulatory Cooperation: TTIP as a Learning Process Toward a Global Policy Laboratory' (2015) 78(4) *Duke University Law and Contemporary Problems Journal* 103, https://scholarship.law.duke.edu/cgi/viewcontent.cgi?article=4742&context=lcp (last accessed 9 March 2020).

[46] See Office of the United States Trade Representative, 'Mission of the USTR', https://ustr.gov/about-us/about-ustr (last accessed 9 March 2020). There was some dispute during TTIP talks about the extent to which USTR could bind regulators.

[47] See Corporate Europe Observatory, 'TTIP: Regulations Handcuffed' (28 January 2015), https://corporateeurope.org/en/international-trade/2015/01/ttip-regulations-handcuffed (last accessed 9 March 2020).

[48] Richard Parker and Alberto Alemanno, 'Towards Effective Regulatory Cooperation under TTIP: A Comparative Overview of the EU and US Legislative and Regulatory Systems' (Centre for European Policy Studies, 2014), www.ceps.eu/ceps-publications/towards-effective-regulatory-cooperation-under-ttip-comparative-overview-eu-and-us/ (last accessed 9 March 2020). This report was for example prepared with Commission support.

part was to address the feeling that regulators may need the impetus of outside pressure to reach agreements. Article x.6 then expands this public engagement to a Joint Annual Regulatory Cooperation Program, supported by domestic advisory groups.

There was considerable debate on the issue of sub-central coverage in TTIP, since EU Member States simultaneously sought access to regulatory agencies in heavy regulating states like California without giving this in return. In the end some loose text was proposed, but this may not have survived further negotiation. Concerns about the text in general meant that as per the GRP text, dispute settlement was not intended to apply.

The draft EU chapter concludes with a placeholder for institutional arrangements, including such matters as political accountability, coordination and transparency. These were never fully fleshed out, but do serve to demonstrate the seriousness with which the EU took this part of TTIP. For the EU and Member States the regulatory cooperation provisions were to be the way to tackle regulatory alignment, and the US approach of focusing on Good Regulatory Practices was never well understood in this context.

It should be finally noted that US negotiators did not share any text or papers with EU Member States or other stakeholders during the TTIP negotiating process. Unlike the EU, we therefore have little by way of a paper trail of documentation. This is in large part due to the US's own well established provisions of only sharing documentation with approved individuals,[49] but has also made comparative analysis difficult.

V. Conclusions

On the surface the approach taken by the EU and US to the issue of regulatory coherence in TTIP was completely different. For the US the most important element was to strengthen public consultation and transparency mechanisms, building on existing Technical Barriers to Trade disciplines. For the EU the important element was early stage dialogue between regulators, coupled with a degree of political, public and business engagement to help drive the process.

Yet we can see a large similarity underlying this approach, which is to project regulatory approaches and opportunities for their companies through trade agreements. For the EU, where the regulatory function is so bound in with the Commission, providing regulators with the opportunities to influence others to follow EU rules is a clear projection of external power. Similarly for a US regulatory environment shaped by quite rigid public consultation and engagement with powerful US companies, extending this system to other countries also demonstrates regulatory power.

[49] See https://ustr.gov/about-us/advisory-committee.

Another similarity is that for both the US and EU their approach in TTIP could be justified by being a 'good' global governance actor. For the US, demands on Good Regulatory Practice are in line with WTO Technical Barriers to Trade principles. For the EU similarly a dialogue between regulators is in line with those same principles. Certainly in the period 2013 to 2016 both were concerned about being seen to be protective of the global system.

Through careful design, both the EU and US could have gained from TTIP being completed with Good Regulatory Practices and Regulatory Coherence chapters. There would have been a balance between the two, and precedents for their own offensive interests, not to mention potentially putting in place the structure to finally deliver greater regulatory coherence between the EU and the US. It wasn't these chapters that caused TTIP to fail, since more fundamental problems lay in the areas of public procurement, where the US is relatively closed, and agriculture, where the EU has strong protectionist interests.

Yet as the timeline above indicates, both sides took a time to accept the offensive interests of the other. The Commission was not keen to make commitments on Good Regulatory Practice, just as the US did not really want to see a new transatlantic regulatory structure. The time and effort taken to get to a place where there was some common ground arguably detracted from difficult issues elsewhere. Both sides, however, may also argue that they were concerned about precedents with other countries.

TTIP talks were suspended in November 2016, yet regulatory initiatives continued. The agreement on mutual recognition of good manufacturing practice inspections in pharmaceuticals went fully live in 2019, and discussions continue on a broader agreement on mutual recognition of conformity assessments. These achievements were somewhat lower than originally envisaged under TTIP, but at least serves as some reward for the huge efforts put into the subject.

Considering the subsequent protectionist moves from President Trump, including against the EU, it is possible that TTIP was the high-point of a transatlantic attempt to control the global trade architecture, with both sharing the benefits. It was also a rare attempt to tackle the trade difficulties from divergent regulation. At some stage there is likely to be another effort to create an EU-US trade agreement, and when that happens the draft GRP and regulatory coherence chapters can at least serve as a starting point.

8

EU External Relations and International Law: Divergence on Questions of 'Territory'?

PAUL JAMES CARDWELL AND RAMSES A WESSEL

I. Introduction

The European Union is not a state. Yet, it is increasingly involved in territorial questions, either of its own or of other states. Notions of territory and jurisdiction are central in international law.[1] Indeed, state sovereignty implies that states are the sole rule makers and rule enforcers within a jurisdiction that is intrinsically linked to their physical territory. This is obviously different for international organisations,[2] also considering that during the process of drafting the Convention on the Law of Treaties, the International Law Commission (ILC) had difficulties in accepting the existence of a 'territory of the organization'.[3] While the EU will largely leave internal border disputes to be settled on the basis

[1] *cf* Cedric Ryngaert, *Jurisdiction in International Law* (Oxford University Press, 2015).

[2] *cf* Article 29 (on the 'Territorial scope of treaties') of the 1986 Vienna Convention essentially copied Article 29 of the 1969 Convention and provides: 'Unless a different intention appears from the treaty or is otherwise established, a treaty between one or more States and one or more international organizations is binding upon each State party in respect of its entire territory.' It is interesting to note that, while international agreements concluded by international organisations are included, the obligations are imposed on 'each State party' only.

[3] The 1982 ILC Commentary explains this choice in the following terms: 'Is it possible to imagine a parallel provision concerning the obligations of international organizations? Despite the somewhat loose references which are occasionally made to the "territory" of an international organization, we cannot speak in this case of "territory" in the strict sense of the word. However, since this is so and since account must nevertheless be taken of the variety of situations which the multiple functions of international organizations may involve, it seemed preferable to avoid a formula which was too rigid or too narrow. If the draft articles said that, in the case of an international organization which is a party to a treaty, the scope of application of the treaty extended to the entire territory of the States members of that organization, the draft would diverge from article 29 of the Vienna Convention by raising the question of the scope of application of a treaty, which is not expressly covered by that Convention.'

of international law,[4] territorial questions are increasingly important, not just in relation to the changing role of borders in its internal market, but also in the context of its role as a global actor. As a maturing legal system, the possibility of divergence from international law is thus pertinent.[5] In that context, the main question that this chapter explores is if and how the Court of Justice of the European Union (CJEU) has used international law in the adjudication of (incidental) territorial matters that have arisen in the course of interpreting agreements with third states.

The competences of the EU to make and enforce rules within a given 'territorial space' are undisputed.[6] These days we are witnessing an extension of that 'territorial space'. The increasing membership of the EU is the most obvious factor causing the territorial scope of the Union to change. Needless to say, a decrease in official members via the exit of the UK from the EU is an unprecedented situation, though less so when framed in terms of 'territory' rather than 'membership'.[7] But the 'global reach' of EU law,[8] and the extent to which external territories fall within that scope, is even more important and less definable by reference to physical territory. Citizenship, boundaries and jurisdiction are three interlocking elements that have strong relationships to 'territory'. Nonetheless, the EU is treaty-bound not only to respect, but to uphold international law:[9] an obligation which has come under increased scrutiny.[10] All of this leads to the conclusion that the special nature of the EU and the transfer of a number of competences from the Member States to that organisation, cause it to be more active in relation to territorial questions than 'regular' organisations. As the EU does not exist in isolation, but is very well connected to other areas and levels of international law, the EU cannot escape these questions.[11]

Therefore, rather than convergence as a process, we are looking primarily at divergence. Since EU law was, at the outset at least, a creation of international law then the starting point would be that on such fundamental questions as territory,

[4] See Case C-457/18 *Republic of Slovenia v Republic of Croatia* ECLI:EU:C:2020:65 in which the Court on 31 January 2020 held that the issue of geographical determination of borders between those two states is a matter of public international law.

[5] See the Introduction by Elaine Fahey to this volume.

[6] We leave aside the fact that there continue to exist territorial disputes between EU Member States, eg between the UK and Spain (Gibraltar), or Slovenia and Croatia.

[7] Greenland, though remaining part of the Kingdom of Denmark, left the EU in 1984. Further back still, former various territories *de facto* left the EEC/EU when gaining independence: most notably Algeria (previously a full part of France) in 1962.

[8] Elaine Fahey, *The Global Reach of EU Law* (Routledge, 2016). See also Anu Bradford, *The Brussels Effect: How the European Union Rules the World* (Oxford University Press, 2020).

[9] Article 3(5) Treaty on European Union (TEU).

[10] Jed Odermatt, 'The Court of Justice of the European Union: International or Domestic Court' (2014) 3 *Cambridge Journal of International and Comparative Law* 3, 696–718.

[11] See for instance the various contributions to Bart Van Vooren, Steven Blockmans and Jan Wouters (eds), *The EU's Role in Global Governance: The Legal Dimension* (Oxford University Press, 2013); as well as, in particular, Arts 3(5), 21 and 22 of the TEU. See more extensively: Ramses A Wessel, 'Flipping the Question: The Reception of EU Law in the International Legal Order' (2016) *Oxford*

definitions should be the same. However, in the context of the EU as a maturing legal system, the aim of the present chapter is to consider the extent of *divergence* between EU and international law. There are two strands to the chapter. First of all – using an *internal* perspective – it will examine the effects of EU norms and rules by looking through a 'territorial' lens and by considering the EU's own definition and understanding of territory in its legal order. Second – using an *external* perspective – it will specifically look at the response by one of the EU institutions, the CJEU, in cases where international territorial questions have arisen. These have generally arisen when the Court of Justice has been faced with the highly problematic matters of the territorial application of EU law and bilateral agreements with third states as indications. The continued prevalence of occupied (or at least disputed) territories around the globe has resulted in a line of case law before the Court which at times seems to force it into deciding matters which go beyond the role envisaged for it in the original Treaty. Though questions on territorial scope are some of the most politically-charged in international law, they often emerge through seemingly mundane and technical matters of trade. This part of the chapter explores the extent to which the Court, which was set up to deal with matters of EU law and not to resolve 'general' international law quandaries, has developed its own methods to grapple with such inherently 'political' and thorny questions. Although the Court is only one institution in the EU framework, its judgments reveal the legal position of the Union on an increasing number of territorial questions.

II. Internal EU Territorial Issues

A first step to assess divergence with international law is to map the various ways in which territorial questions come up within the European Union and to what extent the Union has understood the notion of territory. The present section will subsequently address various dimensions related to territory: nationality and citizenship, and jurisdiction and extra-territorial effects. First, however, we will briefly revisit how the EU treaties deal with questions of territory.

Yearbook of European Law; Ramses A Wessel, 'Studying International and European Law: Confronting Perspectives and Combining Interests' in Sacha Garben and Inge Govaere (eds), *The Interface between International and EU Law* (Hart Publishing, 2018). See further: Fahey (n 8); Dimitry Kochenov and Fabian Amtenbrink (eds), *The European Union's Shaping of the International Legal Order* (Cambridge University Press, 2013); Jed Odermatt, *The European Union as a Global Actor and its Impact on the International Legal Order*, PhD thesis (University of Leuven, 2016); Penelope Nevill, 'The European Union as a Source of Public International Law' (2013) *Hungarian Yearbook of International Law and European Law* 281–95 (Eleven International Publishing, 2014); Frank Hoffmeister, 'The Contribution of EU Practice to International Law' in Marise Cremona (ed), *Developments in EU External Relations Law* (Oxford University Press, 2008) 37–127. On the EU and other international organisations, see Ramses A Wessel and Jed Odermatt (eds), *Research Handbook on the European Union and International Organisations* (Edward Elgar Publishing, 2019).

A. Territorial References

The European Union has considered territorial questions from the outset and there are many references to 'territory' in the EU Treaties. Yet, most of these are related to the Member States' territories.[12] Article 52(2) of the Treaty on European Union (TEU) points to the territorial scope of the Treaties as specified in Article 355 of the Treaty on the Functioning of the European Union (TFEU), which in turn lists the overseas territories belonging to some of the Member States and the extent to which EU law does or does not apply.[13] While it is mainly in this context that references by the Court to the 'territory of the EU' may be found,[14] it has been claimed that 'it is clearly possible to speak of the emergence of the concept of Union territory, given the autonomous demarcation of the territorial application of EU law defined in the Treaties'.[15] Indeed, one may also find some hints at the possible existence of an 'EU territory' in the Treaties. Thus, Article 3(3) TEU refers to the Union's objective to 'promote economic, social and territorial cohesion, and solidarity among Member States'. At the same time 'It shall respect its rich cultural and linguistic diversity, and shall ensure that Europe's cultural heritage is safeguarded and enhanced.' References like these are meant to create unity while preserving diversity, and the objective of 'territorial cohesion' has merely been the driver behind the allocation of the so-called cohesion funds aimed at 'reducing disparities between the levels of development of the various regions and the backwardness of the least favoured regions'.[16] In a way, 'economic, social and territorial cohesion' intends to view the territories of the Member States as a whole, which is reinforced by the commitment to remove internal frontiers (for example, Article 3(2) TEU on the area of freedom, security and justice).

[12] See extensively as well as much more in detail on these provisions, Dimitry Kochenov, 'European Union Territory from a Legal Perspective: A Commentary on Articles 52 TEU, 355, 349, and 198–204 TFEU' in Manuel Kellerbauer, Marcus Klamert and Jonathan Tomkin (eds), *The EU Treaties and the Charter of Fundamental Rights – A Commentary* (Oxford University Press, 2019); also available as University of Groningen Faculty of Law Research Paper 2017-05; available at SSRN https://ssrn.com/abstract=2956011 (last accessed 13 March 2020).

[13] Two Declarations (43 and 60) are attached to the Treaty, both of which concern potential future changes to the status of French and Dutch territories.

[14] See for instance the frequent use of the term 'Community territory' in Case 177/95 *Ebony Maritime SA and Loten Navigation Co Ltd v Prefetto della Provincia di Brindisi and others* ECLI:EU:C:1997:89. Other cases in point may be Case C-34/09 *Gerardo Ruiz Zambrano v Office national de l'emploi* ECLI:EU:C:2011:124 and Case C-434/09 *Shirley McCarthy v Secretary of State for the Home Department* ECLI:EU:C:2011:277. *cf* Dimitry Kochenov, 'A Real European Citizenship; A New Jurisdiction Text; A Novel Chapter in the Development of the Union in Europe' (2011) 18 *Columbia Journal of European Law* 56.

[15] Kochenov (n 12).

[16] Art 174 TFEU.

Yet, the absence of a *genuine* EU territory – or at least an acceptance of the continued existence of state territories – is underlined by the Treaty on European Union:

> The Union shall respect the equality of Member States before the Treaties as well as their national identities, inherent in their fundamental structures, political and constitutional, inclusive of regional and local self-government. *It shall respect their essential State functions, including ensuring the territorial integrity of the State*, maintaining law and order and safeguarding national security. In particular, national security remains the sole responsibility of each Member State.[17]

At the same time, these Member State territories are to be defended on the basis of a *collective* security rule: 'If a Member State is the victim of armed aggression on its territory, the other Member States shall have towards it an obligation of aid and assistance by all the means in their power [...]'.[18]

Similarly, the EU's security and defence policy may be used in 'the fight against terrorism, including by supporting third countries in combating terrorism in their territories', and the so-called 'solidarity clause' calls upon both the Union and its Member States to 'act jointly in a spirit of solidarity if a Member State is the object of a terrorist attack or the victim of a natural or man-made disaster'.[19]

More clear notions of a possible 'EU territory' can be found when the 'territorial application' of the Treaties is concerned. First of all, the Treaties apply to the EU Member States (which are all mentioned by name).[20] This is further specified in relation to the so-called countries and territories overseas, which leads to an extension of the territorial scope of the EU.[21] This latter provision provides that EU law in principle, applies to Guadeloupe, French Guiana, Martinique, Mayotte, Réunion, Saint-Martin, the Azores, Madeira and the Canary Islands. For all other overseas countries and territories (including those of the UK, the Åland Islands, the Faeroe Islands, or the Netherlands's Antilles) specific rules are to be found in Art 355 and in particular in Annex II of the Treaty. That one could perhaps indeed see this as an 'upscaling' of 'European territory' is underlined by Art 198 TFEU:

> The Member States agree to associate with the Union the non-European countries and territories which have special relations with Denmark, France, the Netherlands and the United Kingdom. These countries and territories (hereinafter called the 'countries and territories') are listed in Annex II. The purpose of association shall be to promote the economic and social development of the countries and territories and to establish close economic relations between them and the Union as a whole.

This association brings the non-European countries and territories clearly within the reach of EU law and policies. They have a right to the same treatment as the

[17] Art 4(2) TEU. Emphasis added.
[18] Art 42(7) TEU.
[19] See Arts 43 TEU and 222 TFEU respectively.
[20] Art 52 TEU.
[21] Art 355 TFEU.

EU Member States, for instance in relation to trade and investment.[22] At the same time, the existence of overseas territories may have territorial implications under, for instance, the law of the sea, in particular where these territories may result in an additional economic exclusive zone (EEZ) to be used for fishing and possible mining activities. Thus, while Greenland is not part of the EU, its location does make it a place of interest to the EU in terms of debates on the future of the Arctic area.

In addition, EU 'territory' is also extended *within* Europe as 'The provisions of the Treaties shall apply to the European territories for whose external relations a Member State is responsible' (para 3). Although the geographic scope of the EU has undergone seven rounds of enlargement between 1973 and 2013 (with the additional incorporation of the former German Democratic Republic into the Federal Republic of Germany), it should be noted that the scope has also shrunk. Although the United Kingdom was the first Member State to leave the EU, Greenland left the Union in 1984 (though it remains part of the Kingdom of Denmark) and the independence of former colonies – such as Algeria from France – have changed the political map of Europe, and its frontiers.

Although we cannot see a divergence from international law approaches as such, the approach of the EU Treaties to 'territorial questions' is quite specific and largely deals with the (extended) territories of Member States and primarily in relation to the application of EU law. Despite the fact that the Treaties do not refer to 'EU territory' as such, some territorial concepts clearly hint in that direction, as will also be considered below.

B. European Citizenship

The 'idea' of EU territory comes back in the clear link between territory, nationality and citizenship. While in international law, *nationality* is related to statehood, *citizenship* can also be granted to others living on the territory of that state.[23] It is the latter notion that returns in EU law and 'European citizenship' is a key element of the process of European integration. Art 30(2) TFEU inter alia provides: 'Citizens of the Union shall enjoy the rights and be subject to the duties provided for in the Treaties. They shall have […] the right to move and reside freely within the territory of the Member States'. Indeed, the territory of *all* Member States; the rights of European citizens have largely been harmonised and European citizenship is frequently used by the CJEU to rule on extensive rights for individuals. Citizenship has thus become an essential element in the right to seek or accept

[22] Art 199 TFEU.

[23] *cf* Kay Hailbronner, 'Nationality in Public International Law and European Law' in Rainer Bauböck, *Acquisition and Loss of Nationality: Policies and Trends in 15 European States* (Amsterdam University Press, 2006).

jobs, to start a business or to provide cross-border services. At the same time, European citizenship entails

> the right to enjoy, *in the territory of a third country* in which the Member State of which they are nationals is not represented, the protection of the diplomatic and consular authorities of any Member State on the same conditions as the nationals of that State [...].[24]

Hence, outside the EU a European citizen may rely on the help of another EU Member State. Thus, the traditional national diplomatic and consular assistance is extended to an EU-wide system of protection of European citizens abroad. Links with international diplomatic and consular law become ever more visible. New developments in EU diplomacy indeed reveal at least an ambition of the EU to act on behalf of its Member States in situations of diplomatic protection and consular assistance. European Union Delegations can increasingly be compared to national Embassies.[25]

While currently the idea of 'supranational citizenship'[26] can most easily be seen as a dimension of the European integration process, it has been argued that the existence of the phenomenon could allow for a more general separation between states and (single) citizenship:

> This belonging to a polity, expressed in purely legal terms, is the real novelty of the European model, replicable in other geographical areas or global organizations – which could generate – one day – their one partial citizenships – and it opens the door to multiple and cumulative citizenships, not conflicting among each other, to communities partially overlapping.[27]

While 'European citizenship' could thus be seen as deviating from the clear link between statehood and nationality that can be found in public international law, it is at the same time clear that EU citizenship does not endow the EU with competences states would generally have under international law to protect their nationals. In international diplomatic and consular law, the notion of nationality remains crucial. New developments in EU diplomacy reveal at least an ambition of the EU to act on behalf of its Member States in situations of diplomatic protection and consular assistance. This clearly highlights the parallels between being a national of a state and a European citizen.[28] The Brexit debate in the UK has similarly highlighted how citizens perceive the addition of EU citizenship to

[24] Art 23 TFEU. Emphasis added.

[25] Pia Kerres and Ramses A Wessel, 'Apples and Oranges? Comparing the European Union Delegations to National Embassies' *CLEER Papers*, No 2, 2015.

[26] See Francesca Strumia, *Supranational Citizenship and the Challenge of Diversity: Immigrants, Citizens and Member States in the EU* (Brill| Nijhoff, 2013).

[27] Susanna Cafaro, 'Peculiarities of a Supranational Citizenship' (21 November 2016), available on www.linkedin.com/pulse/peculiarities-supranational-citizenship-susanna-cafaro (last accessed 13 March 2020).

[28] Ramses A Wessel, 'Can the European Union Replace its Member States in International Affairs? An International Law Perspective' in Inge Govaere, Erwan Lannon, Peter Van Elsuwege and Stanislas Adam (eds), *The European Union in the World: Essays in Honour of Marc Maresceau* (Martinus Nijhoff Publishers, 2013) 129–47; Ramses A Wessel and Bart Van Vooren, 'The EEAS' Diplomatic Dreams and the Reality of International and European Law' (2013) 9 *Journal of European Public Policy*, 1350–67.

national citizenship, and the intrinsic difficulties in retaining rights obtained by virtue of EU citizenship.[29]

Overall, the notion of 'European citizenship' does not seem to have led to changes in the international law notions on nationality and the rights states have in the protection of the rights of their nationals abroad.[30]

C. Jurisdiction and 'Extra-Territorial' Effects of EU Law

So-called 'extra-territorial effects' of EU law and their impact on international law receive more and more attention in EU legal scholarship.[31] As phrased by Joanne Scott:

> the EU makes frequent recourse to a mechanism that may be labelled 'territorial extension.' The practice of territorial extension enables the EU to govern activities that are not centered upon the territory of the EU and to shape the focus and content of third country and international law.[32]

This may also lead to jurisdictional questions, eg with respect to international law notions of the concept.[33]

While the EU rules are, obviously, primarily related to relations between the EU Member States, these rules often affect or influence other legal systems. While part of this is related to an intentional 'export' of norms (see our earlier references to the notion of the EU as a 'normative actor'), other effects flow from an adoption of norms of standards by other states to, for instance, allow access to the EU market. This is usually referred to as 'the global reach of EU law'.[34] As Fahey argues, this

[29] Willem Maas, 'EU Citizenship and Free Movement after Brexit' in Scott Greer and Janet Laible (eds), *Europe after Brexit* (Manchester University Press, forthcoming in 2020).

[30] In that context, Advocate General Maduro emphasised the principle of international law that 'questions of nationality are in principle within the reserved domain of States'. Case C-135/08 *Janko Rottman v Freistaat Bayern* ECLI:EU:C:2009:588.

[31] *cf* Joanne Scott, 'Extraterritoriality and Territorial Extension in EU Law' (2014) 62 *American Journal of Comparative Law*; Joanne Scott, 'The New EU Extra-Territoriality' (2014) 51 *Common Market Law Review* 1343; Bradford (n 8).

[32] Scott, 'Extraterritoriality and Territorial Extension', *ibid* at 89. In this paper, Scott is actually challenging the notion of 'extra-territoriality' as it is commonly used in the literature, and draws attention to 'territorial extension': 'a measure will be regarded as extraterritorial when it imposes obligations on persons who do not enjoy a relevant territorial connection with the regulating state. By contrast, a measure will be regarded as giving rise to territorial extension when its application depends upon the existence of a relevant territorial connection, but where the relevant regulatory determination will be shaped as a matter of law, by conduct or circumstances abroad' (*ibid* at 90). For the present contribution it suffices to note that both notions are relevant to underline the need to understand both international and EU law systematics.

[33] A case in point was formed by the *Ebony Martime* case, where the question arose of the compatibility of an EU Regulation on the enforcement of sanctions and the freedom of the high seas under international law. See *Ebony Maritime* (n 14).

[34] Fahey (n 8).

includes the effects of EU regulatory standards on, for instance, US rules in the realm of inter alia genetically modified foods, data privacy standards and chemical safety rules or even the transposition of EU environmental standards in some US states.[35] This is believed to stretch the EU's legal influence beyond its own territory, and could perhaps indeed be seen as an 'upscaling' of the EU's territorial jurisdiction. In the words of Fahey:

> Included in these theorisations is the view that the size and scale of the EU, as a market and as a polity, has generated what is understood here as 'rule-transfer'. It has entailed that the EU has adopted rules and standards that other polities and markets have in turn adopted, compelled to do so or acting out of sheer necessity.[36]

Debates on this issue are related to the question to what extent the EU can be a global normative actor. The brief – reflected in for instance Articles 3(5) and 21 TEU – is quite well known. At the same time questions of the extra-territoriality of the EU's own Charter of Fundamental Rights seem to have remained unsolved, since the territorial scope of the Charter is undefined. In fact, the issue of extra-territoriality of the Charter and the opposing views of Advocate General (AG) Mengozzi in *X and X v Belgium* (against the adoption of the extra-territoriality standard developed by the European Court of Human Rights (ECtHR) and in favour of an autonomous understanding of the territorial scope of the Charter) and the one of AG Wathelet (adopting the effective control standard developed by the ECtHR) shows the potential of divergence from the notion of human rights law 'jurisdiction'.[37]

Questions of 'extra-territoriality' indeed imply questions of jurisdiction. At least as far as enforcement is concerned, in international law, state jurisdiction is traditionally quite closely linked to territorial notions, and it has also been discussed by both the CJEU and the International Court of Justice (ICJ) as such.[38] In fact, jurisdiction can be seen as the exclusive competence of states to set and enforce the rules on its territory.[39] It is well-known that part of these

[35] Fahey (n 8) at 1.

[36] Fahey (n 8) at 1.

[37] Violeta Moreno-Lax and Cathryn Costello, 'The Extraterritorial Application of the Charter: From Territoriality to Facticity, the Effectiveness Model' in Steve Peers, Tamara K Hervey, Jeff Kenner and Angela Ward (eds), *Commentary on the EU Charter of Fundamental Rights* (Hart Publishing, 2014) 1657–83; Cedric Ryngaert, 'EU Trade Agreements and Human Rights: From Extraterritorial to Territorial Obligations' (2018) 20 *International Community Law Review* 374; Lorand Bartels, 'The EU's Human Rights Obligations in Relation to Policies with Extraterritorial Effects' (2015) 25 *European Journal of International Law* 1071–91.

[38] Jed Odermatt, 'The International Court of Justice and the Court of Justice of the European Union: Between Fragmentation and Universality of International Law' in Achilles Skordas (ed), *Research Handbook on the International Court of Justice* (Edward Elgar Publishing, forthcoming in 2020); also available as Jed Odermatt, 'The International Court of Justice and the Court of Justice of the European Union: Between Fragmentation and Universality of International Law'; *iCourts Working Paper Series* No 158, available at SSRN: https://ssrn.com/abstract=3369613 (last accessed 13 March 2020).

[39] See, much more extensively: Ryngaert (n 1).

jurisdictional competences has been transferred to the EU, both where the creation and the enforcement of norms is involved. Fahey has argued that the merger of sovereignty, territoriality and jurisdiction in a global world is an emerging matter for EU law.[40] In the case of enforcement, we do however see differences. Where enforcement of competition law is clearly in the hands of EU institutions (or national authorities acting as agents of the EU), enforcement of criminal law, for instance, is still left to the Member States.[41] Yet again territorial jurisdiction is stretched as, under certain conditions, Member State authorities may operate on the territory of other Member States.[42]

The question is to what extent these developments will push the jurisdiction back to a more controllable territory and in that sense to a closer convergence of EU law and traditional international law notions of jurisdiction. But in order to appreciate the full extent of the extra-territorial nature of EU law, it is also necessary to examine the specific implications of EU law when questions relating to the territories of third states come to light.

III. The CJEU and External Territorial Implications of EU Law

The above section aimed to provide insight into how questions of territory form part of, and have been defined in, the context of the EU's internal set up. Next to 'internal' questions of territory, the European Union's expanding activities as a global actor increasingly force it to be engaged in international territorial questions. These external territorial implications of EU law can arise in a number of ways. As the EU's competences have expanded, the EU finds itself dealing with 'newer' areas, such as migration from third countries and the interface with international law in both a general sense and in its more specific dimensions (eg protection of refugees). The closeness of relationships between the EU and third states, whether those in the European Economic Area (Norway, Iceland, Liechtenstein), complex bilateral agreements (Switzerland), neighbouring countries in Eastern Europe, the Mediterranean or, indeed, across the North Sea, brings into focus the uncertainty surrounding territorial scope. This section focuses on the capacity to make international agreements, ie when the EU enters into a contractual agreement with a third state and how this can lead to considerations of 'territory' to which the CJEU in particular has had to confront.

[40] Fahey (n 8) at 12.

[41] See for instance Art 88(3) TFEU: 'Any operational action by Europol must be carried out in liaison and in agreement with the authorities of the Member State or States whose territory is concerned. The application of coercive measures shall be the exclusive responsibility of the competent national authorities.'

[42] *cf* Art 89 TFEU.

The EU benefits from both express and implied competences to conclude international agreements. Express competences to conclude agreements are littered throughout the Treaty, and include: Article 8(2) TEU on agreements with neighbouring countries; Article 37 TEU on the Common Foreign and Security Policy (CFSP); Article 79(3) TFEU on readmission of third country nationals; Article 207 on common commercial policy; Article 212 TFEU on economic, financial and technological cooperation with third countries; and Article 216–219 TFEU on a general competence for international agreements. The *ERTA* doctrine[43] established long ago the principle of implied external competence when the EU benefits from internal competence.[44]

As such, there are estimated to be over 1,100 agreements concluded by the EU with almost all states around the world.[45] Almost inevitably, therefore, the EU and its power to make agreements is likely to be caught up in questions of application to territory. This is particularly the case since many territorial disputes, occupied territories and breakaway regions are found in Europe and its neighbourhood.[46] An agreement may cover the territorial scope of the provisions, but this is unlikely if the international consensus and the view of the third state on where frontiers lie do not align.

It is futile, however, to suggest that the EU is merely a technocratic body, with the Court of Justice merely applying rules to specific situations. The whole project of European integration, and its increasing focus on developing its role as an external actor in international affairs, means that these inevitably collide. The EU's considerable economic weight, the values it seeks to promote via its external (and internal) identities and its legal/contractual relations with third states mean the Court is not merely responding to disputes but doing something more. As Kontorovich has commented, 'the European Union is a self-consciously "normative power," channelling its economic policies to reflect substantive legal norms'.[47]

Where complex and multi-faceted questions relating to territory arise in international relations, political means are often deployed to find a compromise or middle ground. For example, neither the EU nor its Member States have official diplomatic relations with Taiwan: as such, the EU does not have a Delegation in Taipei but rather an 'Economic and Trade Office' which serves much the same function. Similarly, in recognition of the fact that not all EU Member States recognise the statehood of Kosovo, EU documentation relating to Kosovo (which is nevertheless recognised as a potential candidate for future EU

[43] Case 22/70 *Commission of the European Communities v Council of the European Communities (ERTA)* ECLI:EU:C:1971:32.

[44] See more extensively Ramses A Wessel and Joris Larik (eds), *EU External Relations Law: Text, Cases and Materials* (Hart Publishing, 2020) Ch 4.

[45] See EU Treaties database available at http://ec.europa.eu/world/agreements/default.home.do (last accessed 13 March 2020).

[46] Eugene Kontorovich, 'Economic Dealings with Occupied Territories' (2015) 53 *Columbia Journal of Transnational Law* 584, 588.

[47] *Ibid.*

membership) makes consistent references to United Nations Security Council (UNSC) Resolution 1244/1999 and the ICJ Opinion on the Kosovo declaration of independence.[48]

The Court of Justice has been faced with questions of territorial scope on a number of occasions. Courts are, of course, able to find means to 'fudge' all kinds of difficult matters, but the purpose of a court is to render a definitive decision, which makes the possibility of an inability to find a compromise on a significant territorial question pertinent. The Court therefore needs to tread carefully if it is to ensure that its decisions do not amount to an effective change in the relationship between the EU and its Member States and the third country/ies or territories in question. This can involve not in fact characterising the issue as one essentially relating to territory at all. For instance, *Anastasiou*[49] was a case concerning Cyprus, before it became an EU Member State, and its preferential trade agreement for goods. The Commission's policy on accepting certificates from Turkish Cypriot authorities was not consistent. When faced with a preliminary reference case concerning direct imports from northern Cyprus, the CJEU refused to recognise export certificates from authorities other than those belonging to the Republic of Cyprus (that is to say, those which bear the name 'Turkish Republic of Northern Cyprus' ('TRNC')) under the EC-Cyprus agreement. To do so would represent 'a denial of the very object and purpose of the system', ie of the agreement concluded by the (then) EC with the Government of Cyprus.[50] The Court did not engage with points made by Greece that recognition of certificates issued by TRNC would amount to a violation of Security Council resolutions calling upon all states not to recognise the entity.[51] However, it did emphasise, 'The existence of different practices among the Member States [that] creates uncertainty of a kind likely to undermine the existence of a common commercial policy and the performance by the Community of its obligations'.[52] Thus, this decision allowed the Court to adopt a cautious approach[53] to avoid the territorial dimension and the accompanying political elements by relying on the lack of recognition of the 'TRNC' rather than the reasons or justification for the non-recognition.[54]

[48] See, eg, Commission, '2019 Communication on EU Enlargement Policy: Kosovo* 2019 Report' COM(2019) 260 final (29 May 2019) available at https://ec.europa.eu/neighbourhood-enlargement/sites/near/files/20190529-kosovo-report.pdf (last accessed 13 March 2020).

[49] Case C-432/92 *Anastasiou (Pissouri) and Others* ECLI:EU:C:1994:277.

[50] *Ibid*, para 41.

[51] Panos Koutrakos, 'Legal Issues of EC-Cyprus Trade Relations' (2003) 52 *International and Comparative Law Quarterly* 2, 489–98.

[52] *Anastasiou (Pissouri)* (n 49) para 53.

[53] Marise Cremona, 'Case C-432/92, R. v. Minister of Agriculture, Fisheries and Food, ex parte S.P. Anastasiou (Pissouri) Ltd. and others, Judgment of 5 July 1994' (1996) 33 *Common Market Law Review* 1, 125–13.

[54] Stefan Talmon, 'The Cyprus Question before the European Court of Justice' (2001) 12 *European Journal of International Law* 4, 727–50.

In *Brita*, the Court was faced with a similar but more complex question than in *Anastasiou* of whether goods originating from the West Bank could be included within the EU's free trade agreement signed with the State of Israel[55] and benefit from the preferential treatment allowed for Israeli products in the EU. The EU also has an interim agreement with the Palestinian authority.[56] This was referred to the CJEU by the Hamburg *Finanzgericht* after Brita attempted to annul the customs duties which the German authorities said were owed, due to the products (listed as being from Israel) coming from the West Bank.[57]

AG Bot[58] and the Court of Justice were both of the view that the German Court should not allow the goods to benefit from the preferential treatment regime allowed under the agreement. However, their reasoning was rather different. AG Bot put great emphasis on the context of the Euro-Mediterranean partnership (of which the EU, Israel and Palestine are all part) and the question of how to be certain as to the 'real' origin of products. The Court of Justice, on the other hand, started its decision with reference to the Vienna Convention on the Law of Treaties 1969 and 'general international customary law'. It found that although there is a general level of trust required behind contracting parties, this does not prevent the Member State authorities from peering behind the verification of goods to ascertain their actual origin. Given that the Israeli authorities had not responded to clarification requests by the German authorities, the Court found that the latter could not simply make an 'elective determination' as to whether the goods should enter under the agreement or not. This would mean the national authorities unilaterally interpreting the scope of the agreement.

The Court in *Brita* was willing to refer to international law, but only so far. The AG explicitly referred to Security Council resolutions calling upon Israel to withdraw from the occupied territories for the purpose of determining the territorial scope of the Agreement.[59] However, the Court did not engage with this. Rather, it relied on the principle of the relative effect of treaties to interpret the agreement, which some commentators found unconvincing.[60] The Court underlined the importance of the respect for customary international law as a justification for its decision. The Court did not refer to the 'internal' position of the EU via the Commission's notice, but rather placed the emphasis on the 'locations which have

[55] Euro-Mediterranean Agreement Establishing an Association between the European Communities and their Member States, of the one Part, and the State of Israel, of the other part (2000) OJ L146.

[56] Euro-Mediterranean Interim Association Agreement on trade and cooperation between the European Community, of the one part, and the Palestine Liberation Organization (PLO) for the benefit of the Palestinian Authority of the West Bank and the Gaza Strip, of the other part, (1997) OJ L187.

[57] Case C-386/08 *Brita GmbH v Hauptzollamt Hamburg-Hafen* ECLI:EU:C:2010:91.

[58] Opinion of AG Bot, C-386/08 *Brita GmbH v Hauptzollamt Hamburg-Hafen* ECLI:EU:C:2009:674.

[59] *Ibid* paras 108–12.

[60] Enzo Cannizzaro, 'A Higher Law for Treaties?' in E Cannizzaro (ed), *The Law of Treaties Beyond the Vienna Convention* (Oxford University Press, 2011) 425, 432; Guy Harpaz and Eyal Rubinson, 'The Interface between Trade, Law and Politics and the Erosion of Normative Power Europe: Comment on *Brita*' (2010) 35 *European Law Review* 551, 562; Paul James Cardwell, 'Adjudicating on the Origin of Products from Israel and the West Bank: Brita GmbH v Hauptzollamt Hamburg-Hafen' (2011) 17 *European Public Law* 37, 45.

been placed under Israeli administration since 1967' as understood in international law. In a sense, therefore, international law came to the 'rescue' of the CJEU, even though the Vienna Convention does not formally bind the EU or all its Member States. It is hardly overstating the obvious that neither the German courts nor the CJEU would wish to be seen as defining the borders of Israel, but in this case the Court avoided adopting a unilateral European view on territory. Neither did the Court – unlike AG Bot – appear to fully use the content of the UNSC Resolutions to underline its position. Yet, interpreting this as a *divergence* from international law would be unfair. International law arguments do form the background of decisions like these and it is hard to find examples of a clear deviation of EU law.

Another case in point is the *Front Polisaro* saga. In December 2016, the Court of Justice[61] set aside a judgment of the General Court,[62] which had annulled a Council Decision on an agreement with Morocco for reciprocal liberalisation measures on agricultural products, in so far as it applied to the territory of Western Sahara. The Front Polisaro, a liberation movement in the Western Sahara, brought an action for annulment in the General Court via Article 263 TFEU. The contested decision was an agreement for an Exchange of Letters between the EU and Morocco on agricultural liberalisation measures amending and replacing protocols of the EU-Morocco Association Agreement. This differed from *Brita* because the EU has not concluded association agreement concerning products from Western Sahara with any other state.[63] The agreement referred only to the 'territory of the Kingdom of Morocco'. Front Polisaro brought an action based on 11 pleas in law, claiming that the decision approving the application of the agreement to Western Sahara was unlawful. The General Court dismissed the pleas, but nevertheless annulled the decision in so far as it approved the application to Western Sahara. The Court's decision was based on the failure of the Council to 'fulfil its obligation to examine all the elements of the case before the adoption of the contested decision' which related to the commitment to fundamental rights in the EU Charter, a reasoning noted as 'a somewhat surprising move'.[64]

Of interest here is the question posed by the General Court:

> whether there is an absolute prohibition against concluding an international agreement on behalf of the European Union which may be applied to a territory in fact controlled by a non-Member State, without the sovereignty of that State over that territory being recognised by the European Union and its Member States or, more generally, by all other States ('the disputed territory') and, where relevant, the existence of discretion of the EU institutions in that regard, the limits of that discretion and the conditions for its exercise.[65]

[61] Case C-104/16 *Council v Front Polisario* (2016) EU:C:2016:973 (Court of Justice).

[62] Case T-512/12 *Front Polisario v Council* (2015) ECLI:EU:T:2015:953 (General Court).

[63] *Front Polisario* (General Court), *ibid* para 97.

[64] Sandra Hummelbrunner and Anne-Carlijn Prickartz, 'It's not the Fish that Stinks! EU Trade Relations with Morocco under the Scrutiny of the General Court of the European Union' (2016) 32 *Utrecht Journal of International and European Law*, 19–40.

[65] *Front Polisario* (General Court) (n 62) para 117.

The Court responded in the negative, finding that there is no absolute prohibition on concluding an agreement with a third state which may be applied to a disputed territory.[66] Furthermore, there was a marked reluctance in this instance to defer to international law. This 'might partly be motivated by its reluctance to imply that the EU may have acted in violation of international law, which in turn could bring with it questions as to the EU's international responsibility'.[67]

The Council successfully appealed to the Court of Justice, which set aside the decision of the General Court. The Court noted in its decision that 'the Association Agreement did not include any interpretation clause or any other provision which would have the consequence of excluding that territory from its scope'.[68] Furthermore, the Court's view that the General Court found that the agreement also applies to the territory of Western Sahara was based, 'not on a finding of fact, but on a legal interpretation of that agreement made by the General Court on the basis of Article 31 of the Vienna Convention'.[69] The Court felt the General Court erred in law that the Western Sahara was tacitly included in the Association Agreement.[70]

For the purposes of the discussion here, the Court's analysis of 'territory' is worth citing in full:

> it thus follows from that rule [the customary rule codified in Article 29 of the Vienna Convention], placed in the context of the interpretation of Article 94 of the Association Agreement, that a treaty is generally binding on a State in the ordinary meaning to be given to the term 'territory', combined with the possessive adjective 'its' preceding it, in respect of the geographical space over which that State exercises the fullness of the powers granted to sovereign entities by international law, to the exclusion of any other territory, such as a territory likely to be under the sole jurisdiction or the sole international responsibility of that State.
>
> In that regard … it follows from international practice that, where a treaty is intended to apply not only to the territory of a State but also beyond that territory, that treaty expressly provides for it, whether it is a territory 'under [the] jurisdiction' of that State, … or in any territory 'for whose international relations [that State] is responsible.[71]

With this in mind, the Court appeared to back away from its view in *Brita*, where the consideration of the entry of goods under the separate agreement with the Palestinian Authority was a factor in the Court's reasoning. Here, the Court appeared to place less emphasis on assessing what the EU's commitments were towards a territory effectively controlled by a partner state, whilst at the same time reaffirming that it was upholding international law. The difficulty, as some have noted, is that it means in effect that the CJEU has de facto

[66] *Front Polisario* (General Court) (n 62) para 215.
[67] Hummelbrunner and Prickartz (n 64) at 40.
[68] *Front Polisario* (Court of Justice) (n 61) para 84.
[69] *Front Polisario* (Court of Justice) (n 61) para 81.
[70] *Front Polisario* (Court of Justice) (n 61) para 108.
[71] *Front Polisario* (Court of Justice) (n 61) paras 95–96.

allowed the EU to be complicit in 'over a decade long infringement of the right to self-determination'.[72]

The way in which the Court, somewhat selectively, applied international law in this case, has been criticised in the literature. As argued by Kassoti,

> … the Court's artificial and selective reliance on international law in *Front Polisario* adds a new dimension to the ever-burgeoning debate on the relationship between international and EU law. In the past, the Court has arguably shown a great deal of judicial recalcitrance towards international law and a tendency to guard its own identity and the autonomy of the EU legal order through its reluctance to engage with international law. However, the *Front Polisario* judgment manifests a different and more worrisome judicial strategy. While seemingly anchoring its findings in international law, the Court, in essence, showed here a great degree of willingness to stretch international rules on treaty interpretation to a breaking point in order to avoid addressing the political disinterest that the EU has demonstrated in relation to the situation in Western Sahara.[73]

Front Polisario was followed up by a similar case one year later. In *Western Sahara*,[74] the Court again had to assess the validity of an international agreement (the EU-Morocco Fisheries Partnership Agreement (FPA) and its 2013 Protocol) and the EU implementing acts. Again, the question concerned application of the agreement to the territory of and products originating in Western Sahara. In *Western Sahara*, the Court again extensively applied international law, also to determine the EU's own obligations. By accepting Morocco's sovereignty over the Western Saharan waters, the EU would, inter alia, accept Morocco's breach of the right to self-determination of Western Sahara (and thus, the EU might also be found responsible for that breach by way of complicity).[75] As in *Front Polisario*, a way out was found in arguing that 'Moroccan fishing zones' did not include Western Sahara territory; hence, the agreements did not, in the eyes of the Court, apply to any illegally occupied territory.

The issue of rules of origin relating to Israel returned to the Court of Justice following a preliminary reference from the French *Conseil d'Etat* in a decision

[72] Vivien Kube, 'The Polisario Case: Do EU Fundamental Rights Matter for EU Trade Policies?' (*EJIL:Talk*, 3 February 2017), available at www.ejiltalk.org/the-polisario-case-do-eu-fundamental-rights-matter-for-eu-trade-policies/ (last accessed 13 March 2020).

[73] Eva Kassoti, 'The *Council v. Front Polisario* Case: The Court of Justice's Selective Reliance on International Rules on Treaty Interpretation (Second Part)' (2017) 2 *European Papers* 23–42, 40.

[74] Case C-266/16 *Request for a preliminary ruling under Article 267 TFEU from the High Court of Justice (England & Wales), Queen's Bench Division (Administrative Court) (United Kingdom), made by decision of 27 April 2016, received at the Court on 13 May 2016, in the proceedings The Queen, on the application of: Western Sahara Campaign UK v Commissioners for Her Majesty's Revenue and Customs, Secretary of State for Environment, Food and Rural Affairs* EU:C:2018:118.

[75] But again the Court seems to have been selective in using international law arguments. See Eva Kassoti, 'The ECJ and the Art of Treaty Interpretation: Western Sahara Campaign UK' (2019) 56 *Common Market Law Review* 209.

delivered in November 2019.[76] AG Hogan, in his opinion of 13 June 2019, pointed to 'the need to make a clear distinction between products originating in the territory of Israel and those originating in the West Bank'[77] as the Court had decided in *Brita*. But the emphasis on Israeli settlement policy as being 'a manifest breach of international law'[78] is striking, alongside his reminder to the Court of the EU's Treaty-based commitment to the strict observance of international law.[79] The Grand Chamber of the Court decided that foodstuffs originating in a territory occupied by the State of Israel must bear not only the indication of that territory but also, where those foodstuffs come from a locality or a group of localities constituting an Israeli settlement within that territory, the indication of that provenance. In doing so, the Court considered the settlements to be 'in violation of the rules of general international humanitarian law'.[80] Whilst the rationale for doing so was the important aspect of consumer choice, the Court engaged in a more direct assessment of what constitutes a 'state' and 'territory' and explicitly referring to the ICJ and UNSC resolutions, which seem to have been welcomed by international lawyers.[81] In this case, although concerning the same geographical area, the law in question was different from *Brita*. But it does show that the Court was less inclined to avoid or ignore international law and on this basis, in a somewhat unlikely setting of ruling on consumer choices, convergence between EU and international appears to be a reality.

How the CJEU views 'territory' is a prism through which to understand the relationship between EU and international law. The very fact that in *Western Sahara*, the CJEU made the case to be one about territory is significant. The CJEU framed the issue to be one of territorial application of the agreements (and tied issues of standing to that question). It could have also framed the question of whether the EU policy had effects on the right to self-determination; whether it legally recognised an illegal situation, etc. However, in the Court's mind, it frames the issues in terms of territory in these cases.[82] If the view of commentators since *Kadi* is that the Court is 'much less open to international law',[83] then we can also expect that the Court uses the sources of international law and opinion as a means of justifying its normative choices. *Front Polisaro* and *Western Sahara* suggest

[76] Case C-363/18 *Organisation Juive Européenne, Vignoble Psagot Ltd v Ministre de l'Économie et des Finances* ECLI:EU:C:2019:954. See on this case also the Special Section – *What's in a Name? The Psagot Judgment and Questions of Labelling of Settlement Products*, edited by Eva Kassoti and Stefano Saluzzo (2019) 4 *European Papers* 3.

[77] Opinion of AG Hogan in Case C-363/18 *Organisation Juive Européenne, Vignoble Psagot Ltd v Ministre de l'Économie et des Finances* ECLI:EU:C:2019:494, para 57.

[78] *Ibid* para 55.

[79] *Ibid* para 58, citing Article 3(5) TEU.

[80] *Organisation Juive Européenne* (n 77) para 48.

[81] Joseph Weinzierl, 'An Unlikely Couple: Informed Consumer Choice in EU Law and the Middle East Conflict' (*Völkerrechtsblog*, 14 November 2019).

[82] We are grateful for discussions with Jed Odermatt on this point.

[83] Odermatt (n 10) at 697.

that the Court has also shifted somewhat from its post-*Brita* characterisation as adopting a 'dualist' approach to international law in the EU legal order. However, this does not make the CJEU particularly different from national courts, which are often required to rule on the effects of international law too. And as decisions demonstrate, both the quantity and quality of international law for the Court to draw on has increased dramatically.[84] By contrast, the recent *Organisation juive européenne* decision once again shows that it is difficult to generalise and that the Court continues to have in its cannon a number of approaches to questions of territory (including avoiding the discussion of territory completely) which leave it open to charges of inconsistency.[85]

IV. Conclusion

The very existence of the EU itself has posed a challenge to our understanding of what constitutes 'territory' and its association with citizenship, boundaries and jurisdiction. The fact that the Court is now increasingly faced with complex and politically sensitive questions relating to the territory of third states can be traced back to the Court's own assertion of the 'new legal order' of EU law back in *Van Gend en Loos*.[86] Had the Court not done so, then it may not have attracted the type of preliminary references, such as in *Brita* and *Organisation juive européenne*, that would have allowed it to develop the autonomous legal order concept of the EU. A doctrine by which the Court does not hear 'political' cases would in all likelihood not be helpful, since the very cases which it has been confronted with have been of a technical nature and relating to the physical import of goods. What remains open to the Court is often the possibility to find ways of avoiding answering questions head on which would have ramifications far beyond the confines of EU law. The cases above show where this technique has been deployed, but with the risk of inconsistency of practice that give much less direction to the other institutions as to how such questions should be treated in the law.

Therefore, an equally surprising point in considering the notion of 'territory' is that the focus of discussion is on the Court of Justice and not the other, 'executive'-led institutions. A view on what constitutes the territory of a third state would normally be expected to come from a government/executive branch.

[84] Christina Eckes, 'International Law as Law of the EU: The Role of the ECJ' (November 2010) in Enzo Cannizzaro, Paolo Palchetti and Ramses A Wessel (eds), *International Law as Law of the European Union* (Martinus Nijhoff Publishers, 2011) CLEER Working Paper 2010/6 17 available at SSRN https://ssrn.com/abstract=2096203 (last accessed 13 March 2020).

[85] Olia Kanevskaia Whitaker, 'EU Labelling Practices for Products Imported from Disputed Territories' (2019) TILEC Discussion Paper No 2019-15, available at <https://papers.ssrn.com/sol3/papers.cfm?abstract_id=3421419 (last accessed 13 March 2020).

[86] Case C-26/62 *Van Gend en Loos v Administratie der Belastingen* ECLI:EU:C:1963:1.

In the EU sense, it is even more stark that the Court has been left to give a ruling on an essential matter of foreign policy, since the CFSP is deliberately functioning on the basis of distinct rules and procedures – and with a more limited scope granted to the Court to oversee it.[87] The ability of the Court to impact on what the other institutions have in mind when dealing with territorial disputes may be limited[88] – but is dependent of course on the Court having the opportunity to do so. As per the case law above, these opportunities often arise from unlikely areas in relation to foreign policy, such as consumer choice.

It is difficult to see, however, how the Court could do anything other than a case-by-case resolution depending on the highly context-specific nature of the cases. It would be futile to suggest, for example, that the Court could spearhead a singular view of how EU agreements apply to third countries. But it is equally futile to suggest that the Court of Justice would be any more at ease with defining the borders of Israel than the national German court that referred the *Brita* dispute to it. In this respect, it seems that the Court's oscillation between asserting the autonomous legal order of the EU and examining the purpose of the agreements as well as their scope, to relying on a more deferential approach to international law, can be explained by its desire to find a normative solution to a technical problem.

In short, understanding the internal and external aspects of the EU through a prism of 'territory' is enlightening – both of the unsettled nature of the international system on seemingly basic questions as to what constitutes a 'territory' and also the EU's contribution to the legal order, which goes beyond what was originally intended as a role for the Court. Our short overview of internal and external dimensions of the way in which territorial questions are approached by the EU, not only underlines the 'specificities' of the EU as a non-state entity in a state-centred world, but also reveals the attempts by the Court and other institutions to find arguments within the realm of public international law. The tendency not to *create* divergence is fully in line with the well-known open attitude of the EU towards international law and its so-called '*Völkerrechtsfreundlichkeit*'.[89] The question is whether the further development of the Union as an international and diplomatic actor will not force the international legal system to accept a certain deviation.

[87] See Christophe Hillion and Ramses A Wessel, 'The Good, the Bad and the Ugly: Three Levels of Judicial Control over the CFSP' in Steven Blockmans and Panos Koutrakos (eds), *Research Handbook on the EU's Common Foreign and Security Policy* (Edward Elgar Publishing, 2018) and Paul James Cardwell, 'On Ring-Fencing the Common Foreign and Security Policy in the Legal Order of the European Union' (2013) 64 *Northern Ireland Legal Quarterly* 443–463.

[88] See, eg, the contributions to Marco Balboni and Giuliana Laschi (eds), *The European Union Approach towards Western Sahara* (Peter Lang, 2017).

[89] See on this discussion already Cannizzaro, Palchetti and Wessel (n 84).

9

The Global Compact on Migration: Convergence or Divergence with EU Policies?*

JUAN SANTOS VARA AND LAURA PASCUAL MATELLÁN

I. Introduction

The process that led to the adoption of the Global Compact for Safe, Orderly and Regular Migration (hereinafter, 'Global Compact') was initiated with the New York Declaration for Refugees and Migrants (hereinafter, 'Declaration'), adopted unanimously by the UN General Assembly Resolution on 19 September 2016.[1] Two processes of intergovernmental consultations and negotiations were launched, leading to the adoption of the Global Compact on Refugees and the Global Compact on Migration, respectively. The High Commissioner for Refugees was in charge for the negotiation of the Compact on Refugees. The UN Special Representative for International Migration, assisted by the International Organisation for Migration (IOM), was responsible for the development of the Global Compact on Migration. From the beginning, the Declaration was considered a step forward since the UN has not developed in the past a coherent framework within which states should frame their response to international migration.[2] The objective of the Declaration was to develop a framework for comprehensive international cooperation on migrants and human mobility. The Declaration acknowledged 'the important contribution made by migrants and migration to development in countries of origin, transit and destination, as well as the complex interrelationship between migration and development'.[3]

* This contribution has been written within the framework of the research project on 'The externalisation and informalisation of the EU migration, asylum and border management policies: new legal challenges' (EUMABEXT), funded by the Spanish Government (RTI2018-099097-B-I00).

[1] UN General Assembly, New York Declaration for Refugees and Migrants, Resolution A/71/L.1, 19 September 2016.

[2] E Guild and S Grant, 'What Role for the EU in the UN Negotiations on a Global Compact on Migration?' CEPS Research Report N° 2017/05, March 2017, p 2.

[3] NY Declaration Annex II, para 3.

The Global Compact on Migration was finalised in July 2018 and was formally adopted by 164 states at the Intergovernmental Conference of Marrakech that took place on 10–11 December 2018, and some days later it was endorsed by the UN General Assembly (UNGA) in its Resolution 73/195.[4] The Compact represents the first attempt at introducing a comprehensive framework on migration on a global level. The Global Compact on Migration establishes a range of principles, commitments and understandings among UN Member States regarding all dimensions of international migration. The Global Compact introduces a 'cooperative framework' on migration that 'upholds the sovereignty of States and their obligations under international law'.[5] The commitment to improve cooperation on international migration has to be based on a common understanding and shared responsibilities since no country can address the challenges of this global phenomenon on its own.[6]

The process that led to the adoption of the Global Compact on Migration put the emphasis on reaching political and practical compromises and not on developing a binding legal instrument. It seems that states were only willing to support the development of the Global Compact if the document would have a non-binding nature. However, the Global Compact may have a considerable impact on the field of international migration, despite not having binding effects.[7] There is no doubt that the Compact will facilitate international cooperation to manage future migration challenges. It is not excluded that the Compact could subsequently lead to the adoption of legal instruments on specific aspects of migration or some of the commitments included in the Global Compact might become binding in the form of customary international law.[8]

The aim of this chapter is to analyse the convergence or divergence between the Global Compact and EU migration policies and the implications arising from the internal division between Member States as regards the implementation process. First, the controversy about whether the Global Compact creates legal obligations will be examined. It will be shown that the lack of binding effects does not necessarily mean that a soft law instrument is irrelevant (section II). Second, the role played by the EU in the negotiation process that led to the adoption of the Global Compact will be explored (section III). Third, the breach of the unity in the international representation of the EU in the last months of the negotiation process will be analysed (section IV). Fourth, the last section will be devoted to the analysis

[4] UNGA Res 73/L.66.

[5] Global Compact (n 1) Preamble 7.

[6] Global Compact (n 1) Preamble 10 and 11.

[7] See TG Hansen, 'The Normative Impact of the Global Compact on Safe, Orderly and Regular Migration' in Elspeth Guild, Isobel Roele, Marion Panizzon, Thomas Gammeltoft-Hansen and Violeta Moreno-Lax (eds), *What is a Compact? Migrants' Rights and State Responsibilities Regarding the Design of the UN Global Compact for Safe, Orderly and Regular Migration* (Raoul Wallenberg Institute, 2017) 7.

[8] See Report of the Special Representative of the Secretary-General on Migration (Sutherland Report) Sutherland Report, UN Doc A/71/728 of 28 December 2016.

of the implications of the divergence among EU Member States as regards the implementation of the Global Compact.

II. The Legal Effects of the Global Compact

The Global Compact includes four parts introduced by a Preamble: a Vision and Guiding Principles; 23 objectives; a part on the implementation; and a follow-up and review. As regards the Vision and Guiding principles, 'the Compact is based on the international human rights law and upholds the principles of non-regression and non-discrimination. By implementing the Global Compact, we ensure effective respect, protection and fulfilment of the human rights of all migrants'. Each of the 23 objectives contain a commitment, followed by a set of actions, including policy instruments and best practices that are considered relevant to achieve safe, orderly and regular migration.[9] The Global Compact points out on several occasions that all of them must be carried out in accordance with the competences and will of states. The objectives are framed in a very broad language varying from the collection of accurate and disaggregated data (objective 1), enhancing the availability of pathways for regular migration (objective 5), to saving lives (objective 8) or using migration detention as a last resort (objective 13), to invest in skills development (objective 18) or facilitating safe and dignified return and readmission (objective 21). The objectives are just guidelines for states to ensure that migration happens in a safe, orderly and regular manner. However, there are many references in the Compact to the existing international human rights instruments that are applicable in the area of migration.[10] It has been held that

> the Compact represents a delicate balancing exercise between the protection of the rights of migrants and strong calls for effective returns, and addressing the drivers of migration, or, more or less, the interest of the global South, on the one hand and the global North, on the other.[11]

The Compact does not create the obligation for States to admit migrants nor the right to migrate to another country. On the contrary, one of the Compact's objectives is 'to cooperate in facilitating safe and dignified return and readmission' of migrants. The states of origin 'commit to ensure that our nationals are duly received and readmitted'.[12] The disinformation campaign across the EU that preceded the adoption of the Compact has led to a controversy about whether the document creates new legal obligations for the states signing it and, in particular, the right

[9] Global Compact (n 1) para 16.
[10] See Global Compact (n 1) para 1.
[11] J Wouters and E Wauters, 'The UN Global Impact for Safe, Orderly and Regular Migration: Some Reflections', Working Paper n° 210 – February 2019.
[12] Global Compact (n 1) objective 21, para 37.

to migration.[13] The decisive criteria to determine whether or not legal obligations arise from an international instrument are the intention of the parties. The International Court of Justice (ICJ) and the European Court of Justice (ECJ) have constantly held that the question of whether a text constitutes an international treaty does not depend on the form but on its content and the context in which the text was drawn up.[14] The analysis of the Compact leads to the conclusion that the intention of the participating states was not to bind themselves legally. Even though the Compact was elaborated as it was a treaty in a typical international conference, it was merely adopted at the Conference of Marrakech, and some days later it was endorsed by the UN General Assembly. As regards the content, the Global Compact emphasised in the Preamble that it establishes 'a non-legally binding, cooperative framework'. The Compact also 'reaffirms the sovereign right of states to determine their national migration policy and their prerogative to govern migration within the jurisdiction'.[15] In addition, there is no provision on the ratification of the instrument at national levels. It seems clearly that the intention of the parties was not to create legally binding obligations.

It is not completely excluded that an instrument that is not legally binding can lead to the creation of new rights and obligations in the future. The former UN Special Rapporteur on Migrants' Rights, Francois Crépeau, affirmed that the Global Compact can develop 'from a normative framework to a binding document' which occurred with the Universal Declaration of Human Rights.[16] However, from the vague language used in the Compact and the opposition by a group of relevant countries to it in the last phase of the adoption, it is not very likely to give rise to new rights and obligations in the future. The lack of binding effects does not necessarily mean that a soft law instrument is irrelevant.[17] Non-binding texts such as the Global Compact can be used as a guideline for the

[13] S Carrera, K Lannoo, M Stefan and L Vosyliūtė (2018a), 'Some EU Governments Leaving the UN Global Compact on Migration: A Contradiction in Terms?', CEPS Policy Insight nº 15, 2018; S Carrera and R Cortinovis, 'EU's Role in Implementing Global Compact on Refugees: Contained Mobility vs. International Protection', ReSOMA Discussion Brief/ CEPS nº 4, 2019; L Vosyliūtė, What is the EU's Role in Implementation of the Global Compact for Migration? No 2019-12, December 2019.

[14] See Opinion 1/75, EU:C:1975:145, p 1630, y 2/92, EU:C:1995:83, para 8; C-327/91 *France v Commission* EU:C:1994:305, para 27; *Aegean Sea Continental Shelf Case (Greece v Turkey), Jurisdiction of the Court*, ICJ Reports, 1978, p 39; *Delimitation and Territorial Questions between Qatar and Bahrein, Jurisdiction and Admissibility*, ICJ Reports, 1994, p 112, para 23.

[15] Global Compact (n 1) paras 7 and 15.

[16] See Report of the Special Representative of the Secretary-General on Migration, (Sutherland Report) UN Doc A/71/728 of 28 December 2016.

[17] Soft law is traditionally understood as non-legally binding norms that might have in practice legal relevance. See for instance A Peters, 'Soft Law as a New Mode of Governance' in U Diedrichs, W Reiners and W Wessels (eds), *The Dynamics of Change in EU Governance* (Edgar Elgar Publishing, 2011); L Senden, *Soft Law in European Community Law* (Hart Publishing, 2004); J Santos Vara, 'Soft International Agreements on Migration Cooperation with Third Countries: A Challenge to Democratic and Judicial Controls in the EU' in J Santos Vara, S Carrera and T Strik (eds), *Constitutionalising the External Dimensions of EU Migration Policies in Times of Crisis. Legality, Rule of Law and Fundamental Rights Reconsidered* (Edward Elgar Publishing, 2019); F Snyder, 'The Effectiveness of European Community Law: Institutions, Processes, Tools and Techniques' (1994) *Modern Law Review* 19–54.

interpretation of national law or can even replace legally binding commitments.[18] Also, the Global Compact could have legal effects if it is able to decisively influence the content of the legislation adopted by the EU legislature.[19] In conclusion, the negotiation of the Compact put the emphasis on reaching political and practical compromises. However, the Global Compact may have a considerable impact on the field of international migration, despite not having binding effects. There is no doubt that the Compact can facilitate international cooperation to manage future migration challenges.

III. The Role of the EU in the Elaboration of the Global Compact

It is not surprising that the EU and its Member States have actively participated in the elaboration of the Global Compact, working closely in order to ensure that EU interests were reflected in the final text. During the two years of intensive consultations and negotiations at UN level that preceded the adoption of the Compact, the EU representative addressed the conference on several occasions on behalf of the EU and its Member States and managed to present a common position. For instance, on 20 February 2018, the EU representative made a statement on the Global Compact Zero Draft.[20] He pointed out the need to further reflect in the final text the following issues: first, the distinction between regular and irregular migrants and, second, the states' responsibilities to readmit their own nationals. On another occasion, the EU called for the reinforcement of 'the principles of solidarity and shared responsibility in managing large movements of migrants'.[21] Also, the EU Member States presented sometimes individual contributions complementing the EU position. The EU and its Member States continuously emphasised during the negotiations that the final document should not be legally binding. It seems that the Union and its Member States presented a common position between November 2016 and May 2018.

In March 2018, when the negotiation process of the Compact was almost finished, Hungary expressed for the first time its opposition to the content of the Compact. Hungary argued that migration is an unfavourable and dangerous

[18] T Fajardo del Castillo, 'El Pacto Mundial por una Migración Segura y Regular: un instrumento de soft law para una gestión de la migración que respete los derechos humanos' (2019) 38 *Revista Electrónica de Estudios Internacionales* 12; M Gatti, 'EU States' Exit from the Global Compact on Migration: A Breach of Loyalty' (EU Immigration and Asylum Law and Policy, December 2018); A Peters, 'The Global Compact for Migration: To Sign or not to Sign? (EJIL:Talk, 21 November 2018).

[19] European Commission, Opinion of the Legal Service on 'The Legal Effects of the Adoption of Global Compact for Safe, Orderly and Regular Migration' (Brussels, 1 February 2019).

[20] On the Zero Draft, see Guild and Grant (n 2).

[21] EU Statement – United Nations Global Compact for Migration: General Statement on the Zero Draft (20 February 2018).

process, which caused serious security challenges in many regions of the world.[22] As a result of the fact that Hungary changed its position, the EU presented a statement on behalf of 27 Member States in May 2018.[23] It should be pointed out that all Member States supported the EU position until the finalisation of the text of the Global Compact, with the exception of Hungary in the last months. It could legitimately be concluded that 'significant internal coordination on the Global Compact did take place and there are indeed official documents proving the common position of the EU and its Member States'.[24] The Commission held in March 2018 that 'since 2016, the Union has been strongly and continuously engaged in the process of elaboration of the Global Compact for Migration, delivering EU coordinated statements through the EU delegations in the consultative and stocktaking phase'.[25]

Despite the engagement in the process of the elaboration of the Global Compact, several Member States decided not to support the final text of the document.[26] The Hungarian Government stated in October 2018 that the document is at odds with the interest to restore European Security.[27] The Austrian Government, holding in the second semester of 2018 the EU rotating Presidency, also left the Compact in October 2018 stating that migration is not and should not become a human right. The withdrawal of both countries was followed by similar declarations by the governments of Poland, Bulgaria and the Czech Republic. They made references to the principle of separating legal and illegal migration, the right to independently decide who they choose to accept and the damages to national interests. Also, the Compact was rejected by Slovakia and Latvia at the end of 2018. The Global Compact was also subject to intense political debates in other EU countries, such as Germany, Estonia, Croatia, the Netherlands, Slovenia and Belgium. The last country that decided not to support the Compact was Italy. The former Minister of Interior, Matteo Salvini, announced in November 2018 that Italy would not take part in the Marrakech Conference. In total, nine Member States did not attend the Marrakesh Conference and did not approve the

[22] Security First Proposals by Hungary to the UN's Global Compact on Migration, available at https://ensz-newyork.mfa.gov.hu/assets/91/89/30/afcddc20c5314d7d87fd4f3874e36932e7bb016f.pdf.

[23] GCM – 4th Round of Negotiations: In-depth Discussion on International Cooperation (15 May 2018), available at https://refugeesmigrants.un.org/sites/default/files/eu_proposal_on_international_cooperation.pdf.

[24] Gatti (n 18) 3.

[25] Proposal for a Council Decision authorising the Commission to approve, on behalf of the Union, the Global Compact for Safe, Orderly and Regular Migration in the area of immigration policy, COM(2018) 168 final, 21 March 2018.

[26] The United States quit the negotiation process of the Global Compact on 2 December 2017. The US Permanent Representative to the UN argued that 'our decisions on immigration policies must always be made by Americans and Americans alone. We will decide how best to control our borders and who will be allowed to enter our country. The global approach in the New York Declaration is simply not compatible with US sovereignty'.

[27] Hungarian Government, 'Hungary is Exiting the Adoption Process of the Global Compact for Migration' (Ministry of Foreign Affairs and Trade, 18 July 2018), available at www.kormany.hu/en/ministry-of-foreign-affairs-and-trade/news/hungary-is-exiting-the-adoption-process-of-the-global-compact-for-migration.

Global Compact: Austria, Bulgaria, the Czech Republic, Estonia, Hungary, Italy, Latvia, Poland and Slovakia. The vote of the EU Member States at the UN General Assembly revealed clearly the division at the EU internal level. Only five countries voted against the final text of the Global Compact at the General Assembly: the Czech Republic, Hungary, Poland, Israel and the United States. Five Member States abstained in the final vote: Austria, Bulgaria, Italy, Latvia and Romania. Slovakia is among the countries that did not attend the vote at the UN General Assembly.

There is no logical explanation for the internal division of the EU Member States in the final phase of the elaboration of the Global Compact. As it was pointed out above, the Member States and the EU Delegation to the UN were very active in ensuring that the content of the document was compatible with national and EU interests. Indeed, many of the priorities of the EU are reflected in the final text, such as cooperation in facilitating safe and dignified return and readmission.[28] As the Commission noted, the EU approach resulted in a 'draft of the Global Compact for Migration which largely reflects EU acquis and policy, and reflects the Union's objective to promote multilateral solutions to common problems, in particular in the framework of the United Nations'.[29] The New York Declaration of 2016 already contained the main elements of the Global Compact that were later criticised by a group of EU Member States. Jean Claude Juncker declared that 'those countries that decided they are leaving the UN Migration Compact, had they read it, they would not have done it'.[30] The confusion and disinformation about migration driven by populist and anti-immigration parties led the reversal of some EU Member States.[31] Even the Opinion of Commission's Legal Service on the legal effects of the adoption of the Global Compact was subjected to a disinformation campaign.[32]

It seems that the European populist parties did not oppose specific elements of the document, but they rejected the Global Compact as a whole.[33] They consider migration as a threat or danger to their countries. The EU Member States that opposed the adoption of the Compact were against one the main objectives of the document which is 'making migration work for all'.[34] As the Special Representative for International Migration, Louise Arbour stated, the Compact cannot be considered an infringement on State sovereignty, because 'it is not legally binding, it is a framework for cooperation'.[35]

[28] Global Compact (n 1) objective 21.
[29] Proposal for a Council Decision (n 25).
[30] Georgi Gotev, 'Six EU Countries – and Counting – Back Out From the Global Migration Pact (*Euroactiv*, 12 November 2018).
[31] Carrera et al (n 13).
[32] See Vosyliūtė (n 13).
[33] Gatti (n 18) 6.
[34] Global Compact (n 1) para 5.
[35] Francois Murphy, 'Austria to Shun Global Migration Pact, Fearing Creep in Human Rights' (*Reuters*, 31 October 2018).

IV. The Breach of the Unity in the International Representation of the EU

The opposition of a group of Member States to the adoption of the Global Compact negatively affects the unity in the international representation of the EU and encroaches upon the duty of sincere cooperation.[36] After two years of internal consultations and international negotiations, their behaviour is not coherent. As it has been pointed out, 'one could expect EU Member States to approve the Compact, or, at least, to disagree only with those aspects of the Compact that had not been discussed at the EU level', but not rejecting the Global Compact as a whole.[37] The fact that three EU Member States opposed the Compact in contradiction to the EU official position and five abstained, may constitute a violation of the duty of sincere cooperation, which entails that Member States are subject to duties of action and abstention.[38] These duties of action and abstention are especially important in matters falling within both the scope of EU competences and Member States' competences as is the case of the Compact.[39] The Compact covers a broad range of issues that are shared competence between the EU and its Member States: legal pathways for migration, prevention and fight against human trafficking and migrant smuggling, return and readmission border management, among others. The duty of sincere cooperation was very relevant in the context of the adoption of the Global Compact, since the EU was not able to formally adopt the document. According to the Modalities for Intergovernmental Negotiations of the Global Compact, only states could approve the Compact at the Marrakesh Conference.[40] In addition, the Compact was approved by the UN General Assembly, where the EU is merely an observer.[41]

In my opinion, the Compact should have been negotiated by the Commission on behalf of the EU on the basis of a negotiation mandate approved by the Council. The Global Compact largely reflects EU acquis and policies. However, the negotiation process of the Compact was led by the European External Action Service (EEAS) leaving aside the Commission. In the *Swiss Memorandum* case, the Court argued that it cannot be considered that the signing of a non-binding agreement is an act of external representation under Article 17 of the Treaty on European

[36] See P Melin, 'The Global Compact for Migration: Lessons for the Unity of EU Representation' (2019) 2 *European Journal of Migration and Law* 194–214.

[37] Gatti (n 18) 6.

[38] *Commission v Kingdom of Sweden*, ECLI:EU:C:2010:203, Judgment of the Court (Grand Chamber) of 20 April 2010, paras 73 and 103.

[39] See P García Andrade, 'External Competence and Representation of the EU and its Member States in the Area of Migration and Asylum' (EU Immigration and Asylum Law and Policy, 18 January 2018); European Commission (n 19).

[40] UN General Assembly, 'Modalities for the Intergovernmental Conference to Adopt the Global Compact for Safe, Orderly and Regular Migration', A/72/L.67, 31 August 2018.

[41] UN General Assembly, 'Participation of the European Union in the Work of the United Nations', Resolution n° 65/276, 10 May 2001.

Union, which cannot be adopted in the absence of the Council's prior approval.[42] From the principle of institutional balance enshrined in the Treaties, the Court held that the 'signature of a non-binding agreement entails the assessment by the Union of whether the agreement still reflects its interest, as defined by the Council in particular in the decision to open negotiations on the conclusion of the agreement'.[43] The institutional balance enshrined in the Treaties should have been respected despite the fact that the Global Compact is deprived of legal binding force.

Due to its marginalisation during the negotiation process of the Compact, the Commission tried at a late stage to approve the Global Compact on behalf of the Union and requested the Council to give such authorisation based on the competences in the area of migration (Art 79 of the Treaty on the Functioning of the European Union (TFEU)) and in the area of development cooperation (Article 209 TFEU). The Commission stated that the Global Compact reflects the Union's objective to promote multilateral solutions to common problems, in particular in the framework of the United Nations.[44] The Commission argued that the Compact would contribute to the EU's commitment to achieve the Sustainable Development Goals agreed at UN level. However, the strategy of the Commission to represent the EU and its Member States at the end of the process did not succeed. The controversies surrounding the adoption of the Global Compact led the Member States not to approve the Commission's request for authorisation to approve the Global Compact, and the proposal was later withdrawn by the Commission. In theory, the Commission could have brought an infringement procedure before the Court of Justice to sanction the infringement of the duty of loyalty. If the Council had adopted the Commission's request for authorisation to approve the Global Compact, it would have been much easier to sanction the EU Member States that acted in contradiction to the EU official position.[45] Since the Council did not approve the Commission's proposal and the Global Compact goes beyond EU competences, the declaration by the Court that a group of Member States infringed the principle of sincere cooperation would not have any effects in practice. Probably, the Commission preferred to avoid the intervention of the Court in a much politicised topic, such as the Global Compact.

The opposition to the Compact by a group of EU Member States not only violated the principle of unity in the international representation of the Union, but may also hamper the EU cooperation with third countries in the field of migration.

[42] Case C-660/13 *Council v Commission* (*Swiss MoU*), ECLI:EU:C:2016:616 paras 30 and 38. See P García Andrade, 'The Role of the European Parliament in the Adoption of Non-Legally Binding Agreements with Third Countries' in J Santos Vara and SR Sánchez-Tabernero (eds), *The Democratization of EU International Relations Through EU Law* (Routledge, 2018) 115–31; Santos Vara (n 17); T Verellen, 'On Conferral, Institutional Balance and Non-binding International Agreements: The *Swiss MoU* Case' (2016) 1 European Papers (*European Forum*, *Insight*, 10 October 2016) 1225–33.

[43] *Swiss MoU*, *ibid* para 42.

[44] Proposal for a Council Decision (n 25).

[45] Gatti (n 18).

The cooperation between the Member States themselves as well as between the Member States and the Union is crucial in order to involve third countries in the management of migration. As the Commission argued in its draft proposal for a Council Decision authorising the Commission to approve the Compact,

> over the past years, the Union has built a comprehensive long-term strategy on migration covering all aspects of this phenomenon (…). This strategy is built on partnership and close cooperation with partner countries and organisations such as the African Union, the United Nations and its Agencies.[46]

The reputation and credibility of the EU on the international stage has been clearly endangered in the area of migration. It has even been argued that the opposition to the Compact by a group of EU Member States means that they are questioning internationally agreed human rights and international labour standards and EU legal principles, such as non-discrimination, equal solidarity and respect for fundamental rights.[47]

V. The Implications of the Divergence among EU Member States as Regards the Global Compact

The Global Compact on Migration reflects several elements of the EU migration policy. This outcome is not surprising since the EU and its Member States have supported the Global Compact and have substantially contributed to its development. The EU and its Member States demonstrated in the past a great degree of convergence in the external dimension of migration.[48] The difficulties surrounding the conclusion of readmission agreements have led the EU and its Member States to look for practical arrangements in the management of migration with third countries.[49] The EU has adopted several policy initiatives, including mobility partnerships, common agendas on migration and mobility, compacts, migration dialogues and statements. A common trait of these instruments is that they have an increasing relevance in practice in governing EU migration cooperation with third countries. Mobility partnerships encompass a broad range of instruments offered by the EU and some Member States to a third country including visa facilitation, projects and actions on mobility, legal migration and development in exchange for commitments on border control and readmission.[50] Mobility partnerships are conceived as flexible instruments that intend to address both the EU's interests and the partner countries' needs in the management of migration.

[46] Proposal for a Council Decision (n 25).
[47] Vosyliūtė (n 13) 9.
[48] Gatti (n 18).
[49] Santos Vara (n 17).
[50] See European Commission, 'Communication on circular migration and mobility partnerships between the European Union and third countries' COM(2007) 248 final.

However, the content of the mobility partnerships is clearly determined by the interests of the former, giving priority to the fight against irregular migration over legal migration.[51] The adoption of the Migration Partnership Framework in 2016 represents a key step in the process of informalisation of EU external migration policy, in particular in the area of readmission.[52] The objective of the Migration Partnership Framework is to develop 'win-win' relationships with the EU's partners to tackle the shared challenges of migration and development.[53] There are other recent developments that underline the unity of the EU and its Members States on the external dimension of migration. The Joint Way Forward on migration issues between Afghanistan and the EU aims to step up cooperation between the EU and Afghanistan on addressing and preventing irregular migration, and on return of irregular migrants.[54] The EU Turkey Statement of 2016 is the most well-known example of convergence between the EU and its Member States in the area of migration.

The Compact emphasises that cooperation on return and readmission constitutes an important element of international cooperation on migration. The return of migrants who do not have the legal right to stay on another state's territory should take place 'in full respect for the human right to return to one's country and the obligation of States to readmit their own nationals'.[55] Any type of return, whether voluntary or otherwise, must be consistent with international human rights law and, in particular, the principle of *non-refoulement*. In order to reach this objective, the UN Member States commit to 'develop and implement bilateral, regional and multilateral cooperation framework and agreements, including readmission agreements'.[56] The EU and its Member States strongly advocated for the inclusion of the obligation of states 'to take back their own nationals without any conditions and actively cooperate to facilitate returns and readmission'.[57] As a result of the opposition of a group of EU Member States to the Global Compact, it may happen that the EU may confront more difficulties in the future when trying to get third countries involved in the adoption of formal or informal readmission agreements.

The Global Compact also refers to the need to reduce 'the incidence and negative impact of irregular migration through international cooperation and a

[51] M Cremona, 'Circular Migration: A Legal Perspective' (2008) *CARIM Analytic and Synthetic Notes 2008/30*, 7.

[52] European Commission, 'Communication on establishing a new Partnership Framework with third countries under the European Agenda on Migration' COM(2016) 385 final.

[53] See C Bauloz, 'The EU Migration Partnership Framework: An External Solution to the Crisis?' (*EU Migration and Asylum Law blog*, 31 January 2017).

[54] See European Commission, European External Action Service, 'Joint Way Forward on Migration Issues between Afghanistan and the EU' (Kabul, 2 October 2016) <https://eeas.europa.eu/sites/eeas/files/eu_afghanistan_joint_way_forward_on_migration_issues.pdf.

[55] Global Compact (n 1) objective 21.

[56] Global Compact (n 1) objective 21 (a).

[57] EU Statement (n 21).

combination of measures put forward in this Global Compact'. The EU has insisted through the negotiation process of the Compact on the need to distinguish between regular and irregular migrants.[58] It has been stated that 'the EU's focus on the "negative implications" of irregular migration feeds into the discourse which criminalises and dehumanises migrants with irregular status'.[59] The influence of the EU on making reference to the negative impact of irregular migration does not mean that the Compact condones the repressive policies adopted by some EU Member States towards migrants.

Finally, it should be analysed if the policies and operational activities developed by the EU, in particular in the external dimension of migration, are fully compatible with the objectives of the Compact. One of the more relevant objectives of the Compact is to expand the possibilities for legal migration. According to objective 5, states commit 'to enhance availability and flexibility of pathways for regular migration'. It must be acknowledged that progress in the area of legal migration since the so-called refugee crisis has been very limited.[60] The EU still lacks a coherent and well developed policy in the area of legal migration. It has been stated that 'the cumulative effects of EU Visa policies, bi-lateral agreements, and qualification recognition procedures still make regular migration into the EU very challenging', even for highly qualified migrants.[61] The aim to facilitate safe, orderly and regular migration and mobility of people includes the creation and expansion of safe, regular pathways for migration. The EU and its Member States are still far away from establishing a comprehensive migration policy that covers all stages and addresses the root causes of migration and open regular pathways for migration, among other issues.

The EU and its Member States have resorted very often to the externalisation of migration policies with the aim to prevent the access of irregular migrants and persons in need of international protection to the territory of the Member States. The externalisation in the management of migration prioritises the prevention of migrants reaching the territory of the Member States over the protection of human rights.[62] As a result of the transfer of responsibilities to third countries in the management of migration, migrants and persons in need of international protection are often obliged to stay in the territory of third countries with a questionable

[58] EU Statement (n 21).

[59] E Guild and KT Weatherhead, 'Tensions as the EU Negotiates the Global Compact for Safe, Orderly and Regular Migration' (2018) *EU Immigration and Asylum Law and Policy*.

[60] S Carrera, *An Appraisal of the European Commission of Crisis: Has the Juncker Commission Delivered a New Start for EU Justice and Home Affairs?* (CEPS Paperbacks, 21 January 2019).

[61] Vosyliūtė (n 13).

[62] See Parliamentary Assembly of the Council of Europe, 'Human Rights Impact of the "External Dimension" of European Union Asylum and Migration Policy: Out of Sight, out of Rights?', Doc 14575, 13 June 2018; V Guiraudon, 'Before the EU Border: Remote Control of the Huddle Masses' in K Groenendijk, E Guild and P Minderhoud (eds), *In Search of Europe's Borders* (Kluwer Law International, 2003) 191–214; JA Gonzalez Vega, '*Non-refoulement* at Risk? Asylum's Disconnection Mechanisms in Recent EU Practice' in Santos Vara, Carrera and Strik (eds) (n 17); V Mitsilegas, 'Extraterritorial Immigration Control, Preventive Justice and the Rule of Law in Turbulent Times: Lessons from the

human rights record. The so-called refugee crisis has led the EU and its Member States to intensify the externalisation in the management of migration. In the current political context, priority is given to reduce the influx of migrants arriving to the Southern Mediterranean countries. There is a clear tension between the externalisation of EU migration policies and some of the objectives of the Global Compact, in particular with objective 11 (manage borders in an integrated, secure and coordinated manner), objective 13 (use immigration detention only as a measure of last resort and work towards alternatives) and objective 23 (strengthen international cooperation and global partnerships for safe, orderly and regular migration).

VI. Concluding Remarks

The Global Compact on migration does not entail any restriction of national sovereignty. It is not an international agreement and will therefore have no legal binding effect on national legal systems and neither do obligations which arise from it. However, the above analysis shows that the lack of binding effects does not necessarily mean that the Global Compact is irrelevant. It can be used as a guideline for the interpretation of national law or could decisively influence the content of the legislation adopted by the UN Member States. Apart from it, the Compact could facilitate international cooperation to manage migration challenges in the future. The signatory states agreed on a series of mechanisms for implementation. Governments will exchange and share progress achieved at the International Migration Review Forum, a platform to be held every four years as of 2022.

Throughout the negotiation process, the EEAS regularly informed the UN Working Party (CONUM) instead of fully involved other working groups such as the High-Level Working Group on Asylum and Migration (HLWG) and the Commission. The analysis of the role played by the EU in the negotiation process of the Global Compact reveals that this approach was not correct. The Compact should have been negotiated by the Commission on behalf of the EU on the basis of a negotiation mandate approved by the Council. It has been rightly pointed out that

> the EU will have to do a good deal of critical introspection and soul-searching in light of the three-split vote of its membership at the UNGA in December 2018. All of this has the potential to complicate the implementation process and undermine cooperation within the EU.[63]

Since nine Member States did not attend the Marrakesh Conference and did not approve the Global Compact, it is not clear what role the EU should play in the

Anti-Smuggling Crusade' in Santos Vara, Carrera and Strik (eds) (n 17); J Ripjma, 'External Migration and Asylum Management: Accountability for Executive Action Outside EU-Territory' (2017) *European Papers: A Journal on Law and Integration* 2, 2, 1.

[63] Wouters and Wauters (n 11) 16.

implementation process. The level of support for their implementation differs inside the EU.[64] The division between the EU Member States raises the question of whether the EU and, in particular, the Commission and the working groups of the Council on UN and migration issues should play an active role in coordinating the implementation of the Global Compact. It has been argued that it would be more useful to use informal settings such as gathering government representatives, or using platforms such as the European Migration Network or the European Return and Reintegration Network to discuss specific issues.[65] These platforms could facilitate a more coherent implementation across EU Member States and avoid clashes between them.

The Commission and the European Parliament expressed an interest in supporting the implementation during the negotiation process of the Global Compact. However, under the Romanian and Finish Presidencies of the Council in 2019, the implementation of the Compact has not progressed at EU level. This is unlikely to change in 2020 under the Croatian Presidency because of the remaining tensions between Member States as regards the Global Compact and, in general, the future of EU migration and asylum policies. The controversies surrounding the adoption of the Global Compact in the last months of 2018 and the lack of consensus among them have probably led EU Member States not to discuss it at EU level, to avoid re-opening Pandora's Box. In other words, the EU institutions and the Member States have opted to remain silent as regards the implementation process at EU level. The risk of this silence is the potential lack of coherence in the implementation of the Compact among the EU Member States. A more active engagement by the EU in the implementation of the Global Compact would contribute to the clear assertion that the EU is a relevant player on migration on an international level. The New Pact on Migration and Asylum that will be presented by the Commission in the first months of 2020 offers a unique opportunity for finding common ground on migration and creating a comprehensive long-term strategy for the implementation of the Global Compact.

[64] See European Council on Refugees and Exiles and Platform for International Cooperation on Undocumented Migrants, 'Implementing the Global Compact on Refugees and the Global Compact on Safe, Regular and Orderly Migration – What Role for the EU?' (6 February 2019).

[65] N Cascone, 'Implementing the Global Migration Compact in EU Member States: A Long and Winding Road?' (*ECDPM blog*, 12 September 2019), https://ecdpm.org/talking-points/implementing-global-migration-compact-eu-member-states/.

10

Convergence and Divergence of the Principle of Solidarity

MAGDALENA FOROWICZ

I. Introduction

The past few years have been marked by the rapid arrival of foreigners crossing international borders to seek safety from war and other threats to their rights. This mass influx of migrants and asylum-seekers rarely occurred in the past and the receiving States were largely unprepared. The major factor behind this movement was the state of origin's inability or unwillingness to protect its own population. Further, the maintenance and restoration of law and order in the country of origin was uncertain. As part of the failing Dublin System,[1] the EU Member States found themselves in a situation where stemming the flow of refugees without one another's help would be very difficult. Many governments have raised needs for external assistance but have underscored the fact that their needs have gone unsatisfied. Efforts to undertake actions and initiatives to cooperate in the past have been launched but they have been usually met with low commitment in practice. Such efforts were largely based on overseas resettlement schemes, which arranged for further emigration into safe third countries, externalising the problem.

A momentum may have been reached where international consensus to further strengthen international cooperation measures in times of mass movement of migrants is no longer an option. While there is much opposition from various countries against solidarity measures, there is a strong appeal from different circles to increase efforts in helping asylum-seekers in safer countries. With multiplying armed conflicts, natural disasters and other humanitarian emergencies, political consensus may be sufficiently ripe to step up the measures used thus far and to rely on more drastic measures and assistance. This situation is further

[1] The Dublin System was established by the Dublin Regulation, which provides criteria and mechanisms for determining which EU Member State is responsible for examining an asylum application. While the rules aim to ensure quick access to asylum procedure and the examination of an application by a single Member State, they were not designed to ensure a fair sharing of responsibility for asylum applications across the EU.

compounded in Europe by the mounting dissatisfaction with the inadequacies of the Dublin System. The malfunctioning of EU law and politics became apparent at the international level as the migration crisis unfolded. Due to deeply entrenched inadequacies of the Dublin System, the EU and individual Member States were forced to reach out for new solutions. The measures proposed and/or adopted as part of the crisis broke new ground, both at the EU and at the international levels.

The aim of this chapter is to evaluate whether EU and International law converge in the area of solidarity measures and contribute to the development of the principle of solidarity. In section II, the chapter reviews the development of the principle of solidarity in international law and evaluates how it has been implemented as part of the newly concluded Global Compact on Refugees. In section III, this contribution evaluates the evolution of the principle of solidarity and EU law and then reviews how it was implemented as part of the EU's response to the recent crisis. In section IV, the chapter compares the findings of the previous sections with the aim is to assess whether there is convergence between the international and EU levels.

II. The Principle of Solidarity

A. International Refugee Law

i. Legal Foundations and Doctrinal Interpretations

The meaning of the principle of solidarity in international law is ambiguous. The concept is scarcely mentioned in any significant international treaty and is missing from statements articulating the general practice of States accepted as law – custom.[2] It has been viewed as a 'value-driven principle'[3] with 'a strong ethical underpinning'.[4] Legal scholarship tried to pin down more precisely the evolution of the principle of solidarity in an international context. The idea that the principle of solidarity should guide State relations appeared between the sixteenth and nineteenth centuries.[5] In the eighteenth century, Emer de Vattel

[2] Philipp Dann, 'Solidarity and the Law of Cooperation' in Rudiger Wolfrum and Chie Kojima (eds), *Solidarity: A Structural Principle of International Law* (Springer, 2010) 55, 78.

[3] Anne Peters, 'Compensatory Constitutionalism: The Function and Potential of Fundamental International Norms and Structure' (2006) 19 *Leiden Journal of International Law* 579, 601.

[4] Erika de Wet, 'The Emergence of International and Regional Value Systems as a Manifestation of Emerging International Constitutional Order' (2006) 19 *Leiden Journal of International Law* 611.

[5] Rüdiger Wolfrum, 'Solidarity' in Dinah Shelton (ed), *Oxford Handbook of International Human Rights Law* (Oxford University Press, 2013) 402; Ulrich Scheuner, 'Solidarität unter den Nationen als Grundsatz in der gegenwartigen internationalen Gemeinschaft' in Ipsen Delbruck Jost, Rauschning Dietrich Knut (eds), *Recht im Dienst des Friedens. Festschrift für Eberhard Menzel* (Drucker & Humbolt, 1975).

referred to the principle of solidarity as a moral duty not giving rise to rights of affected States but merely to legitimate expectations.[6] In the nineteenth century, French sociologist Émile Durkheim expanded its sociological dimension by distinguishing between *solidarité mécanique* and *solidarité organique*.[7] Léon Duguit imported the concept into French administrative and constitutional law based on the distinction between objective and subjective law.[8] George Scelle extended this theory in the field of international law.[9]

Most modern scholars accept that the principle of solidarity operates within the framework of international law. However, they disagree about its nature and normative character. Wolfrum argued that a general obligation to cooperate had not yet been established, but he pointed out that certain universal treaties contain an obligation to cooperate.[10] His contribution raised an important point that States did not agree on a general obligation to cooperate, but they did agree to an obligation to cooperate in specific treaties.[11] He considered that solidarity is a multifunctional principle and provided useful input on how to assess the operation of the principle.[12] In his view the principle reflected a transformation of international law into a value based international legal order.[13] Wellens affirmed that the principle of solidarity constitutes one of the 'common constitutional characteristics'[14] between the various branches of international law. According to him, solidarity is more than an inspirational principle.[15] It is a constitutional principle, which performs a combination of functions depending on the degree of interpenetration in various branches of international law.[16] Other scholars tried to find evidence in treaties of the emergence of an international legal principle.[17] Recently, Dann has proposed to re-define the notion of international solidarity in more practical terms. He suggested that the notion of solidarity should be conceived as

[6] Karel Wellens, 'Revisiting Solidarity as a (Re-)Emerging Constitutional Principle: Some Further Reflections' in Wolfrum and Kojima (n 2) 3, 5, referring to, Otto Kimmich, 'Die Genfer Flüchtlingskonvention als Ausdruck globaler Solidarität' (1991) 29 *Archiv des Völkerrechts* 261, 265.

[7] Von Bogdandy, 'Opening Address' in Wolfrum and Kojima (eds)(n 2) 1.

[8] 'Discussion Following the Presentation by Philipp Dann' in Wolfrum and Kojima (eds) (n 2) 79, 81.

[9] Von Bogdandy (n 7) 2; 'Discussion Following the Presentation by Philipp Dann', *ibid* 79, 92.

[10] Jost Delbrück, 'The International Obligation to Cooperate' in Holger Hestermeyer, Doris König et al (eds), *Coexistence, Cooperation and Solidarity: Liber Amicorum Rüdiger Wolfrum, Volume I* (Martinus Nijhoff, 2012) 3, 4.

[11] *Ibid.*

[12] Rüdiger Wolfrum, 'Solidarity amongst States: An Emerging Structural Principle of International Law' in Pierre-Marie Dupuy (ed), *Völkerrecht als Weltordnung, Festschrift für Christian Tomuschat* (Engel, Kehl a. Rhein, 2006) 1087.

[13] *Ibid.*

[14] Wellens (n 6) 3, 30; Christian Walter, 'International Law in a Process of Constitutionalization' in Janne Nijman and André Nollkaemper (eds), *New Perspectives on the Divide between National and International Law* (Oxford University Press, 2007) 191, 214.

[15] Wellens (n 6) 30.

[16] Wellens (n 6).

[17] Abdul Koroma, 'Solidarity: Evidence of an Emerging International Legal Principle' in Hestermeyer and König et al (eds) (n 10) 103, 120.

a *non-legal* concept,[18] enabling the notion as a tool of critical analysis.[19] According to his interpretation, solidarity contains three elements: it is an obligation (1) to provide help to another in order to advance a common objective; (2) based on the recognition of the equality of partners involved; and (3) refers to the mutuality of obligations.[20] This interpretation captures the gist of the problem of defining the concept of solidarity at the international level.

ii. Implementation of the Solidarity Principle in International Refugee Law

a. The 1951 Refugee Convention

The principle of solidarity has existed for a long time in international refugee law. It is, however, insufficiently defined and entrenched in order to give rise to meaningful legal rights and obligations. Article 35 of the 1951 Refugee Convention[21] and Article II of the 1967 Protocol[22] contain an explicit obligation to cooperate. Pursuant to Article 35 (1),

> [t]he Contracting States undertake to cooperate with the Office of the High Commissioner for Refugees (…) and shall in particular facilitate its duty of supervising the application of the provisions of this Convention. 'According to para 2, the Contracting States undertake to provide them in the appropriate form with information and statistical date requested concerning: (a) the condition of refugees, (b) the implementation of this Convention, and (c) laws, regulations and decrees which are, or may hereafter be, in force in relation to refugees'.

This obligation entails that Member States have agreed to cooperate within a framework with the United Nations High Commissioner for Refugees (UNHCR). This article deals with administrative means used to facilitate the UNHCR mandate of supervising State compliance and implementation of obligations under the Refugee Convention. Member States are required to provide the UNHCR with information concerning the condition of refugees and the implementation of the Convention. The mandate of the UNHCR is to act in cases of a refugee crisis. The UNHCR cannot act in isolation and requires cooperation of the other Member States. However, Article 35 does not allow the UNHCR to require States to provide assistance to refugees and to grant asylum. Additionally, the Refugee Convention contains non-binding statements of intent or political commitment in the Preamble. For instance, the Member States have recognised in para. 4 that 'the

[18] Dann (n 2) 55, 61.

[19] *Ibid.*

[20] *Ibid.*

[21] Convention Relating to the Status of Refugees (adopted 28 July 1951, entered into force 22 April 1954) 189 UNTS 137 (Refugee Convention).

[22] Protocol relating to the Status of Refugees (entered into force 4 October 1967) 606 UNTS 267 (Refugee Protocol).

grant of asylum may place unduly heavy burdens on certain countries, and that a satisfactory solution of a problem of which the United Nations has recognized the international scope and nature cannot therefore be achieved without international cooperation'.

The UNHCR Executive Committee (ExCom) has underlined the importance of international cooperation, solidarity and burden-sharing as essential components of an effective international protection system.[23] The consensus reached by ExCom in the course of discussions is expressed in the form of Conclusions on the international protection of refugees (ExCom Conclusions). They are formally non-binding, but relevant to the interpretation of international refugee law. Reached by consensus, they constitute authoritative expressions of opinion which are representative of the views of the international community.

b. The New York Declaration and the Global Compacts

Recently, consultations have been conducted to find a concrete arrangement where States could cooperate to alleviate the problems associated with a mass influx of migrants. Solidarity and sharing of responsibility became key aspects of the 2016 Agenda on Humanity,[24] becoming a stepping-stone for subsequent initiatives. On 19 September 2016, the United Nations General Assembly (UNGA) adopted a set of commitments to enhance the protection of refugees and migrations in the New York Declaration for Refugees and Migrants.[25] The New York Declaration reaffirmed the commitment of Member States to strengthen mechanisms to protect persons on the move. The document intended to pave the way towards two global compacts in 2018, one on refugees and another on safe, orderly and regular migrations.

The New York Declaration contains the main aspects of a Comprehensive Refugee Response Framework (CRRF) to be applied to large-scale movements of refugees and protracted refugee situations.[26] The Framework is centred on the idea

[23] UNHCR Executive Committee Conclusion No 77 (XLVI) (1995) para (o); UNHCR Executive Committee Conclusion No 80 (XLVII) (1996) paras (e), (e)(iii); UNHCR Executive Committee Conclusion No 85 (XLIX) (1998) para (p); UNHCR Executive Committee Conclusion No 87 (L) (1999) para (I); and UNHCR Executive Committee Conclusion No 100 (LV) (2004).

[24] New York Declaration, 'One Humanity: Shared Responsibility, Agenda for Humanity', Annex to the Report of the Secretary-General for the World Humanitarian Summit (A/70/709), 30 January 2016, 1, www.agendaforhumanity.org/sites/default/files/AgendaforHumanity.pdf (last accessed 16 March 2020.

[25] UNGA, Resolution by the General Assembly on 19 September 2016, 71/1 New York Declaration for Refugees and Migrants, UN Doc A/RES/71/1, 3 October 2016.

[26] UNGA, Resolution from 19 September 2019, New York Declaration for Refugees and Migrants, UN Doc A/RES/71/1, Annex 1. For further information and comments: Randall Hansen, 'The Comprehensive Refugee Response Framework: A Commentary' (2018) 31 (2) *Journal of Refugee Studies* 31; Volker Türk and Madeline Garlick, 'From Burdens and Responsibilities to Opportunities: The Comprehensive Response Framework and Global Compact on Refugees' (2016) 28 (4) *International Journal of Refugee Law* 656; Manisha Thomas, 'Turning the Comprehensive Refugee Response into Reality' (2017) 56 *Forced Migration Review* 69.

that refugees should be included in the communities from the beginning. Refugees should gain access to education and labour markets, allowing them to acquire further skills and to become self-reliant whilst contributing to local economies. The aim of the Framework is to ease the pressure on countries that host refugees, build the self-reliance of refugees, expand access to resettlement in third countries, enabling conditions where refugees voluntarily return to their home countries. The negotiations leading towards the New York Declaration demonstrated that wealthier countries firmly rejected any specific target or binding obligations on refugee resettlements numbers. The measures described as part of the CRRF are broadly phrased and leave a broad margin of decision.

Pursuant to the New York Declaration, the Global Compact on Refugees[27] was adopted in 2018 as a voluntary initiative to provide a more equitable responsibility-sharing arrangement among countries of origin, transit and destination to address large movements of refugees. It provides a framework for applying existing norms in a large-scale influx based on the principles of international cooperation and responsibility-sharing.

The first part consists of an introduction to the guiding principles and objectives. The second part includes the CRRF, agreed in Annex I of the New York Declaration. The third part consists of a programme of action setting out actions that can be taken to support the application of the CRRF and to ensure that it is fully implemented equitably. The programme of action lists broadly-formulated measures consisting of global arrangements taken as part of a periodic Global Refugee Forum, at ministerial level for all UN Member States with all relevant stakeholders. These arrangements consist of making pledges and contributions that take different forms, including financial, material or technical assistance, resettlement places and complementary pathways for admission to third countries. Significantly, a review mechanism of the Global Compact on Refugees has been put into place: a Global Refugee Forum every four years at the Ministerial level (2019), to announce concrete pledges and contributions towards the Refugee Compact's objectives and to consider opportunities for enhancing responsibility-sharing (paras 17, 103). There will be an interim high-level officials' meeting every two years (from 2021), and indicators to measure success towards the achievement of the Refugee Compact's four objectives (paras 19, 102, 104).

The New York Declaration also provided for the adoption in a Global Compact for Safe, Orderly and Regular Migration ('the Global Compact on Migration').[28] In contrast to the situation of refugees, there is no specialised comprehensive legal regime concerning migrants, and no agreed framework for addressing large movements of migrants. The starting point for achieving greater predictability

[27] United Nations, Report of the United Nations High Commissioner for Refugees, Part II, Global Compact on Refugees, UN Doc A/73/12 (Part II), 13 September 2018.

[28] 'Global Compact for Safe, Orderly and Regular Migration', Final Draft, 11 July 2018, https://refugeesmigrants.un.org/sites/default/files/180711_final_draft_0.pdf (last accessed 16 March 2020).

and responsibility-sharing for refugees is different from achieving a common approach to international migration. The Global Compact on Migration is an intergovernmental, non-legally binding cooperative framework founded on various international human rights legal instruments (para 2). It sets out a common understanding of migration, guiding principles, shared responsibilities and purpose (paras 3–15). Moreover, it contains a list of 24 objectives to be achieved, including a number of collaborative measures (para 16).

Significantly, the Global Compact on Migration reaffirms the adherence to 'the sovereign right of States to determine their national migration policy and their prerogative to govern migration within their jurisdiction, in conformity with international law' (para 15). It leaves States discretion to decide on distinguishing between regular and irregular migration status and determining their legislative and policy measures for the implementation of the Global Compact on Migration (para 15). As with the Global Compact on Refugees, a formal review mechanism was established. The progress in implementation of the goals and measures agreed as part of the Global Compact on Migration is assessed in a four-yearly International Migration Review Forum (from 2022). A UN network on migration will work to ensure effective and coherent system-wide support to implementation, follow-up and review (paras 45, 49).

While the New York Declaration, the Global Compact on Migration and the Global Compact on Refugees represent a step forward in establishing consensus and forming a political will, they are not aimed at changing existing legal obligations. They are unlikely to break new ground in regard to the nature of the principle of solidarity and to its development. Further, they are grounded in the doctrine of State sovereignty with the intention of maintaining the status quo and margin of discretion for States. They are meant to facilitate the operationalisation of the existing legal obligations by providing a structured framework and greater monitoring of the commitments. They are of little assistance in pinning down the normative character of the principle of solidarity, which appears to have a structuring character. While these documents are based on various international human rights instruments, they are phrased in terms of burden-sharing, management or containment. Such an approach does not reflect preoccupations which lie at the heart of a genuine human rights-based approach, aiming to address the precarious situation of asylum-seekers, refugees and migrants. On a positive note, the two Global Compacts contain concrete frameworks for action wherein States can be held to account politically, through new formal review mechanisms. This is a step forward in the operationalisation of the agreed cooperation measures and goals.

c. The Draft Declaration on International Solidarity

Promising efforts to further develop the principle of international sovereignty were made under the auspices of the United Nations Human Rights Council (HRC). An international expert on international solidarity was appointed by the

HRC to develop a Draft Declaration on the Right of Peoples and Individuals to International Solidarity. According to the Draft Declaration,[29] 'International solidarity is the expression of a spirit of unity among individuals, peoples, States and international organization, encompassing the union of interests, purposes and actions and the recognition of different needs and rights to achieve common goals' (Art 1 (1)). It is a foundational principle underpinning contemporary international law (Art 1 (2)) consisting of three concepts: preventive solidarity, reactive solidarity and international cooperation (Art 2). Article 6 identifies all States as primary duty bearers and international organisations and non-state actors as entities that have to respect the right to international security. Article 8 spells out the broad obligations of these actors as part of the implementation of the rights to international solidarity. The Independent Expert emphasised that these already exist in obligations under international human rights treaties.

In context, the right to international solidarity is a right to demand the implementation of international solidarity so that benefits can be derived. The Independent Expert's position is that the right to international solidarity is a claimable right by virtue of its relationship with international human rights law.[30] The Independent Expert emphasised that not all rights are complete from the moment they are established:

> (…) our understanding of human rights cannot be perfect and complete from the very start, as exemplified by the international human rights treaties that were not enforceable even as they entered into force. Human rights can be realized as enforceable claims only through the continuous work and efforts of legal and political institutions as well as human rights mechanisms at [all] levels.[31]

B. European Union Law

The whole European Union project was inspired by the idea of solidarity – one of the main ideas behind the integration movement following the Second World War. The principle of solidarity is enshrined in various provisions of EU primary law. According to the sixth preambular provision of the Treaty of the European Treaty (TEU), the Member States express their desire 'to deepen the solidarity between their peoples while respecting their history, their culture and their traditions'.

i. Legal Foundations and Doctrinal Interpretations

On the basis of Article 2 TEU, solidarity alongside human dignity, freedom, democracy, equality, the rule of law and the respect for human rights, pluralism,

[29] UNGA, Report of the Independent Expert on Human Rights and International Solidarity, Human Rights Council, 6–23 June, UN Doc A/HRC/35/35, 25 April 2017, p 15 Annex.
[30] *Ibid*, para 65, p 14.
[31] *Ibid*.

non-discrimination and justice constitute the foundational values of the EU. These values are shared by the Member States and must prevail in the process of creating an ever-closer Union. The normative nature and the legal standing of these values were recognised by the Court of Justice of the European Union (CJEU).[32] In the *Kadi* case, they were elevated to the status of 'constitutional principle' of EU Law.[33] They were found to be of such critical importance to the EU that treaties 'in no circumstances permit any challenge to the principles that that form part of the very foundations of the Community legal order'.[34] Regarding their implementation, the CJEU has mentioned that

> Member States must not only implement their national law in a manner consistent with (EU) law but must also make sure they do not rely on an interpretation of wording of secondary legislation which would be in conflict with (…) general principles of (EU) law.[35]

Solidarity and the other values contained in Article 2 are meta-principles of European integration as well as 'constitutional paradigms' which transcend the interpretation, application and implementation of EU law.[36]

This fundamental constitutional principle is streamlined in EU Treaty Articles regulating specific areas of EU competences. According to Article 3(3) TEU, the EU aims at promoting 'economic, social and territorial cohesion, and solidarity among Member States'. Eight provisions in the TEU and in the Treaty on the Functioning of the European Union (TFEU) refer expressly to this principle, while many others give expression indirectly (ie Articles 21, 24 paras 2 and 3, 42(7) of the TEU and Articles 67, 80, 122, 194 and 222 of the TFEU). The whole Chapter IV of the EU Charter on Fundamental Rights refers to solidarity. These provisions do not contain a unified definition of solidarity, but they appear to be applications of the same principle.

There are different types of solidarity in legal provisions and case law. They include solidarity among Union citizens, between the Union and the Member States, between Member States, between the Union Institutions and between the Union and third countries.[37] In broader terms, solidarity can be conceived

[32] Violeta Moreno-Lax, 'Solidarity's Reach: Meaning, Dimensions and Implications for EU (external) Asylum Policy' (2017) 24(5) *Maastricht Journal of European and Comparative Law* 740, 746.

[33] *Ibid.*

[34] C-402/05 and C-415/05 *Yassin Abdullah Kadi, Al Barkaat International Foundation v Council of the European Union, Commission of the European Communities, United Kingdom of Great Britain and Northern Ireland*, Court of Justice, OJ C-285 (2008) 2 para 304.

[35] C-305/05 *Ordre des barreaux francophones et germanophones v Council of Ministers*, ECLI:EU:C:2007:383, para 28.

[36] Moreno-Lax, referring to Malcolm Ross, 'Solidarity – A New Constitutional Paradigm for the EU?' in Malcolm Ross and Yuri Borgmann-Prebil (eds), *Promoting Solidarity in the European Union* (Oxford University Press, 2010) 23 (n 32) 747.

[37] Eglė Dagilytė, 'Solidarity: A General Principle of EU Law? Two Variations on the Solidarity Theme' in Andrea Biondi, Eglė Dagilytė, Esin Küçük (eds), *Solidarity in EU Law: Legal Principle in the Making* (Edward Elgar, 2018) 61, 63.

as horizontal, vertical and systemic.[38] Horizontal solidarity corresponds to inter-State relations, vertical solidarity relates to State-individual relations. Systemic solidarity concerns the State-regime requiring commitment to an international, EU, State or other framework.[39] Despite elaborate dichotomy, most EU law Articles on solidarity refer expressly to relationships between Member States – horizontal solidarity.[40]

In contrast to international refugee law, the principle of solidarity has stronger legal foundations in EU law. Due to the nature of the EU legal order, consisting of legally binding and enforceable primary and secondary law, unsurprisingly, the principle of solidarity benefits from stronger foundations and is more entrenched than in the international refugee law regime. The EU has strong federal characteristics that contributed to a stronger establishment of this principle. In many federations around the world, the principle of solidarity or cooperation is fundamental for the good functioning of the country. Similarly, the idea of European integration is based on solidarity and cooperation, more so than the Refugee Convention. The principle of solidarity has a foundational, quasi-constitutional nature under EU law. The same cannot be affirmed about the principle of solidarity in the Refugee Convention, which does not have a foundational or constitutional character. Due to a greater number of references to this concept, there are also more types of solidarity in EU law giving rise to a more comprehensive concept of solidarity. Though the EU legal regime also protects fundamental human rights, it has for many decades pursued other aims, primarily economic integration. The nature of the principle of solidarity therefore has other strains related to those economic aims, non-existent under the Refugee Convention.

The EU concept of solidarity is not isolated from international refugee law. The EU Charter on Fundamental Rights has the same legal value as the Treaties (Art 6 (1) TEU) and it reaffirms 'the rights as they result, in particular, from the (…) international obligations common to the Member States' (Preamble to the Charter). Moreover, Article 18 of the Charter stipulates that '[t]he right to asylum shall be guaranteed with due respect to the rules of the Geneva Convention (…)'. Article 78 (1) TFEU also provides that '[t]he Union shall develop a common policy on asylum, subsidiary protection and temporary protection (….)' which must be in accordance with 'the Geneva Convention of 28 July 1951 and the Protocol of 31 January 1967 relating to the status of refugees, and other relevant treaties'. From a systemic view, the EU principle of solidarity should be established, interpreted and applied in compliance with its counterpart in international law.

[38] Lax-Moreno (n 32) 743. For different classifications of EU solidarity, see Andrea Sangiovanni, 'Solidarity in the European Union' (2013) *Oxford Journal of Legal Studies* 5; Floris De Witte, *Justice in EU Law: The Emergence of Transnational Solidarity* (Oxford University Press, 2012) 705–10 or Dagilytė, *ibid* 63–71.

[39] Lax-Moreno (n 32).

[40] Jürgen Bast, 'Deepening Surpanational Integration: Interstate Solidarity in EU Migration Law' in Biondi, Dagilytė and Küçük (eds) (n 37) 114, 116.

This is problematic given the nature and level of development of the EU principle of solidarity, which is more entrenched and developed. Its constitutional character should not be weakened through an interpretation based on international refugee law. However, as will be seen in the next section, such a case will probably not occur. The implementation of the solidarity principle in EU law exhibits several problems, which need to be redressed in accordance with the 1951 Geneva Convention. The convergence with international refugee law is therefore an important aim that must not be treated as a matter of *lege feranda*.

ii. Implementation of the Solidarity Principle in EU Asylum Law

The legal obligations of Member States regarding solidarity law are formulated generally in EU primary law. According to Article 67 (2) TFEU, the EU 'shall frame a common policy on asylum, immigration and external border control, based on solidarity between Member States, which is fair towards third-country nationals'. Article 80 TFEU requires the Union policies on border checks, asylum and immigration and their implementation to be governed by the principle of solidarity and fair sharing of responsibility, including its financial implications, between the Member States. Whenever necessary, the acts of the Union must contain appropriate measures to give effect to this principle. Pursuant to Article 78 (3) TFEU, 'in the event of one or more Member States being confronted with an emergency situation characterised by a sudden inflow of nationals of third countries, the Council, on a proposal from the Commission, may adopt provisional measures for the benefit of the Member State(s) concerned', subject to consultation of the European Parliament.

These principles have not been implemented in accordance with the core characteristics of the principle of solidarity. Most EU efforts in the area of asylum and immigration giving effect to the principle of solidarity are not based on a human rights approach. Their primary aim is not to ensure or to improve the protection of the persons concerned. Rather, the EU efforts based on solidarity constitute short-term measures aimed at responding to an emergency or a crisis. They aim at preventing, containing, managing or controlling migration movements and even at outsourcing and externalising them so that they do not reach the EU territory.

a. The Inadequacy of the Dublin System

The Dublin System, one of the cornerstones of the Common European Asylum System, was not conceived as system of solidarity.[41] It was established as a

[41] *Ibid* 122, referring to European Commission, Green Paper on the future of Common European Asylum System, COM(2007) 301 final (6 June 2007) sub.4.1 and to Reinhardt Marx, 'Ist die Verordnung (EG) Nr. 343/2003 (Dublin-II-VO) noch-reformfähig?' (2012) 32 *Zeitschrift für Ausländerrect und Auslädnerpolitik* 188, 189.

delimitation of responsibilities without a sharing of burdens between the States.[42] The principle of the country of first asylum is ill-suited to function as a rule establishing solidarity. It does not compensate for the uneven burdens of the Member States' geographic locations and by established migration patterns.[43] It intensifies these effects by making movement within Europe more difficult.[44] The Dublin System has not only been criticised for not respecting human rights,[45] but even found by the European Court of Human Rights (ECtHR) to violate crucial provisions of the European Convention on Human Rights.[46] The Commission launched reforms of the Common European Asylum System, including of the Dublin System, in May 2016. These reform plans resulted in a deadlock due to the Member States' inability to reach an agreement in the Council. It remains to be seen whether the newly elected European Parliament (2019) will pursue the reached agreements.

Following up on a Commission Recommendation, in 2015, EU Member States, together with Iceland, Liechtenstein, Norway and Switzerland, adopted the Council Conclusions establishing the resettlement of 22,504 individuals in need of international protection over the period 2015–2017, through multilateral and national schemes. A temporary emergency relocation scheme was established in two Council Decisions in September 2015,[47] in which Member States committed to relocate up to 160,000 people from Italy and Greece (and from other Member States) by September 2017. During mid-late 2017, the European Commission launched a new resettlement pledging exercise and called on EU Member States to resettle at least 50,000 persons in need of international protection by October 2019. This was intended to address the gap following the end of the resettlement scheme under the 2015 Council Conclusions in mid-2017. These measures represent a step towards introducing more binding physical cooperation measures under EU law, but they are problematic as they are founded on short-term emergency considerations and do not take into account the rights of the persons of concern enough.

[42] Bast (n 40), referring to Daniel Thym, *Mirgationsverwaltungsrecht* (Mohr Siebeck, 2010) 354, 364.

[43] Bast (n 40).

[44] Bast (n 40), referring to Agnes Hurwitz, *The Collective Responsibility of States to Protect Refugees* (Oxford University Press, 2009) 165.

[45] See Joanna Lenart, 'Fortress Europe: Compliance of the Dublin II Regulation with the European Convention for the Protection of Human Rights and Fundamental Freedoms' (2012) 28 (75) *Utrecht Journal of International and European Law* 4 or Juss Satvinder, 'The Post-Colonial Refugee, Dublin II, and the End of Non-Refoulement' (2013) 20 (2) *International Journal on Minority and Group Rights* 307.

[46] See, eg, *MSS v Belgium and Greece* (2011) (App No 30696/09) GC or *Trakhel v Switzerland* (2014) (App No 29271/12) GC.

[47] Council of the European Union, Resolution of the Representatives of the Governments of the Member States meeting within the Council on relocating from Greece and Italy 40 000 persons in clear need of international protection, Doc No 11131/15, Brussels, 22 July 2015; Council of the European Union, COUNCIL DECISION establishing provisional measures in the area of international protection for the benefit of Italy and Greece, Doc No 12098/15, Brussels, 22 September 2015.

b. The EU-Turkey Statement

The resettlement measures taken were insufficient to relieve the EU system from the mass migration movement that started in 2015. In an attempt to stem the flow of migrants and asylum-seekers to the EU, Turkey agreed in March 2016 'to accept the rapid return of all migrants not in need of international protection crossing from Turkey to Greece and to take back all irregular migrants intercepted in Turkish waters'.[48] Pursuant to the arrangement, all migrants arriving in Greece were to be duly registered and their asylum applications processed in accordance with the EU Asylum Procedures Directive 2013/32/EU.[49] For every Syrian readmitted to Turkey from Greece, another Syrian would be resettled from Turkey to the EU. At the same time, Turkey would take any necessary measures to prevent new sea or land routes for illegal migration opening from Turkey to the EU and cooperate with neighbouring states as well as the EU to this end. In return, the fulfilment of the visa liberalisation roadmap would be accelerated vis-à-vis all participating Member States, with a view to lifting the visa requirements for Turkish citizens.

The EU-Turkey Statement was made under the presumption that Turkey is a 'safe third country'. This presumption can be questioned due to the fact that Turkey denies any possibility to request protection under the Refugee Convention to persons coming from non-European countries. They can only obtain a temporary status under the Turkish law on Foreigners and International Protection.[50] Significantly, the EU-Turkey Statement was not negotiated under an official EU mandate. The General Court of the CJEU found that it lacks jurisdiction to hear and determine the actions of annulment brought against the EU-Turkey Statement.[51] The CJEU considered that the Statement can only be attributed to the Heads of State or Government of the EU Member States, not to the European Council. As there was no act of a European Institution, the Court found that it did not have competence to adjudicate the case. It was pointed out that similarly to the Dublin System, the EU-Turkey Statement 'shifts, rather than shares, responsibility on the basis of geographical proximity to the country of origin of refugee flows without considering relevant protection or capacity-related criteria'.[52] It gives rise to a misconstrued 'externalisation-based solidarity' that prevents, rather than facilitates, access to asylum.[53]

[48] European Council, EU-Turkey Statement No 21, 18 March 2016, www.consilium.europa.eu/en/press/press-releases/2016/03/18/eu-turkey-statement (last accessed 17 March 2020).

[49] Directive 2013/32/EU of 26 June 2013 on common procedures for granting and withdrawing international protection (recast) [2013] OJ L180/60.

[50] Law on Foreigners and International Protection, Ministry of Interior, Turkey, Law on Foreigners and International Protection, Ministry of the Interior, Turkey, www.goc.gov.tr/files/files/eng_minikanun_5_son.pdf (last accessed 17 March 2020).

[51] Order of the General Court, T-192/16 *NF v European Council* ECLI:EU:T:2017:128; Order of the General Court, T-193/16 *NG v European Council* ECLI:EU:T:2017:129; Order of the General Court, T-257/16 *NM v European Council* ECLI:EU:T:2017:130.

[52] Lax-Moreno (n 32) 753.

[53] Lax-Moreno (n 32) 753.

c. The Italy-Libya Memorandum of Understanding

Another example of a false or misconstrued solidarity measure aimed at keeping asylum-seekers and migrants away from the EU territory is the Italy-Libya Memorandum of Understanding (MoU) signed in February 2017.[54] Italy has previously cooperated with Libya on migration during the 2000s. At that time, both countries concluded agreements aiming to curb migratory flows and enhancing readmission. This partnership was suspended in 2012 as a result of the collapse of the Government as well as the ECtHR *Hirsi Jamaa* judgment,[55] finding that Italy violated the principle of *non-refoulement* and the prohibition of collective expulsions. The new MoU adopts very generic language and does not reveal much about the precise projects supported or the amount and origin of funds. The MoU outlines two main objectives: the control of migratory flows and the support of the development of the region. It appears that the immediate actions focus on reducing entries to Italy. The MoU repeats that its goal is to stem the flow of migrants from Libya to Europe and securitise Libya's borders to prevent departure. It lacks any reference to international human and international protection. Moreover, It does not contain any initiative aimed at identifying individuals eligible for international protection and establishing an appropriate system of protection. The negotiators of the MoU ignored the poor human rights situation in Libya, especially as it does not recognise a right to asylum.[56] The MoU is a worse version of the EU-Turkey Statement aiming at externalising migration control to a transition country. However, despite these deficiencies, the EU endorsed the Italy-Libya Memorandum.[57]

d. New Resettlement Framework

Following on from the Common European Asylum System reform process, the Commission presented a proposed Regulation setting up a Union Resettlement Framework.[58] The Commission emphasised that resettlement is one of the avenues allowing persons in need of protection to enter the Member States legally and safely in order to receive protection as long as needed.[59] It was considered a tool

[54] Italy-Libya Memorandum of Understanding (2017), http://eumigrationlawblog.eu/wp-content/uploads/2017/10/MEMORANDUM_translation_finalversion.doc.pdf (last accessed 18 March 2020). See: Sergio Carrera, Vara Santos and Juan Strik Tineke, *Constitutionalising the External Dimensions of EU Migration Policies in Times of Crisis: Legality, Rule of Law and Fundamental Rights Reconsidered* (Edward Elgar, 2019); Mariagiulia Giuffré, 'State Responsibility beyond Borders: What Legal Basis for Italy's Pushbacks to Libya?' (2012) 24 (4) *International Journal of Refugee Law* 692; Marina Mancini, 'Italy's New Migration Control Policy: Stemming the Flow of Migrants from Libya Without Regard for Their Human Rights' (2018) XXVII *Italian Yearbook of International Law* 259; Anna Liguori, *Migration Law and the Externalization of Border Controls: European State Responsibility* (Routledge, 2019).

[55] *Hirsi Jamaa and Others v Italy* (2012) (App No 27765/09) GC.

[56] Mancini (n 54) 262–65.

[57] *Ibid* 265–66.

[58] European Commission, Proposal for a Regulation of the European Parliament and of the Council establishing a Union Resettlement Framework and amending Regulation (EU) No 516/2014 of the European Parliament and the Council COM/2016/0468 final – 2016/0225 (COD) (3 July 2016).

[59] *Ibid* 2.

of international solidarity and responsibility-sharing with third countries, within which large numbers of persons in need of protection have been displaced.[60]

The proposed legislation aims to create 'a more structured (…) and permanent framework for resettlement'[61] and introduce a unified resettlement procedure across the EU. According to the proposal, annual EU resettlement plans adopted by the Council, based on a Commission proposal, will identify the broad geographical priorities for resettlement and the maximum total number of individuals to be resettled, detailing the participation and contributions of Member and Associated Schengen States (Article 7). The proposal lays out the standard eligibility criteria and exclusion grounds for resettlement (Articles 5 and 6), the type of procedure – either ordinary or expedited – applied, and the status granted to individuals resettled under the Framework (Articles 10 and 11). These procedures build on existing resettlement experience and standards of the Member States, including the Standard Operating Procedures[62] guiding the implementation of the resettlement scheme with Turkey set out in the EU-Turkey Statement of 18 March 2016.

The ordinary procedure is based on a full refugee status determination in a third country and in a Member State granting to the resettled third-country nationals refugee or subsidiary status. Member States identify persons for whom they intend to carry out the resettlement procedure either through referral by the UNHCR, the European Agency for Asylum, relevant international bodies or by themselves. As part of the expedited procedure, specific humanitarian grounds or urgent legal or physical protection warrants a rapid admission of third-country nationals to the territory of the Member States. The procedure should be conducted within four months from the moment of registration.

Despite being intertwined with international refugee law, resettlement under the proposal is tainted by the EU's own objectives. It is framed as a win-win solution, which is part of the larger objective to reduce irregular migration and block dangerous routes used to obtain protection. While the proposal refers in many articles to human rights, international protection and solidarity, it is not founded on a comprehensive human rights approach.

III. Convergence or Divergence Trends as Regards the Principle of Solidarity

A. The Nature of the Area Considered

Before comparing EU and international solidarity, it is crucial to note that the regulation and implementation of these notions at the international and EU level

[60] *Ibid.*
[61] *Ibid.*
[62] Council of the European Union, Standard Operating Procedures implementing the mechanism for resettlement from Turkey to the EU as set out in the EU-Turkey Statement of 18 March 2016, Brussels, 5 April 2016, www.statewatch.org/news/2016/apr/eu-council-EU-Turkey-Standard-operating-procedures-resettlement-7462-16.pdf (last accessed 18 March 2020).

is influenced by the nature of the competence being considered. Immigration and asylum are areas where it has been difficult to agree on binding standards and where broad, non-binding standards have been preferred. Both fields are typical landmarks of State sovereignty and States have always been reluctant to cede competences. Letting migrants into a country has important consequences on its social, employment and economic policies, which explains why the Member States prefer to retain control over law and policy-making. Other impeding factors for agreeing on common binding standards are the divergences appearing at the national level – the different immigration histories, cultures and legal, political and economic systems of the Member States. Migration is a complex phenomenon, very difficult to control due to the unpredictable nature of the push-factors leading to migratory movements. Due to the complexity of the subject matter, the national divergences as well as the difficulty in reaching a certain degree of generality and indeterminacy of standards has prevailed. It became evident that legal instruments do not suffice in themselves to reach the desired policy objectives in the context of immigration and asylum. Practical cooperation was instituted at various levels in order to improve the coherence of decision-making and to achieve convergence.

The strong emphasis on State sovereignty in the area of immigration and asylum conflicts with the principle of solidarity. Apparent from the reviewed solidarity measures and instruments, State sovereignty limited the efforts towards adopting solidarity measures. These measures are anchored in the principle of State sovereignty and are to be implemented in accordance thereto. They either barely limit or preserve States' sovereignty; there are no solidarity measures which limit or take precedence over State sovereignty. This explains why many of the efforts result in measures which are based on false or misconstrued solidarity. Further, it is the reason why the principle of solidarity has not been developed further as part of the implementation efforts at the international and EU levels. In order to establish measures based on human rights and international protection, a greater limitation of State sovereignty would be required.

The lack of common binding standards can be attributed to the patchy EU competence in the area of migration and asylum. Migration and asylum are competences shared by the Union and its Member States. Member States may exercise their competences until the adoption of common rules by the Union that is until the Union has not entirely 'pre-empted the field'. For instance, the EU enjoys exclusive external competences on short-term visas and borders on the basis of the *ERTA* case law.[63] The adoption of common internal rules in these fields prevents Member States from concluding international agreements, affecting their uniform application. Further, Union competences are concurrent with Member States on

[63] C-22/70 *Commission v Council (ERTA)*, 31 March 1971 [1971] ECR 263. The *ERTA* judgment recognised the existence of implied powers of the European (Economic) Community to conclude treaties under public international law. For further case law on the 'ERTA doctrine', see the following cases: Opinion 1/76, 26 April 1977 [1977] ECR 741; Opinion 1/75, 11 November 1975 [1975] ECR 1355; Opinion 1/78 4 October 1979 [1979] ECR 2871.

readmission. The exercise by the Union of this explicit external competence will exclude Member States' external action from the moment the Union concludes an agreement with a given third country or even since the adoption by the Council of a negotiation mandate for that purpose. Union competences can be qualified as concurrent regarding legal migration and migrants' integration, fields in which the conclusion of Union agreements is subject to legal and political constraints. Decisions on the volumes of admission of economic migrants from third countries pertain to the exclusive remit of Member States. Solidarity concerns most of the named competences, where EU and Member States competence is not uniform.[64]

B. The Need to Ensure Systemic Convergence

EU asylum law and policy is extensively based on existing international human rights and refugee law. This is due to the fact that the 1951 Refugee Convention is currently applicable law and *lex specialis* in the area of refugee status determination. This field is already almost 'pre-empted' at the international level and the EU cannot override existing norms. As a result, the EU common policy on asylum had to be established in accordance with the 1951 Geneva Convention and the Protocol. The EU transposed the requirements of the 1951 Geneva Convention as part of the relevant Qualification Directive[65] adopted on 13 December 2011. There is a systemic legal necessity (and lower margin of State discretion) to ensure convergence between EU law and international refugee law.

The need to ensure convergence applies *a fortiori* to the principle of solidarity in EU asylum law and in international refugee law. From a systemic standpoint, the EU principle of solidarity must establish, interpret and apply in compliance with its counterpart in international refugee law. This is problematic given the nature and level of development of the principle of solidarity in EU law, which has stronger legal foundations as part of the EU legal order than international solidarity under the 1951 Geneva Convention. The foundational and constitutional character of the EU principle of solidarity should not be weakened through an interpretation based on international refugee law. This may be an area where the EU could contribute to the conceptual development of the principle of solidarity

[64] Mauro Gatti, 'Too Much Unity in the European Union's External Migration Policy?' (*EU Immigration and Asylum Law and Policy*, 20 July 2018), http://eumigrationlawblog.eu/too-much-unity-in-the-european-unions-external-migration-policy/ (last accessed 18 March 2020); Paula Garcia Andrade, 'External Competence and Representation of the EU and its Member States in the Area of Migration and Asylum' (*EU Immigration and Asylum Law and Policy*, 17 January 2018), http://eumigrationlawblog.eu/external-competence-and-representation-of-the-eu-and-its-member-states-in-the-area-of-migration-and-asylum/ (last accessed 18 March 2020).

[65] Directive 2011/95/EU of the European Parliament and of the Council of 13 December 2011 on standards for the qualification of third-country nationals or stateless persons as beneficiaries of international protection, for a uniform status for refugees or for persons eligible for subsidiary protection, and for the content of the protection granted (2011) OJ L337/9–26.

at the international level. It would not be the first time that the EU contributes to the development of international refugee law; it has done so by providing an explicit legal base for granting subsidiary protection on EU territory and thus filling gaps under the 1951 Geneva Convention. It would be possible for the EU to do the same with regard to the principle of solidarity and close the numerous gaps that remain at the international refugee level.

C. Convergence Trends

There is evidence of convergence regarding resettlement at the EU and international levels: the applicable standards converge on most aspects, though they vary in relation to the type of instruments used to set standards. While international refugee law contains few binding standards relating to resettlement, EU law would contain a stronger legal framework if the proposed Directive on Union Resettlement was to pass. At the time of writing, it is not certain whether this proposal will be accepted in Parliament and enter into force. The difference in approach between the EU and international level is due to the type of actor imposing the standards. While the EU can impose binding standards and enforce them, the UN is barely capable of imposing any binding standards. Its enforcement mechanisms are either inexistent or weak. The UNHCR has nonetheless a long-standing experience in the area of resettlement. It developed detailed standard operating procedures which can be followed and adapted to the specific situation of a UNHCR field office in cases of resettlement. The UNHCR is aiming to create coherence through practical cooperation rather than binding standards. Setting binding standards within immigration and asylum is an extremely difficult task and may not even lead to the desired results.

It is possible that the practical cooperation instituted under the EU auspices as part of the recent migration crisis had an influence on the development of the CRRF under New York Declaration and the Global Compact on Refugees. There are clear parallels between efforts at the international and EU levels. It is logical that the experience and lessons flowing from the application of the Dublin System, its subsequent failure and the corresponding adoption of complementary resettlement measures influenced the establishment of cooperation measures at the international level. It would be peculiar if this experience had gone unnoticed and there was no convergence, at least in terms of the resettlement measures agreed and due to the political consensus. In both cases, the political momentum and urgency obliged the EU and the international community to adopt measures, which may have led to some convergence.

A general move towards convergence on politically (albeit not legally) binding physical (not financial) burden-sharing measures between the international and EU levels can be noted in the form of relocation and resettlement measures. These have also been prompted in greater part by the political momentum and the urgency of the situation resulting from the migration crisis. While these physical burden-sharing measures are not devoid of criticism in terms of their compliance with human rights, they represent an improvement in comparison to measures existing before the mass migration crisis. The development of these measures gave rise to a parallel 'brake' reaction of States reasserting their unwillingness to go beyond existing legal obligations. This reaction concerns State sovereignty and an unwillingness to concede more than required to control the mass movement of persons of concern. Finally, many of the measures proposed have an ad hoc and piecemeal character aiming to reach a win-win situation among actors which pays regard to national and regional interests. The current status quo may not be ideal, as it is not grounded on a genuine human rights-based approach (giving rise to legally claimable and enforceable rights) but based on measures meant to deter and to restrain the onward movement of asylum-seekers and migrants to the EU territory. It does represent an overall improvement developing physical burden-sharing measures. Hopefully, this improvement will develop further in the right direction.

D. Divergence Trends

An overview of the legal foundations and interpretations of the principle of solidarity as part of EU law and international refugee law reveals several divergences. First, the legal character of the EU and international principle of solidarity differs. The principle of solidarity has stronger constitutional and legal foundations under EU law than its counterpart. The principle of solidarity established under the 1951 Geneva Convention is not binding and lacks constitutional and legal force. It is worth mentioning that important efforts have been deployed at the international level to improve political (albeit not legal) accountability through the establishment of review mechanisms. Second, the normative nature of the principle of solidarity at the EU and international levels varies. The EU principle of solidarity is strongly entrenched in the EU legal framework and obeys its specific systematic dynamics, including the EU's own aims and objectives. The EU is marked by strong federative elements contributing to the establishment of stronger cooperative and solidarity mechanisms. The principle of solidarity in international refugee law is based on a human rights approach (especially under the Draft Declaration on International Solidarity). According to the latest efforts of the UN International Expert to develop the principle of international solidarity, it was considered that solidarity is a claimable and enforceable human right, which is not yet complete and needs to be developed further. The EU principle of solidarity obeys a certain human rights rationale but takes into greater account (than its international counterpart does) national and EU aims and objectives.

Several divergences appear between implementation measures taken at the EU and international levels. A number of EU or EU-backed initiatives departed from international refugee law. The EU-Turkey deal and the deal with Libya are the best examples of this departure. The EU attempted to outsource and to contain movements of people of concern and actively tried to prevent them from crossing the Member States' border. The strategy of containment pushed it to send people to a country, which can hardly be called a 'safe third country'. Instead of reforming the Dublin System or replacing it with more efficient mechanisms, the EU outsourced the migration problem while disregarding international refugee law. Both deals seemed to externalise and outsource responsibility rather than make genuine efforts to share responsibility among the EU Member States.

The lack of convergence in the matter can be attributed to patchy EU competence in the area of migration and asylum. Migration and asylum are competences shared by the Union and its Member States. They may therefore exercise their competences until the adoption of common rules by the Union that is until the Union has not yet entirely 'pre-empted the field'. As already mentioned, solidarity measures or burden-sharing measures concern areas, where EU and Member States competence is not uniform.[66] With no clear legal basis granting competence to the EU, it becomes difficult to adopt common binding standards, which gives rise to adoption of weaker instruments.

Overall, the divergences between the international and the EU level are not a positive development for the systemic convergence that should ensue from the requirements imposed by EU law and the aim to avoid fragmentation. While the EU went further than the international community in developing common binding standards, the requirements developed at the international level go further than their EU counterparts in a normative sense (in being based on a human rights approach). This difference can be attributed to the fact that the international community was able to discuss and/or agree on requirements that are more progressive because they are non-binding. Such a state of affairs is not ideal but not entirely negative, as it shows that there is an evolution in consensus and a greater recognition of the importance of solidarity. The efforts made as part of the negotiations on the Draft Declaration on International Solidarity are especially important, as they break new ground in terms of recognising – albeit incomplete and in progress – solidarity as a claimable and enforceable right.

More alarming are the divergences evidenced as part of implementation measures adopted at the EU and international levels. By departing from international refugee law in at least two instances (deals with Turkey and Libya), the EU followed its own aims and disrespected the need to ensure systematic convergence with the 1951 Geneva Convention. It could be that the urgency of the situation or the need to ensure its own survival led the EU to act this way. Its discourse was heavily tainted with 'solidarity language', but the measures adopted bore no resemblance to solidarity in international refugee law. The resulting 'misconstrued' or 'false' solidarity concept is new and has been developed by the EU to serve its own interests and to contain while externalising the mass migration crisis.

[66] Gatti (n 64); Garcia (n 64).

11

Epilogue: The EU as a Selective and Conflicted Converger

GABRIEL SILES-BRÜGGE

As Elaine Fahey states in the Introduction, the starting 'premise' of this volume is that 'the EU epitomises the concept of convergence and is arguably one of the ultimate convergence actors in contemporary global politics'.[1] Given this context, this part of the book has focused on the interaction between the EU and the global legal order. While the contributors do show that the EU has often been proactively engaged in international institutionalisation efforts, to me they have also highlighted two important features of the EU's convergence efforts. The first is that the EU has been highly *selective* when it comes to the question of striving for convergence with international rules. The second is that this reflects the '*conflicted*' nature of the EU as a convergence actor.

Turning to the first point, Paul James Cardwell and Ramses Wessel's chapter highlights different attitudes in the jurisprudence of the Court of Justice of the European Union (CJEU) with respect to the status of international law. They cite evidence to suggest that it has been 'selectively' applied in regard to the question of the territorial application of agreements with third parties. The Court has 'oscillat[ed] between asserting the autonomous legal order of the EU and [...] relying on a more deferential approach to international law'.[2] Magdalena Forowicz, meanwhile, highlights how despite there being some convergence around the concept of 'solidarity' between international refugee and EU asylum law, the EU's conception of solidarity has largely underpinned 'short-term measures aimed at responding to an emergency'; it also lacks the normative depth of the international legal concept.[3] Also writing on EU approaches to global migration law, Juan Santos Vara and Laura Pascual Matellán highlight the piecemeal adoption of the Global Compact on Migration by the EU, with only some Member States signing on to this soft law instrument. In trade policy, David Henig shows that while in

[1] See Introduction by Elaine Fahey, p 1.
[2] See chapter 8 by Paul James Cardwell and Ramses Wessel, p 161.
[3] See chapter 10 by Magdalena Forowicz, p 187.

the Transatlantic Trade and Investment Partnership (TTIP) talks the EU was keen on regulator-led substantive alignment, it was also open to converging towards the US's preferred approach to regulation epitomised by 'good regulatory practices'.

This of course does not belie the significance of the EU as a global convergence actor; when it comes to the question of the Single Market alone, its size and importance are powerful drivers of the 'Brussels effect' of externalising EU rules.[4] Rather, recognising the EU has been more of a *selective* converger is about acknowledging that the EU's pursuit of convergence, of multilateralism and international cooperation is not an end in itself but tied to *conflicting* sets of political objectives and normative visions.

Ben Rosamond's re-reading of Ian Manner's concept of 'normative power Europe' is quite helpful in drawing out this point. In his original article, Manners defines the EU's normative power as being fundamentally about the 'ability to shape conceptions of "normal" in international relations'.[5] In a departure from much of the subsequent literature on the concept, Rosamond suggests that we cannot reduce the idea of normative power Europe to 'liberal-cosmopolitan' values, or to the idea that the EU does not act strategically.[6] Instead, Rosamond argues that 'value-driven' and 'strategic action' are not incompatible in the EU's external action, which also juggles multiple and 'potentially contradictory' liberal normative visions. These three 'modes of liberalism' are a desire to foster markets; the promotion of 'peace' by reducing the probability of war between states and the EU's sense of 'cosmopolitan duty', where it is concerned with protecting fellow human beings. While the EU's external trade policy might fall under the first mode of promoting market-marking, enlargement policy is associated with the second mode of liberalism, and EU human rights policy with the third. Moreover, Rosamond suggests that the first, market mode of liberalism needs to be further unpicked to highlight the 'struggle and delicate balancing act between German ordoliberalism, Anglo-American neoliberalism and French Colbertism' characterising 'EU economic liberalism'.[7]

A 'normative' Europe can therefore mean any number of things depending on the policy area – reflecting an on-going internal political struggle over the form of liberalism embodied by the European project. In the literature on EU external relations others have similarly spoken about the challenge of achieving EU policy coherence – including 'horizontal coherence' (between policy areas) and 'vertical coherence' (between EU and Member State policies).[8] Analogous to the argument that Sophie Meunier and Kalypso Nicolaïdis have made about the EU as

[4] A Bradford, 'The Brussels Effect' (2012) 107 *Northwestern University Law Review* 1–68.

[5] I Manners, 'Normative Power Europe: A Contradiction in Terms?' (2002) 40(2) *Journal of Common Market Studies* 235–58, 239.

[6] B Rosamond, 'Three Ways of Speaking Europe to the World: Markets, Peace and Cosmopolitan Duty and the EU's Normative Power' (2014) *British Journal of Politics and International Relations* 16 (1), 133–48, 133–35.

[7] *Ibid* 135, 137, 139–43.

[8] M Carbone, 'Mission Impossible: The European Union and Policy Coherence for Development' (2008) 30(3) *Journal of European Integration*, 323–42, 326.

a 'conflicted trade power', which faces incongruencies between 'its own guiding principles' as well as disagreements between Member States, the EU is also a conflicted converger.[9]

A few examples from the contributions to this part of the book might help draw out these conflicts over the EU's role in global (legal) convergence. Cardwell and Wessel's chapter highlights how the CJEU has taken different approaches to the question of territory in its judgments. Beyond the point they make about the specificity of each of these cases, the CJEU's jurisprudence in this area has arguably also reflected different 'modes of liberalism' at work. These have sometimes been in tension. For the *Organisation juive européenne* case,[10] Cardwell and Wessel show that the CJEU ruled that goods must indicate their origin in Israel or an Israeli settlement, citing international humanitarian law in the context of consumer choice (invoking both cosmopolitan duty and market logics). In contrast, they also illustrate that the CJEU's reliance on some elements of international law when it comes to the definition of territory in the *Polisario* case,[11] where it had previously stressed the autonomy of the EU legal order, was criticised as an abnegation of EU cosmopolitan duty altogether. It was seen as reflecting a dismissal of concerns regarding the exercise of Moroccan sovereignty over Western Sahara.

As Forowicz highlights, tensions can also be observed between the different forms of solidarity found in the EU's legal framework. Drawing on relevant literature, she identifies three types of solidarity: horizontal (inter-state); vertical (between the state and individuals) and systemic (the congruence between a state's regime and that of a supranational/international entity). She argues that it is ultimately the more limited horizontal solidarity between *Member States* of the EU that is most prevalent – and which has constrained the EU's response to the migration crisis. More 'cosmopolitan', vertical understandings of solidarity have been subscribed to by EU Member States in various international conventions – but the EU's 'principle of solidarity' has yet to be interpreted in light of these international 'counterparts'. Santos Vara and Pascual Matellán, meanwhile, have highlighted how, despite Member States and the EU actively participating in the elaboration of the Global Compact on Migration, this was ultimately opposed by several states: Austria, Bulgaria, the Czech Republic, Estonia, Hungary, Italy, Latvia, Poland and Slovakia.

Henig's chapter, in turn, concludes by arguing that the TTIP negotiations can be seen as an attempt by the EU and the US to 'project [their respective] regulatory approaches […] through trade agreements'.[12] But arguably the TTIP negotiations have also exposed tensions between different modes of market liberalism

[9] S Meunier and K Nicolaïdis, 'The European Union as a Conflicted Trade Power' (2006) 13(6) *Journal of European Public Policy* 906–25, 907.

[10] Case C-363/18 *Organisation Juive Européenne, Vignoble Psagot Ltd v Ministre de l'Économie et des Finances* ECLI:EU:C:2019:954.

[11] Case C-104/16 *Council v Front Polisario* (2016) EU:C:2016:973.

[12] See chapter 7 by David Henig, p 141.

at the heart of the European Single Market.[13] The non-governmental organisation (NGO) campaign against TTIP was successful in politicising the agreement by invoking the perceived threat of the agreement – notably its investor protection and regulatory cooperation provisions – to standards established through the Single Market, undermining the European social market economy.[14] TTIP itself, however, was the product of a very different, 'neoliberal' vision of EU trade policy and the Single Market. As I have argued with Ferdi De Ville, it was 'driven by both a philosophy and a discourse that idealise the efficient operation of markets and seek to minimise the constraints imposed by democratic decision-making in public policy'.[15]

All of this points to the importance of seeing convergence not in terms of a linear process, but rather, as Fernanda Nicola argues, 'through its dialectics with different types of resistance'.[16] She maps out four types of *local* resistance to the global convergence efforts pursued by the EU and other international organisations (IOs): 'local differentiation'; institutional path dependencies; resistance to Eurocentric convergence and 'democratic resistance' to the entrenching of neoliberalism – the latter of which I recognise in the anti-TTIP protests. Her contribution's focus on the *local* invites us to pay greater attention to this level of policymaking in assessing global convergence efforts and the role of the EU therein. For example, one of the central elements of the anti-TTIP campaign in Europe is that NGOs focused on persuading municipalities to pass hundreds of critical motions; some – including municipalities in Brussels, even went as far to declare themselves TTIP-free zones.[17] Local governments in Europe have also been involved in supporting undocumented migrants in the face of restrictive immigration and asylum policies.[18]

As I finish writing this epilogue on Brexit day, such debates about the nature of the EU as a global convergence actor are particularly resonant. As Rosamond has highlighted, despite its general liberal personality, the EU's external action is not the product of a unitary set of political values or objectives – even if some, such as myself, have pointed that there has been a move towards more neoliberal (external) policies over time.[19] This runs counter to many of the essentialising

[13] N Jabko, *Playing the Market: A Political Strategy for Uniting Europe, 1985–2005* (Ithaca, NY, Cornell University Press, 2006).

[14] G Siles-Brügge, 'Transatlantic Investor Protection as a Threat to Democracy: The Potency and Limits of an Emotive Frame' (2017) 30 (5–6) *Cambridge Review of International Affairs*, 464–88, 472.

[15] F De Ville and G Siles-Brügge, *TTIP: The Truth about the Transatlantic Trade and Investment Partnership* (Cambridge, Polity Press, 2016) 131.

[16] See chapter 6 by Fernanda Nicola, p 126.

[17] G Siles-Brügge and M Strange, 'Municipal Level Trade Contestation: Activists and Local Governments from the MAI to TTIP' in J Broschek and P Goff (eds), *Multilevel Trade Politics: Configurations, Dynamics, Mechanisms* (Toronto, University of Toronto Press, 2020).

[18] A Lundberg and M Strange, 'Struggles over Human Rights in Local Government – the Case of Access to Education for Undocumented Youth in Malmö, Sweden' (2012) 11(2) *Critical Policy Studies* 146–65.

[19] Rosamond (n 6).

arguments expressed by both right-wing Brexiteers and Lexiteers that the EU is, respectively, either an over-regulated Social Democratic space or simply a 'capitalist club'.[20] What approach the EU takes to global convergence is ultimately the product of broader political struggles. We could still see the flagship European Green Deal push the EU in a more environmentally sustainable direction, with the carbon border adjustment mechanism allowing the EU to push global convergence towards lower carbon intensity.

[20] D Baker, A Gamble and D Seawright, 'Sovereign Nations and Global Markets: Modern British Conservatism and Hyperglobalism' (2002) 4(3) *British Journal of Politics and International Relations* 399–428; J Hilary, 'It's Time the Left Saw the EU for What it Really is' (*politics.co.uk*, 8 January 2016). See www.politics.co.uk/comment-analysis/2016/01/08/comment-it-s-time-the-left-saw-the-eu-for-what-it-really-is (last accessed 9 March 2020).

PART III

When is EU Law and Policy More 'Inside-Out' than 'Outside-In'?

12

Regulatory Cooperation in EU FTAs: Linking Legalisation to Convergence

KORNILIA PIPIDI-KALOGIROU

I. Introduction

The new generation free trade agreements (hereinafter FTAs), symptoms of the renewed and ambitious trade agenda set by the EU Commission with its 2006 Global Agenda,[1] have changed decisively the landscape of international trade regulation and not only because of the EU's normative power.[2] Most importantly, the innovation lies in the inclusion of features that marginally touch upon hard core trade questions, as is for example the extension of trade to sustainable development and the insistence to connect trade liberalisation to the domestic regulatory agenda. A feature that falls under the latter category are the chapters on regulatory cooperation, outlined in detail especially in the Comprehensive Economic and Trade Agreement (hereinafter CETA)[3] and the EU-Japan Economic Partnership Agreement[4] (hereinafter JEEPA), which shall be the focus of the present contribution.

Of course, regulatory cooperation has been on the table long before its inclusion in the FTAs, with a long list of bilateral political agreements promoting it between the EU and the US.[5] Under its present form though, it represents

[1] Commission of the European Communities, 'Communication from the Commission to the Council, the European Parliament, the European Economic and Social Committee and the Committee of the Regions Global Europe: Competing in the World' COM(2006) 567 final (4 October 2006), https://eur-lex.europa.eu/LexUriServ/LexUriServ.do?uri=COM:2006:0567:FIN:en:PDF (last accessed 11 March 2020).

[2] Ian Manners, 'Normative Power Europe: A Contradiction in Terms?' (2002) 40 *Journal of Common Market Studies* 235.

[3] Comprehensive Economic and Trade Agreement (CETA) between Canada, of the one part, and the European Union and its Member States, of the other part [2011] OJ L11/23.

[4] Agreement between the European Union and Japan for an Economic Partnership [2018] OJ L330/3.

[5] For a comprehensive outline of the regulatory cooperation initiatives between the EU and the US, see Tamara Takaks, 'Transatlantic Regulatory Cooperation in Trade' in Elaine Fahey (ed), *A Transatlantic Community of Law* (Cambridge University Press, 2014).

an original shift. However, one would wonder about the reasons for this change. In order to understand this, I will borrow a phrase that Professor Cottier used in his keynote address at the University of Birmingham's Institute of European Law conference 'Transatlantic Perspectives', on 28 June 2018, which focused on Regulatory Cooperation. He suggested that academic research needs to 'go back to the foundations' in order to be able to give answers to political problems.[6] With this statement, he urged the necessity to examine the core issue behind a political choice in order to be able to develop an appropriate narrative for its legal/political solution. And the core issues behind regulatory cooperation are no secret.

Ever since traditional tariffs were disqualified as being the number one hurdle to international trade, the global focus has been reoriented and agendas have been updated in the search for the remaining obstacles to frictionless trade. However, this reorientation follows not only the impressive reduction of tariffs but also market regulation. Global trade is all the more dominated by the so-called global value chains, the sequence of production in which not all components of a final product originate from the same country but instead transcend borders for the final accumulation.[7] It is thus a paradox when these chains, which are created in order to minimise component costs, and thus the cost of the final product, face regulatory barriers when crossing borders, which usually generate extra costs. The competitive advantage is lost. Of course, this paradox is not the only reason why contemporary trade focuses on addressing regulatory barriers. As they are the only substantial impediment left, the need to properly address them in order to maximise trade gains is imperative.

This narrative, while hardly capturing the magnitude of the problem, certainly reveals the importance of putting aspects of the domestic regulatory agenda on the negotiating table. Given the significance of the matter and the shortcomings of similar exercises in the bilateral political arena (especially the transatlantic saga on regulatory cooperation) but also in the multilateral scene (indeed the Agreements on Technical Barriers to Trade and Sanitary and Phytosanitary Measures can only be taken so far), the EU opted for a change in terms of confronting regulatory cooperation as part of its new trade policy.

It is exactly this change that this chapter tries to capture. For this exercise it shall use the conceptual tool of 'Legalisation'. The choice of 'Legalisation' as a concept created by International Relations scholars draws insights from different disciplines, particularly political science and international relations, in order to

[6] Thomas Cottier, 'The Changing Structure of International Economic Law and the Future of Regulatory Cooperation' Keynote Address at the University of Birmingham's Institute of European Law Conference 'Transatlantic Perspectives', 28 June 2018, www.youtube.com/watch?v=lcQYgk9c5nA (last accessed 11 March 2020).

[7] Bernard Hoekman and Charles Sabel, 'Trade Agreements, Regulatory Sovereignty and Democratic Legitimacy', EUI Working Papers, RSCAS 2017/36, 4.

methodologically present legal argumentation through 'borrowed' lenses, thus gaining in:

- coherence, as far as concepts are being used;
- comprehensiveness, as far as factors that escape a narrow doctrinal analysis are taken into consideration; and
- accessibility, as far as the content becomes comprehensible to non-legal scientists.

Its use is also in harmony with an overarching question of the book, whether making use of other disciplines is methodologically sound in addressing legal questions.

In essence, this is a question that follows the inaugural call for the 'interdisciplinary marriage' of International Law and International Relations, advocated by Kenneth Abbot in his seminal 'wake-up call' towards lawyers two decades ago in an effort to bring together the two, estranged after the Cold War disciplines.[8] The call was successful given that, in the years that followed, actors from both sides walked on the road that Abbot had paved.[9] The development of the concept of 'legalisation', first presented at the symposium on 'Legalisation and World Politics' and later hosted as a special issue in International Organisation, counts as the most significant contribution from the International Relations side.[10] The concept was constructed in such a way as to allow 'a better understanding of this variation in the use and consequences of law in international politics'.[11] As per its instigators, the term 'legalisation' aims to capture the augmenting tendency of sovereign states to constrain themselves in various domains.[12]

This tendency, depicted as far as regulatory cooperation is concerned in the inclusion of the relevant chapters in the FTAs, can be based on the insisting trade-distorting effect of non-tariff barriers to trade as explained above. While this is one of the reasons explaining the turn to legalisation, it does not explain how this legalisation takes place, meaning on what elements legalisation is measured and the significance of each element.

It is this gap that the present contribution will try to fill. In so far as this contribution seeks to unlock a better understanding of the use of law in the

[8] Kenneth W Abbot, 'Modem International Relations Theory: A Prospectus for International Lawyers' (1989) 14 *Yale Journal of International Law* 336.

[9] For an overview of the Canonical Interdisciplinary Literature, see Jeffrey L Dunoff and Mark A Polack, 'International Law and International Relations' in Jeffrey L Dunoff and Mark A Polack (eds), *Interdisciplinary Perspectives on International Law and International Relations: The State of Art* (Cambridge University Press, 2012) 10ff.

[10] Kenneth W Abbott, Robert O Keohane, Andrew Moravcsik, Anne-Marie Slaughter and Duncan Snidal, 'The Concept of Legalisation' (2000) 54 *International Organisation* 401.

[11] Judith Goldstein, Miles Kahler, Robert O Keohane and Anne-Marie Slaughter, 'Introduction: Legalisation and World Politics' (2000) 54 *International Organisation* 385, 386.

[12] *Ibid.*

regulatory cooperation chapters of CETA and JEEPA and its consequences upon the enhancement of regulatory convergence, it shall use the concept of 'legalisation' as the methodological key. The present contribution understands regulatory convergence as the gradual process of approximation of regulatory orders, both process and results-wise. Regulatory convergence is distinguished from regulatory cooperation in the sense that the latter is the means to achieve the former. By placing regulatory cooperation under the lens of legalisation, we ask the question if and how the founding elements of the legalisation concept – precision, obligation and delegation – picture the promotion of regulatory cooperation practices that target regulatory convergence. Precision measures exactly how precise the provisions are. As a first step, this element serves as an analytical tool to map subjects and objects of regulatory cooperation. Obligation informs us about the type of obligation and its stringency. We shall make use of this element, in order to comment upon the legal nature of the commitments and reflect on how their legal nature promotes convergence. Finally, we will base the last part of the chapter on the delegation element, in order to discuss whether there is a dynamic element in the whole arrangement to promote convergence results-wise.

Before diving into each separate section, we need to justify the choice of examining regulatory cooperation as is present in the two particular FTAs, CETA and JEEPA. Indeed, the choice of these two agreements is a conscious one, and it is based on two criteria: the presence of regulatory cooperation in an FTA and the similarity of commitments. On the basis of the first criterion we can exclude the analysis of non-FTA regulatory cooperation as well as other FTAs for which we do not yet have a final text (for example the Transatlantic Trade and Investment Partnership (TTIP)). The second criterion excludes from our scope of analysis FTAs that don't have a separate chapter on regulatory cooperation as a horizontal procedure or that go as far as including only regulatory coherence commitments (for example the EU-South Korea FTA[13] and EU-Singapore FTA[14] have a strong sectoral focus). The difference between the two lies in the fact that while regulatory coherence aims mostly in ensuring the quality of the regulatory process and the produced regulations internally, regulatory cooperation is a process that encompasses specific activities jointly undertaken by the regulators of two (or more) parties on existing or future regulations.[15] We are thus interested in examining opportunities for convergence regarding a very specific form of

[13] Council Decision (EU) 2011/265 of 16 September 2010 on the signing, on behalf of the European Union, and provisional application of the Free Trade Agreement between the European Union and its Member States, of the one part, and the Republic of Korea, of the other part [2011] OJ L127/6.

[14] Council Decision (EU) 2019/1875 of 8 November 2019 on the conclusion of the Free Trade Agreement between the European Union and the Republic of Singapore [2019] OJ L294/1.

[15] Regulatory Coherence & Cooperation in the Transatlantic Trade and Investment Partnership (TTIP), The US Chamber of Commerce, www.uschamber.com/sites/default/files/regulatory_coherence_regulatory_cooperation_-chamber_ttip_paper-final_2.pdf (last accessed 11 March 2020).

regulatory cooperation, the characteristics of which – bilateral and part of an FTA – create a new mode of governance in the sphere of the EU's international relations.

II. Precision: Mapping the Subjects and Objects of Regulatory Cooperation

Regulatory Cooperation as a general term encompasses a broad range of activities of varying intensity, undertaken by actors located in the public and private domain. For example, Regulatory Cooperation may implicate coordination not only of regulators as state agents but also of industry actors and standardisation bodies, which may but also may not be attached to the public domain. Accordingly, the object of the cooperation may vary. Having this plurality in mind, the present section aims to map the main protagonists of regulatory cooperation in the FTAs under analysis and their working material.

A. Defining the Subjects of Regulatory Cooperation

The different nature of the two FTAs under consideration, with JEEPA being an EU-only agreement and CETA being a mixed one, is seen on various occasions. One illustration is the difference regarding the concerned regulators in the workings of regulatory cooperation. Thus, while regulatory cooperation in JEEPA remains centralised, with the concerned Japanese authority being the Government of Japan and for the European Union, the European Commission,[16] CETA seems to opt for the inclusion of national regulators as well, at least in theory. In this regard, while JEEPA gains in precision, a concrete reference is missing from Chapter 21 of CETA. Nevertheless, an answer can be extracted by context.

First, as mentioned, CETA is a mixed agreement which means that the inclusion of national regulators is at least possible. Second, the repartition of regulatory competences in the Canadian regulatory system, which gives substantial independence to provincial regulators, makes their inclusion a functional necessity since it is very often provincial legislatures that have to translate international commitments into domestic law and action.[17] Last but not least, as we mentioned, Chapter 21 does not directly name the implicated regulators. However, as the TTIP negotiations have also shown, precision as an instrument is preferred over silence in concretising the policy choices of the parties. Article x2 of the TTIP

[16] Article 18.2 (a) JEEPA.

[17] Stanko S Krstic, 'Regulatory Cooperation to Remove Non-tariff Barriers to Trade in Products: Key Challenges and Opportunities for the Canada-EU Comprehensive Trade Agreement' (2012) 39 *Legal Issues of Economic Integration* 14.

draft Chapter on Regulatory Cooperation mentioned in a similar way to JEEPA that the implicated regulators were the only ones at a centralised level.[18] After a comparative analysis of those two examples with CETA's Chapter 21, one can safely perceive the absence of precision in the latter as advocating for the inclusion of national regulators, at least on paper.

B. Connecting Subjects to Objects

Thus, precision is more than an accessibility tool to each separate provision. As shown already, its utility extends beyond that, for example to the facilitation of comparative analyses, as it will also be used later. These functions of the tool are however not exclusive. Precision can also serve as an interpretation mechanism. To make this clearer, the results that we extract from a precise provision can be of importance to others. This function is illustrated best by the co-relation between subjects and objects. Indeed, the depiction of the subjects is not only important of and by itself; it also provides us with a first definition of the object of cooperation, the material on which regulators are called to work, and the legal tools with which they will work.

The analysis for each agreement will proceed as follows: The first limb of the term 'objects' will, as mentioned, refer to the substantive material. This will always fall within the limits of each regulator's substantive competence. For the EU, this means that a first delimitation is done on the basis of the Union's competences, the geography of which corresponds to a primary match in the regulation.[19] The substantive material is further crystallised by the scope as agreed by the parties and found in the relevant chapter provisions. The crystallisation of the term will be completed by examining its second limb, the legal tools which will be subject to regulatory cooperation.

i. Objects of Regulatory Cooperation in CETA

Starting with the substantive material subject to regulatory cooperation in CETA, one can as a first step make the connection between the broadness of participating regulators and their material competence. This means that the latter is, at least in theory not confined only to EU-only areas of competence. It is however limited by the scope of application. Stated in Article 21.1, the scope of application enumerates in a non-exhaustive manner some chapters whose subjects fall within the material

[18] See Article x2 of the TTIP-EU proposal for Chapter: Regulatory Cooperation, as submitted for discussion by the EU, http://trade.ec.europa.eu/doclib/docs/2016/march/tradoc_154377.pdf (last accessed 11 March 2020).

[19] Consolidated versions of the Treaty on European Union (TEU) and the Treaty on the Functioning of the European Union (TFEU) [2016] OJ C202/1, Arts 2–6.

scope of regulatory cooperation. Although limiting the vast area that could in theory fall under regulatory cooperation, the scope of application remains quite broad, justifying the identity of the new generation FTAs as going beyond traditional trade matters but also embracing behind-the-border issues of domestic regulation.

Based on similar thinking, regulatory cooperation could also encompass and concern every legal tool, including the legislative acts. Should one want to have a first idea of potential 'candidates', one could identify which legal acts are mostly used to include technical aspects of regulation that could act as regulatory barriers. For example, we could presume that delegated and implementing acts, that treat technical/non-essential aspects of a regulation, could be potential candidates.[20] However, this is purely hypothetical. According to the ambition of the parties in each case, activities could either relate to technical aspects or touch upon more substantial issues that are usually enshrined into formal legislation.

ii. Objects of Regulatory Cooperation in JEEPA

Thus, in an EU-only Agreement, such as JEEPA, regulatory cooperation is primarily defined by the competence scope of the Union, while JEEPA similarly adopts an 'open-list' approach which includes 'every measure susceptible to affect trade and investment'.[21] A closer look is required though for defining the legal tools that are subject to the Agreement's regulatory cooperation.

The official answer is stated in Article 18.2b. Regulatory cooperation provisions shall concern a) laws, b) cabinet orders and c) ministerial ordinances, while for the EU, regulatory cooperation extends to regulations and directives of Article 288 of the Treaty on the Functioning of the European Union (TFEU) and delegated and implementing acts of Articles 290 and 291 respectively. Should one read the provision carefully, one will remark that legislative acts of the EU, one of the legal acts of Article 288 TFEU adopted according to one of the legislative procedures of Article 289 TFEU, seem to be excluded from the scope of cooperation.

This comes as a consequence of Article's 18.2b silence regarding Article 289 TFEU and the importance of the latter provision in the EU legal order. Indeed, in the EU legal system, as legislative acts or legislation qualify only the instruments enumerated in Article 288 (regulations, directives and decisions) that have been adopted under a legislative procedure in accordance with Article 289 TFEU.[22] In fact, regulations, directives and decisions can stand as legal acts without having

[20] Deirdre Curtin and Tatevik Manucharyan, 'Legal Acts and Hierarchy of Norms in the EU' in Anthony Arnull and Damien Chalmers (eds), *The Oxford Handbook on EU Law* (Oxford University Press, 2015).

[21] JEEPA Art 18.3.

[22] Alexander H Türk, 'Law-making after Lisbon' in Andrea Biondi, Piet Eeckhout and Stefanie Ripley (eds), *EU Law after Lisbon* (Oxford University Press, 2012) 67 ff.

been adopted by a legislative procedure, either ordinary or special. For example, the so-called delegated and implementing acts, while not adopted under Article 289 TFEU and thus not qualifying as legislation *stricto sensu*, can take the form of one of the acts mentioned in Article 288 TFEU.[23]

The precision by which TTIP negotiations were carried are once more helpful in offering a comparative background for a better understanding of the will of the parties. According to Article x2b of the negotiating document on Regulatory Cooperation of the TTIP Agreement, regulatory acts at central level were meant to include

> Regulations and Directives within the meaning of Article 288 of the Treaty on the Functioning of the European Union, including: i. Regulations and Directives adopted under a legislative procedure in accordance with the Treaty; ii. Delegated and Implementing acts adopted pursuant to Articles 290 and 291 of that Treaty.

Under such a formulation, the parties considered the nature of the EU's legislation in order to add legislation *stricto sensu*. It is exactly this preciseness in the negotiating history of the Union that creates doubt as to whether legislative acts are excluded from both the regulatory coherence and cooperation activities.

Despite this interpretation of the omission of Article 289 TFEU, it is for reasons of reciprocity that we cannot accept this reading. In other words, EU legislation *stricto sensu* must be included since from the side of Japan, laws fall under the ambit of the Chapter, as per Article 18.2 g. In this case, not mentioning Article 289 TFEU creates legal uncertainty, since it casts legal doubts on issues that cannot stand politically, illustrating perfectly another aspect of preciseness.

C. Inference on the Role of Precision in Discovering the Subjects and Objects

As explained in the Introduction, the use of the concept of 'legalisation' and its components shall be used to serve various purposes simultaneously. It is however only after unbundling each element that we can understand its multiple significance in the analysis. Very importantly, the categorisation according to the various elements helps in gaining analytical clarity in presenting the changes in regulatory cooperation coherently. Thus, by employing precision we primarily attempt to map subjects and objects, which is *conditio sine qua non* in our understanding of the level of regulatory convergence through FTAs. Indeed, broader participating actorness, which is also given an extended working palette, signifies a more integrated and committed approach towards convergence. However, precision proved to be much more than a categorisation facilitator. Through the precision of provisions, or better the absence thereof, this section highlighted legal uncertainties

[23] Curtin and Manucharyan (n 20) 111 ff.

that could arise from incomplete references, as was the omission to refer to the concerned regulators in Chapter 21 of CETA and the non-reference to Article 289 TFEU in Article 18.2g of JEEPA. In such cases of uncertainty, the precise formulation of similar negotiating documents proved helpful in understanding the will of the parties. In a similar fashion, the next sections will proceed with the remaining legalisation elements.

III. Obligation: Enhancing Convergence of Processes

Regulatory convergence is primarily a matter of stabilisation of processes. While it can be gradual, generalised and achieved over time, by enhancing the compatibility of regulatory regimes, it can also be 'fast-forwarded' with concrete and intense cooperation activities. This difference in the chosen type of convergence is reflected in the two agreements under analysis, with JEEPA focusing on the former and CETA on the latter. This difference corresponds to the division between regulatory cooperation and regulatory coherence.

A. A Solid Legal Status of the Commitments

Regardless of the type of convergence that is advanced within the respective agreements, commitments in both cases qualify as legal international ones, undertaken under public international law, whose overarching framework applies. Their quality as such should not be questioned on the basis of a declaration of voluntary character or a possible absence of dispute settlement. Indeed, legality should not be confused with 'substance', meaning the degree to which parties agreed to change their behaviour, par example with a clause on voluntary initiation.[24] Equally importantly, legality should be distinguished from structure. The choice to submit an obligation of an agreement to dispute settlement is in fact part of the structure of the agreement, rather than part of the nature of the obligation.[25]

The legal nature of the commitments is instead tied to fundamental norms that constitute the cornerstones of the international legal system and that inform us of the consequences that derive from the nature of the obligations undertaken by the regulatory cooperation chapters. The fundamental principle of *pacta sunt servanda*, codified in Article 26 of the Vienna Convention on the Law of Treaties, along with its sister provision Article 27, both extracted from the imperatives

[24] Kal Raustalia, 'Form and Substance in International Agreements' (2005) 99 *The American Journal of International Law* 584.

[25] Andrew Guzman, 'The Cost of Credibility: Explaining Resistance to Interstate Dispute Settlement Mechanisms' (2002) 31 *Journal of Legal Studies* 303.

of *bona fide*,[26] ask for compliance in good faith and invite the parties to honour the terms upon which they have agreed to initiate regulatory cooperation, without invoking internal legislation as an impediment to the fulfilment of their obligations.[27]

It is exactly this principle of good faith, which substantiates the obligation to comply, the key that can 'fill' the gaps that structural and substantial choices as the absence of enforcement and the voluntary initiation can create.[28] Indeed, good faith is a good facilitator in a case like this, where the parties have opted for various safety valves to dress their obligation. Of course, the heart of the chapters entail both the right of the parties to ask for initiation of regulatory cooperation along the agreed lines but also their commitment in good faith to comply should the appropriate circumstances arise, those being for example the identification of cases of mutual interest, or of emerging areas in need of regulation. Should the parties choose not to proceed, they are expected to state the reasons behind their choice. Still though, even with this regime, the parties enjoy a wide margin of discretion, which renders the distinction between conformity and non-conformity a difficult exercise. This in turn hinders the establishment of the international responsibility of the parties,[29] a regime that even if questionable given the insistence to outline regulatory cooperation as voluntary, entails reputational damage in any case.

The consequences arising from the characteristics of the obligation are necessary to be considered mostly in order to have a clear view on the functioning of the obligation. However, two things should be summarised from the above analysis: First, the choices that the parties make regarding the structure and substance of the agreement should not interfere with their legality. Regulatory cooperation commitments remain international obligations with whatever that entails. Instead, those choices that the parties make may hinder the application of the obligations, an impediment which can in any case be confronted with the principle of good faith.

B. Mapping the Substance of the Commitments

The nature of the obligations as such matters from a legal perspective, in so far as it informs us about its status in the international arena and consequences that come

[26] Markus Kotzur, 'Good Faith (Bona Fide)' in Rüdiger Wolfrum (ed), *Max Planck Encyclopedia of Public International Law*, https://opil.ouplaw.com/view/10.1093/law:epil/9780199231690/law-9780199231690-e1412?prd=EPIL (last accessed 11 March 2020).

[27] Anthony Aust, 'Pacta Sunt Servanda' in Rüdiger Wolfrum (ed), *Max Planck Encyclopaedia of Public International Law*, https://opil.ouplaw.com/view/10.1093/law:epil/9780199231690/law-9780199231690-e1449 (last accessed 11 March 2020).

[28] See Kotzur (n 26).

[29] Alain Pellet, 'The Definition of Responsibility in International Law' in James Crawford, Alain Pellet and Simon Olleson (eds), *The Law of International Responsibility* (Oxford University Press, 2010) 4.

hand in hand with it. After having made that clear, this section will analyse what these obligations entail for the parties.

i. CETA's Focus on Concrete Cooperation Activities

Regulatory cooperation in CETA is outlined in a detailed manner. Indeed, CETA's Article 21.4 targets specific activities, which mainly include: exchanging experiences on regulatory tools;[30] consulting and exchanging information on various instances;[31] seeking to gather and enable foreign input through commenting in the regulatory process;[32] examining different ways or alternatives to convergence; and using similar methodological tools to generally promote similarity of results.[33] Their reach is intense. Of varying nature, the commitments are formulated and chosen to touch all aspects of the regulatory circle, beginning with the formulation and extending to review and revise their evaluation, also touching upon the methodology behind the regulatory choices.

ii. JEEPA's Focus on Regulatory Coherence

On the other end of the spectrum, regarding regulatory cooperation, JEEPA chooses to refer only to the procedure to be followed for their initiation, but Chapter 18 in general is mostly dedicated to commitments of regulatory coherence, the reach of which is also expected to be substantial in the regulatory process. This is mostly understood by context, since the nature of some undertaken commitments render them applicable to specific stages of the regulatory process, something that is usually reflected in the text itself as well; for example, while transparency is required at all stages,[34] public consultations and impact assessment refers to the preparatory phase of a regulation,[35] and retrospective evaluation coincides with a later review of regulatory measures. The betterment of the regulatory process through the coherence commitments is better achieved only if it is thorough. Other major trading actors that have included similar commitments in their trade agenda have also opted for a far-reaching intervention in the regulatory circle. An extract from the Trans-Pacific Partnership Agreement's advanced chapter on regulatory coherence, confirms that the good regulatory practices enshrined therein

[30] CETA, Art 21.4.a.(i) to (iv).

[31] CETA, Art 21.4 b, c, f.

[32] CETA, Art 21.4.d, e.

[33] CETA, Art 21.4.i, k, n.

[34] For example, on the basis of Article 18.5, each party is required to make public any material that describes the processes and mechanisms that are used for the preparation, evaluation and review of its regulatory measures.

[35] Article 18.7 on Public Consultations is to be respected 'when preparing major regulatory measures' while Article 18.8 on Impact Assessment obliges the parties to undertake this procedure for 'major regulatory measures under preparation'.

were meant to apply 'in the process of planning, designing, issuing, implementing and reviewing regulatory measures'.[36]

C. Inference on the Role of Obligation in Picturing Convergence of Processes

The role of 'obligation' in depicting how convergence of processes is achieved with regulatory cooperation was twofold. Mainly, the element 'obligation' referred to the nature of the obligations as legal or non-legal. The first part of the analysis established the legal nature of the obligation as well as its particularities. This served as the first step in concluding that, whatever the content may be, the processes enshrined within have taken the form of a legal obligation and thus carry a normative weight. Later, the puzzle was completed by looking into the substance of the obligations. There, we observed differences regarding the processes outlined in each agreement, with CETA focusing on regulatory cooperation activities and JEEPA on regulatory coherence. Both having the same status, their normative capacity to promote convergence is equally strong. What changes is the way that they will impact regulatory convergence, via direct or indirect methods.

IV. Delegation: (Not) Embracing Convergence Results

After having analysed the element of obligation which enhances procedural convergence through the transformation of commitments to legal international ones, what follows is an examination of if and how the regulatory cooperation chapters have foreseen mechanisms that allow for the adoption of regulatory cooperation results that aim at convergence. In other words, we are interested in learning whether and how results of regulatory cooperation are being consolidated. For this we shall use the element of delegation, which was introduced as the quality picturing the presence of a dynamic character in an international arrangement. That dynamic element can, according to the instigators of the concept, either take the form of an adjudicating mechanism with the authority to interpret and apply rules (hereinafter 'Type A Delegation') or of secondary rulemaking (hereinafter 'Type B Delegation').[37] Although regulatory cooperation commitments are subject to Type A Delegation dispute settlement in CETA (but not in JEEPA),[38] the present section will focus on Type B Delegation to examine whether the possibility

[36] Article 25.2.1, Final Text of the Trans-Pacific Partnership Agreement, <https://ustr.gov/sites/default/files/TPP-Final-Text-Regulatory-Coherence.pdf (last accessed 11 March 2020).

[37] See Abbott, Keohane, Moravcsik, Slaughter and Snidal (n 10) 415.

[38] Dispute settlement is excluded from the Regulatory Cooperation Chapter by virtue of Article 18.19 of JEEPA.

of secondary rulemaking which is present in other instances exists with regard to regulatory cooperation.

A. Absence of Decision-Making in the Regulatory Cooperation Specialised Committees

The institutional structure in both agreements is similar, consisting of a central body, better known as the 'Joint Committees' with a general mandate to overview the functioning of the agreements and of the various specialised bodies, whose focus centres upon the particular chapter under which they are founded.[39] The separate bodies relevant for our analysis are the ones foreseen under the Regulatory Cooperation Chapters, the Regulatory Cooperation Forum in the CETA and the Regulatory Cooperation Body in the JEEPA (hereinafter referred to as 'Regulatory Cooperation Bodies').[40] From a first textual analysis of the mandate of the Regulatory Cooperation Bodies enshrined in Articles 21.6 CETA and 18.14 JEEPA, it is easily deductible that this remains confined to implementation and support activities. Indeed, the focus of their activities centres around the coordination and promotion and sustainability of regulatory dialogues,[41] the identification of areas of common interest[42] and the facilitation of forums for the development of those dialogues,[43] whose progress they are also in charge of overseeing.[44] Despite having an active role in the substantial part of the rulemaking, formal decision-making does not seem to be listed among the powers vested to either of those specialised committees. This absence of delegation seems inconsistent when seen under the prism of the *telos* of regulatory cooperation, which is regulatory convergence, and which figures in both agreements as an objective.[45]

B. Absence of Delegated Decision-Making in the Joint Committees

One of the powers of the joint committees is decision-making which can vary from fundamental to technical issues.[46] Relevant provisions within various chapters

[39] See generally Chapter 26 CETA and Chapter 22 JEEPA.
[40] Articles 21.6 CETA and 18.14 JEEPA.
[41] Articles 21.6.2 (a) CETA, 18.14.3 (d) and 18.14.3 (e) JEEPA.
[42] Article 18.14.3 (g) JEEPA.
[43] Articles 21.6.2 (a), 21.6 (d) CETA and 18.14.3 (a) JEEPA.
[44] Articles 21.6.2 (c) CETA and 18.14.3 (i) in combination with 18.16.8 JEEPA.
[45] Article 21.3 (d) and 21.4 (g) CETA and Article 18.14.3 (d) JEEPA.
[46] Wolfgang Weiss, 'Delegation to Treaty Bodies in EU Agreements: Constitutional Constraints and Proposals for Strengthening the European Parliament' (2018) 18 *European Constitutional Law Review* 532, 534.

confirm so. For the joint committees to be able to adopt decisions on matters that fall within a certain chapter, there is a certain procedure that must be followed.

This procedure begins by the submission from the specialised committees of a proposal to the Joint Committee, which will later take the relevant decision. This of course is the case when the specialised committees do not have decision-making powers of their own (some do on the basis of Article 22.5 JEEPA and 26.2.4 CETA but only when the agreements specifically state so). As far as the submission of proposals to the joint committees is concerned, we can extract from the provision that the specialised committees are in principle free to submit proposals, without that being specifically mentioned in each separate chapter. This interpretation follows the positioning of the comma in CETA: 'The specialized committees may propose draft decisions for adoption by the CETA Joint Committee, or take decisions when this Agreement so provides'. The same comma appears in other language versions.[47] It thus becomes clear that specific provision is necessary only for the decision-making part, but not for the submission of proposals. In JEEPA, no such comma exists, however, there is no evidence that supports a different intention of the drafters.

Given the above, it could be supported that the regulatory cooperation fora are in principle allowed to submit for adoption any substantive proposal which would reflect the outcome of a successful cooperation. However, even in this case, joint committees do not enjoy the right of taking decisions on regulatory cooperation issues. Their decision-making capacity stems from Articles 26.3.1, 26.3.2 CETA and 22.2.1 JEEPA, which entitle each one of them to adopt decisions only *when the Agreement so provides*.

This phrase in italics, found also in JEEPA,[48] clarifies that the decision-making capacity in each specific case must be based elsewhere in each agreement, in provisions other than Articles 22.5 JEEPA or 26.2.4 CETA. This is confirmed by the existence of such provisions within certain specialised chapters of both agreements, which allow a decision to be taken by the Joint Committee upon proposal of the respective specialised one. This possibility exists in other cases.[49] Since such a provision is missing from both regulatory cooperation chapters, it seems that decisions are, at least for the time being, excluded.

V. Conclusion

A concluding collective inference on the elements presented above not only reveals to what extent regulatory convergence is advanced, but also allows for a first comparison between the potential of the two agreements to further regulatory

[47] To my understanding Greek, French, Italian, Spanish and German.
[48] In a slightly differently formation '*where provided for in this Agreement*'.
[49] For example, Arts 10.16.2 (a), 2.35 (c) 14.53.3 in JEEPA, or Arts 2.13.2, 6.14.4 CETA.

convergence. First, as international obligations created through the inclusion in an FTA, certainly the conditions under which regulatory cooperation procedures are perceived, implemented and conducted are altered. Indeed, such an obligation carries a heavy legal significance, one that has the power to oversee, prevent and give solutions to internal implementation problems, exactly because of the weight it carries as an international commitment. Second, despite the same degree of obligation, which elevates equally the envisaged procedures to 'legal obligation' status, it becomes apparent that between the two chapters, it is CETA that seems overall more precise, and more comprehensive. We draw this conclusion from its two main differences with JEEPA: first, from the promotion of concrete regulatory cooperation, activities are outlined, and second from the ambition of the envisaged cooperation. Indeed, the participation of national regulators due to the Agreement's mixed character, extends convergence possibilities beyond national borders. If we combine the two elements, we shall observe that the enhanced obligation strengthens the procedures envisaged in each agreement, whichever their nature. In other words, it is the procedure leading to convergence that is strengthened. In contrast to the procedure, the promotion of convergence results is not taking effect through the chapters, which lack an inbuilt mechanism to support secondary rulemaking. There are various reasons behind such a decision that go beyond the scope of this work. Whatever the motives, it is always useful to examine the prospects and limits of new efforts on controversial issues such as regulatory cooperation. It certainly constitutes a development when compared to previous efforts aiming at regulatory cooperation. A successful step by step approach might lead to new developments in the future.

13

Labour Standards in EU-Mexico Trade: An Assessment along Two Narratives of Convergence

AAKRITI BHARDWAJ AND JEFF KENNER

I. Introduction: Identifying the Two Narratives of Convergence

The European Commission has asserted that the *new approach* in the EU's trade policy is directed at promoting 'values like sustainable development human rights, fair and ethical trade and the fight against corruption'.[1] The EU's pursuit of a value-based trade agenda has been a subject of considerable debate from legal and policy perspectives.[2] In its bilateral trade relations, the EU has sought to address these issues in its new generation free trade agreements (FTAs).[3] In these agreements, labour-related obligations of the parties are covered by a Trade and Sustainable Development (TSD) chapter. As a 'common formulation' approach in all FTAs,[4] the EU predominantly focuses on upward convergence with international labour standards as vested in the International Labour Organisation's (ILO) Core

[1] See Foreword by Cecilia Malmström in *Trade for All* (European Commission, 2015).

[2] European Commission, 'The Social Dimension of Globalisation – The EU's Policy Contribution on Extending the Benefits to All' COM(2004) 383 final (18 May 2004); Lotte Drieghe and Diana Potjomkina, 'EU's Value-Based Approach in Trade Policy: (Free) Trade for All?' (2019) 5 *Global Affairs* 63; Olivier De Schutter, *Trade in the Service of Sustainable Development* (Hart Publishing, 2015); Emily Reid, *Balancing Human Rights, Environmental Protection and International Trade* (Hart Publishing, 2015); Melo Araujo, *The EU Deep Trade Agenda* (Oxford University Press, 2016); Lore Van den Putte and Samantha Velluti, 'The Promotion of Social Trade in the EU's External Trade Relations' in Sangeeta Khorana and María García (eds), *Handbook on the EU and International Trade* (Edward Elgar, 2018).

[3] European Commission, 'Report From The Commission To The European Parliament, The Council, The European Economic And Social Committee And The Committee Of The Regions On Implementation Of Free Trade Agreements' COM(2017) 654 final 7 (9 November 2017); European Commission, 'Global Europe: Competing in the World' (Commission Staff Working Document) COM(2006) 567 final 16 (4 October 2006).

[4] James Harrison and others, 'Labour Standards Provisions in EU Free Trade Agreements: Reflections on the European Commission's Reform Agenda' (2018) *World Trade Review* 1.

Conventions, the Declaration of Fundamental Principles and the Rights at Work 1998 and the Decent Work Agenda. This is the first strand of convergence, which we identify as vertical convergence.

The Commission has expressed the need to improve the TSD chapters in EU FTAs.[5] As a result, the EU mentioned its intent to further enable civil society participation and to identify country priorities which 'address priorities for each partner country'.[6] Recent developments in EU-Mexico trade relations demonstrate an advancement of the EU's Agenda in both these respects. The EU-Mexico FTA will be the first one with an extended role for the civil society and a chapter on anti-corruption.[7] Anti-corruption is a public concern in respect of Mexico and may have been necessitated by the various 'patterns' of corruption in Mexico which co-existed.[8] Moreover, corruption has entrenched trade unions, impacting public interest advocacy within the country.[9] The linkage between labour rights on the one hand and the civil society and corruption on the other, is hard to miss in relation to the obligations on human rights, sustainable development and rule of law which the EU undertakes to promote in its external relations.[10] The coverage of these areas promotes the EU's normative agenda[11] but also gives rise to the want for convergence between provisions of the trade agreement. We identify this strand of convergence as horizontal convergence.

Taking the EU-Mexico FTA as a reference, this chapter asserts that the trade-labour linkage largely depends on the vertical and horizontal narratives of convergence. This premise is tested against theoretical and practical realities of the EU's trade with Mexico. From a theoretical perspective for instance, the EU's requirement on seeking vertical convergence is that Mexico ratify all core conventions of the ILO. There are two points that arise in this respect, first, now

[5] *Non-Paper of the Commission Services Trade and Sustainable Development (TSD) Chapters in EU Free Trade Agreements (FTAs)* (European Commission, 2017), http://trade.ec.europa.eu/doclib/docs/2017/july/tradoc_155686.pdf (last accessed 13 March 2020).

[6] *Non Paper Of The Commission Services: Feedback And Way Forward On Improving The Implementation And Enforcement Of Trade And Sustainable Development Chapters In EU Free Trade Agreements* (European Commission, 2018), http://trade.ec.europa.eu/doclib/docs/2018/february/tradoc_156618.pdf (last accessed 13 March 2020).

[7] The EU and Mexico trace their trading relationship to the Global Agreement (GA) which covers political dialogue, trade relations and cooperation and liberalised trade in goods and trade in services, in 2000 and 2001, respectively. The new EU-Mexico FTA modernises the trade pillar of the GA, see 'New EU-Mexico Agreement: The Agreement in Principle' https://trade.ec.europa.eu/doclib/docs/2018/april/tradoc_156791.pdf (last accessed 13 March 2020).

[8] Such as drug-related corruption, criminal organisation, business-related corruption and governmental corruption, Stephen D Morris, 'Corruption and the Mexican Political System: Continuity and Change' (1999) 20 *Third World Quarterly* 623–43.

[9] Carlos De Buen Unna, 'Mexican Trade Unionism in a Time of Transition' in Joanne Conaghan, Richard Michael Fischl and Karl Klare (eds), *Labour Law in an Era of Globalization* (Oxford University Press, 2004) 402.

[10] Article 3(5) Treaty on European Union (TEU) and Article 21(1) TEU.

[11] Ian Manners, 'Normative Power Europe: A Contradiction in Terms?' (2002) 40 *Journal of Common Market Studies* 235.

that Mexico has ratified all ILO Conventions, it is difficult to establish empirically whether the EU's insistence played a role in the process. The EU's approach is to pursue *ex post* regulatory changes[12] and therefore, it is highly unlikely that Mexico ratified the core convention under the purview of trade negotiations with the EU.[13] Second, ratification is not an indicator of performance, meaning that it does not guarantee the operational efficiency of these fundamental conventions.

Vertical convergence in EU-Mexico trade relations may also be overshadowed in the light of practical and fundamentally political developments in US-Mexico trade relations. This is also explained as 'competitive interdependence' between the EU and US as their firms compete in third markets.[14] The EU and Mexico are renewing their economic ties against the backdrop of anti-globalisation accompanied by economic nationalism prevailing in the United States of America (US). With specific focus on Mexico, the Trump administration renegotiated the North American Free Trade Agreement (NAFTA) based on the argument that the agreement harmed the American economy and its workers particularly in the automobiles manufacturing sector. The negotiations have resulted in the United States-Mexico-Canada Agreement (USMCA) to replace the NAFTA. These factors influence EU-Mexico trade relations because Mexico is a part of asymmetrical regionalism[15] to the advantage of the US which also approaches the trade-labour linkage differently from the EU.[16]

The incorporation of an increased role for the civil society and the anti-corruption chapter may be the EU's effort to transform its present, neoliberal form that is receiving backlash.[17] Alternatively, it demonstrates the expanding scope of the EU's normative agenda based on the domestic factors of the partner country.[18] Worker's organisations have consistently criticised the labour courts in Mexico[19]

[12] Lachlan McKenzie, *'Overcoming Legacies of Foreign Policy (Dis)nterests in the Negotiation of the European Union–Australia Free Trade Agreement' (2018) 72 Australian Journal of International Affairs* 255.

[13] The envisioned clause in the EU-Mexico FTA is based on the ex-post approach. See draft text Article 3(4), TSD Chapter, EU-Mexico FTA.

[14] Alberta Sbragia, 'The EU, the US, and Trade Policy: Competitive Interdependence in the Management of Globalization' (2010) 17 *Journal of European Public Policy* 368.

[15] Robert G Finbow, *The Limits of Regionalism* (Routledge, 2018) 5.

[16] See also analysis of the ILO on the existing labour provisions in US and EU FTAs, *Handbook on Assessment of Labour Provisions in Trade and Investment Arrangements* (International Labour Office – Geneva, ILO, 2017) 124.

[17] Jeff Kenner, 'Economic Partnership Agreements: Enhancing the Labour Dimension of Global Governance?' in Bart Van Vooren, Steven Blockmans, Jan Wouters (eds), *The EU's Role in Global Governance* (Oxford University Press, 2012) 317, 318; María García, 'The European Union and Latin America: "Transformative Power Europe" Versus the Realities of Economic Interests' (2015) 28 *Cambridge Review of International Affairs* 621.

[18] Sandra Lavenex and Frank Schimmelfennig, 'EU Rules Beyond EU Borders: Theorizing External Governance in European Politics' (2009) 16 *Journal of European Public Policy* 791; 'Mexico's Growing Crisis: Reforms and Democracy, but No Rule of Law' (2014) 413 *The Economist* 19.

[19] The Conciliation and Arbitration Boards (CABs, known as *juntas de conciliation y arbitraje*) played the central role as special labour tribunals responsible for settling disputes.

citing inefficiency, political bias and corruption. As noted by the ILO, workers trying to organise independent and democratic trade unions risk life threatening consequences,[20] whereas, active and passive public and private sector corruption is deeply rooted in the country's political history.[21] As a result, the interests of Mexican labour unions have been vulnerable to the 'symbiotic relationship' between the Mexican political system and the industrial relations system.[22] Amidst the constitutional reform on labour in Mexico,[23] upholding rule of law emerges as a priority for ensuring democratic unions, better wages and working conditions, and health and safety at work. In this context, it becomes essential to question whether the EU can advance horizontal convergence for the strengthening rule of law in a partner country.

This chapter will define vertical and horizontal convergences and subsequently, assess these narratives on convergence in respect of labour standards through the EU's trade policy to determine the potential of the EU's approach on the promotion of labour rights as linked to sustainable development, human rights and rule of law.

II. Vertical Convergence: EU-Mexico FTA and International Labour Standards

This form of convergence is concerned with the EU's pursuit of international labour standards in the field of trade. This section is based on the assertion that the EU attempts 'institutional convergence in the global legal order in a systemic sense, beyond its own law-making'.[24] The inquiry is in two directions: what are the factors that motivate the EU to pursue ILO standards in trade and what are the factors that hinder their pursuit in the EU-Mexico trading partnership. On the latter, the discussion on US-Mexico trade is based on the premise that FTAs are predominantly for pursuing political interests of parties.[25] The revision of the trade pillar of the Global Agreement (GA)[26] re-invites attention to the agreement as it 'links the two largest markets in the world: that of the North American Free

[20] Workers Victor and Marcelino Shaunitla Peña and Quintin Salgado were murdered in November 2017 and January 2018, see 'Individual Case (CAS) – Discussion' (*ilo.org*, 2018) www.ilo.org/dyn/normlex/en/f?p=NORMLEXPUB:13100:0::NO::P13100_COMMENT_ID:3953281 (last accessed 13 March 2020).

[21] For historical background, see Herbert S Klein and others (eds), 'Mexico Before 1982: The Political Economy of Authoritarian Rule' in *Mexico since 1980* (Cambridge University Press, 2008) 20–65.

[22] De Buen Unna (n 9) 402; Jorge A Vargas, 'Mexico's Legal Revolution: An Appraisal of Its Recent Constitutional Changes, 1999-1995' (1996) 25 *Georgia Journal of International & Comparative Law* 497.

[23] Ley Federal Del Trabajo 2019.

[24] See the Introduction to this volume by Elaine Fahey.

[25] Michael Trebilcock, Robert Howse and Antonia Eliason, *The Regulation of International Trade*, 4th edn (Routledge, 2013).

[26] See *Non Paper Of The Commission Services: Feedback* (n 6).

Trade Agreement (NAFTA) and the EU'.[27] The US is Mexico's primary trading partner with its economy substantially dependent on its powerful neighbour.[28] The US-Mexico trade agreement differs in its normative content, for instance, it is known that EU law considers human rights as a general principle of law that cannot be overlooked[29] but the same cannot be said for the US. The US is not a champion of either the Universal Declaration of Human Rights (UDHR) or the International Covenant on Civil and Political Rights (ICCPR) and International Covenant on Economic, Social and Cultural Rights (ICESCR). It ratified the ICCPR only after constructing an extensive 'package of provisos' which was accepted without significant challenge by the US Senate[30] and has not, to date, ratified the ICESCR.[31] In this sense, US trade policy is an external factor affecting vertical convergence as sought by the EU.

A. The EU's Approach to Labour Standards in Trade

In framing its approach 'inside-out', starting with the adoption of the European Social Charter 1961, the EU sought to align itself with the standards set by the ILO.[32] However, the focus of the (then) community was to the complete the internal market and therefore, a non-binding set of instruments were adopted such as the Community Charter of the Fundamental Social Rights of Workers and the Social Policy adopted at Maastricht.[33] Moreover, Member States have not pursued harmonisation in the field of labour.[34] Member State practices vary and there is no convergence with international labour standards in areas such as right of association and the right to strike.[35] The cases of *Viking*[36] and *Laval*[37] demonstrate the

[27] Marcela Szymanski and Michael E Smith, 'Coherence and Conditionality in European Foreign Policy: Negotiating the EU-Mexico Global Agreement' (2005) 43 *Journal of Common Market Studies* 171.

[28] Daniel C Levy and Kathleen Bruhn, *Mexico: The Struggle for Democratic Development* (University of California Press, 2001) 180, 243.

[29] Cases C-402/05 P and 415/05 P *Kadi v Council and Commission* [2008] ECR I-6351.

[30] See David P Stewart, 'United States Ratification of the Covenant on Civil and Political Rights: The Significance of the Reservations, Understandings, and Declarations' (1993) 42 *DePaul Law Review* 1183–1207, 1186.

[31] See Philip Alston, 'US Ratification of the Covenant on Economic, Social and Cultural Rights: The Need for an Entirely New Strategy' (1990) 84 *The American Journal of International Law* 365–93.

[32] DJ Harris, 'The European Social Charter' (1964) 13 *The International and Comparative Law Quarterly* 1076.

[33] Catherine Barnard, Simon Deakin and Gillian S Morris (eds), *The Future of Labour Law* (Hart Publishing, 2004) 12.

[34] It is also an area falling under shared competence, see Article 2, Treaty on the Functioning of the EU (TFEU) and Article 151–61, TFEU.

[35] Tonia Novitz, 'In Search of a Coherent Social Policy' in Jan Orbie and Lisa Tortell (eds), *The European Union and the Social Dimension of Globalization* (Routledge, 2009).

[36] Case C-438/05 *International Transport Workers' Federation v Viking Line ABP* [2007] ECR I-10779 (hereinafter, '*Viking*').

[37] Case C-341/05 *Laval un Partneri Ltd v Svenska Byggnadsarbetareförbundet* [2007] ECR I-11767 (hereinafter, '*Laval*').

divergence between international labour standards and EU law. *Viking* upheld a company's freedom of establishment vis-à-vis trade union rights, and in *Laval* the Court found an infringement of EU law on free movement of services thereby favouring the freedom to provide services over the exercise of the right to take collective action.

In framing its approach 'outside-in', the EU worked closely with the ILO on the issues of fundamental principles and rights at work, economic development and trade liberalisation.[38] As evident from the 2002 'Towards a Global Partnership for Sustainable Development' communication, around the time when the Global Agreement was signed, the EU was in the process of factoring 'the external dimension' of its approach to sustainable development.[39] It wasn't until the 2006 'Global Europe' communication that the EU substantially modernised its trade policy to cover sustainable development concerns covering labour rights and decent work for all under a 'new generation' of FTAs.[40]

B. The United States-Canada-Mexico Agreement in Context

NAFTA was the first FTA to expressly address the trade-labour linkage through the North Atlantic Agreement on Labour Cooperation (NAALC), a 'side' agreement to the main agreement. The NAALC, was primarily signed for ensuring political legitimacy of the NAFTA in the US but also initiated trade-related international labour rights advocacy.[41] Under the USMCA that is slated to replace NAFTA and NAALC, labour rights are covered in a core chapter of the agreement.[42] However, the renegotiation of NAFTA signals that trade between US and Mexico is 'politically managed' on account of the new regulations on the rules of origin as linked to labour regulation.[43] The Labour Chapter incorporates international labour standards[44] but the economic nationalism undercurrent prevailing in

[38] Corrigendum to the exchange of letters between the Commission of the European Communities and the International Labour Organization [2001] OJ C165/12. The exchange of letters set the framework for EU-ILO strategic Partnership for Development signed in 2004. See European Commision and International Labour Organisation, 'Memorandum of Understanding', www.ilo.org/wcmsp5/groups/public/---europe/---ro-geneva/---ilo-brussels/documents/genericdocument/wcms_169299.pdf (last accessed 13 March 2020).

[39] COM(2002) 82 final.

[40] COM(2006) 567 final.

[41] Lance Compa, 'NAFTA's Labor Side Agreement and International Labor Solidarity' in Peter Waterman and Jane Wills (eds), *Place, Space and the New Labour Internationalisms* (Blackwell Publishers, 2002) 150.

[42] In addition to enforcing their domestic labour laws, the USMCA obligates the Parties to comply with certain international minimum standards as under the ILO's 1998 Declaration on Fundamental Principles, see Article 23.3, USMCA.

[43] Pierre Lemieux, 'Is NAFTA 2.0 Better than Nothing?' (2018) 41 *Regulation* 12.

[44] The chapter prohibits the importation of goods produced (in whole or in part) by forced or compulsory labour, including forced or compulsory child labour (Article 23.6, USMCA) and carries

the US is reflected in the Rules of Origin Chapter. With specific reference to the automobile sector, 'originating goods' must fulfil a 'labour value content' (LVC) criteria to qualify for duty and restriction-free treatment.[45] To counter any regulatory competition in the industry, the provisions also set a minimum wage rate at $16 per hour for workers directly involved in the production to reduce the wage gap between Mexico and the rest of North America.[46]

Mexico may have accepted these terms to avoid economic breakdown of other industries dependent[47] on the US and until the agreement comes into force, the impact or effectiveness of the provisions is not possible. However, the economic rationale for trade prevails over social rationale. This is especially true for the social inequalities in the aftermath of NAFTA in the context of the Maquiladoras in Mexico as noted by the ILO.[48] Labour issues persist to this day in the lack of trade union protection offered to workers and women workers being particularly vulnerable in employment.[49] While waves of protectionism are not new in US trade policy,[50] the current policy stands to influence the EU's objective of vertical convergence, at least in Mexico.

At the same time, particularly at the moment when the agreements are not in force, it is difficult to conclude whether the policy of the US will influence the EU's normative agenda but it surely reflects a different normative agenda in the field of trade. Then again, this may not be conclusive because at some points there is convergence between the US and EU while at others, the US approach is more ambitious. This is reflected by the provisions that:

I. direct the incorporation of workers' freedom of association and collective bargaining, into Mexican labour law (Annexure 23-A, USMCA); or
II. require Mexico to prohibit employer domination or interference in union activities, discrimination, or coercion against workers for union activity

specific provisions on violence against workers (Article 23.7, USMCA), migrant workers (Article 23.8, USMCA) and sex and gender-identity based discrimination and harassment (Article 23.9, USMCA).

[45] Annex 4-B to the Labour Chapter; the provisions define LVC for passenger vehicles, light and heavy trucks divided into high-wage material and manufacturing expenditures, high-wage technology expenditures and high-wage assembly expenditures. Articles 7(1) and 7(2), USMCA. For the method of calculating these, see Article 7(3), USMCA.

[46] This wage rate does not include 'benefits, of employees directly involved in the production of the part or component used to calculate the LVC, and does not include salaries of management, R&D, engineering, or other workers who are not involved in the direct production of the parts or in the operation of production lines' see fn 76 to Article 7(3)(a), USMCA.

[47] Lemieux (n 43).

[48] Maquiladoras constitute a diverse and heterogenous set of plant operations, technologically segmented within each industry and as a whole and their production is largely exported to the US. See Regina Galhardi, *Maquiladoras Prospects of Regional Integration and Globalization* (ILO, 1997).

[49] Edmé Domínguez Reyes and Cirila Quintero Ramírez, 'The Fight for Improved Labour Standards: Women Labour Organising on the Northern Mexican Border and El Salvador' (2019) 4 *Third World Thematics: A TWQ Journal* 27.

[50] Judith Goldstein, 'Ideas, Institutions, and American Trade Policy' (1988) 42 *International Organization* 179, www.jstor.org/stable/2706774 (last accessed 13 March 2020).

or support, and refusal to bargain collectively with the duly recognised union;[51] or

III. provide conditionality in trade through general dispute settlement mechanisms (Article 23.17.12, USMCA).

III. Horizontal Convergence: Human Rights and Rule of Law Approaches to Labour

This section views convergence of legal orders[52] as they interact on account of the regulatory and governance mechanisms introduced by an FTA. In the light of the increased mobility of non-state actors and particularly, the civil society in EU-Mexico trade, we take to analysing the transnational interaction between legal orders. This presupposes that labour is not a policy field that is studied in isolation which is not justified in the context of the EU's trade policy that is directed at achieving human rights protection and rule of law in its external relations. Accordingly, we look at labour rights from the perspectives of sustainable development and human rights linkage and rule of law as linked to the issues of corruption and participation in the convergence debate.

A. Placing Labour Rights in a Normative Framework: Sustainable Development or Human Rights?

Labour rights have conventionally shared a close relationship with human rights[53] and their linkage to sustainable development is comparatively recent.[54] The UN's 2030 Sustainable Development Agenda ('2030 Agenda') endorses the Decent Work Agenda (DWA) through a standalone goal on Decent Work, which was otherwise not a part of the Millennium Development Goals.[55] The DWA encompasses the objective of job creation, rights at work, social protection and social dialogue. These are the categorical areas of Decent Work, but gender equality is its crosscutting objective.[56] The TSD chapter of the EU-Mexico FTA integrates

[51] Article 2(a), Annex 23-A, USMCA.

[52] See Introduction to this volume by Elaine Fahey.

[53] Philip Alston (ed), *Labour Rights As Human Rights* (Oxford University Press, 2005); Kevin Kolben, 'Labour Rights as Human Rights?' (2010) 50 *Virginia Journal of International Law* 449.

[54] Schutter (n 2).

[55] Draft text EU-Mexico FTA 'Trade and Sustainable Development', https://trade.ec.europa.eu/doclib/docs/2018/april/tradoc_156822.pdf (last accessed 13 March 2020).

[56] ILO, 'Decent Work Agenda', www.ilo.org/global/topics/decent-work/lang--en/index.htm (last accessed 13 March 2020).

DWA through the Declaration on Social Justice for a Fair Globalization, 2008,[57] the 2030 Agenda for Sustainable Development and specific reference to gender equality.[58] The Parties do not seek to harmonise labour standards and also protect their right to regulate domestic labour protection but tie their commitments to the internationally recognised core labour standards, the ILO Constitution and the Declaration on Fundamental Principles and Rights at Work,[59] establishing the vertical convergence with international legal standards.

The institutional mechanism of the chapter provides for inter-party cooperation, consultation and dialogue for its implementation which is government centric. 'Contact points' within the administrative authorities of the Parties are vested with the primary role to facilitate communication and coordination between the Parties.[60] The contact points will also initiate government-to-government dispute resolution process comprising Consultations and the establishment of a Panel of Experts in case the former are unsuccessful.[61] The Panel of Experts is expected to release a non-binding report of advisory value at the end of the proceedings. The provisions do not incorporate positive or negative conditionality in the form of incentives or sanctions for promoting labour standards and rely on the cooperation approach practised by the EU. The civil society may provide its inputs in the implementation and dispute resolution processes but is excluded from participating in the formal sub-committee on TSD that is to monitor the overall implementation of the chapter.[62] Only senior officials and their delegates from each Party will be members of the committee, making its composition substantively bureaucratic.

The GA currently in place has an 'essential elements' clause which is the 'basis of the agreement' that underscores the inalienability of the obligation.[63] The EU's approach on the essential element clause demonstrates the incorporation of conditionality, making labour rights protection a harder obligation.[64] For the same reason it is still arguable that the protections offered by the GA may be more binding in so far as the human rights discourse on labour standards is concerned.[65] At the time of writing the final text of the EU-Mexico FTA is still

[57] ILO, 'ILO Declaration on Social Justice for a Fair Globalization', www.ilo.org/wcmsp5/groups/public/---dgreports/---cabinet/documents/genericdocument/wcms_371208.pdf (last accessed 13 March 2020).

[58] Article 13(e), TSD Chapter, https://trade.ec.europa.eu/doclib/docs/2018/april/tradoc_156822.pdf (last accessed 13 March 2020).

[59] *Ibid.* Articles 2 and 3.

[60] Article 14(7), 'Trade and Sustainable Development' (n 55).

[61] Articles 15–17, 'Trade and Sustainable Development' (n 55).

[62] Article 14(1), 'Trade and Sustainable Development' (n 55).

[63] Article 1, Global Agreement.

[64] Narine Ghazaryan, 'A New Generation of Human Rights Clauses? The Case of Association Agreements in the Eastern Neighbourhood' (2015) 40 *European Law Review* 391.

[65] Myriam Oehri, 'EU External Labour Governance: Pointing Fingers or Lending a Hand?', *US and EU External Labor Governance* (Palgrave Macmillan, 2017) 103. See also Article 1, Global Agreement.

awaited. Since the EU-Mexico FTA is a new generation FTA, we can expect that the essential element clause is omitted from the final text of the agreement. In one way the TSD chapters signify an evolution in the approach to the EU on the trade-labour linkage.[66] Taking three new generation FTAs as our reference, we find that the human rights are affirmed in the recitals, evidently distancing from labour rights.[67] Moreover, there is no guarantee that approaching labour rights from the perspective of sustainable development carries improved protection of labour rights over the human rights discourse.[68]

The question is not so much about covering labour standards under the purview of sustainable development or human rights, but about which of these provides better protection. There is no clear answer on this point for two reasons. First, the essential elements clause may afford better protection because it underscores conditionality. However, this is not without internal challenges on the part of the EU as it is the EU that has largely refrained from initiating conditionality in trade relations.[69] The TSD chapters are also excluded from the general dispute resolution chapter of EU FTAs and there is no specific trade suspension clause within the TSD chapters. However, the Court of Justice of the European Union applied the 'essential elements doctrine'[70] in the case concerning the EU-Singapore FTA namely, *Opinion 2/15*.[71] The Court held that a breach of provisions on the social protection of workers authorises a party to terminate or suspend the FTA.[72] However, under the EU-Korea FTA on potential violations of labour standards, the EU has shown a clear preference for a cooperation-based approach by initiating consultations with Korea.[73]

[66] Adalberto Perulli and Tiziano Treu, *Sustainable Development, Global Trade and Social Rights* (Wolters Kluwer, 2018) 85–86.

[67] See EU-Japan Economic Partnership Agreement, http://trade.ec.europa.eu/doclib/docs/2018/august/tradoc_157228.pdf#page=16 (last accessed 13 March 2020); The EU- Canada Comprehensive and Economic Trade Agreement, https://ec.europa.eu/trade/policy/in-focus/ceta/ (last accessed 13 March 2020); and the EU-Singapore Free Trade Agreement, https://eur-lex.europa.eu/legal-content/EN/TXT/PDF/?uri=CELEX:22019A1114(01)&from=EN#page=1 (last accessed 13 March 2020).

[68] Tonia Novitz, 'Labour Standards and Trade: Need We Choose Between "Human Rights" and "Sustainable Development"?' in Henner Gött (ed), *Labour Standards in International Economic Law* (Springer, 2018).

[69] Nicolas Hachez, '"Essential Elements" Clauses in EU Trade Agreements Making Trade Work in a Way That Helps Human Rights?' (Leuven Centre for Global Governance Studies Working Paper No 158, 2015).

[70] L Ankersmit, 'Opinion 2/15: Adding Some Spice to the Trade and Environment Debate' (European Law Blog, 15 June 2017), http://europeanlawblog.eu/2017/06/15/opinion-215-adding-some-spice-to-the-trade-environment-debate/ (last accessed 16 March 2020).

[71] *Opinion 2/15* ECLI:EU:C:2017:376 (Court of Justice, 16 May 2017), para 161.

[72] *Ibid.*

[73] European Commission, 'EU Team in Korea for Government Consultations over Labour Commitments under the Trade Agreement' (Brussels, 21 January 2019), https://trade.ec.europa.eu/doclib/press/index.cfm?id=1973&title=EU-team-in-Korea-for-government-consultations-over-labour-commitments-under-the-trade-agreement (last accessed 16 March 2020).

B. Rule of Law and Corruption

The 2030 Agenda sets out the rule of law as a cross-cutting goal at the international level.[74] This strengthens policy guidance for the protection of trade unionists and human rights activists. However, the protection of the rule of law in economic relations is primarily sought to maintain stable market activities.[75] In the 'Anti-corruption' chapter of the EU-Mexico FTA, the parties approach the issue of corruption as a non-tariff barrier. The provisions merely reaffirm commitments under various international and regional instruments that Mexico and the EU Member States are parties to.[76] With reference to responsible business conduct, only the Organisation for Economic Co-operation and Development Guidelines for Multinational Enterprises in relation to anti-corruption are referred.[77] Sustainable Development Goal 16 'Promote peaceful and inclusive societies for sustainable development, provide access to justice for all and build effective, accountable and inclusive institutions at all levels' of the 2030 Agenda finds an express mention, but there are no *horizontal* references to the TSD chapter.[78] Some reporting requirements have been stipulated for businesses on non-financial obligations and corporate social responsibility practices. The dispute resolution process relies on cooperation-based approaches for implementation as in the TSD chapter. A prima facie observation is that the agreement approaches corruption with the objective of accomplishing the 'ease of doing business' in Mexico.

A contention requiring further analysis is the fact that this approach does not take into account the 'governance spillovers'[79] resulting from the correlation of labour and corruption activities. This is particularly relevant in the context of Mexico where Union leaders are guaranteed a certain amount of power in the form of political representation, policy influence or other welfare benefits *in exchange* for controlling dissidence among workers.[80] The ILO identifies the role for governments, business and social partners in the fight against corruption.[81] Therefore, indirect effects upon governance require that policy makers direct convergence

[74] Noora Arajärvi, 'The Rule of Law in the 2030 Agenda' (2018) 10 *Hague Journal on the Rule of Law* 187.

[75] Christopher May, 'Market Exchange and the Rule of Law: Confidence in Predictability' (2018) 10 *Hague Journal on the Rule of Law* 365.

[76] The United Nations Convention against Corruption, the Financial Action Task Force, the G20 High Level Principles on asset disclosure by public officials, the APEC Conduct Principles for Public Officials for Mexico and the Council of Europe Recommendation on codes of conduct for public officials for the EU.

[77] The TSD chapter mentions the ILO Tripartite Declaration of Principles concerning Multinational Enterprises and Social Policy, also see Article 9(2)(b) of the TSD chapter.

[78] The Goal informs that trade unionists face violence and death while working towards reforms or generating public awareness.

[79] *Handbook on Assessment of Labour Provisions* (n 16) 122.

[80] Ana Isabel López García, 'After Regime Change: Corporatist Organisations and Political Parties in Mexico' (2017) 61 *The Latin Americanist* 309 at 311–12 (emphasis added).

[81] See ILO Resolution Concerning Decent Work in Global Supply Chains, adopted on 10 June 2016.

of labour policy with other public policies such as anti-corruption to strengthen rule of law. With the ongoing concerns related to corruption in Mexico, the EU wants to ensure that business have access to a credible environment. Neither the EU-Mexico agreement is close to implementation yet nor can we assess the effectiveness of the provisions. However, the sessions held at the Stakeholder Event on the EU-Mexico FTA in Brussels, discussed in the next section, provide more insights in this respect.

C. Civil Society and Participation

Until now EU FTAs facilitate civil society participation for monitoring the implementation of the TSD chapters in EU FTAs. While there are power asymmetries between the non-profit and business actors comprising civil society, there is also overall support for the mechanism.[82] The EU-Mexico FTA enhances the role of the civil society to other parts of the FTA such as the chapter on corruption. Accordingly, the Agreement in Principle envisages that the mechanism will be utilised 'in the prevention and fight against corruption'. Organised on both sides as Domestic Advisory Groups, civil society will be 'able to present proposals on how to better address corruption' under the Agreement.[83] If human rights are the 'silver thread' that run through the EU's external relations, the civil society mechanism could hold the same importance in the implementation of EU FTAs.[84]

While the civil society has the complete support of Mexico and the EU, neither side conclusively answered the question on which party proposed the inclusion of the anti-corruption chapter or how it would link to the TSD chapter in due course.[85] The expanded role for the civil society may be a deliberate effort on the part of the Parties to enhance participation, but the discussion was primarily presided over by groups representing business actors.[86] This makes it impossible to define the civil society as an 'alternative voice to market and state actors'.[87] Business actors

[82] Jan Orbie and others, 'Promoting Sustainable Development or Legitimising Free Trade? Civil Society Mechanisms in EU Trade Agreements' (2016) 1 *Third World Thematics: A TWQ Journal* 526.

[83] 'New EU-Mexico Agreement: The Agreement in Principle' (n 7) 17.

[84] European Commission, 'Human Rights and Democracy at the Heart of EU External Action – Towards a More Effective Approach' COM(2011) 886 final (12 December 2011).

[85] The Mexican representative did, however, reiterate the interest of the country in combating corruption. He stated that the Mexican Government has set four key priorities vis-à-vis economic growth and development: (i) Tackling Corruption; (ii) Reducing Inequality; (iii) Driving Investment and Innovation; and (iv) Revamping National Peace and Security Programme, see 'The Modernised EU-Mexico Global Agreement: Better Rules, Common Values and More Opportunities for Trade and Investment' (Brussels, Madou Auditorium, 20 May 2019), https://trade.ec.europa.eu/doclib/docs/2019/may/tradoc_157887.pdf (last accessed 16 March 2020).

[86] *Ibid.* Three representatives were from business or business lobby groups, one from the ILO.

[87] Jean-Baptiste Velut, 'What Role for Civil Society in Cross-Regional What Role for Civil Society in Cross-Regional Mega-Deals? A Comparative Analysis of EU and US Trade Policies' [2016] *Papers in Political Economy*.

believed the update of the Global Agreement was needed in *strategic* response to the USMCA. On the expectations of the business community, the actors prioritised market access and rules that provide certainty and stability in trade. Trade facilitation issues such as efficient customs processes and related administrative actions at the national levels were highlighted by another representative, alluding to fighting corruption in this respect. The ILO representative's remark was the most relevant in establishing the need for horizontal convergence, stating that labour provisions should not be read in *isolation*.

IV. Conclusions

The EU's pursuit is to ensure that trade co-opts labour as an essential policy area in its trade agreements, seeking first the convergence of economic and non-economic interests and then the convergence of domestic labour law with international labour standards. Vertical convergence is more or less sought by seeking ratification of the core conventions, but the purpose of that clause has already been achieved. Furthermore, ratification may be *sine qua non*, it does not guarantee effective enforcement of labour rights at the national level. This chapter framed the US approach to trade and labour in USMCA as the primary challenge to the EU's objective on seeking convergence. However, there are domestic factors and constraints that will shape convergence. The EU's engagement with Mexico brings forth the challenge of reconciling differing levels of economic development, systemic issues such as comprehensive unionisation in Mexico and eradication of corruption.

Horizontal convergence looked at the provisions of the proposed agreement text from the view that there is definite correlation between labour standards, human rights and rule of law. The agreement categorises them separately, but the civil society has a de facto as well as de jure role in driving convergence. However, the trajectory of convergence is what matters, meaning that business actors may play a stronger role in pursuing their interests which will decide whether and to what extent horizontal convergence materialises.

14

Global Convergence through EU Value Chain Regulation and Voluntary Standards

ENRICO PARTITI*

I. Introduction

The growing institutionalisation of corporate social responsibility (CSR) practices resulting, among other factors, from international soft law instruments,[1] has recognised the importance of the unit of analysis of global value chains (GVCs) in addressing social and environmental externalities connected to global production.[2] In the European Union (EU), regulators have been at the forefront of ensuring 'responsible' or 'sustainable' corporate conduct. This is not just visible through the pioneering efforts of the Commission in the domain of CSR,[3] but also in the acknowledgement by EU institutions of the potentially perverse effects of EU trade policy on GVCs. In a 2017 Resolution, the European Parliament urged the Commission to put GVCs at the centre of EU trade policy and develop mandatory value chain human rights due diligence legislation. The Parliament expressed its support for a 'smart mix'[4] of mandatory rules and voluntary corporate action in

* This contribution was written in the context of a research project that received funding from the European Research Council (ERC) under the European Union's Horizon 2020 research and innovation programme (Grant Agreement No 725798).

[1] Human Rights Council, 'Guiding Principles on Business and Human Rights: Implementing the United Nations "Protect, Respect and Remedy" Framework', A/HRC/17/31 (21 March 2011).

[2] G Gereffi, J Humphrey, T Sturgeon, 'The Governance of Global Value Chains' (2005) 12 *Review of International Political Economy* 78. In legal literature see KB Sobel-Read, 'Global Value Chains: A Framework for Analysis' (2014) 5 *Transnational Legal Theory* 364; The IGLP Law and Global Production Working Group, 'The Role of Law in Global Value Chains: A Research Manifesto' (2016) 4 *London Review of International Law* 57.

[3] As early as 2002. See European Commission 'Communication from the Commission concerning Corporate Social Responsibility: A business contribution to Sustainable Development' COM(2002) 347 final (2 July 2002).

[4] On 'smart mixes' see van J Erp, M Faure, A Nollkaemper, N Philipsten (eds), *Smart Mixes for Transboundary Environmental Harm* (Cambridge University Press, 2019).

GVC regulation and stressed the need for a more prominent role for private initiatives in ensuring responsible and sustainable global production.[5] The Parliament's recent position reflects the broader stance of the Commission in its 2015 'Trade for all' agenda, where high social and environmental standards were put at the core of EU trade policy.[6] With respect to global production practices, convergence with international obligations is a key concern for EU institutions. This concern thus brings to the fore just another instance of the 'convergence ethic' characterising EU action.[7]

What stands out in this 'road-map for convergence' is the Parliament's elevation of private initiatives and voluntary standards as key tools in the regulation of sustainable value chains. While private regulation has long been legitimised as a component in EU law-making,[8] the embrace of highly normative voluntary standards for sustainability and responsible business conduct represents a new step in the EU interaction with private regulators and voluntary regimes, especially in light of their extraterritorial implications. The Parliament position actually crystallises certain trends already visible in EU regulation of responsible and sustainable production. This is the case of measures disciplining value chains such as biofuels, timber and conflict minerals, and as well in more 'horizontal' pieces of legislation such as those disciplining public procurement and non-financial corporate reporting.

As this contribution will discuss, a common feature of these EU instruments is their global reach, capable of affecting the position (and the production methods) of economic operators outside the EU. At varying degrees, these measures rely on private actors, private regulatory instruments, as well as voluntary international standards in achieving their goals – in particular for exercising regulatory effects outside the EU. For example, the 2009 EU Renewable Energy Directive[9] recognises and incorporates voluntary sustainability standards in EU biofuel regulation. Such standards require chain-of-custody certification, which necessitate compliance from all relevant economic operators in a biofuel value chain. External normative material is thus brought *inside* EU measures, and then disseminated *outside* – in upstream value chains – to non-EU economic actors that nevertheless have to comply with EU rules.[10]

[5] European Parliament Resolution of 12 September 2017 on the impact of international trade and the EU's trade policies on global value chains (2016/2301(INI)).

[6] European Commission, 'Trade for All. Towards a More Responsible Trade and Investment Policy' (European Union, 2015) 24.

[7] See Elaine Fahey in the Introduction to this volume.

[8] Council Resolution (EC) of 7 May 1985 on a New Approach to technical harmonisation and standards [1985] OJ C136/1; European Parliament/Council/Commission, Inter-institutional agreement on better law-making [2003] OJ C321/1.

[9] Directive 2009/28/EC of 23 April 2009 on the promotion of the use of energy from renewable sources, as amended by Directive (EU) 2015/1513 of 9 September 2015 (hereinafter referred to as 'RED') [2009] OJ L140.

[10] A Bradford, 'The Brussels Effect' (2012) 107 *Northwestern University Law Review* 1.

As standards seem to be at varying degrees grounded on international law provisions, convergence of production practices with international law could be the final outcome of their use in EU measures. The use of external norms in EU instruments does not just 'export' EU regulatory preferences to those economic actors which want to enter the EU market, but also fosters transnational legalisation which, at least judging from the content of the standards, seems to occur in line with international law. In a similar manner, as it will be explained in section II.C, using standards developed by the Organisation for Economic Cooperation and Development (OECD) in EU regulation subsequently prompts economic actors in an entire GVC to comply with them. OECD instruments may require all corporations in a GVC to act in compliance with a host of requirements, and to exercise due diligence in the domain of human rights, as contemplated by the United Nations Guiding Principles on Business and Human Rights (UNGPs).[11]

This chapter conceptualises convergence as the approximation of different regulatory regimes, either public or private, international, transnational, EU or national. In the forms discussed here, convergence, most often, takes place when one regime 'flows' into another and, possibly, into another again. As will be discussed, international provisions are brought into private standards, which are then incorporated into EU measures. The lowest (and arguably most important) level of convergence is however that between EU provisions 'in the books' and the actual behaviour in their context of operation. The employment of non-EU standards in EU legislation may therefore contribute in bringing about a degree of convergence of production practices at the global stage with provisions of international human rights, environmental and labour law. External normative material is mobilised both as a *source* of, and as a *vehicle* for, EU-stimulated global convergence. From a functionalist perspective, private standards implement international law; corporations exercise implementing and enforcement functions when required to address negative human rights impacts attributable to their suppliers. Such functions can thus be mobilised in the public interest. However, the actual implementation of both private regimes and OECD standards depends on the practice of the companies operationalising them in their operations. This will ultimately determine empirically the extent of convergence 'on the ground'.

This contribution illustrates a series of dynamics of convergence between various regulatory levels, characterised by a crucial role of EU action. Section II depicts two forms of convergence. The first concerns convergence between international law and voluntary private standards, where the former flows into the latter without any direct EU intervention. The second form of convergence stems from an emerging trend in EU regulation, ie the discipline of transnational business conduct with the employment of voluntary private standards which, as seen, are in line with international law obligations. Private standards are used in EU measures; in this sense, convergence of private standards into EU measures

[11] Human Rights Council, 'Guiding Principles' (n 1).

can be observed. As it will be seen, this may even lead to situations where an external standard defines the substance of an obligation under EU law. Using voluntary standards constitutes a peculiar EU strategy to stimulate convergence in global production with international law principles. These measures contribute to foster worldwide producers' compliance with voluntary standards and, in turn, international law obligations in the social and environmental domains.

Secondly, this contribution aims to assess the actual implications of a regulatory approach aiming at convergence which is heavily reliant on private authority. With the assistance of socio-legal scholarship, section III aims at appraising the potential external effects of this approach. It therefore appraises the possible convergence of behaviour 'on the ground' with the standards, as a result of regimes convergence. In particular, it questions whether the extent of convergence which could be inferred by assessing the formal content of the standards is matched by actual convergence 'on the ground', ie in the context of application. It will be shown that it is difficult to hold that, simply because private standards are based on social and environmental agreements, an entity complying with voluntary instruments would be in compliance with international provisions. Similarly, requiring corporations to exercise due diligence hardly ensures human rights compliance in value chains. With a lack of careful measure design, legitimising private regulatory competences may instead further privatisation in the regulation of sustainability, and lead to the prevalence of private interests over public goals. It shall also not be forgotten that private regulation remains a highly normative process which often generates considerable distributional effects, especially from the global South to the global North.[12]

Simultaneously, EU-stimulated global convergence with social and environmental international obligations results in divergence with rules of international trade law. Section IV discusses whether private standards in particular may come into conflict with classic tenets of World Trade Organisation (WTO) law, and allow the EU to get away with trade restrictions linked to human rights and other forms of conditionality that would be rather complex to justify under WTO law – especially where standards require certification of economic actors in the entire value chain. Regardless of whether the EU's use of private standards is part of a deliberate regulatory strategy, private actors' use to create convergence bypasses trade law and its constraints on extraterritorial effects. Convergence with social and environmental international law in GVCs spurred by the EU and its measures therefore occurs at the expense of convergence with other areas such as international trade law. In addition, the use of private regimes may limit the margin of review that WTO law exercises on EU measures. Section V concludes with some methodological reflections on the study of convergence in GVC regulation.

[12] See generally W Mattli and T Büthe, *The New Global Rulers: The Privatisation of Regulation in the World Economy* (Princeton University Press, 2012).

II. Using Standards in GVC Regulation

Voluntary private standards have emerged globally with the goal of harnessing the forces of global production. Private regulatory schemes are established by multi-stakeholder and sectoral organisations to certify that products have been responsibly produced, that inputs and natural resources have been responsibly harvested, or that labour practices and employment conditions are acceptable. They are private in so far that neither their establishment nor operation is formally connected to public authority, as they emerged from the desire of industry or multi-stakeholder groups to establish regulatory regimes to address global common problems and reputational concerns.[13] They are voluntary in so far, formally, that uptake is a free choice of the economic operator seeking certification. The proliferation of voluntary sustainability standards (VSS)[14] has represented an opportunity for public actors to harness the regulatory potential of transnational *private* regulators. As private certification schemes in sectors spanning from biofuels to textile, from forestry to electronic products, and from agricultural commodities to fisheries acquired market success and acceptance among consumers and producers alike, public regulators especially in the EU have become aware of their potential contribution in regulating (global) production.

At face value these standards offer a high degree of norms complementarity to public rules.[15] VSS are based on international law obligations and, in addition, often require that producers are in compliance with all applicable national requirements to obtain certification. For example, VSS in the social domain such as the SA8000 Standard and Fairtrade require compliance with at least the Core International Labour Organisation (ILO) Conventions and human rights treaties.[16] Standards in the domain of sustainable forest exploitation (such as the Forestry Stewardship Council, or the Responsible Forestry Initiative) require compliance with all applicable treaties, conventions and agreements, including the CITES Convention and the Convention on Biological Diversity – as well as all nationally-applicable provisions.[17] By laying down management standards operationalising such requirements, they ingrain compliance within the operations of the economic actors adopting the standard. International obligations

[13] T Bartley, 'Institutional Emergence in an Era of Globalisation: The Rise of Transnational Private Regulation of Labor and Environmental Conditions' (2007) 113 *American Journal of Sociology* 297, 299.

[14] A Marx and J Wouters, 'Competition and Cooperation in the Market of Voluntary Sustainability Standards' in P Delimatsis (ed), *The Law, Economics and Politics of International Standardisation* (Cambridge University Press, 2015) 215–48.

[15] F Cafaggi, 'New Foundations of Transnational Private Regulation' (2011) 38 *Journal of Law and Society* 20, 39–40.

[16] See, eg, Social Accountability 8000 International Standard by Social Accountability International, June 2014, available at www.sa-intl.org/_data/global/files/SA8000Standard2014(3).pdf.

[17] For the Forestry Stewardship Council, see: International Generic Indicators, FSC-STD-60-004, available at https://fsc.org/en/document-center/documents/335.

thus converge into voluntary standards, which then transform them into readily applicable provisions for economic operators.

From a functional perspective, and in the eyes of regulators, VSS thus offer producers specific tools to act in line with international (and national) law provisions. VSS are capable of implementing otherwise general provisions of international law, which become directly applicable for entities normally not considered as subjects of international law. By relying on third-party auditing, standards also exercise monitoring and enforcement functions, especially in contexts where ratification and implementation are lagging behind, or enforcement is weak. As the next section will illustrate, EU regulatory practice has, on occasion, led to the formal recognition of these schemes, or has allowed companies to employ them to implement specific EU measures or demonstrate compliance with sustainability-related requirements. Regulatory effects are thus exercised via a combination of requirements established by EU authorities, as well as external normative material in the form of voluntary standards.

The voluntary standards mobilised by the EU are not just private; non-mandatory standards established by international organisations such as the OECD have also been 'used' on occasion.[18] The OECD has been one of the first multilateral fora for the transnational regulation of business conduct with the elaboration of voluntary standards for members to employ in regulating businesses established in their territories. The first edition of the OECD Guidelines for Multinational Enterprises dates back to 1976, with several notable revisions, the last one taking place in 2011. More recently, implementing Guidance Documents attempt to operationalise the more general content of the Guidelines to specific contexts or sectors. They also bring the OECD Guidelines in line with the concept of human rights due diligence (HRDD) as elaborated in the United Nations Guiding Principles on Business and Human Rights (UNGPs).[19]

The UNGPs are the leading international instrument in the area of 'business and human rights'. They establish and articulate the boundaries of a moral responsibility of corporations to avoid, prevent and remedy negative human rights impact. Such a responsibility is to be operationalised by corporations through human rights due diligence procedures (ie internal management processes) aiming at identifying and remedying negative human rights impact connected to corporate activities and their GVCs. Also OECD standards therefore heavily rely on private actors to achieve their goals. For example, the OECD Guidance on conflict minerals operationalises broader principles of the corporate responsibility to engage in HRDD via corporate management standards and processes.[20] EU measures regulating responsible corporate conduct therefore make use of voluntary standards which,

[18] See generally E Partiti, 'Orchestration as a Form of Public Action: The EU Engagement with Voluntary Sustainability Standards' (2019) 25 *European Law Journal* 94.

[19] Human Rights Council, 'Guiding Principles' (n 1).

[20] OECD, *OECD Due Diligence Guidance for Responsible Supply Chains of Minerals from Conflict-Affected and High-Risk Areas: Third Edition* (Paris, OECD Publishing, 2016).

also in the cases where international *public* standards are contemplated, are closely contingent on private actors and private rule-makers for their operationalisation.

A. EU's Employment of Voluntary Public and Private Standards

The 'business case' for employing external standards in EU measures stems from two different sets of legal and policy considerations. On the one hand, the EU is under the obligation to support the implementation of both the OECD Guidelines and their sectoral instruments,[21] and the UNGPs.[22] Such support ought to entail taking mandatory measures requiring business to comply with the Guidelines and the UNGPs, in addition to softer forms of support such as awareness-raising. It should not be forgotten that these instruments entail no direct obligations for corporations under international law, apart from possessing a strong 'moral' character fostering adoption. Public standards thus spillover 'top-down' from the international to the EU stage, to be then spread out globally via their incorporation in EU measures. On the other hand, the use of VSS is the outcome of an increasingly visible deliberate policy preference from EU institutions, however coherent, for employment and support of private initiatives and market-based instruments of regulation. To varying degrees, such standards have emerged 'bottom-up'; EU action then crystallises and diffuses their regulatory claim in GVCs.[23]

From an initial phase, where VSS became the object of attention from the perspective of internal market regulation, the EU approach towards private standards evolved in a piecemeal fashion. Areas such as organic food products have been the object of early direct harmonisation to ensure the credibility of private organic claims and to protect consumers.[24] A more hands-off approach was however preferred, which anyway acknowledged an important regulatory position for private standards. In two Commission Communications on Fairtrade[25] and in the Communication on best practice guidelines for voluntary certification schemes for agricultural products and foodstuffs,[26] the Commission recognised

[21] See E Partiti and S Van der Velde, 'Curbing Supply-Chain Human Rights Violations through Trade and Due Diligence. Possible WTO Concerns Raised by the EU Conflict Minerals Regulation' (2017) 51 *Journal of World Trade* 1043, 1064–65.

[22] United Nations. Office of the High Commissioner on Human Rights, 'Frequently asked Questions about the Guiding Principles on Business and Human Rights' HR/PUB/14/3 (2014).

[23] D Casey and C Scott, 'The Crystallisation of Regulatory Norms' (2011) 38 *Journal of Law and Society* 76.

[24] Council Regulation (EC) No 834/2007 of 28 June 2007 on organic production and labelling of organic products [2007] OJ L189/1.

[25] Commission Communication, 'Contributing to sustainable development: The role of Fair Trade and non-governmental trade-related sustainability assurance schemes' COM(2009)215 final; See also Commission Communication COM(1999) 619 final on 'fair trade'.

[26] See Commission Communication, 'EU best practice guidelines for voluntary certification schemes for agricultural products and foodstuff' (2010) OJ C 341/04.

goal alignment between public and certain private measures. This would occur where private schemes ensure food health and safety, provide products which conform to societal demand for certain characteristics, and inform consumers about hidden product features.[27] While these measures and policy documents were taken within the domain of the internal market, and focused on the potential positive effects standards could bring about to EU consumers, recent EU practice has enlarged its focus. Private standards have acquired a strong 'external' dimension as EU institutions began noticing their potential in contributing also to EU external action goals, especially in the framework of trade and market access, and called for more systematic support and mobilisation to pursue EU goals.

In a 2017 Resolution, the European Parliament urged the Commission to put GVCs at the centre of EU trade policy. It called for clear rules and responsibilities both for regulating actors and companies.[28] In line with the EU's obligations connected to the OECD Guidelines and the UNGPs discussed above, the Parliament called on the Commission to develop mandatory value chain human rights due diligence legislation. The Resolution also asks the Commission to further promote the uptake of sectoral OECD Guidelines, possibly in EU legislation along the lines of the 2017 Conflict Minerals Regulation.[29] Deference to an international standard and its adoption at the EU level[30] becomes thus a distinct modality for regulating GVCs. The Parliament also expressed its support for a 'smart mix' of regulation and voluntary corporate action in GVC regulation which, according to the Parliament, has yielded positive results in the past.[31] For this reason, parallel to a request for public intervention, the Parliament stresses the need for a more prominent role for private-sector engagement and private initiatives. In particular, the Parliament welcomes the 'many promising initiatives taken by the private sector such as codes of conduct, labelling, self-assessment and social audits'.[32]

As section III will further illustrate, the position of the Parliament may sound a bit naive, in particular as it appears to gloss over the considerable differences existing between schemes,[33] as well as more structural criticism of private regulatory regimes in the domain of sustainability.[34] Standardisation in any domain is far from being the exclusive preserve of dry technocratic deliberation. It is instead a highly politicised battle for prevalence of certain private interests over others, which

[27] See *ibid*.

[28] European Parliament Resolution of 12 September 2017 on the impact of international trade and the EU's trade policies on global value chains (2016/2301(INI)).

[29] Regulation (EU) 2017/821 laying down supply chain due diligence obligations for Union importers of tin, tantalum and tungsten, their ores, and gold originating from conflict-affected and high-risk areas (Conflict Minerals Regulation) [2017] OJ L130/1, Art 4(b).

[30] See E Fahey in the Introduction to this volume.

[31] European Parliament Resolution (n 28) at 11.

[32] European Parliament Resolution (n 28) at 11.

[33] S Mena and C Palazzo, 'Input and Output Legitimacy of Multi-Stakeholder Initiatives' (2012) 22 *Business Ethics Quarterly* 527.

[34] See generally T Bartley, *Rules without Rights. Land, Labor, and Private Authority in the Global Economy* (Oxford University Press, 2018).

end up generating deep distributional effects between producers, and between consumers and producers.[35] The outcome is not improved by limited venues for weak-interests representation in transnational global governance, especially in its private configurations.[36] And even when formal structures for deliberation are contemplated, for example in the more sophisticated multi-stakeholder initiatives, traditional power dynamics in value chains, often dominated by powerful Western retailers, are reflected in standard-setting and standard-governance.[37]

The Parliament's position is however consistent with the stance of the Commission in its 2015 'Trade for all' agenda, where high social and environmental standards were put at the core of EU trade policy. There, the Commission committed to support the implementation of the UNGPs and OECD instruments, as well as promoting 'fair and ethical trade schemes'.[38] While this approach to private standards seems narrower both in focus (ie limited to fair trade schemes only) and in approach (confined to awareness-raising and information campaigns among consumers), the Parliament encourages broader and across-the-board inclusion of non-EU standards in regulation of value chains.

B. Private Standards in EU GVC Measures: VSS

Interestingly, the presence of private standards in EU measures regulating value chains predates both the 2015 'Trade for all' agenda and the 2017 Parliament Resolution on value chains. A number of measures described in this section and in section II.C aim at disciplining value chains in combination with voluntary standards – both private and public – along the lines of a legally structured form of the 'smart-mix' advocated by the Parliament. Measures regulating GVCs have the following in common: that, either through EU economic actors or through voluntary standards, regulatory effects are pushed to the upstream tiers of the value chains. In other words, through the economic incentives offered by marketing in the EU or dealing with EU traders and importers, several actors at different tiers in GVCs are required to comply with EU-recognised rules established in non-EU voluntary standards. Generally, such standards refer to internationally agreed-upon normative material in the domain of human rights, environment and labour. Different from the formal and systematic mandate to define direct product characteristics casted upon technical standard-setters,[39] EU regulators' use of private standards in the domain of sustainability remains *ad hoc*,

[35] Mattli and Büthe (n 12).

[36] RB Stewart, 'Remedying Disregard in Global Regulatory Governance: Accountability, Participation, and Responsiveness' (2014) 108 *American Journal of International Law* 211.

[37] P Paiement, *Transnational Sustainability Laws* (Cambridge University Press, 2017).

[38] European Commission, 'Trade for All' (n 6) 24.

[39] H Schepel, 'The New Approach to the New Approach: The Juridification of Harmonised Standards in EU Law' (2013) 12 *Maastricht Journal of European and Comparative Law* 521.

ie varying from measure to measure and limited to certain sectors, and escaping the traditional legal categories of delegation of regulatory competences to private actors.[40] Regardless of a relative legal informality in their use, private standards play an important role in EU legislation by operationalising requirements defining sustainable production and, simultaneously, monitoring compliance within and outside the EU.

The 2009 Renewable Energy Directive (RED)[41] was the first measure incorporating VSS in EU regulation in view of disciplining the biofuel value chain. Among other obligations, the RED establishes greenhouse gas emission and other general sustainability meta-requirements for biofuels and their inputs in order to account for the Member States' renewable energy targets and qualify for financial support.[42] The Commission is empowered to recognise national or international public and private standards for the measurements of emissions and the implementation of sustainability requirements set up by the Directive. Producers can then use these standards to demonstrate compliance.[43] The possibility of recognition has spurred voluntary standards to converge with EU sustainability requirements in the RED. At the same time, since other requirements in the schemes – for example other environmental and social requirements originating in international law, where present – are not set out in the Directive, the use of private regimes brings in internationally agreed upon criteria into an EU measure, which then spreads them outside the EU.

The Commission has so far recognised 16 schemes, among which private standards such as the Round Table on Responsible Soy (RTRS),[44] the International Sustainability and Carbon Certification System,[45] and also producer association schemes such as 2BSv.[46] While some of these schemes were established by producer organisations in the EU with the aim of meeting the requirements of the RED and are less demanding,[47] other standards also provide for additional compliance with internationally applicable obligations such as a number of ILO

[40] For delegation criteria see Case C-9/56 *Meroni v High Authority* [1958] ECR I-0135.

[41] RED (n 9).

[42] RED (n 9), Art 17.1.

[43] RED (n 9), Art 18.4.

[44] Commission Implementing Decision 2011/440/EU of 19 July 2011 on the recognition of the 'Round Table on Responsible Soy EU RED' scheme for demonstrating compliance with the sustainability criteria under Directives 2009/28/EC and 2009/30/EC of the European Parliament and of the Council [2011] OJ L190/83.

[45] Commission Implementing Decision 2011/438/EU of 19 July 2011 on the recognition of the 'International Sustainability and Carbon Certification' scheme for demonstrating compliance with the sustainability criteria under Directives 2009/28/EC and 2009/30/EC of the European Parliament and of the Council [2011] OJ L190/79.

[46] Commission Implementing Decision 2011/437/EU of 19 July 2011 on the recognition of the 'Biomass Biofuels Sustainability voluntary scheme' for demonstrating compliance with the sustainability criteria under Directives 2009/28/EC and 2009/30/EC of the European Parliament and of the Council [2011] OJ L190/77.

[47] S Ponte and C Daugbjerg, 'Biofuel Sustainability and the Formation of Transnational Hybrid Governance' (2015) 24 *Environmental Politics* 96.

conventions and biodiversity provisions originating from the Convention on Biological Diversity.[48] Recognised biofuel sustainability schemes, albeit at varying extent, may require chain of custody certification. This approach requires all entities in a GVC to be certified under a private standard which, it should be kept in mind, is in line with the EU requirements.[49] For example, this is the case of the RTRS. RTRS-certified economic operators are allowed to sell soy, soy-based biomass, biofuels or bio-liquids as RTRS compliant. Any economic operator in the supply chain making RTRS claims about the output they supply must possess a chain of custody certificate.[50] Therefore, an end-user that delivers RTRS-certified products to the market can only make such claim if each and every step in its value chain has a valid RTRS certificate in line with the RED requirements spelled out in the relevant standards 'RTRS EU RED Compliance Requirements for the Supply Chain' and 'RTRS Chain of Custody Standard'.[51] The chain of custody approach of private standards therefore has the further effect of magnifying the global reach of EU provisions on biofuels sustainability, and spreading them upstream in GVCs outside the EU.

The Public Procurement Directive[52] represents another measure stimulating the employment of private standards and, as a result, convergence with internationally agreed upon instruments in the social and environmental domains. Different from the RED, here are contracting authorities covered by the scope of the Directive that are offered the possibility to use private standards in the context of responsible procurement. In contracting products that are 'sustainable' or 'green', contracting authorities at the EU and national level can simply require that contracting products are 'sustainable'. They can select a private standard, or equivalent forms of certification, to define such a product characteristic. In this way, private standards serve as a technical reference for the identification and description of all relevant sustainability-related features of the products or services a public body is contracting.[53] In other words, what is 'sustainable' is left to the standard to define.

Since non-EU normative material comes to define the substance of a general obligation spelled out under EU (or national) law, this form of use of private regimes highlights the convergence of private regimes into EU law. At the same

[48] See, eg, RTRS Standard for Responsible Soy Production Version 3.1.

[49] This may also entail, as it is often the case, that an original pre-existing standard adjusted its requirements to be in line with the RED baseline requisites.

[50] See RTRS Chain of Custody Standard Version 2.2, Section VII. General Chain of Custody System Requirements for the Supply Chain, Section 1.1.1. Available at www.responsiblesoy.org/wpdm-package/rtrs-chain-of-custody-standard-pdf/?lang=en.

[51] RTRS EU RED System Description V2.4, p 2–3.

[52] Directive 2014/24/EU of 26 February 2014 on public procurement [2014] OJ L94/65, Art 42, 43 and Annex VII.

[53] MA Corvaglia, 'Public Procurement and Private Standards: Ensuring Sustainability under the WTO Agreement of Government Procurement' (2016) 19 *Journal of International Economic Law* 607, 613.

time, outside-EU convergence is also possible. Given the potential of public procurement in steering the practices of producers[54] in combination with the employment of private standards, the practice of contracting authorities creates the potential for an increased convergence of production practices towards a more sustainable approach, in line with the international obligations incorporated into the standard. Remarkable outside-EU regulatory effects are generated for businesses desiring to qualify to the vast EU procurement market. In addition, the employment by contracting authority of private schemes with a chain-of-custody approach stimulates compliance with sustainability requirements in value chains.

Another measure working in tandem with private regulatory authority is the Forest Law Enforcement, Governance and Trade (FLEGT) regime. The EU Timber Regulation in particular aims at ensuring that imported timber products are harvested in compliance with all applicable national and international obligations.[55] Private standards in the domain of forestry certification such as PEFC (the Program for the Endorsement of Forestry Certification) and the FSC (the Forestry Stewardship Council) play an important part in ensuring the functioning of the regime. Traders placing imported timber on the EU market must exercise due diligence in verifying lawfulness of timber products.[56] In doing so, they may employ systems designed by EU-recognised monitoring organisations which routinely use third-party private standards in the risk assessment, ie as evidence of a low risk of non-compliance.[57] FSC, for example, requires compliance also with all international treaties related to protected areas, endangered species, including their habitats and potential habitats, and with CITES (Convention on International Trade in Endangered Species of Wild Fauna and Flora) Permits. In addition, compliance is mandated also with the ILO Declaration on Fundamental Principles and Rights at Work (1998) based on the eight ILO Core Labour Conventions.[58]

The Directive on the Annual Financial Statements, Consolidated Financial Statements and Related Reports of Certain Types of Undertaking[59] imposes an

[54] See generally B Sjåfjell and A Wiesbrock (eds), *Sustainable Public Procurement under EU Law. New Perspective on the State as Stakeholder* (Cambridge University Press, 2016).

[55] Regulation (EU) No 995/2010 of 11 May 2009 laying down the obligations of operators who place timber and timber products on the market [2009] OJ L295/13.

[56] *Ibid*, Art 6.

[57] For Bureau Veritas, see www.en.bureauveritas.cn/home/news/latest-news/cer+article+eutr+and+bureau+veritas+solution+for+trading+tracking?presentationtemplate=bv_master_v2/news_full_story_presentation_did_you_know_v2. For SGS, see www.sgs.com/~/media/Global/Documents/Brochures/SGS%20CBE%20EUTR%20Due%20Diligence%20Guidebook%20LR%20A4%20EN%2016%2009.

[58] See FSC Principles and Criteria and in particular Forest management requirements for Controlled Wood certification, available at https://fsc.org/en/document-center/documents/73.

[59] Directive 2013/34/EU of the European Parliament and the Council of 26 June 2013 on the annual financial statements, consolidated financial statements and related reports of certain types of undertakings [2013] OJ L182/13, Art 19a, as amended by Directive 2014/95/EU of the European Parliament and the Council of 22 October 2014 amending Directive 2013/34/EU as regards disclosure of non-financial and diversity information by certain large undertakings and groups.

obligation on large corporations to report on the development, performance, position and impact of their economic activities relating to environmental, social and employee issues, respect for human rights, anti-corruption and bribery. Several types of private standards are permitted to be employed for this purpose, including reporting initiatives such as the United Nations Global Compact and ISO 26000, the International Organisation for Standardisation's (ISO) first sustainability/responsibility standard. While these standards do not contemplate certification, and the Global Compact has been criticised in particular for a lack of real 'teeth', a common feature is their connection to internationally-recognised human rights obligations, international labour rights as protected through ILO provisions, and principles of international environmental law such as a precautionary approach to environmental risks and the polluter-pays principle.

C. Public Standards in EU and Member States' Measures: OECD Guidelines and Human Rights Due Diligence

EU regulation of GVCs does not just unfold through the employment of private standards. Also, public standards for responsibility may be incorporated in public measures. This section will focus on standards centred on human rights due diligence (HRDD) in light of its implication for GVC regulation. A global regulatory preference for HRDD has emerged since the adoption of the UNGPs. HRDD is an ongoing and holistic attempt to ensure companies incorporate respect for human rights within the heart of their operations; it also represents a moral expectation of all corporations.[60] Corporations have to operationalise specific information-gathering strategies in order to have a comprehensive overview of actual and potential negative human rights impacts connected to their operations. These strategies also allow them to devise approaches to end, remedy, and communicate about these negative impacts.[61] These include impacts caused by a corporation alone, in combination with, and through another, business or non-business entity. Only through the implementation of HRDD, are corporations in the position to 'know and show' that there are no human rights impacts connected to their activities.[62]

Remarkably, HRDD responsibilities of corporations extend also to those negative impacts that can be directly connected to them, their products and operations, even if they did not directly contribute to, but that are instead directly linked to their products and business activities.[63] To this extent, transnational businesses

[60] United Nations, 'Frequently Asked Questions' (n 22) 9–10.

[61] Human Rights Council, 'Guiding Principles' (n 1) Principles 16 and 17.

[62] JG Ruggie, 'Global Governance and "New Governance Theory": Lessons from Business and Human Rights' (2014) 20 *Global Governance* 5.

[63] Human Rights Council, 'Guiding Principles' (n 1) Principle 13.

have to ensure that their suppliers and, on occasion, also the suppliers of their suppliers, fully respect all human rights obligations. If this is not the case, through the use of economic and non-economic leverage, corporations should prompt their lower-tier suppliers to comply with human rights – ultimately by discontinuing commercial relations. Under HRDD, corporations are thus required to act as GVC regulators, gathering information about their suppliers, designing strategies for their monitoring, and enforcing sanctions through disengagement if necessary.[64]

The emergence of EU legislation that makes HRDD mandatory for EU-based corporations will prompt businesses to establish internal procedures that, among other goals, ensure that their trading partners and in particular their suppliers respect human rights. As seen above, there are two main standards adopted by international organisations on corporate responsibility, the UNGPs and the OECD Guidelines. From the OECD Guidelines, a number of sectoral Guidance documents have been drafted which refer to, and incorporate, HRDD aspects as spelled out in the UNGPs. Such standards can then be incorporated in EU measures as it occurs with the Conflict Minerals Regulation. HRDD obligations imposed on economic actors such as EU minerals importers (or, perhaps in the future, EU textile manufacturers,[65] and importers of agricultural commodities impacting on deforestation[66]) have a strong potential to pursue public objectives in GVCs under the pressure of downstream economic entities. As legislations making HRDD mandatory has been approved in France, the UK and the Netherlands,[67] it is likely to be a matter of time before the EU implements its international obligation to support the adoption of the UNGPs and HRDD.[68]

The Conflict Minerals Regulation sets up a comprehensive supply chain due diligence system for EU importers of certain ores and minerals often associated with the financing of armed conflict and extensive human rights violations in Central African countries. Such importers have to implement a model supply chain policy[69] aligned to the OECD Due Diligence Guidance. In the context of

[64] For further conceptualisation on this regulatory function of corporations see: GA Sarfaty, 'Shining Light on Global Supply Chains' (2015) 56 *Harvard International Law Journal* 419.

[65] European Parliament Motion for a Resolution on the EU flagship initiative on the garment sector. 27 April 2017, A8-0080/2017.

[66] Ecofys, Milieu and COWI, 'Feasibility Study on Options to Step up EU Action Against Deforestation'. Final Report (Study financed by the European Commission, 2018) 20, available at http://ec.europa.eu/environment/forests/pdf/feasibility_study_deforestation_kh0418199enn_main_report.pdf.

[67] Loi n° 2017-399 du 27 mars 2017 relative au devoir de vigilance des sociétés mères et des entreprises donneuses d'ordre; Modern Slavery Act 2015 c. 30, Section 54; Wet Zorgplicht Kinderarbeid, vergaderjaar 2016–2017, 34 506.

[68] On the possible presence of an obligation to implement mandatory due diligence legislation, see UN Committee on Economic, Social and Cultural Rights (CESCR), General comment No 24 (2017) on State obligations under the International Covenant on Economic, Social and Cultural Rights in the context of business activities, 10 August 2017, E/C.12/GC/2.

[69] Conflict Minerals Regulation (n 29) Art 4(b).

their risk-management obligation – and in line with the concept of HRDD in the UNGPs – importers have to identify whether minerals may originate from conflict-affected and high-risk areas and, if so, must adopt measures which may include the suspension of trading or disengagement with a supplier.[70] Trading in conflict-minerals is condemned by a United Nation Security Council Resolution, which also called upon the exercise of due diligence by all economic actors involved in their trade.[71] In a way, the OECD Due Diligence Guidance serves as a tool for corporations to ensure implementation of the UN Security Council Resolution on conflict minerals.

The OECD Guidance was incorporated by reference in the EU Regulation, while stipulating the importers' traceability obligations, explicitly requires additional documentation to be provided in case minerals originate from conflict-affected and high-risk areas.[72] The burden for compliance is therefore not limited to EU economic operators, and other entities in a mineral's value chain have to comply with additional requirements. In order to trade with EU importers and allow them to comply with their traceability obligations, upstream companies from conflict-affected areas must comply with the OECD Guiding Note for Upstream Companies Risk Assessment. This instrument requires the implementation of detailed procedures affecting daily business operations on the ground and ensuring that minerals connected to human rights violation are not traded into the EU market. Due to the pressure from EU importers, non-EU producers and traders several tiers away from the EU market are thus prompted to act in line with international standards from the OECD which, ultimately, implement the UN Security Council Resolution. Regardless of the fact that the EU Regulation does not formally address non-EU economic actors, the resulting effect is a likely on-the-ground convergence of behaviour (i.e the eradication of trade in conflict-minerals) with the standard. Reliance on a non-EU voluntary standard is therefore essential in meeting the objective the Regulation.

III. Is there Convergence on the Ground?

EU Member States' reliance on external normative material does not necessarily generate proliferation and divergence of regulatory outcomes according to the substantive nature of the standard employed. To employ international standards for business conduct such as those drafted by international organisations like the OECD ensures convergence between EU and international provisions. Private regimes are grounded on international law obligations. In establishing criteria to determine, for example, what practices constitute responsible exploitation of

[70] Conflict Minerals Regulation (n 29) Art 5(1).
[71] Security Council of the United Nations, Resolution 1952(2010) S/RES/1952(2010).
[72] Conflict Minerals Regulation (n 29) Art 4(f)(v).

forestry resources,[73] acceptable workplace conditions,[74] or sustainable fishery management,[75] these schemes routinely refer to international environmental law obligations, human rights treaties, and to ILO instruments and conventions.[76] From a functionalist perspective, private standards in the domain of sustainability have the effect of providing implementation, and even interpretation, to international social and environmental obligations, their monitoring and enforcement.

All these standards, to varying degrees, share a potential to result in an increased alignment of production practices in line with the broad principle of international obligations on which they are based, and to which implementation they contribute. In order to understand the actual impact on the ground requires, however, a more careful appraisal. However tempting a functionalist approach may be in discussing divergence and convergence,[77] it remains exposed to the risk of missing crucial dynamics especially in the presence of multiple actors involved in rule-setting and implementation, and in multi-level constructs such as the transnational legal space. In the first place, not all standards share the same proximity to international legal obligations: schemes established by industry organisations, for example, have been observed to be more relaxed than schemes established by multi-stakeholder organisations.[78] Most importantly, however, it must be acknowledged that the normative material contained in the standards, even where used by EU authorities, interacts with the behaviour of other actors, a number of legal requirements and specific conditions 'on the ground' which filter and impact on the application and effectiveness of the standard. They may therefore contribute substantially to the effective presence of convergence.

In the first place, and perhaps more obviously, third party auditing operates under the doubtful assumption that auditors are capable of operating independently from the business entities which pay for their services. In spite of its almost structural employment in several different contexts, third party auditing puts an undue emphasis on auditors' actual technical capacity to identify cases of non-compliance.[79] It should not be forgotten that some of the brands whose subcontractors' production site was located at the Rana Plaza complex held valid Business Social Compliance Initiative and SA8000 certifications providing

[73] See, among the many the schemes established by the Forestry Stewardship Council, the Programme for the Endorsement of Forestry Certification and the Sustainable Forestry Initiative.

[74] Among which Social Accountability's SA8000 standard (n 16) is the most popular.

[75] See the Marine Stewardship Council,

[76] For an exhaustive empirical appraisal, see O Perez and O Stegmann, 'Transnational Networked Constitutionalism' (2018) 45 *Journal of Law and Society* S135.

[77] For a discussion of functionalism in comparative law, see F Chirico and P Larouche, 'Conceptual Divergence, Functionalism, and the Economics of Convergence' in S Prechal and B van Roermund (eds), *The Coherence of EU Law: The Search for Unity in Divergent Concepts* (Oxford University Press, 2008).

[78] A Kalfagianni and P Pattberg, 'Participation and Inclusiveness in Private Rule-Setting Organisation: Does it Matter for Effectiveness?' (2013) 26 *Innovation* 213.

[79] RM Locke, *The Promise and Perils of Private Power: Promoting Labour Standards in a Global Economy* (Cambridge University Press, 2013). In particular, on the risks of auditing, see RM Locke, M Amengual and A Mangla, 'Virtue Out of Necessity? Compliance, Commitment, and the Improvement of Labor Conditions in Global Supply chains' (2009) 37 *Politics and Society* 319.

assurance that the factory complied with adequate standards concerning worker safety. The standards in question did not include requirements for building safety.[80] In addition, auditors have been extremely creative in certifying compliance with all ILO requirements, including freedom of association, also in countries such as China or Vietnam where free trade unions are not allowed.[81] An additional layer of actors, ie those entrusted with monitoring compliance with the standards, is therefore capable of glossing over whether actual convergence occurs according to the context in question. The presence of certification may signal apparent convergence of behaviour with standards in compliance with ILO requirements (including those for worker safety) where, in fact, this does not occur.

Secondly, from a more constructivist perspective, private standards do not operate in a vacuum, but they are exposed to numerous interactions and influences from different factors in their context of operation which reconfigure the extent of convergence. National legal requirements, political contexts, and even sourcing practices of retailers deeply influence the operation of private regimes. Standards may simply be incapable of affecting labour and land-management practices strictly controlled by State actors, for example when they claim to guarantee land tenure rights to indigenous communities.[82] Authoritarian States may suppress and make invisible conflicts connected to production or resource exploitation which would otherwise impede certification. The lack of strong civil society movements in the country of operations may fail to counterbalance corporations' frequent minimalistic understanding of compliance with a standard.[83] All these factors are crucial in determining the actual degree of convergence in the context of application of a standard, but can be easily glossed over in the presence of certification stating that a given producer, factory or product is fully compliant with the requirements of the scheme.

It is quite disappointing that the European Parliament Resolution discussed above accepts private standards as positive *per se*, without urging for, or supporting, rigorous public benchmarking of labelling schemes and private standards in their different contexts of application, or measures establishing the financial independence of social auditors from the entities they certify. In addition, EU measures recognising private schemes contain very limited requirements for the selection of which private standard to employ, in spite of their differences in terms of stringency, governance structure and association to the industry.[84] Clear criteria for employment, encompassing both substantive and procedural requirements of the schemes, as well as close verification of compliance by EU institutions will be

[80] See Clean Clothes Campaign, 'BSCI 10th Anniversary Shame over Rana Plaza', https://cleanclothes.org/news/2013/06/25/bsci-10th-anniversary-shame-over-rana-plaza.

[81] P Paiement, 'Jurisgenerative Role of Auditors in Transnational Labour Governance' (2019) 13 *Regulation and Governance* 280.

[82] T Bartley, 'Transnational Governance as the Layering of Rules: Intersections of Public and Private Standards' (2011) 12 *Theoretical Inquiries in Law* 517.

[83] See generally Bartley (n 34).

[84] Partiti (n 18) in particular at 112–15.

required in order to fully exploit the potential of private regimes. Arguably this shows that EU institutions are not fully aware of the ramifications on the ground of private regimes, and seem satisfied with a potentially shallow operationalisation of their requirements. This could be explained by the urgent need to address transnational phenomena even at the cost of adopting sub-optimal solutions.

Similarly as with voluntary standards, also the external effects of EU measures incorporating public standards such as the OECD Guidelines may be difficult to predict 'on the ground'. This is largely due to the open-ended character of HRDD, arguably the transnational regulatory approach of choice in mitigating the negative impacts of globalisation, and incorporated in the OECD Guidelines. As with private standards, the extent of global convergence closely depends on the actual practice of businesses and a number of contextual issues. In this case, corporation-specific HRDD strategies – especially those addressing their suppliers – will be key in determining the extent of compliance with human rights obligation upstream the value chain. HRDD has been criticised both for its substantive breadth (applying to *all* human rights) and for its somewhat hortatory character.[85] The UNGPs themselves acknowledge that corporations may prioritise on which human rights impact to focus their efforts, for example on the most severe ones, or those with the highest likelihood of occurrence. While EU and Member State measures may stimulate compliance with HRDD, the actual convergence of human rights practices outside the EU will depend on how corporations will structure their management processes and internal governance according to company-specific priorities, contexts, and even internal understanding of HRDD.

Preliminary empirical appraisals seem to point towards considerable variety of approaches, in particular of stringency, in operationalising due diligence.[86] In addition, monitoring the quality of HRDD processes, appraising their effectiveness, and ultimately exposing cases of insufficient due diligence, depend on the monitoring efforts of civil society and, in particular, non-governmental organisations. A key problem with HRDD is that it pushes away from public regulators important competencies concerning the regulation of upstream entities in value chains, and conceals them into corporate processes basically inaccessible to the public. The success of the incorporation of HRDD in EU regulation will require very clear guidance about what actions shall be taken by corporations in specific circumstances, monitoring tools to ensure that such actions are in fact taken, as well as enforcement mechanisms.

While the use of different forms of private authority is indispensable if the EU is to exercise influence and generate convergence on production practices outside the EU territory, the reliance on private standards and corporations' due diligence

[85] S Deva and D Bilchitz, 'The Human Rights Obligations of Business: A Critical Framework for the Future' in S Deva and D Bilchitz (eds), *Human Rights Obligations of Business: Beyond the Corporate Responsibility to Respect?* (Cambridge University Press, 2013).

[86] K Salcito and M Wielga, 'What does Human Rights Due Diligence for Business Relationships Really Look Like on the Ground?' (2018) 3 *Business and Human Right Journal* 113.

systems remains complicated in light of the lack of effective mechanisms that can support, steer and ensure proper implementation in their context of application. The necessity to use *private* forms of monitoring and enforcement, the natural interaction of private regimes with other legitimate regimes and practices, as well as the large degree of freedom enjoyed by corporations in structuring and operationalising their due diligence, does not just weaken the extent of convergence, but also exposes normative questions about the effective trustworthiness of private regimes in the pursuit of public goals in association with public measures. In particular, given the impact on various sets of interests determined by private action, it is essential that mechanisms for ensuring that the interests of those affected are established, especially where public authority makes direct and explicit use of private forms of rule-making.[87]

IV. Divergence with International Trade Obligations

An analysis of EU measures which, ultimately, have the ability to affect and even determine market access must also encompass the dimension of international trade law. In the end, such measures must be in compliance with the WTO tenets of non-discrimination and unnecessary trade-restrictiveness. However, the use of private authority makes the appraisal more complex. The emergence and proliferation of private regulatory regimes in the domain of sustainability can also be seen as a response to State inaction. For example, the emergence of forest certification was linked to the inability of the international community to come up with a regime against trade in illegal timber.[88] Such inaction is also connected to the constraints of international trade law, in particular stemming from WTO law, which have been traditionally perceived as limiting the tools available to public authority to affect actors located extraterritorially and the regulation of processes and production methods (PPMs).[89]

Particularly in social and environmental matters, multilateral solutions are the most appropriate venue and should be sought in good faith by WTO Members before proceeding with establishing unilateral trade-restrictive measures.[90] In spite of common misunderstandings, PPM-based measures are not prohibited *per se* under WTO law.[91] In particular, origin-neutral PPMs (ie that do not

[87] E Partiti, 'Trust in Global Governance. Ensuring Trustworthiness of Transnational Private Regulators' (2020) 52 *NYU Journal of International Law and Politics* 415.

[88] E Meidinger, 'The Administrative Law of Global Private-Public Regulation. The Case of Forestry' (2006) 17 *European Journal of International Law* 50–51.

[89] L Ankersmit, *Green Trade and Fair Trade in and with the EU. Process-Based Measures within the EU Legal Order* (Cambridge University Press, 2017).

[90] United States – Import Prohibition of Certain Shrimp and Shrimp Products (US – Shrimp), WT/DS58/AB/R, adopted 12 October 1998.

[91] J Potts, *The Legality of PPMs under the GATT. Challenges and Opportunities for Sustainable Trade Policy* *Winnipeg, Manitoba, International Institute for Sustainable Development, 2008) 3.

discriminate on the basis of the territory of origin of products) should not be problematic. However, the regulation of social and environmental requirements taking the form of PPMs may structurally generate detrimental impacts for certain producers, for example from developing countries. It must therefore be carefully designed in order to avoid breaches of the non-discrimination principle.[92] Also directly monitoring compliance with EU requirements may not always be possible, nor permissible in foreign jurisdictions, to EU entities. Convergence in global production via voluntary standards as stimulated by the EU thus enters into a collision course with international trade rules.

Private standards regulating social and environmental issues have, since their early days, been criticised by developing countries for their trade restrictiveness and their detrimental effect on the competitiveness of their producers.[93] Among other criticisms, food quality and safety standards have been routinely debated by WTO Members since 2005 within the Sanitary and Phytosanitary Measures Committee.[94] Private standards addressing environmental concerns have been steadily on the agenda of the Committee on Trade and Environment since 2007. Developing countries repeatedly voiced a number of concerns relating to the standards' excessive stringency in pursuing legitimate objectives, and especially concerning the limited compliance capacity with respect to the complex and burdensome requirements frequently incorporated in the standards.[95] In any event, it has been argued extensively elsewhere that private standards in the social and environmental domain may fall under the discipline of the Technical Barriers to Trade (TBT) Agreement, and may under some circumstances considered to be compliant with its criteria.[96]

The association of private standards to public authority however greatly enhances the fictitious voluntary character of schemes that are already basically mandatory to enter into certain markets due to the preferences of consumers and retailers.[97] Especially when coupled with chain-of-custody requirements, public use of private standards may result in a *de facto* ban, or at the very least in detrimental treatment, for products that do not fall under the definition of

[92] See the General Agreement on Tariffs and Trade (GATT) Arts I:1 and III:4.

[93] Among the many: SW Chang, 'GATTing a Green Trade Barrier. Eco-Labelling and the WTO Agreement on Technical Barriers to Trade' (1997) 31 *Journal of World Trade* 137; M Joshi, 'Are Eco-Labels Consistent with World Trade Organisation Agreements?' (2004) 38 *Journal of World Trade* 69; R Bonsi, AL Hammet and B Smith, 'Eco-Labels and International Trade: Problems and Solutions' (2008) 42 *Journal of World Trade* 407.

[94] Committee on Sanitary and Phytosanitary Measures. Summary of the meeting held on 29–30 June 2005. Note by the Secretariat, 24 January 2007. G/SPS/R/37.

[95] SR Gandhi, 'Regulating the Use of Voluntary Environmental Standards within the World Trade Organisation Legal Regime: Making a Case for Developing Countries' (2005) 39 *Journal of World Trade* 855.

[96] For exhaustive discussion see E Partiti, '*What Use is an Unloaded Gun?* The Substantive Discipline of the WTO TBT Code of Good Practice and its Application to Private Standards Pursuing Public Objectives' (2017) 20 *Journal of International Economic Law* 829.

[97] J Wouters and D Geraets, 'Private Food Standards and the World Trade Organisation: Some Legal Considerations' (2012) 11 *World Trade Review* 479.

'sustainable' or 'ethical' as identified by the combination of private and public requirements. This is indeed the purpose of the measure itself. However, long-lasting WTO debates have failed to settle whether 'green' and 'brown' products are 'like products',[98] as well as the precise margins for Members to lawfully regulate processes and production methods.[99] This lack of clarity notwithstanding, it may occur that social and environmental criteria end up favouring domestic producers in compliance with stricter social and environmental standards. This is inherent in the nature of standard-setting and, generally, private rule-making. Power dynamics in standard-setting, often dominated by Western players, in turn, exacerbate concerns for interest representation of developing countries and small producers, thereby further impacting negatively on their competitive advantage. Using private regimes can therefore be a tool to strategically level the playing field, and impose regulatory burdens that will affect non-EU producers more than they affect EU ones. Convergence is thus forced on actors not seeking it, and even actively resisting it.[100]

Furthermore, EU measures which simply permit the employment of private standards without their formal recognition, or that encourage by varying degrees their use, escape classic categories for attribution of private conduct under public international law[101] and their transposition to WTO law.[102] It is therefore difficult to establish State responsibility for negative effects on trade stemming from *private* authority. Granted, WTO Members are under an obligation under Art 4 of the TBT Agreement to discipline standards in line with the substantive and procedural principles contained in the TBT Code of Good Practice for the Preparation, Adoption and Application of Standards. The relevance of procedural and substantive requirements for standards, including international standards as provided in a TBT Committee Decision,[103] has been asserted in a relatively recent Appellate Body ruling on tuna certification.[104] However, such an obligation to support procedural and substantive best practices is merely phrased along the lines of a 'best effort' obligation with respect to non-governmental standards established in Members' territory.

[98] DP Stewart, 'First WTO Judicial Review of Climate Change Subsidies Issues' (2013) 107 *American Journal of International Law* 875.

[99] See generally, CR Conrad, *Processes and Production Methods (PPMs) in WTO Law: Interfacing Trade and Social Goals* (Cambridge University Press, 2011).

[100] See E Fahey, in the Introduction to this volume.

[101] Draft Articles on Responsibility of States for Internationally Wrongful Acts, with commentaries. Yearbook of the International Law Commission, 2001, vol II, Part Two, in particular Arts 4, 5, 8 and 11.

[102] Panel Report, *Japan – Measures Affecting Consumers Photographic Film and Paper (Japan – Film)* WT/DS44/R, adopted 31 March 1998, para 10.56.

[103] TBT Committee Decision on Principles for the Development of International Standards, Guides and Recommendation with Relation to Arts 2, 5, and Annex 3 to the Agreement, in WTO document G/TBT/1/Rev 10, Decisions and Recommendations adopted by the WTO Committee on Technical Barriers to Trade since Jan 1, 1995, June 9, 2011, 46–48.

[104] Appellate Body Report, *United States – Measures Concerning the Importation, Marketing and Sale of Tuna Products (US – Tuna II)* WT/DS381/AB/R, adopted 16 May 2012.

Members are also under an obligation not to take measures which have the effect of, directly or indirectly, requiring or encouraging such standardising bodies to act in a manner inconsistent with WTO principles – but the extent of this potentially far reaching obligation has never been clarified, nor tested in WTO dispute settlement. In fact EU practice shows that the employment and recognition of private regimes takes place under a minimalistic appraisal of both procedural and substantive requirements provided under the TBT Agreement.[105] The use of highly normative private regimes in public regulation may then bring large chunks of these measures, ie the entire private component, outside WTO review especially in the presence of legal informality in the recognition process. As a consequence, the venues for multilateral dispute resolutions are further limited.

Finally, also international organisations' standards may generate concerns under WTO law. On the one hand, the elaboration of international standards and guidelines covering responsible business conduct by the OECD and the UN testify to the allocation of social and environmental regulation away from the WTO towards institutions that, in the context of fragmentation of international law, are arguably better placed to do so. On the other hand, it should not be discounted that both the OECD Guidelines and the UNGPs embrace management practices and discretionary business conduct in delivering regulatory outcomes, a strategy that in itself reflects the regulatory preference of corporations and that may put an undue burden of compliance on their suppliers. Similarly as with the use of private standards, the mobilisation of corporations in GVC regulation will be very difficult to square with international rules of attribution and thus ensure WTO review of EU measures affecting trade.[106] In addition, while OECD standard-setting is increasingly open to non-OECD Members, the growing adoption rate of OECD Guidance documents and their value chain regulatory effects will have an impact on economic actors from countries which did not, or only very limitedly, contribute to their elaboration and drafting – thereby enhancing possible trade restrictiveness and discriminatory character.

V. Conclusion

Consistent with its role as 'normative power',[107] the EU is increasingly occupied with GVCs regulation to ensure responsible corporate conduct. Because of Treaty provisions defining a normative role for the EU in global governance and the frequent 'altruistic purposes' characterising the EU as a benign hegemonic actor

[105] Partiti (n 18) 105–106.

[106] This does not mean, however, that the HRDD is *per se* inconsistent with WTO law. See E Partiti, 'Regulating Trade in Forest-Risk Commodities' (2020) 54 *Journal of World Trade* forthcoming.

[107] I Manners, 'Normative Power Europe: A Contradiction in Terms?' (2002) 40 *Journal of Common Market Studies* 235.

on the global stage,[108] this activity is likely to continue, and perhaps even increase, in the near future. In light of legal and practical complexities in regulating global production, GVC discipline has taken experimental forms jointly performed by public authority and non-mandatory private and public standards. Frequently, transnational corporations are casted upon regulatory competences. In this framework, the effects of measures impacting on non-EU producers or the behaviour of other businesses – either directly, or indirectly through private standards – represent an instance of EU-led global convergence of production practices with human rights and other international obligations. In GVC regulation, the EU plays the role of a convergence actor of production practices and human rights. It does so though the use of voluntary private and public standards incorporating international law obligations. Yet, the global convergence on the ground is more difficult. While these measures, at face value, are aligned to international obligations, or themselves adopt and implement international obligations as in the case of HRDD, the extent of actual convergence may differ, and be more elusive to determine. In addition, convergence with international obligations in the social and environmental domain may occur at the expense of international obligations in the area of trade.

It is tempting to adopt a functionalist characterisation of transnational private regulation and private authority to justify their use in public measures. However, by focusing on *functions*, such an approach conceals differences among functionally-similar regimes and their actual effects. Crucial blind spots of functionalism include the actual performance of voluntary schemes, their distributional effects, and the actual practice of corporations implementing HRDD. At least in regulatory matters, interactions between different normative materials (EU-private standards based on international law/ EU-OECD Guidelines and UNGPs) may seem to prompt convergence of production practices globally. However, only moving beyond functionalism allows us to get a more nuanced picture of extent and effects of public use of private standards, and to evaluate whether convergence is superficial, apparent or non-existent altogether. An analysis of global convergence in production practices stimulated by EU action cannot thus be disassociated from sociological, socio-legal and empirical appraisals inquiring into the *praxis* and motives of many co-regulating actors. This endeavour would also permit the generation of badly-needed insights on the effectiveness of the combination of public and private regimes – especially where public authority explicitly relies on private authority and private actors in bringing about global convergence.

[108] Bradford (n 10) 37.

15

The EU Equivalence Regime as a Mechanism of Convergence: Financial Regulation and EU Law

FRANCESCO PENNESI

I. Introduction

The global financial crisis led to fundamental transformations in the regulation and supervision of capital markets in the European Union (EU). In order to respond to the post-crisis imperative of preserving EU financial stability, EU Member States have pooled together their financial sovereignty at an unprecedented level, transferring many of their regulatory and supervisory powers to the EU.[1] EU institutions, together with the European Securities and Market Authority (ESMA), have now greatly substituted national authorities in the regulation of financial markets, with the EU single financial rulebook governing capital markets in lieu of national legislations. Also the supervision of non-bank market actors, although still a responsibility of national authorities, is coordinated at the EU level and, in certain specific circumstances, even directly conducted by the ESMA.[2] The centralisation of regulatory and supervisory processes at the European level has strengthened the global clout of the EU in the area of capital markets regulation, but also increased the need to protect this complex multi-jurisdictional and multi-level governance framework from the external risks of regulatory arbitrage and international competition.[3]

[1] For a general overview of the post-crisis reforms in the area of EU capital markets regulation and supervision, see Marco Lamandini and David Ramos Muñoz, *EU Financial Law: An Introduction* (Wolters Kluwer, 2017); Niamh Moloney, *EU Securities and Financial Markets Regulation* (Oxford University Press, 2014).

[2] To understand the change of perspective in the supervision of banking and capital markets firms in the EU before and after the crisis, see Eilis Ferran, 'Financial Supervision' in Daniel Mügge, *Europe and the Governance of Global Finance* (Oxford University Press, 2014).

[3] There is a rich scholarship on the rise of the EU as global financial regulator due to the centralisation of regulatory and supervisory powers in the hands of EU authorities. Chris Brummer, *Soft Law and the Global Financial System Rule Making in the 21st Century* (Cambridge University Press, 2012); Lucia Quaglia, *The European Union and Global Financial Regulation* (Oxford University Press, 2014).

In particular, the EU has sought to increase not only its capacity to resist the influence of other jurisdictions ('power as autonomy'), but also its ability to extraterritorially export EU regulatory preferences at the international level ('power as influence').[4] The present contribution analyses one of the main legal mechanisms employed by the EU to achieve this twofold objective, the EU equivalence regime.[5] Equivalence empowers the European Commission to grant market access to third countries whose regulatory and supervisory framework is equivalent to the one adopted within the EU. It is thus a sophisticated procedural mechanism through which the EU can require a foreign authority to align its regulatory regime or its supervisory practices to EU standards in exchange for market access.

Although equivalence constitutes an important case study of the academic and policy discourse on the 'global reach of EU law', its effectiveness as a mechanism to promote international convergence with EU standards is not clear.[6] To what extent can the EU impose a foreign authority to internalise EU regulatory preferences in exchange for market access? The question has become extremely relevant after the decision of the United Kingdom (UK) to leave the EU. Brexit constitutes in fact an existential challenge to the EU regulatory power in the area of capital markets regulation. When it comes to market-based finance, the UK is not a Member State like every other. Benefitting from economies of scales and a friendly regulatory environment, the UK and in particular the City of London has become the 'investment banker' of Europe, hosting a staggering amount of capital market providers of systemic relevance for the Single Market.[7] The EU is therefore running the risk of becoming a 'regulator without a market', with the main financial centre of the continent soon leaving the Single Market. However, since Brexit will entail the transformation of the UK into a third country, extraneous to the EU legal order, the level of market access enjoyed by the UK financial sector

[4] Eric Helleiner and Stefano Pagliari, 'The End of an Era in International Financial Regulation? A Postcrisis Research Agenda' (2011) 65(1) *International Organization* 169, 177.

[5] The EU equivalence regime is not the only legal mechanism employed by the EU to influence the financial rule-making of third countries. The EU also seeks to extraterritorially expand its regulatory clout influencing the rule-making activities of global transnational regulatory networks, such as the Group of Twenty and the Financial Stability Board. The EU also has bilateral regulatory exchanges with third countries, such as the EU-US Financial Regulatory Forum and the EU-Switzerland Financial Regulatory Dialogue. For a legal analysis of the legal mechanisms employed by the EU, see Paul L Davies, 'Financial Stability and the Global Influence of EU Law' in Marisa Cremona and Joanne Scott (ed), *EU Law Beyond EU Borders. The Extraterritorial Reach of EU Law* (Oxford University Press, 2018). The main difference is that, whereas those multilateral and bilateral legal mechanisms are all based on non-binding, soft law principles and high-level standards, equivalence decisions are powered by a binding regulatory and institutional framework. Equivalence is in fact based on EU financial regulation and managed by EU Institutions.

[6] For a political science perspective on this academic discourse, see Chad Damro, 'Market Power Europe' (2012) 19(5) *Journal of European Public Policy* 682; for a legal perspective, see Anu Bradford, 'The Brussels Effect' (2012) 107 *Northwestern University Law Review* 1; Elaine Fahey, *The Global Reach of EU Law* (Routledge, 2016).

[7] Niamh Moloney, 'Brexit, the EU and its Investment Banker: Rethinking "Equivalence" for the EU Capital Market' (2017) LSE Legal Studies Working Paper No 5/2017, 8.

to the rest of the EU will depend upon equivalence decisions adopted unilaterally by the EU Commission.[8] Henceforth, not only is equivalence bound to play a fundamental role in the context of Brexit, but the regulatory degree of convergence between the EU and the UK will most probably be determined by how the two jurisdictions conceptualise and apply the principle of equivalence in their third country regimes.

Taking the perspective of EU law and relying on a legal analysis of the EU equivalence regime, the present contribution claims that the future fitness of equivalence as a convergence mechanism after Brexit will chiefly depend upon two factors. A first determinant will be the amount of discretion and autonomy the EU institutional ecosystem will be willing to leave in the hands of the EU Commission, in a period where the institutional and political monopoly of this institution over equivalence policies is increasingly contested. The convergence and extraterritorial effects of equivalence will also depend on the effectiveness of recent legislative reforms adopted by the EU to turn equivalence into a more flexible instrument, to respond to the needs of the EU Commission in the volatile and overly complex context of EU financial relations with third countries.

II. What is the EU Equivalence Regime?

The EU equivalence regime is a legal and procedural mechanism governing third country access to the EU Single Market, and its main objective is to facilitate cross-border financial integration between the EU and selected financial partners.[9] The EU equivalence process sees the Commission assessing whether the regulatory regime of a third country for a specific financial service is equivalent to EU standards and can thereby be directly sold to EU clients or EU counterparties.[10] In certain cases, a positive equivalence determination also alleviates the regulatory and capital requirements that EU financial firms must comply with to provide services or to use a financial infrastructure in third countries.[11] Taking stock from the painful

[8] In EU law jargon, 'third countries' are all the jurisdictions which are not part of the EU, and are therefore extraneous to the EU legal order.

[9] For an institutional and regulatory analysis of the EU equivalence regime, see Kern Alexander and others, *Brexit and Financial Services: Law and Policy* (Bloomsbury Publishing, 2018); John Armour, 'Brexit and Financial Services' (2017) 33(suppl_1) *Oxford Review of Economic Policy* S54; David Howarth and Lucia Quaglia, 'Brexit and the Single European Financial Market' (2017) 55(S1) *Journal of Common Market Studies* 149; Moloney (n 7).

[10] Andy Tarrant, Peter Holmes and Daniele Kelemen, 'Equivalence, Mutual Recognition in Financial Services and the UK Negotiating Position' (2019) Briefing paper 27, UK Trade Policy Observatory (UKTPO).

[11] Moloney categorises EU equivalence regimes between 'access' and 'export' rules. The former group allows financial firms established outside the Single Market to provide services in the EU, whereas the latter facilitates the opposite scenario, namely the provision of financial services outside the Single Market for financial firms located in the EU. Moloney (n 7) 5.

experience of the financial crisis, the EU promotes cross-border financial integration only with third countries whose regulatory and supervisory framework is deemed 'equivalent' to the EU regulatory regime, in order to ensure a level playing field within the Single Market and to shield the latter from competitive distortions and financial risks.[12] According to the EU Commission, equivalence does not aim at liberalising international trade in financial services, but it is rather a key instrument to 'effectively manage the cross-border activity of market players in a safe and secure environment'.[13] The equivalence concept has therefore the underlying objective of protecting EU financial stability and EU regulatory autonomy in global capital markets.[14]

The legal basis through which the Commission can adopt equivalence determinations is established in EU secondary law, and the substantive procedure that third country firms must follow in order to provide services under equivalence diverge in every piece of EU financial legislation. There is no common approach to equivalence access, but rather each EU legislative act, governing a specific financial sector, also establishes the conditions and requirements according to which third country firms may provide the financial service regulated thereof without establishing a subsidiary in the Single Market.[15] Certain EU legislative acts do not even include equivalence provisions, with the consequence that not every market activity is available through equivalence. In addition, equivalence allows third country financial firms to service only professional and eligible clients, whereas retail clients can be catered for only by financial firms authorised in the Single Market, either under EU law or under a national regime.[16] Finally, the extent to which a third country firm established in an equivalent jurisdiction can rely on its home country regulation and supervision to operate in the EU depends on each legislative act, and it diverges significantly for each financial activity.

[12] Ferran (n 2) 23.

[13] European Commission, 'EU Equivalence Decisions in Financial Services Policy: An Assessment', Commission Staff Working Paper, SWD(2017) 102 final (27 February 2017).

[14] Using the words of Michel Barnier during his time as Commissioner for Internal Market and Services, the post-crisis EU equivalence regime was established with the purpose of preserving the 'sovereignty' and 'autonomy' of the EU in the area of financial services. See House of Lords, European Union Committee, *The Post-Crisis EU Financial Regulatory Framework, do the Pieces Fit?*, 5th report of session, HL 2014–2015, 103, oral evidence given by Michel Barnier: 'We are not trying to establish extraterritoriality here, just as we do not accept extraterritorial measures that the Americans sometimes implement. What we want are common standards, interoperability of rules and equivalence when it comes to supervision in particular. That is what we are working on. The Americans are quite reticent about the issue of equivalence, but we have to stick to our guns and impose it to ensure that we are not subjected to the rules and supervision of others. Europe needs to keep its autonomy and sovereignty in this area.'

[15] Casper de Vries and others, 'Implications of Brexit on EU Financial Services', study for the ECON Committee (European Parliament, 2017) 23.

[16] Eddy Wymeersch, 'Brexit and the Equivalence of Regulation and Supervision' (European Banking Institute Working Paper Series, 2017) no 15, 2.

The Commission has thus no general authority to grant equivalence access to third countries, but it can only act under the rules and procedures established in each equivalence clause envisaged under EU secondary legislation. However, the 'salami-sliced' nature of the EU equivalence regime is counterbalanced by the uniformity of the EU administrative procedure leading to an EU equivalence decision.[17] In the great majority of cases, in fact, equivalence is singlehandedly managed by the EU Commission, which adopts a unilateral decision in the form of an implementing act (Art 291 of the Treaty on the Functioning of the European Union (TFEU)) after a technical and non-binding assessment by ESMA. The Commission is accountable for its equivalence policies to the representatives of EU Member States, who must approve equivalence decisions under the comitology procedure.[18] The institutional monopoly over equivalence policies gives extensive powers to the EU Commission, which has unsurprisingly made equivalence a central piece of its external relations policy in the area of financial services.[19] Among 40 pieces of EU financial legislation, 15 of them contain equivalence empowerments. Moreover, equivalence plays a specific importance in the area of capital markets, given the transnational and cross-border nature of market-based finance. Within this field, the Commission can grant 'passport-like' market access to the Single Market to central counterparties and trade repositories (EMIR), investment firms (MIFIR), alternative investment funds (AIFMD), credit rating agencies (CRAs), central securities depositories (CSDR), trading venues (MIFID II/MIFIR) and financial benchmarks (BMR).[20]

[17] Moloney (n 7) 14.

[18] In the area of capital markets, draft equivalence decisions must be submitted by the EU Commission to the European Securities Committee, composed of high level representatives of Member States. Representatives from the European Central Bank, ESMA, EFTA (European Free Trade Association) and candidate countries may be invited to attend as observers. See: https://ec.europa.eu/info/business-economy-euro/banking-and-finance/financial-reforms-and-their-progress/regulatory-process-financial-services/expert-groups-comitology-and-other-committees/european-securities-committee_en.

[19] European Commission, 'Equivalence in the Area of Financial Services', Communication from the Commission to the European Parliament, the Council, the European Central Bank, the European Economic and Social Committee and the Committee of the Regions, COM(2019) 349, 2.

[20] Regulation of the European Parliament and of the Council No 648/2012 of 4 July 2012 on OTC derivatives, central counterparties and trade repositories (EMIR) [2012] OJ L2012, Arts 25 and 75; Regulation of the European Parliament and of the Council No 600/2014 of 15 May 2014 on markets in financial instruments (MIFIR) [2014] OJ L173, Arts 23, 28, 33, 38 and 47; Directive of the European Parliament and the Council 2014/65/EU on markets in financial instruments (MIFID II) [2014] OJ L173, Art 25; Directive of the European Parliament and of the Council 2011/61/EU of 8 June 2011 on Alternative Investment Fund Managers (AIFMD) [2011] OJ L174, Arts 35, 36, 39 and 42; Regulation No 462/2013 on credit rating agencies (CRAR) [2013] OJ L146/1, Art 5; Regulation No 909/2014 of the European Parliament and of the Council of 23 July 2014 on improving securities settlement in the European Union and on central securities depositories (CSDR) [2014] OJ L257, Art 25; Regulation of the European Parliament and of the Council No 2016/1011 of 8 June 2016 on indices used as benchmarks in financial instruments and financial contracts or to measure the performance of investment funds [2016] OJ L171, Art 30.

III. Equivalence as a Mechanism of Regulatory Convergence

The political science and legal scholarship has identified in equivalence a mechanism of regulatory convergence through which the EU can 'transfer' or 'cross-load' EU financial rules into other jurisdictions.[21] Equivalence allows the EU to leverage its market size and institutional capacity to extend its regulatory clout vis-à-vis third countries seeking market access for their financial sector. First of all, the mere existence of an equivalence clause constitutes an incentive for foreign regulators to seek regulatory convergence with the EU, as they know *ex ante* that incorporating EU financial standards in their legislation is a requirement to obtain market access. Second, in order to obtain equivalence, foreign authorities usually start long negotiations with the EU Commission.[22] The Commission must in fact verify the equivalence between the regulatory and supervisory frameworks, as well as assess whether all the legal requirements to grant equivalence established under EU law are satisfied by the relevant jurisdiction. Within those informal negotiations, the Commission can leverage its large administrative experience with the principle of cross-border legal recognition as well as the market size of the EU to demand regulatory concessions in exchange for equivalence.[23] Third, an equivalence decision imposes on third countries a *dynamic* regulatory alignment with EU financial standards, as they otherwise risk seeing their positive assessment being withdrawn by the Commission. On one hand, equivalence access constitutes a *de facto* standstill clause because third countries positively assessed by the Commission cannot unilaterally change their standards without triggering a new evaluation. On the other hand, third countries must continuously align their regulatory framework to EU standards, as failure to closely follow EU regulatory reforms may lead to the withdrawal of an equivalence determination. This for example occurred in the area of credit rating agency regulation, where several third countries lost preferential access to the Single Market after their failure to keep up with the latest EU regulatory reform.[24]

[21] On the ability of great powers to influence the standards adopted by smaller jurisdictions, see Daniel W Drezner, *All Politics is Global: Explaining International Regulatory Regimes* (Princeton University Press, 2008); Quaglia (n 3)).

[22] Kalypso Nicolaidis and Gregory Shaffer, 'Transnational Mutual Recognition Regimes: Governance without Global Government' (2004) 68 *Law & Contempary Problems* 263.

[23] *Ibid.*

[24] The Commission has repealed previously adopted equivalence decisions under the Credit Rating Agency Regulation in favour of Canada, Brazil, Singapore, Argentina and Australia. The decision to withdraw those equivalence determinations arrived after negotiations with the relevant third countries and their failure to update their regulatory framework in light of the latest reform of the EU regulatory and supervisory framework for Credit Rating Agencies. See 'EU Decisions on Equivalence Set to Heighten UK Post-Brexit Fears' *Financial Times*, 28 July 2019, www.ft.com/content/a8f46a2c-b111-11e9-8cb2-799a3a8cf37b.

Naturally, the capacity of the EU to employ equivalence as a mechanism of global convergence towards EU standards is dependent upon the difference in market size and regulatory capacity between the EU and the relevant third country.[25] In the financial relationship between the EU and smaller jurisdictions, where there is a financial and institutional asymmetry in favour of the EU, equivalence is a unidirectional tool where the EU can transfer its technical expertise and often regulatory preferences to the recipient third country in exchange for market access. When however equivalence is employed in favour of jurisdictions with a sophisticated regulatory system and developed financial markets, it becomes a mechanism of 'cooperative governance', facilitating regulatory and supervisory solutions to common problems.[26] In other words, equivalence increases the EU 'power as influence' with smaller jurisdictions, and the EU 'power as autonomy' with other regulatory powers. In both cases, however, equivalence provides the EU with the necessary tool, which it would otherwise lack, to extend and preserve its regulatory clout at the global level.

IV. What is the Required Level of Regulatory Convergence with EU Law to Third Countries?

Given the importance of equivalence in the financial relationship between the EU and third countries, this mechanism is naturally bound to also play a central role in the context of Brexit. The EU Commission has recently issued two policy documents on EU equivalence policies: a working staff paper and a political communication.[27] Without expressly mentioning Brexit, they describe how the Commission intends to employ equivalence access vis-à-vis the UK. The Commission forcefully reiterated that the adoption of an equivalence decision constitutes a 'unilateral and discretionary act of the EU'.[28] Although third countries may express interest in obtaining market access, equivalence provisions do not confer a 'right to be assessed or receive a positive determination'.[29] The Commission also claims to have absolute flexibility in granting equivalence to a third country. In particular, equivalence decisions can be granted 'in full or in part'.

[25] Market size and institutional capacity are the two main determinants of state power in global regulatory cooperation in the area of financial services, identified by the political science scholarship. For the importance of market size in global regulatory coordination, see Drezner (n 21). Regulatory capacity has been defined by the political science literature as the 'capacity to define, monitor and defend a specific set of rules', David Bach and Abraham L Newman, The European Regulatory State and Global Public Policy: Micro-Institutions, Macro-Influence' (2007) 14(6) *Journal of European Public Policy* 827, 831.

[26] For the importance of power asymmetries in mutual recognition agreements between the EU and third countries, see Nicolaidis and Shaffer (n 22) 310.

[27] European Commission Working Paper (n 13).

[28] European Commission Working Paper (n 13) 8.

[29] European Commission Working Paper (n 13) 8.

The Commission can thus allow market access for all the services covered by an equivalence regime, or limit the equivalence determination to certain activities or financial products, or even impose further conditions to the relevant third country in exchange of market access.[30] Equivalence decisions can also have an 'indefinite or time-bound duration', in so far as the EU Commission can adopt equivalence determinations whose validity is restrained to a certain period of time, and subject to specific conditions for renewal.[31] Finally, and most importantly, the discretionary nature of equivalence allows the Commission to change or even withdraw equivalence determination 'at any moment'.[32]

The Commission has often maintained that, in order to be assessed as equivalent, third countries do not have to copy and paste EU financial legislation. Rather than demanding a word-by-word equivalence between the two regulatory regimes, EU authorities only verify whether the two regimes achieve the same outcomes.[33] However, the level of regulatory convergence required by the EU Commission varies on a country by country basis, in a process that is presented as holistic, but substantially driven by competitive as much as stability concerns. The assessment of the Commission is based on a proportionality and risk-based approach. Relying on the technical advice provided by ESMA, the Commission firstly identifies the specific financial risks arising from opening the Single Market to a third country through equivalence. Then the Commission demands that the third country's regulatory proximity with EU legislation is proportionate to the risks identified. This means that jurisdictions with a high level of financial integration with the EU are subjected to closer scrutiny during the equivalence negotiations, and their regulatory framework is required to be more aligned with EU standards in order to obtain equivalence.[34] The more the balance sheet of EU financial markets, infrastructures and firms is interconnected with the one of financial entities located in the relevant third country, the greater will be the need of regulatory convergence between the two parties, in order to preserve the level playing field within the Single Market and avoid interjurisdictional arbitrage. However, financial stability is not the only benchmark employed by the Commission when assessing a third country, as the competitive consequences of cross-border market access is also taken into consideration.[35]

[30] European Commission Working Paper (n 13) 9.

[31] European Commission Working Paper (n 13) 9.

[32] The EU Commission must simply notify its intention to withdraw an equivalence decision to the affected third country 30 days in advance.

[33] European Commission Working Paper (n 13) 4.

[34] See European Commission Political Communication (n 19): 'the equivalence process is primarily a risk management exercise. It invariably involves managing any risks associated with the cross-border activity of market participants (i.e. impacts on EU financial stability, market integrity, investor protection and the level-playing field in the EU internal market), while exploiting the benefits of an open and globally integrated EU financial market'.

[35] The Commission highlighted in both the working staff paper and the political communication that equivalence decisions are adopted to facilitate cross-border financial trade for EU financial market actors seeking to provide cross-border services to third countries.

The implementation of the equivalence regime for third country central clearing counterparties (CCPs) under EMIR constitutes an insightful example of how the EU Commission applies the principle of proportionality in its equivalence assessment.[36] The regulatory and supervisory regime adopted by Japan and Singapore for their domestic CCPs was recognised by the Commission as equivalent on the same day in 2014.[37] However, the adoption of an equivalence decision in favour of the US regulatory regime for CCPs took over two years of intense negotiations. US CCPs were finally allowed to provide clearing services to EU clients under equivalence only after a difficult and precarious agreement between the Commission and the Commodity Futures Trading Commission (CFTC), the US regulator competent for the oversight of CCPs.[38] Singapore and Japan had broadly followed US financial standards in drafting their regulatory framework for CCPs, and all three jurisdictions had implemented global regulatory standards in their regimes.[39] Why then this stark difference in treatment between regulatory frameworks which were largely convergent? The Commission justified the different approach between the US and other countries with the principle of proportionality: US CCPs were much more integrated with the Single Market than any CCP regulated in Asia, serving a high number of EU banks and financial firms. Since the failure of a US CCP could severely impact EU financial stability, the conditions attached to equivalence decisions in favour of the US were different, and less favourable than the one established for Japan or Singapore, even if their regulatory regimes were largely equivalent.[40] The decision was also driven by the need of the EU Commission to defend the global competitiveness of EU CCPs. Since the US and the EU are hosting the most important markets for derivatives contracts, the two jurisdictions were actively competing to impose their financial standards in the global arena.[41] Therefore, transatlantic authorities were extremely

[36] EMIR (n 20) Art 25.

[37] The adoption of multiple equivalence decisions on the same day is not exceptional as the EU Commission usually works in 'batches', assessing multiple jurisdictions simultaneously in order to reduce the administrative costs of the process. European Commission, 'Implementing Decision No 2014/753 of 30 October 2014 on the equivalence of the regulatory framework of Singapore for central counterparties'; European Commission, 'Implementing Decision No 2014/752 of 30 October 2014 on the equivalence of the regulatory framework of Japan for central counterparties'.

[38] See the EU Commission press release which followed the informal agreement leading to the mutual recognition of regulatory and supervisory frameworks for CCPs between the EU and the US CCPs regulated by the CFTC: https://europa.eu/rapid/press-release_IP-16-281_en.htm.

[39] Eric Helleiner, Stefano Pagliari and Irene Spagna, *Governing the World's Biggest Market: The Politics of Derivatives Regulation after the 2008 Crisis* (Oxford University Press, 2018).

[40] This explanation was also provided by Olivier Guersent, Director General at DG FISMA of the EU Commission, at the conference 'Financial Regulation and Stability after Brexit', 21 November 2018, Brussels.

[41] For an analysis on the transatlantic turf battle on the regulation of derivatives markets, see Andrew Godwin, Ian Ramsay and Edwin Sayes, 'Assessing Financial Regulatory Coordination and Integration with Reference to OTC Derivatives Regulation' (2017) 12(1) *Capital Markets Law Journal* 36–65; Peter Knaack, 'Innovation and Deadlock in Global Financial Governance: Transatlantic Coordination Failure in OTC Derivatives Regulation' (2015) 22(6) *Review of International Political Economy* 1217.

reticent to open their financial markets to their main competitor, a stalemate that the EU Commission and the CFTC were able to overcome only after years of intense negotiations with a complex agreement for the regulation and supervision of cross-border clearing services.

Those past equivalence practices and the recent policy documents adopted by the EU allow us to hypothesise how the EU Commission will adapt the principles of proportionality and risk-prevention in view of Brexit. In order to be deemed equivalent, the UK will most probably have to closely follow the EU single rulebook, delivering a degree of regulatory convergence never required to any other third country. What are the reasons behind this 'super equivalent' approach adopted by the European Commission? Like every transnational mutual recognition regime, equivalence always entails a certain loss of regulatory and supervisory autonomy from the EU. Adopting an equivalence decision, the EU *de facto* delegates the regulation and supervision of financial firms operating in the Single Market to the home authorities where those entities are located.[42] Given the manageable number of financial entities that have so far benefitted from equivalence access, this 'delegation' has never compromised EU regulatory autonomy and the capacity of EU authorities to adopt rules for the Single Market.

In the Brexit context, however, capital market firms regulated and supervised in the UK ('the home country') would be allowed to provide services in the Single Market ('the host jurisdictions') under equivalence. Given the concentration of capital market activities in London, the EU would be exposed to the 'host's dilemma': it would mainly become a 'host' jurisdiction, being affected by intense market activities and market firms regulated and supervised in the 'home' jurisdiction, the UK. The EU would be unable to autonomously preserve financial stability within the Single Market, as an unhealthy amount of financial services and institutions of systemic relevance for the EU would be regulated and supervised in a third country, the UK, upon which it would have little jurisdictional control.[43]

Equivalence was never devised to accommodate market access and manage cross-border integration between the EU and a former Member State, moreover hosting the most developed and liquid capital market of the continent. Given the level of geographical proximity and financial interconnectedness between the EU and the UK, granting equivalence access without close regulatory alignment could compromise the EU regulatory autonomy and disrupt the level playing field within the Single Market. From the perspective of the EU, requiring the UK to adopt a 'super-equivalent' regulatory framework as a condition for market access responds to a clear stability and political rationale: preserving regulatory autonomy vis-à-vis UK authorities and regulatory control over its own financial system.

[42] An equivalence decision entails 'the transfer of regulatory authority from the host country- where a transaction takes place–to the home country–from which the firm originates', Nicolaidis and Shaffer (n 22) 264.

[43] Katharina Pistor, 'Host's Dilemma: Rethinking EU Banking Regulation in Light of the Global Crisis' (Columbia Law and Economics Working Papers, 2010) No 378.

V. The Role of the Commission in the Management of Equivalence Policies: The Case of Switzerland

The recent documents adopted by the Commission in view of Brexit have both an internal and external effect on the EU equivalence institutional framework. Externally, they attest to foreign jurisdictions and market actors the intention of the Commission to ensure for itself extensive discretionary powers, including the authority to use equivalence decisions as a political tool to obtain policy concessions in exchange for market access. Internally, they seek to reinforce the institutional role of the Commission within the EU equivalence governance. However, both those external and internal effects are deeply contested, primarily by the relevant third countries, against which the equivalence machine risks becoming excessively politicised, and secondarily by other EU actors, which are increasingly challenging the institutional prerogatives of the Commission and its monopoly over the equivalence procedure.

A clear case study of the opposition of third countries against the increasing politicisation of the equivalence regime can be exemplified by Switzerland, another jurisdiction economically and financially integrated with the EU but nevertheless seeking to escape the EU regulatory clout.[44] The relationship between the EU and Switzerland has been governed by a multitude of bilateral agreements, which have allowed the latter to enjoy a relatively stable market access to the EU without the need to dynamically incorporate the *acquis communautaire*. As a consequence, Switzerland has been able to partially 'pick and choose' EU law, avoiding the implementation of EU standards which proved politically unpalatable to Swiss voters, especially in relation to the rights of EU workers in Switzerland.[45] The EU has sought for a number of years to substitute this flux of bilateral treaties with a more comprehensive institutional and regulatory framework without much success. However, the Brexit vote has provided the Commission with the right incentive to both change the relationship with Switzerland, as the privileged

[44] Since 1992, when the Swiss people rejected the possibility of joining the EU through a public referendum, the relationship between the EU and Switzerland has been governed by a series of bilateral treaties based on international law. Although those agreements grant Switzerland a relatively stable access to EU markets, they do not impose the dynamic incorporation of the Acquis Communautaire in the Swiss jurisdiction. Despite the benefits originating from those bilateral treaties, Switzerland has often been able to 'pick and choose' EU law, refusing to incorporate into its jurisdiction EU standards not considered in line with Swiss interests. In a political context extremely remindful of Brexit, Switzerland has for example followed behind EU legislation governing the free movement of persons, especially the extensive interpretation of those norms provided by the Court of Justice. The EU has therefore demanded, as a requisite for market access, the adoption of a new 'institutional framework agreement' which would compel Switzerland to dynamically adapt its jurisdiction to EU standards. An overview of the bilateral agreements between the EU and Switzerland can be found at: www.eda.admin.ch/dea/en/home/bilaterale-abkommen/ueberblick.html.

[45] For a legal overview of the current relationship between the EU and Switzerland, see Christa Tobler, 'Internal Market beyond the EU: EEA and Switzerland' (2010) Briefing paper of the European Parliament think tank.

position of the Helvetic country may constitute a dangerous precedent during the Brexit negotiations, as well as to test the effectiveness of equivalence decisions as political tools.

MIFIR allows EU investment firms to systematically trade shares in foreign trading venues only when they are recognised by the EU Commission through an equivalence decision.[46] In December 2017, the Commission recognised the regulatory framework for trading venues of Switzerland as equivalent, but limited the validity of this equivalence decision to one year.[47] This was in stark contrast with other equivalence decisions adopted in favour of other third countries such as the USA, Hong Kong and Australia, whose trading venues were recognised without any time limitation.[48] In its equivalence decision, the Commission recognised that the regulatory and supervisory standards applicable to trading venues in Switzerland were largely equivalent to the one adopted by the EU, but nevertheless decided to adopt a time-bound equivalence determination to verify the process made by Switzerland towards 'the signature of an agreement establishing a common institutional framework'.[49] The Commission conditioned the renewal of the equivalence determination to a positive development of the political negotiations between the EU and Switzerland to replace the bundle of bilateral treaties currently governing their relationship with a single and comprehensive institutional framework.[50] As pointed out in a draft resolution of the European Parliament, this was the first time that the EU Commission decided to use equivalence in a 'political' manner to 'gain leverage in a separate policy matter'.[51] Indeed, the most striking element

[46] MIFIR (n 20) Art 23(1) requires investment firms to ensure that the trades they undertake in shares admitted to trading on regulated markets, or traded on trading venues should take place on regulated markets, multilateral trading facilities (MTFs) or systematic internalisers, or third-country trading venues assessed by the Commission as equivalent in accordance with MIFID II (n 20) Art 25(4)(a). See ESMA frequently asked questions dated 13 November 2017, www.esma.europa.eu/press-news/esma-news/esma-clarifies-trading-obligation-shares-under-mifid-ii. The EU equivalence regime to recognise the regulatory framework of third countries for foreign stock exchanges is established in Art 25(4)(a) of MIFID II.

[47] European Commission, 'Implementing Decision No 2017/2441 of 21 December 2017 on the equivalence of the legal and supervisory framework applicable to stock exchanges in Switzerland in accordance with Directive 2014/65/EU of the European Parliament and of the Council', Art 1.

[48] The equivalence decisions recognising as equivalent the trading venues of those jurisdictions can be found at: https://ec.europa.eu/info/sites/info/files/business_economy_euro/banking_and_finance/documents/mifid2-equivalence-decisions_en.pdf.

[49] European Commission, Implementing Decision (n 47) Recital 30.

[50] The action of the Commission was strongly supported by the European Council, see European Council, conclusions on EU relations with the Swiss Confederation, 19 February 2019: 'The Council emphasises that the conclusion of the Institutional Framework Agreement on the basis of the present text is a precondition for the EU for the conclusion of future agreements on Swiss participation in the EU's internal market and also an essential element for deciding upon further progress towards mutually beneficial market access. This will allow for a consolidation of the bilateral approach, in such a way as to ensure its sustainability and further development.' See www.consilium.europa.eu/en/press/press-releases/2019/02/19/council-conclusions-on-eu-relations-with-the-swiss-confederation/.

[51] See European Parliament, 'Draft EU Parliament Report on Relationships between the EU and Third Countries Concerning Financial Services Regulation and Supervision (2017/2253(INI)) Committee on

of the 'Swiss case' is that the EU Commission plainly used equivalence to obtain a policy objective that was not even strictly related to financial services regulation and supervision, but concerned more generally the political relationship between the EU and a third country.

The Swiss case constitutes an insightful example of the potential and limitations of equivalence as a convergence mechanism. Similarly to the UK, the financial sector plays an important role in the Swiss economy. Financial services are not extensively covered by any EU-Swiss bilateral treaty, save the exception of an agreement concerning non-life insurance services.[52] As a consequence, equivalence plays an important role for the Swiss financial sector. Without a positive equivalence determination, EU investment firms are not allowed to trade shares of Swiss companies in Swiss trading venues, where they are the most liquid, but only in EU or equivalent trading venues. In the long term, the lack of equivalence access could compromise the liquidity of equity shares of Swiss companies as well as having negative effects on the competitiveness of Swiss stock exchanges.[53]

The decision of the Commission to adopt a time-limited equivalence decision against Switzerland has yielded ambivalent results. On one hand, negotiating 'on the shadow of equivalence' has pressured the Swiss Government into concluding the institutional agreement in 2018, whose talks had begun in 2014.[54] However, the threat of withdrawing market access has not been sufficient to overcome the political resistance of the Swiss Parliament, which has refused to ratify the agreement and demanded a renegotiation of the deal. In response, the EU Commission has decided to not renew its equivalence decision for Swiss trade venues, promising

Economic and Monetary Affairs, 4 April 2018, para 12, where the rapporteur Brian Hayes proposed the following drafting: 'the EU Parliament notes that the Commission's decision of 21 December 2017 to grant equivalence to Swiss share trading venues – limited to a 12-month period with the possibility of an extension provided sufficient progress is made on a common institutional framework – was primarily political, and used to gain leverage in a separate policy matter; deplores the fact that Parliament had no input into this decision EU Parliament'. See www.europarl.europa.eu/doceo/document/ECON-PR-619408_EN.pdf?redirect. The final report approved by the Committee was more nuanced, simply recognising the 'political nature' of the equivalence decision, European Parliament, 'Report on Relationships between the EU and Third Countries Concerning Financial Services Regulation and Supervision' (2017/2253(INI)) Committee on Economic and Monetary Affairs, 18 July 2018, para 15, www.europarl.europa.eu/doceo/document/A-8-2018-0263_EN.pdf.

[52] Agreement between the European Economic Community and the Swiss Confederation on direct insurance other than life assurance [1991] OJ L205/0003 -0027.

[53] See Federal Department of Finance, 'Guidance to the Ordinance on the Recognition of Foreign Trading Venues for the Trading of Equities Securities of Companies with Registered Office in Switzerland', p 5 of the 'Absent the stock exchange equivalence, EU investment firms would, in principle, be disallowed from continuing trading shares in such companies with registered office in Switzerland on Swiss trading venues, and thereby on the entire Swiss stock exchange infrastructure as an essential element of the Swiss financial system'.

[54] For the legal and economic implications of 'negotiating at the shadow of equivalence, see Armour (n 9). For a precise timeline of the negotiations, see the page of the Swiss Government concerning Switzerland's European policy, and more specifically the Institutional agreement: www.fdfa.admin.ch/dea/en/home/verhandlungen-offene-themen/verhandlungen/institutionelles-abkommen.html.

to restore market access only after the ratification of the institutional agreement.[55] The Swiss saga thus shows the shortcomings of employing equivalence as a blunt weapon to influence third countries. The political approach to equivalence has caused a public outcry in Switzerland, where the decision of the Commission has been seen as a direct challenge to Swiss sovereignty. The Swiss Government has pondered whether to challenge the decision before the dispute settlement mechanism of the World Trade Organisation but finally decided otherwise, so as not to further exacerbate the political tensions between the two parties.[56] In a clear retaliation against the decision of the EU Commission, Switzerland has also modified its third country regime, conditioning the recognition of non-Swiss trading venues to the principle of reciprocity.[57] Swiss law now prevents Swiss investment firms from trading Swiss equity shares in trading venues regulated under EU law, in a tit-for-tat situation harming both sides.[58]

Resistance against the employment of equivalence as a political tool has also risen within the EU, in particular by the two co-legislators. The EU Parliament has protested the attempt of the Commission to manage equivalence policies without strict democratic oversight, claiming that the administrative procedure leading to equivalence decisions would lack parliamentary accountability.[59] From an EU institutional perspective, equivalence decisions are non-legislative acts adopted by the European Commission to implement the legislation in which each equivalence clause is encapsulated. Non-legislative acts can take the form of delegated (Art 290 TFEU) or implementing (Art 291 TFEU) acts, each following a different accountability procedure. Whereas the European Parliament has the power to veto ex ante or block ex post delegating acts, it cannot do the same when the Commission adopts implementing acts. Since the vast majority of equivalence regimes require the Commission to adopt equivalence determination in the form of implementing acts (Art 291 TFEU), the Parliament has no decision-making power in the management of equivalence policies. Representatives of the EU Parliament participate in

[55] See 'EU-Based Traders Caught in Swiss Equivalence Spat' *Financial Times*, 30 June 2019, quoting a Commission spokesperson 'At this stage we have no indication about any intention of our Swiss partners to make further progress and hence there is no justification to extend the current equivalence decision beyond 30 June' www.ft.com/content/41091f2c-9ad0-11e9-9c06-a4640c9feebb.,.

[56] There is an ongoing discussion concerning the compatibility of the EU equivalence regime and a differentiated treatment of third countries under equivalence policies and World Trade Organisation (WTO) rules. For an in depth analysis, see Andrew Lang, 'The Default Option? The WTO and Cross-Border Financial Services Trade after Brexit' in Kern Alexander and others (eds), *Brexit and Financial Services: Law and Policy* (Bloomsbury Publishing, 2018).

[57] Federal Council, Switzerland, Ordinance on the recognition of Foreign Trading Venues for the Trading of Equity Securities of Companies with Registered Office in Switzerland.

[58] Although the short-term market consequences of this tit-for-tat situation seems to be minimal, the effects on the long term remain difficult to quantify. See Michael Baltensperger, 'The Consequences of Switzerland's Lost Equivalence Status' (*Bruegel blogpost*, 25 July 2019), https://bruegel.org/2019/07/the-consequences-of-switzerlands-lost-equivalence-status/.

[59] European Parliament Report on Relationships (n 51) 12, the equivalence 'process for granting equivalence would benefit from more transparency towards the European Parliament'.

the Securities Regulatory Committee, the comitology-based organ responsible for approving equivalence decisions, but only as observers without voting rights.

With the political salience of equivalence increasing because of Brexit, the European Parliament is claiming a more decisive role in the ex ante and ex post control of equivalence policies. In a recent resolution, the Parliament has requested to be consulted in every phase of the equivalence process. It has also called for more transparency and predictability in the implementation of equivalence powers, encouraging the Commission to adopt 'guidelines regarding the recognition of third country regulatory frameworks'.[60] The Resolution goes as far as proposing a broad legislative reform of the current regime. Supported by ESMA, the Parliament has advocated the establishment of a 'structured, horizontal and practical' framework, a single piece of legislation governing equivalence access, which would replace the current patchwork of divergent procedures and requirements.[61]

However, the European Parliament is not the only institutional stakeholder contesting the monopoly so far enjoyed by the European Commission. National governments are also showing signs of increasing uneasiness against the tendency of the Commission to centralise equivalence policies. The greater the powers of the European Commission to manage equivalence at the supranational level, the less national authorities can control market access to their own jurisdiction. In force of the principle of conferral, EU equivalence regimes pre-empt Member States to adopt their own market access procedures.[62] When EU secondary law establishes a clause empowering the European Commission to manage EU-level access to the Single Market for third countries, national authorities cannot establish a similar framework at the national level, unless they are expressly allowed to do so by EU law. In principle, this loss of regulatory power is acceptable for EU Member States, as representatives of national governments have to give the green light to draft equivalence decisions and have therefore the power to control equivalence policies. However, those powers have so far not been sufficient to reign in the discretionary power and institutional activism of the European Commission.

[60] European Parliament Report on Relationships (n 51) 12.

[61] European Parliament Report on Relationships (n 51) 12. Steven Maijoor, the Chair of the ESMA, has made similar remarks. See, eg, Steven Maijoor, 'Review of the European Supervisory Authorities: Opportunities to ensure a safe and sound financial system', speech at the ALDE Seminar on the Review of the European Supervisory Authorities: 'The EU third country framework needs to be overhauled. First, there is no generic third country framework: it is a patchwork of arrangements varying across the various pieces of legislation. No arrangement is identical and they are mixtures of equivalence, endorsement, recognition, third country passporting or no arrangement at all. While some differentiation seems inevitable to respond to the different nature of various financial market activities, based on the experience of the past few years it would be beneficial to see greater consistency.'

[62] For a legal analysis on the relationship between EU (equivalence regimes) and National (national regimes) rules of market access for third country firms in the area of financial services, see Norton Rose Fulbright, 'Examining Regulatory Equivalence', Briefing Paper for the Financial Services Negotiation Forum, 12 January 2017.

Given the emergency situation created by Brexit and the technical nature of equivalence decisions, Member States are not in the driving seat when it comes to equivalence policies, but are rather forced to have a passive role in the implementation and management of equivalence. Eleven national governments sent a public letter to the Commission, complaining about the fact they were given only four working days to approve the politically heated equivalence decision recognising Swiss stock exchanges, signalling the political intention to exercise a stronger oversight on the discretion of the Commission in the future.[63]

VI. Limitations of the EU Equivalence Regime as a Convergence Mechanism

The Swiss case clearly shows how the current governance mechanics of the EU equivalence regime are still unfit for the purpose as envisaged by the EU Commission for this instrument, namely promoting regulatory and even political convergence towards EU standards and objectives. First, EU equivalence clauses lack consistency, in so far as every piece of EU secondary legislation establishes different regulatory and supervisory conditions according to which third country financial firms can access the Single Market through equivalence. For certain capital market actors, like UCITS funds (the most important investment fund vehicle for retail clients), or activities, like payment services, equivalence access is not even available.[64] This inconsistent patchwork of rules weakens the potential of equivalence to work as a convergence mechanism, as third countries will have no incentive to follow EU legislation in those financial sectors where equivalence access to the Single Market is not available.

Second, using equivalence as a convergence mechanism entails a problem of enforcement, namely how to ensure that regulatory alignment is preserved not only at the moment of assessing a third country regime, but also afterwards.[65]

[63] See email sent by the Finance Ministries of Latvia, Estonia, Hungary, Slovak Republic, Republic of Slovenia, Czech Republic, United Kingdom, Austria, Luxembourg, Netherlands and Germany to EU Commission, DG FISMA,

[64] However, equivalence is not the only legal avenue through which third countries' entities can provide financial services to the Single Market. For example, the UCIT Directive allows asset managers established in a third country to provide investment management functions to UCITs located in the EU through delegation (Art 13 of Directive 2009/65/EC of the European Parliament and of the Council of 13 July 2009 on the coordination of laws, regulations and administrative provisions relating to undertakings for collective investment in transferable securities, UCITS). Although legal rules governing outsourcing and delegation of functions to third countries are technically different to equivalence rules, they can *de facto* achieve similar effects. However, any market access technique different from equivalence, either provided by EU law or national legislation, falls outside the scope of the present chapter, which focuses exclusively on equivalence. For a general review of the financial services available under the EU equivalence regime, see J Deslandes and others, 'Third Country Equivalence in EU Banking and Financial Regulation' (European Parliament Think Tank In-Depth Analysis, 2019).

[65] Pierre-Hugues Verdier, 'Mutual Recognition in International Finance' (2011) 52 *Harvard International Law Journal* 55.

Ensuring post-equivalence regulatory alignment between the EU and relevant third countries has become a pressing concern since Brexit. At the moment of exiting the Union, the UK will be 'the most equivalent third country in the world', having 'on-shored' in its post-Brexit regulatory framework the entirety of the EU financial rulebook.[66] The problem of ensuring post-equivalence regulatory alignment may nevertheless arise in the medium and long term, when the UK may lower its financial standards in order to preserve its global market share and prevent the relocation of financial firms to the rest of the EU.[67] For the EU Commission it is thus extremely important to make sure that equivalence access is granted only in exchange for a dynamic regulatory alignment to EU standards, and even more so in the Brexit context.

The reform of the European supervisory authorities founding regulation, recently agreed between the EU Parliament and the Council, delegates to the ESMA the responsibility to 'monitor' the regulatory and supervisory framework of equivalent third countries, and inform the European Parliament, the Council and the Commission of the results on a confidential basis.[68] The new legislation is however silent on how the ex post monitoring of equivalent third countries should be carried out in practice by the ESMA and the Commission. This legislative void may cause tensions between the two institutions, as the ex post monitoring of equivalence policies raises many political issues. Monitoring regulatory and market developments in equivalent third countries constitutes a time and resource consuming activity, requiring familiarisation with a legal and financial system animated by different principles than the EU legal order.[69] Since the EU has adopted equivalence for more than 30 countries, the ESMA and the Commission will need to decide how to organise and prioritise their finite administrative resources in their monitoring efforts.

Moreover, the challenge of monitoring equivalence decisions will depend on the level of dynamic regulatory alignment required to third countries after the initial assessment. Until now, the European Commission has required third countries to internalise, or to show comparability in terms of outcome, to EU secondary legislation, and its tolerance to deviations has been quite high. Brexit may however lead the EU to change its stance, requiring convergence not only to binding standards, but rather to the entire EU single financial rulebook, including soft law

[66] The list of the financial services legislation that the UK is prepared to 'onshore' after Brexit can be found at www.gov.uk/government/collections/financial-services-legislation-under-the-eu-withdrawal-act.

[67] See the speech of Andrew Bailey, Chair of the Financial Conduct Authority, 'The Future of Financial Conduct Regulation', proposing to go back to 'principle-based' financial regulation and distancing the UK model from the 'rule-based' framework established under EU law. See www.fca.org.uk/news/speeches/future-financial-conduct-regulation

[68] On 21 March 2019, the European Parliament and the Council reached a political agreement on the text reforming the European supervisory authorities founding regulations. See https://europa.eu/rapid/press-release_IP-19-1655_en.htm?locale=en. A preliminary text can be found at http://www.europarl.europa.eu/doceo/document/TA-8-2019-0374_EN.html#title2.

[69] See Maijoor (n 61).

instruments adopted by the ESMA to ensure EU supervisory convergence and a common playing field within the Single Market.[70] Overall, despite the attempt of the EU to present the monitoring of equivalence as a technocratic activity, the ESMA and the Commission are called to carry out a difficult political exercise, as third country governments are not eager to have their regulatory regime checked and balanced by foreign authorities.[71]

Another limitation of equivalence as a governance mechanism is its inflexible and binary nature. Under the current equivalence framework, the only manner through which the EU can control the regulatory and supervisory behaviour of third countries is to withdraw, or threaten to withdraw, equivalence access. This may be a possible reaction when a foreign jurisdiction adopts a new regulatory framework inconsistent with EU financial standards, but it does not help the EU in case of less macroscopic deviations from the EU single rulebook.[72] Moreover, the EU will be able to influence the behaviour of third country authorities only if they believe that the EU can actually, as a decision of last resort, withdraw equivalence access for their financial sector. This 'nuclear option' must be perceived as credible by the relevant third country and its financial sector. The problem is that, when it comes to capital market services, this 'threat' often carries little credibility. When a financial firm has gained a stable market presence in the EU due to an equivalence decision, restraining its access to EU markets and clients can create cliff-edge risks for the EU as much as for the relevant third country.[73] This is especially the case for financial market infrastructures. Since they process a staggering amount of financial trades, they cannot suddenly be excluded from a financial system without causing operational, liquidity and legal risks to all the financial entities using them, regardless of the jurisdiction in which they are located.

UK CCPs constitute a clear example of the difficulty of withdrawing equivalence from a financial stability and market perspective, as forcing a sudden relocation of those financial market infrastructures would create instability in the Single Market

[70] For the co-existence of binding and non-binding standards within the EU financial rulebook and their importance to ensure a level playing field within the Single Market for financial services, see Stefano Cappiello, 'The Interplay between the EBA and the Banking Union' (EUI Working Paper RSCAS 2015/77, 2015).

[71] See, eg, the strong reaction of Christopher Giancarlo, the Chair of the CFTC, on the EU proposal to strengthen the EU equivalence regime for central counterparties. Christopher Giancarlo, 'CROSS-BORDER SWAPS REGULATION VERSION 2.0 A Risk-Based Approach with Deference to Comparable Non-U.S. Regulation' (White Paper, 2018), www.cftc.gov/sites/default/files/2018-10/Whitepaper_CBSR100118_0.pdf.

[72] For example, the supervisory authorities of equivalent third countries need to routinely cooperate with EU authorities and share information for the common supervision of cross-border firms and activities in a timely manner. Supervisory cooperation is included in equivalence policies through the adoption of Memorandum of Understandings. However, those soft law instruments cannot ensure coordination and cooperation between EU and third country authorities as they are a 'gentlemen's agreement' without binding effects on the signing parties.

[73] See International Swap and Derivatives Association (ISDA), 'Brexit – CCP Location and Legal Uncertainty' (August 2017).

and hinder the capacity of EU capital market firms to clear risky financial products as prescribed by EU Law. After a period of uncertainty, the EU Commission was reluctantly forced to temporarily and conditionally grant equivalence access for UK CCPs to the Single Market, as ejecting them from the Single Market would have damaged the EU as much as the UK.[74] The binary nature of equivalence decisions thus hinder their capacity to influence third country authorities and market actors, as the latter will often perceive the threat of withdrawal as a non-credible policy action. The self-granted discretionary power of the Commission to adopt 'time-bound' or conditioned equivalence decisions may lessen, but not eliminate the lack of flexibility of equivalence decisions. Equivalence is too blunt a convergence instrument, as it entails an 'all or nothing' approach, which is unfit for the purpose of shaping a complex financial relationship such as the one between the EU and neighbouring countries like the UK and Switzerland.

VII. Changing the EU Equivalence Regime in View of Brexit

Mindful of the aforementioned limitations of the current regime, the EU is reforming equivalence in order to enhance its convergence and extraterritorial effects. Brexit constitutes the main motive behind the reform of the equivalence engine, but those changes will also affect the financial relationship between the EU and other third countries, as the Swiss case abundantly testifies. The EU Commission is redesigning equivalence using both hard and soft law sources. On one hand it has successfully proposed EU legislators to review EU secondary legislation, strengthening equivalence rules for central counterparties and investment firms.[75] On the other, as we have seen, the Commission is reforming equivalence through soft law documents, such as the already mentioned working staff paper and the political communication, changing already established equivalence procedures and practices.

First, the EU Commission is seeking to embed EU equivalence policies in a more developed and transparent institutional framework. Currently, the administrative

[74] CCPs and central depositories were the only market actors towards which the EU granted equivalence in case of Brexit for a limited span of time, with the possibility of extension. See European Commission, Implementing Decision No 2018/2031 of December 2018 and European Commission, Implementing Decision No 2018/2030 of 19 December 2018.

[75] For the review of the equivalence regime for central counterparties, see European Commission, 'Capital Markets Union: Agreement on More Robust Supervision of Central Counterparties, Press Release (Brussels, 13 March 2019), https://europa.eu/rapid/press-release_IP-19-1657_en.htm, For the review of the equivalence regime for investment firms, see European Commission, 'Investment Firms: Presidency and Parliament Agree on a New Regulatory and Supervisory Framework', Press Release (Council of the EU, 26 February 2019), www.consilium.europa.eu/en/press/press-releases/2019/02/26/investment-firms-presidency-and-parliament-agree-on-a-new-regulatory-and-supervision-framework/.

process leading to equivalence decisions lacks transparency and does not give any administrative rights to the third countries involved, a situation which can create legitimacy and credibility concerns for the EU, especially if equivalence policies are bound to become fundamental in shaping its financial relationship with key financial partners such as the UK and Switzerland. Henceforth, the EU Commission aims at giving participatory rights to third countries seeking access to the Single Market, granting them the possibility to engage in regulatory and supervisory dialogue with the EU Commission before the adoption of an equivalence decision, as well as the right to be heard in case of withdrawal.[76] In the draft political declaration adopted in the Brexit context, for example, the EU committed itself to 'close and structured cooperation on regulatory and supervisory matters' with the UK, which should include 'transparency and appropriate consultation in the process of adoption, suspension and withdrawal of equivalence decisions, information exchange and consultation on regulatory initiatives and other issues of mutual interest'.

Presumably, similar to what the EU had proposed to the US during the Transatlantic Trade and Investment Partnership (TTIP) negotiations, the UK would acquire the right to be consulted every time the EU Commission presents a new legislative proposal, in order to have the necessary time to decide whether to dynamically adapt its regulatory framework to the new EU legislation, or lose market access. In addition, the 'right to be consulted' would grant the UK the possibility to give its opinion on new regulatory proposals adopted by the Commission, without however the right to participate in the internal EU decision-making process or any right to vote.[77] Similarly, the UK would be under the obligation to inform the EU on every modification to its regulatory framework, in order to put the Commission in the position to evaluate whether the modifications proposed by the UK could endanger equivalence access. Moreover, the UK would acquire the right to be notified of the EU's intention to suspend or withdraw an equivalence decision in its favour, with the duty of the EU to specify the reasons and granting the UK not only the right to answer, but also the possibility to change its regulatory and supervisory behaviour to retain market access. Although very Brexit-based, those administrative rights could be extended to other, interested third countries. Legally speaking, those 'tailored' adjustments of the equivalence regime would not need to be enshrined in EU secondary law, but they could form part of future trade agreements, or even established through a Memorandum of Understanding between the two parties. Those procedural obligations would not entail any binding commitment of the parties to recognise the regulatory framework of the other as equivalent. Equivalence would still constitute a unilateral mechanism, and both

[76] See European Commission Political Communication (n 19) and Council of the European Union, 'Political Declaration Setting out the Framework for the Future Relationship between the European Union and the United Kingdom (Brussels, 22 November 2018), www.consilium.europa.eu/media/37059/20181121-cover-political-declaration.pdf.

[77] Laura Puccio, 'TTIP and Regulation of Financial Markets: Regulatory Autonomy versus Fragmentation, In-Depth Analysis' (European Parliamentary Research Service, 15 June 2015) 25.

parties' 'right to regulate' would be preserved.[78] Nevertheless, they would enhance the transparency and legitimacy of EU equivalence policies, giving more participatory rights to the involved third countries, and it would create a platform through which the EU could continuously monitor regulatory developments in equivalent jurisdictions.

Second, the EU is attempting to make equivalence a more flexible governance instrument. In its current form, the manner in which the EU can leverage its market size through equivalence is rather limited, given the binary nature of equivalence decisions. The financial relationship between the EU and key financial partners like Switzerland and the UK is extremely complex, and its management requires the resolution of a multitude of regulatory and supervisory issues of a political and technocratic nature. In its current form, equivalence only allows the EU to demand regulatory or (as in the case of Switzerland) political concessions in exchange for market access. But it is a rather blunt instrument, which prevents the EU from taking an incremental and targeted approach to collective cooperative challenges. The common preservation of EU financial stability, a public common good which requires the cooperation of important key partners like the UK and Switzerland, cannot be achieved with a black-or-white instrument. It rather requires a 'panoply' of regulatory and supervisory tools. In addition, the 'all or nothing' nature of equivalence exposes the EU to political and legitimacy criticisms that may ultimately weaken, rather than strengthen, its relationship with third countries. As a consequence, the EU is modifying equivalence rules in order to give EU institutions a panoply of intermediate tools, besides the 'reversibility' option, to influence third countries seeking access to the Single Market.

The recent decision of the EU legislator to modify the equivalence regime of third countries' CCPs in EMIR constitutes an example of how equivalence can be transformed into a more flexible and adaptable governance instrument.[79] Under the current regime, CCPs regulated and supervised by third countries can provide clearing services in the Single Market only after a two-step process. First, the jurisdiction where they are located must become the recipient of an equivalence decision adopted by the European Commission. Second, CCPs established in equivalent countries must apply for recognition to the ESMA.[80] Despite this two-level procedure, the EMIR regime is extremely liberal, allowing

[78] For the 'prudential carve-out' or 'right to regulate', established under both WTO law and preferential trade agreements to preserve the right of jurisdictions to adopt prudential rules and more generally non-discriminatory financial standards without violating trade law obligations, see Carlo Cantore, *The Prudential Carve-Out* (Cambridge University Press, 2018).

[79] For a provisional text of the legislative review of EMIR (EMIR 2.2), recently agreed between the EU Parliament and the Council, see European Parliament legislative resolution of 18 April 2019 on the proposal for a regulation of the European Parliament and of the Council amending Regulation (EU) No 1095/2010 establishing a European Supervisory Authority (European Securities and Markets Authority) and amending Regulation (EU) No 648/2012 as regards the procedures and authorities involved for the authorisation of CCPs and requirements for the recognition of third-country CCPs (COM(2017)0331 – C8-0191/2017–2017/0136(COD)).

[80] The entire procedure is established under Art 25 EMIR.

third countries' CCPs to access EU markets, fully relying on their home country regulation and supervision.[81] Once the EU Commission has adopted an equivalence decision, ESMA has very limited legal powers to refuse the recognition of CCPs established in an equivalent jurisdiction. Moreover, EMIR does not give the ESMA any monitoring or enforcing mechanism to obtain data and information from recognised CCPs, nor has it any instrument to address potential systemic risks originating from those market infrastructures. This deferential approach is in stark contrast to the one applied by US authorities. The CFTC has, under the Dodd-Frank Act, extensive extraterritorial regulatory and supervisory powers vis-à-vis non-US CCPs registered to service US clients.[82]

Despite those shortcomings in terms of regulatory and supervisory control, the equivalence regime under EMIR has been by far the most employed in the area of capital markets. The Commission has recognised 15 third countries, whereas 32 CCPs established in those jurisdictions have been authorised by the ESMA to provide clearing services to EU clients. However, the ESMA has lamented the limited powers it has in the field of information collection and risk assessment. Instead of relying on foreign authorities, the ESMA has asked to be assigned sufficient supervisory powers to properly monitor the resilience of foreign CCPs providing clearing services in the Single Market under equivalence.[83]

The lack of regulatory and supervisory authority against third countries' CCPs operating in the Single Market is particularly troubling, as those market infrastructures have acquired systemic relevance after the global financial crisis, given the G20-mandated obligation to rely on them to clear a staggering number of derivatives contracts.[84] However, this weakness will be exacerbated after Brexit, as the most systemic CCP operating in the Single Market is located in the UK.[85]

[81] Maijoor (n 61), 'The EU is an *island* of third-country reliance in a world that has mostly opted for individual registration of CCPs that want to do cross-border business. Therefore, third country CCPs have benefited from the EU's system, while internationally active EU CCPs must be authorized and are subject to the supervision of third country regulators. This was not the intended result when designing the equivalence mechanism'. See also the White Paper issued by the then CFTC Commissioner Christopher Giancarlo (n 71).

[82] For the different approach of EU and US regulators on the supervision of cross-border CCPs, see also Edward Greene and Ilona Potiha, 'Issues in the Extraterritorial Application of Dodd-Frank's Derivatives and Clearing Rules, the Impact on Global Markets and the Inevitability of Cross-Border and US Domestic Coordination' (2013) *Capital Markets Law Journal*, Volume 8, Issue 4, 338–94, and Stuart Weinstein, 'Transatlantic Extraterritoriality and the Regulation of Derivatives: The Need for an Integrated Approach between Washington and Brussels, the Uncertainties of Brexit and new Directions in the US' (SWIFT Institute Working Paper No 2013-003).

[83] See Maijoor (n 61).

[84] Helleiner, Pagliari and Spagna (n 39), see Weinstein (n 82).

[85] Only LCH, the biggest CCP located in London, clears around one trillion of euro in financial contracts. Its resilience is therefore of systemic importance not only for the UK, where it is located, but also for the EU and the US. See Weinstein (n 82), and also the International Monetary Fund, Country Report No 16/156, United Kingdom: Financial Sector Assessment Program- Supervision and Systemic Risk Management of Financial Market Infrastructures, www.imf.org/en/Publications/CR/Issues/2016/12/31/United-Kingdom-Financial-Sector-Assessment-Program-Supervision-and-System ic-Risk-Management-43967.

The EU legislators have thus agreed to review the legal regime for equivalent CCPs (EMIR 2.2), in order to enhance the institutional capacity of the EU to control third country CCPs providing services in the Single Market.[86] The new legislative framework establishes fundamental changes in the recognition procedure that third country CCPs must follow in order to provide clearing services in the EU. The ESMA will in fact acquire the power to divide third country CCPs into two different categories, namely 'Tier 1' and 'Tier 2' CCPs. The tiering will be based on the systemic relevance of each CCP applying for recognition. Third country CCPs will be considered 'Tier 1' when considered to not pose a material threat to EU financial stability, and they will be allowed to operate in the EU under the regulation and supervision of their home country. However, the ESMA will have the power to classify CCPs having a systemic relevance for EU financial stability as 'Tier 2' CCPs. Falling under this category will have strong repercussion on the regulatory and supervisory treatment of those market actors, as they will have to comply with the EU financial rulebook (the requirements set out under EMIR for CCPs) when they service EU clients, as well as demonstrate compliance with the requirements imposed on them by the European Central Bank. Moreover, 'Tier 2' CCPs will be subject to the direct supervision of the ESMA, which will acquire enforcement powers to oversee their operations as a requirement to obtain recognition. Lastly, a CCP may be considered by the EU to be of such systemic importance as to impose its subsidiarisation in the EU to provide services in the Single Market, imposing a *de facto* relocation policy.

The EMIR 2.2 approach transforms EU equivalence from a binary and inflexible governance instrument, mainly based on the continuous threat of the EU to withdraw market access, into a variegated and diverse tool. It provides EU authorities' managing equivalence policies with a 'panoply' of different instruments through which the EU can interact with third countries. In addition to withdrawal, the EU can decide the extent and magnitude of regulatory and supervisory oversight over third country market actors, equipping itself with intermediate and incremental tools to influence the regulatory activities of equivalent jurisdictions. In order to be effective, it will require strong institutional coordination between all the EU authorities involved in the new legislative framework. The EU Commission – responsible for the adoption of jurisdiction-based equivalence decisions – will have to coordinate its equivalence policies with the ESMA and the European Central Bank – which have supervisory competences over individual third country CCPs. If properly managed, however, the new approach under EMIR 2.2 ensures a truly proportionate and risk-based employment of equivalence policies, allowing the EU to diversify its equivalence treatment to third country firms according to the stability risks they create in terms of EU financial stability.

[86] See n 79.

VIII. Conclusion

The present chapter has analysed the strengths and limitations of the EU equivalence regime as a convergence mechanism to drive foreign jurisdictions towards EU regulatory preferences in the area of capital markets regulation. As we have seen, the institutional, regulatory and supervisory features of the EU equivalence regime are currently being transformed by both hard law and soft law sources ignited by the EU Commission to strengthen its grip over equivalence policies in the Brexit context. However, as the Swiss case abundantly testifies, transformations to the EU equivalence regime will also affect the financial relationship between the EU and other jurisdictions. Those transformations are increasingly contested by both foreign authorities, which are directly affected by those changes, and EU institutional actors (EU Parliament, the ESMA, EU Member States) which would like to reign in the discretionary powers so far enjoyed by the EU Commission.

As a consequence of those internal and external contestations, the EU Commission is seeking to change its approach to equivalence, adopting a more proportionate and risk-based model. The reform of the equivalence process to recognise the regulatory and supervisory framework for CCPs, EMIR 2.2, constitutes the main example of this new equivalence paradigm. This reform equips the EU with a 'panoply' of tools to enhance the negotiating position of the EU vis-à-vis third countries, as well as empowering the ESMA to directly oversee systemic risks originating from equivalent jurisdictions. EMIR 2.2 seems a welcome change of paradigm compared to the inflexible nature of other third country clauses, as it enhances the capacity of equivalence to work as both a stability and convergence mechanism. Although it is certainly true that each market activity has its own specificity, requiring to a certain extent a differentiated and tailored equivalence approach, the flexibility and proportionality that the EU is trying to enshrine into the regulatory and supervisory treatment of third country CCPs under EMIR could be extended to other pieces of financial legislation. The 'tiering' of market actors according to their systemic relevance is particularly fitting for the supervision of cross-border CCPs, as those market infrastructures are limited in number, and only a very handful of them have a systemic importance for the EU. A similar, albeit simpler, model has already been adopted for the supervision of third country investment firms, whereas the ESMA has advocated a 'tiering system' for third country trading venues as well.[87]

Finally, Brexit and the departure of the main continental financial centre from the Single Market is bound to constitute a powerful determinant over the future

[87] For the review of the equivalence regime for investment firms, see European Commission, 'Investment Firms: Presidency and Parliament' Press Release (n 75). The ESMA Chair has advocated the adoption of a 'comprehensive regime for third country trading venues in view of Brexit', see Steven Maijoor, 'Mifid II Implementation – Achievements and Current Priorities', speech for the FESE Convention, Vienna 2018.

of the EU equivalence regime. If the EU seeks to lessen its financial dependency on London, then equivalence is likely to play a smaller role in the EU-UK's future relationship, and more generally in EU external relations policy in the area of financial services. National governments seeking to disentangle the Single Market from the City have so far opposed the hypothesis of harmonising the regulatory and supervisory features of equivalence clauses, as well as extending equivalence to financial activities currently uncovered by this legal mechanism.[88] If, however, London continues to play the part of the 'investment banker of Europe', then equivalence will need further legal reforms in the same direction as EMIR 2.2 in order to be an effective instrument of regulatory convergence.

[88] The French Government and French supervisory authorities, in particular, are considering Brexit as an opportunity to lessen the financial dependency of continental Europe on the City of London and finally develop a fully-fledged Capital Market Union. See, eg, the Chair of the AMF, the French securities regulator, Robert Ophele, 'La regulation financière à l'épreuve du Brexit', speech at the Club finance, HEC Paris, 20 February 2019: 'Le Brexit (perte du centre financier majeur et développement de multiples centres financiers dans l'UE) renforce la nécessité d'avoir une véritable Union des Marchés de Capitaux dans l'UE afin de ne pas dépendre de décisions prises en dehors de l'UE pour le placement de notre épargne financière ou pour le financement de nos entreprises; ce qui est tout particulièrement nécessaire en période de crise.'

16

'A Deep Trade Agenda': The Convergence of Trade and Fundamental Rights

ISABELLA MANCINI

I. Introduction

The study of the European Union (EU) in the global legal order implies a complex exercise from a methodological point of view. The EU is famously described as a *sui generis* entity, with at times competing objectives; not least a mutating actorness and status across disciplines and contexts. Attempts to order and make sense of this complexity prove even more challenging when studying the EU in its relations with the wider world. EU external trade is a case in point where different interests and objectives are likely to collide. In line with the theme of the book, this chapter wants to probe the usefulness of 'convergence' as a methodological device to study the EU as a global actor in external trade *and* fundamental rights. This chapter focuses on the EU's latest trade negotiations with other developed countries, which for their ambition have resulted in so-called 'deep' trade agreements. The specific methodological problem addressed here lies in the study of the concept of 'deep' in relation to fundamental rights. The central question of this chapter asks how convergence can help the exploration and understanding of 'deepness of fundamental rights' in the new generation of EU trade agreements. Unlike the literature on the EU as a normative actor, which sees trade agreements as vehicles to pursue a human rights policy externally, this chapter is interested in the methodology of exploring 'deepness' in terms of what would be necessary, in the context of trade agreements, for the safeguard of fundamental rights; which could be understood, more broadly, as convergence of two regimes, namely trade and fundamental rights. The chapter starts by outlining the methodological challenges of understanding and exploring the concept of deepness of fundamental rights in EU trade agreements. Next, it investigates the usefulness of 'convergence' as a methodological device for such enterprise. Finally, it applies the methodological framework of convergence to a specific case study, looking at convergence of trade and labour via treaty bodies and their actors. The chapter concludes that while convergence can justify the targeting of certain analytical elements as opposed to others, its usefulness remains limited for more normative explorations.

II. The Methodological Challenges of Understanding and Exploring 'Deepness of Fundamental Rights' in EU Trade Agreements

The concept of 'deepness' finds its origin in the context of international economic law and in the literature on economic integration. When speaking of 'deep' trade agreements, 'deepness' has been understood in several different ways: in economic terms, to refer to the extent of liberalisation in a wider array of issue-areas, as well as in legal terms, to refer to trade agreements dealing with issues that would add to or go beyond the framework of the World Trade Organisation (WTO).[1] 'Deepness' has also been employed to refer more broadly to the degree of integration sought via the trade agreement, thereby also involving explorations of institutional and legal mechanisms, created under the trade agreement with a view to integrating the market further.[2] A similar interpretation understands 'deep' as the extent to

[1] Some scholars have compared free trade agreements (FTAs) by looking at the number of these provisions in the trade agreements and their legal enforceability (Henrik Horn, Petros C Mavroidis and André Sapir, 'Beyond the WTO? An Anatomy of EU and US Preferential Trade Agreements' (Volume VII, Bruegel Blueprint Series, 2009); Claudia Hofmann, Alberto Osnago and Michele Ruta, 'Horizontal Depth: A New Database on the Content of Preferential Trade Agreements' (Policy Research Working Paper 7981, World Bank Group, 2017)). Other scholars have drawn from the notion of deepness developed by Downs et al and looked at the extent to which States liberalise trade and go beyond what they would have done in their absence (George W Downs, David M Rocke and Peter N Barsoom, 'Is the Good News about Compliance Good News about Cooperation?' (1996) 50 *International Organization* 379; Andreas Dür, Leonardo Baccini and Manfred Elsig, 'The Design of International Trade Agreements: Introducing a New Dataset' (2014) 9 *Review of International Organization* 353; Leonardo Baccini, Andreas Dür and Manfred Elsig, 'The Politics of Trade Agreement Design: Revisiting the Depth-Flexibility Nexus' (2015) 59 *International Studies Quarterly* 765). Some have also combined the interpretation employed in the market integration literature with the interpretation under international economic law: in such cases, deep trade agreements would be understood as those including provisions on both behind-the-border barriers to trade and an extensive range of (also non-trade) issues beyond WTO law (see Kim Soo Yeon, 'Deep Integration and Regional Trade Agreements' in Lisa Martin (ed), *The Oxford Handbook of the Political Economy of International Trade* (Oxford University Press, 2015)).

[2] World Trade Organisation, 'The WTO and Preferential Trade Agreements: From Co-existence to Coherence' (World Trade Report, 2011); Edward Best in Vincent Vicard, 'Trade, Conflicts, and Political Integration: Explaining the Heterogeneity of Regional Trade Agreements' (2012) 56 *European Economic Review* 54; Damian Raess, Andreas Dür and Dora Sari, 'Protecting Labor Rights in Preferential Trade Agreements: The Role of Trade Unions, Left Governments, and Skilled Labor' (2018) 13 *The Review of International Organizations* 143.

which trade agreements reach domestic policies,[3] for instance by dealing with procedural issues and behind-the-border measures.[4]

In the context of trade agreements negotiated by the EU, it is since the so-called 'new generation' that trade agreements have gained the label 'deep'.[5] With the adoption of the strategy 'Global Europe: Competing in the World', EU trade negotiations have sought deeper integration and marked the beginning of a new trade politics.[6] The aim of the strategy was further openness and integration, where the EU should have played a central role:[7] trade agreements were conceived as strategic vehicles to extend the EU's regulatory market to the outside and thus to globalise the EU's regulatory standards.[8] The strategy hence placed the EU at the forefront for driving and shaping globalisation.[9] Developed countries in North America and Asia were targeted as the ideal partners for more ambitious trade negotiations. Following what has been called a 'deep trade agenda',[10] the EU Commission started negotiating with such countries as the US, Canada, South Korea, Singapore and Japan. With the exception of the failed Transatlantic Trade and Investment Partnership, the resulting trade agreements are extremely ambitious. They are more complex in scope, as they include disciplines, and involve commitments, going significantly beyond WTO law; and they also create mechanisms for regulatory alignment and new institutions.[11] They can thus be said to reflect aims of 'deep integration'[12] according to the understandings outlined above. Up to now, however, research

[3] Robert Z Lawrence, *Regionalism, Multilateralism and Deeper Integration* (Brookings Institution, 1996); Finn Laursen and Christilla Roederer-Rynning, 'Introduction: The New EU FTAs as Contentious Market Regulation' (2017) 39 *Journal of European Integration* 763; Christopher SP Magee, 'New Measures of Trade Creation and Trade Diversion' (2008) 75 *Journal of International Economics* 349; Aaditya Mattoo, Alen Mulabdic and Michele Ruta, 'Trade Creation and Trade Diversion in Deep Agreements' (World Bank Policy Research Working Paper No 8206, 2017); Vincent Vicar observes that, by introducing an additional step of regional integration and reducing intraregional trade costs, 'more integrated arrangements provide for deeper trade integration'. See Vincent Vicard, 'On Trade Creation and Regional Trade Agreements: Does Depth Matter?' (2009) 145 *Review of World Economics* 167.

[4] Andreas Dür and Manfred Elsig, 'Introduction: The Purpose, Design, and Effects of Preferential Trade Agreements' in Andreas Dür and Manfred Elsig (eds), *Trade Cooperation: The Purpose, Design, and Effects of Preferential Trade Agreements* (Cambridge University Press, 2015) 7.

[5] See European Commission, 'Global Europe: Competing in the World' COM(2006) 567 (4 October 2006). Available at https://eur-lex.europa.eu/legal-content/EN/TXT/?uri=celex:52006DC0567.

[6] Alasdair R Young, 'Liberalizing Trade, not Exporting Rules: The Limits to Regulatory Co-ordination in the EU's "New Generation" Preferential Trade Agreements' (2015) 22 *Journal of European Public Policy* 1253.

[7] Euroepan Commission (n 5) 8.

[8] Marise Cremona, 'Expanding the Internal Market: An External Regulatory Policy for the EU?' in Bart Van Vooren and others, *The EU's Role in Global Governance: The Legal Dimension* (Oxford University Press, 2013).

[9] See European Commission, 'Reflection Paper on Harnessing Globalisation' COM(2017) 240 (10 May 2017). Available at https://ec.europa.eu/commission/publications/reflection-paper-harnessing-globalisation_en.

[10] Billy A Melo Araujo, *The EU Deep Trade Agenda: Law and Policy* (Oxford University Press, 2016).

[11] *Ibid* 22; Alasdair R Young, 'Not your Parents' Trade Politics: The Transatlantic Trade and Investment Partnership Negotiations' (2016) 23 *Review of International Political Economy* 345.

[12] Alasdair Young, 'The Politics of Deep Integration' (2018) 30 *Journal Cambridge Review of International Affairs* 453.

has tended to focus on the economic aspects of 'deepness', and there has been no discussion about what the concept would mean for fundamental rights in the context of trade agreements.

While trade agreements have been said to be *deepening* in so far as they seek further liberalisation and economic integration, the scope of this *deepening* has not been explored with respect to fundamental rights. So far, little is known about its understanding and meaning in relation to fundamental rights. There exists no exploration as to whether – and if so, how – fundamental rights have deepened along the deepening of trade, and what this would mean. The question then arises as to what 'deep' means for fundamental rights in the context of trade: in the new generation of EU 'deep' trade agreements, what would a deep agenda for fundamental rights in trade look like? How should we understand and explore the 'deepness' of fundamental rights? Asking these questions implies a transposition of a concept that has traditionally been employed with reference to economic integration, onto an understanding of that concept in relation to fundamental rights in the context of trade agreements. From a fundamental rights perspective, 'a deep trade agenda for fundamental rights' would be one that took into consideration fundamental rights across different new features and dimensions of these 'deep' trade agreements. The aim would be to ensure their protection, by preventing potential negative impacts on their enjoyment. From here, the next question could be: in so far as the EU's 'deep' trade agenda aims at further economic integration, what place and consideration are (and should be) given to fundamental rights in these trade agreements?[13]

Unlike the literature on the EU as a normative power, which would think of trade agreements as tools for the EU's promotion of human rights abroad,[14] the exploration of 'deepness' in relation to fundamental rights allows changing perspective: one that *also* looks inward, in the sense of being critical about how the trade agreements themselves, by deepening and becoming more complex and far-reaching, could become vehicles of downward pressures on the protection of fundamental rights. Such perspective would then also lead one to question what should be present, in the trade agreements, for the protection of fundamental rights. The EU has traditionally included human rights requirements as a sort of EU political messianism,[15] which considered human rights as exogenous features

[13] See similarly Araujo (n 10) 4.

[14] See for instance, Sophie Meunier and Kalypso Nicolaidis, 'The EU as a Trade Power' in Christopher Hill and Michael Smith, *International Relations and the European Union* (Oxford University Press, 2011) 276–77; Sophie Meunier and Kalypso Nicolaidis, 'The European Union as a Conflicted Trade Power' (2006) 13 *Journal of European Public Policy* 906; Ian Manners, 'Normative Power Europe Reconsidered' (2004) Paper presented at the CIDEL Workshop 'From Civilian to Military Power: The European Union at a Crossroads?'; Ian Manners, 'Normative Power Europe: A Contradiction in Terms?' (2002) 40 *Journal of Common Market Studies* 235; Karen E Smith, 'The End of Civilian Power EU: A Welcome Demise or Cause for Concern?' (2000) 35 *International Spectator* 11.

[15] Joseph HH Weiler, 'In the Face of Crisis: Input Legitimacy, Output Legitimacy and the Political Messianism of European Integration' (2012) *34 Journal of European Integration* 825.

of the trade agreement, and whose protection could nonetheless be promoted through trade. Conversely, some have argued that today 'fundamental rights' represent defensive interests of the EU as a result of deep trade relations with other developed countries.[16] In this sense, the language of 'fundamental rights' from an EU perspective, as opposed to 'human rights', allows one to go beyond an understanding of the linkage between trade and rights that looks at core human rights as a development issue or as a problem for the trade partner alone. The perspective suggested here instead brings one to consider the relevance of fundamental rights across new 'deep' features and mechanisms of EU trade agreements, and the potential impact of these features and mechanisms on the protection of fundamental rights.

Second, the fact that the EU's trade partners are economically developed countries also prompts more fresh explorations as to the understanding of fundamental rights in trade beyond core human rights: it enables one to embrace broader conceptualisation of linkages between trade and issues such as inequality and social protection, in a context of increasing '*globalised discontent*' with globalisation and free trade.[17] While international trade law and human rights have traditionally been kept separate, there seems to be a 'social question' emerging that calls for them to converge, and to understand their relevance and impact on one another.[18] And while there is no framework for human rights under WTO law, the EU Treaties have recently provided the EU with an important normative mandate to respect and safeguard fundamental rights in its external trade relations.[19] Unlike many other regional organisations and actors, the EU is a global actor in trade which is expected to respect and promote fundamental rights in its external relations. From here, broader questions then arise as to what kind of global actor the EU is in terms of trade: how can the EU be a global actor in trade *and* fundamental rights? Exploring the concept of 'deepness' in relation to fundamental rights – in the sense of trying to understand what should be present, in deeper trade agreements, for the protection of fundamental rights – can provide new perspectives on the role of the EU in global economic governance.

[16] Vincent Depaigne, 'Protecting Fundamental Rights in Trade Agreements between the EU and Third Countries' (2017) 42 *European Law Review* 562, 563.

[17] Joseph Stiglitz, 'The Globalization of Our Discontent' (*Project Syndicate*, 5 December 2017) available at www.project-syndicate.org/commentary/globalization-of-discontent-by-joseph-e--stiglitz-2017-12?barrier=accesspaylog. See also Frank J Garcia and Timothy Meyer, 'Restoring Trade's Social Contract' (2017) 116 *Michigan Law Review Online*.

[18] Anne Orford, Fifth Annual TMC Asser Lecture on November 28 at the Peace Palace in The Hague, see www.asser.nl/about-the-institute/asser-today/watch-the-full-annual-asser-lecture-by-prof-anne-orford/; see also Anne Orford, 'I Want to Put the Social Question Back on the Table' – An Interview with Anne Orford (*Opinio Juris*, 27 November 2019), available at https://opiniojuris.org/2019/11/27/i-want-to-put-the-social-question-back-on-the-table-an-interview-with-anne-orford/.

[19] A combined reading of Article 207 TFEU and Articles 3(5) and 21 TEU implies that, in its trade relations with third countries, the EU is obliged to observe and promote fundamental rights. See Vivian Kube, 'The European Union's External Human Rights Commitment: What is the Legal Value of Article 21 TEU?' (EUI Department of Law Research Paper No 2016/10, 2016) 10–13.

Reflecting upon what deepness could mean for fundamental rights raises a number of methodological challenges. The concept of 'deepness' has been employed in the realm of trade liberalisation and economic integration, but its meaning in terms of fundamental rights in the context of (deep) trade agreements has not been explored before. This also implies that there exists no real definition of it or conceptualisations providing guidance for its exploration. Even though the indeterminateness of the concept leaves room for such exploration, 'deepness of fundamental rights' is something that does not exist as such. And because this exploration involves transposing the concept of 'deepness' from its traditional understanding in economic terms to its understanding in relation to fundamental rights, trying to conceptualise and 'capture' it becomes methodologically challenging. This is even more so since fundamental rights typically represent an omission in trade agreements; and second, the deepening of trade occurs in a regime complex involving different actors, standards and levels of trade-law making (from the negotiation to the treaty itself, and its implementation), which complicate an organic analysis and clear targets and parameters for such exploration.

Asking 'how to explore and understand the deepness of fundamental rights' can indeed be understood as a methodological question per se, in the sense of how to go about this exploration and understanding: where the focus should be and what could be left out of the analysis. It is a task for the researcher to unfold deepness of fundamental rights methodologically, and in this sense, *develop* a methodological framework for its understanding. When asking 'how to explore and understand', 'exploring' is held here to relate to the search of the analytical elements of deepness. The challenge then would be how to design an analytical framework for its exploration; namely, to pinpoint elements where deepness is to be studied and contributing to the normative construction of the concept. The absence of operationalisations and analyses of what deep would mean in relation to fundamental rights inevitably poses a conceptual problem of how to frame it and break it down to analytical components for the purpose of its study. The challenge of developing an analytical framework has an impact on how we go about exploring deepness and where we seek it, from a methodological perspective.

Regarding the second element, 'understanding' is held here as pointing at the normativity of deepness, in the sense of how we should think about fundamental rights in trade agreements; how to conceptualise their linkage, and operationalise such linkage with a view to protect fundamental rights. As a result, even where the researcher was able to develop an analytical framework for the exploration of deepness, the challenge would still remain as to the normative stance: what should deepness ultimately mean and look like for fundamental rights? Is it possible to pinpoint cases of deepness? The researcher would have to construct such knowledge and develop a particular normative understanding or perspective. A conceptual challenge in depicting this normative understanding is whether 'deepness' means looking at whether fundamental rights permeate new deep dimensions of trade agreements (and in this sense, stick to the economic understanding of deep trade agreements and infusing in fundamental rights) or whether deepness of fundamental rights in trade means something that works for fundamental rights; or in fact, a combination of both. Possibly, the first understanding would be more closely related to the analytical dimension of deepness, while the latter to the broader normative stance.

III. Convergence as a Methodological Device

Having provided the methodological challenges of studying the concept of 'deepness' from a fundamental rights perspective, this section engages in an exploration of how 'convergence' could be useful as a methodological device for such enterprise. The turn to 'convergence' in relation to the study of the law is more recent and can be understood as a response to phenomena and literature on 'fragmentation'.[20] Particularly in the field of international law (IL), fragmentation has been described in its substantive, institutional and methodological manifestations: respectively, the mushrooming of sub-fields of IL; the proliferation of non-hierarchical courts and non-traditional actors beyond States; and the emergence of new types of norms besides established sources of IL.[21] Some have problematised it, studied its causes, discussed its potentials and categorised different types of it: from functional to geographical fragmentation; from institutional to ideational; not least fragmentation in law-making and fragmentation in law-application.[22] The focus has been on competing actors of law-making or competing objectives and sources of laws. However, focusing on divergences is perhaps a straightforward descriptive exercise, and with limited usefulness from a normative point of view.[23] Highlighting why, how, over what and towards what 'convergence' happens (and should happen) is possibly a more challenging and informative approach.[24]

[20] See Eyal Benvenisti and George W Downs, 'The Empire's New Clothes: Political Economy and the Fragmentation of International Law' (2007) 60 *Stanford Law Review* 595; John H Merryman, 'On the Convergence (and Divergence) of the Civil Law and the Common Law' (1981) 17 *Stanford Journal of International Law* 357; Jan Klabbers, 'Reluctant Grundnormen: Articles 31(3)(c) and 42 of the Vienna Convention on the Law of Treaties and the Fragmentation of International Law' in Matthew Craven, Malgosia Fitzmaurice Maria Vogiatzi (eds), *Time, History and International Law* (Brill, 2007); International Law Commission, 'Report of the Study Group of the International Law Commission, Fragmentation of International Law: Difficulties Arising from the Diversification and Expansion of International Law, UN Doc A/CN.4/L.682 (2006).

[21] See Jed Odermatt, 'Book Review' (2016) 14 *International Journal of Constitutional Law* 776; Anne Peters, 'The Refinement of International Law: From Fragmentation to Regime Interaction and Politicization' (2017) 15 *International Journal of Constitutional Law* 671; Anne van Aaken, 'Fragmentation of International Law: The Case of International Investment Law' (2008) 17 *Finnish Yearbook of International Law* 91; Eyal Benvenisti and George W Downs, *Between Fragmentation and Democracy: The Role of National and International Courts* (Cambridge University Press, 2017).

[22] Peters, *ibid.*

[23] See Elaine Fahey in the Introduction to this volume.

[24] *Ibid.*

Despite the predominant lexicon of fragmentation, some have pointed out how 'convergence' can be usefully employed as a framework 'for the analysis of [the] global'.[25] This framework would then act as a compass to help navigate through a sea of fragmentation and plurality, and capture spaces of convergence, beyond spaces of fragmentation. A lexicon of convergence, as opposed to divergence, can help identify patterns in 'shifts in the global legal order' against a context of global *dis*order.[26] It allows movement from a narrative of competition and disparity (eg competing legal orders and standards) to a more positive narrative of cooperation (eg rapprochement of law and practice). At the same time, adopting convergence 'as a methodological device' leads to a vicious cycle whereby the researcher is inevitably induced to look for convergence as a 'factual object' of research, which raises questions as to the added value of convergence as a methodological device.

It is argued here that a methodological framework of convergence contributes to the consideration of different aspects of convergence beyond its factual state of being: not only would it enable one to focus on agents, mechanisms and reasons for convergence, but it could also lead one to assess and weigh up factual states of convergence against possible alternative available options; from here, reflect upon normative directions of convergence in a context of global fragmentation; and perhaps even challenge and counter states and processes of convergence.[27] As a methodological device, convergence is understood as having the potential to raise such questions as: what is the object of convergence, ie what is converging? Why do we see convergence? Who and what explains convergence? Where do we see the descriptive and normative meeting points of convergence? Convergence can thus potentially provide new conceptual lenses through which to study *how* and *why* the law develops as it does in a globalised world,[28] not least the role of the EU therein.

The framework of 'convergence' can help us to answer the question of how we can methodologically understand and study the EU in the global legal order. As a methodological device, it allows to filter and focus on *patterns* in law and practice, and look at the role and place of the EU therein. Convergence can help capture the EU's legal reach in the world; situate legal orderings in relation to the EU; and in this sense, explore the extent to which the global legal order is shifting closer to the EU or vice versa. In this sense, it resonates with studies that have explored the global reach of EU law and the so-called 'Brussels effect'. More

[25] David Cox and Andrew O'Neil, 'The Unhappy Marriage between International Relations Theory and International Law' (2008) 20 *Global Change, Peace & Security* 201.

[26] Fahey (n 23).

[27] As convergence has been pointed out by some as not always being desirable, see Jürgen Kurtz, *The WTO and International Investment Law: Converging Systems* (Cambridge University Press, 2016).

[28] Rob van Gestel, Hans-W Micklitz and Miguel Poiares Maduro, 'Methodology in the New Legal World' (EUI Working Paper LAW, 2012/13).

broadly, convergence provides a frame to appreciate the EU's role and contribution as a participant in global legal orderings. What is interesting for this chapter is to look at the role of the EU in nudging convergence between two regimes, trade and fundamental rights, which at the international level have typically been kept separate.[29] Following this understanding, the investigation would focus on how the EU, via its bilateral trade agreements, embeds (or could embed) fundamental rights considerations in a way that trade agreements respect and safeguard the protection of fundamental rights. Such perspective would enhance our understanding of the EU's contribution to a more socially legitimate global economic order in a context of social backlash to globalisation and free trade.

While the EU is a global actor in trade, convergence can provide the conceptual framework to engage in an exploration of the EU as a global actor in trade *and* fundamental rights. It is posited here that this macro-level marriage of fundamental rights *and* trade would be indicative of the deepness of fundamental rights in trade agreements. As explained, while EU trade agreements have deepened and account for further economic integration, the fundamental rights dimension of this deepening has remained largely unexplored. The deepness of fundamental rights in the context of trade agreements could be equated with cases where certain features of deep trade agreements converged with fundamental rights. Convergence can possibly help to focus on mechanisms and spaces of trade agreements where convergence with fundamental rights would be possible. It can lead one to identify elements that either reflect a state of convergence, as could be objectives or provisions related to fundamental rights within the trade agreements; or it could also steer one towards the identification of processes and mechanisms that could have the potential to nudge convergence: for instance, the creation of joint-institutions and mechanisms for exchanges and dialogues between different actors; or commitments to cooperate on regulatory matters, not least parallel political agreements for cooperation on a wide range of matters, are held as examples of such elements. Convergence as a methodological device would thus direct attention to those places and mechanisms of convergence: from objectives and standards, to actors, institutional practices and regulatory cooperation activities, or the promotion of good governance principles and good regulatory practices. A frame of convergence allows one to focus on analytical elements that could trigger convergence of trade and fundamental rights or where convergence could potentially be found. The next section thus turns to the exploration of a case study, chosen because it consists of a space which could potentially nudge such convergence.

[29] See, eg, Robert Howse and Mutua Makau, 'Protecting Human Rights in a Global Economy: Challenges for the World Trade Organization' in Hugo Stokke and Anne Tostensen (eds), *Human Rights in Development Yearbook 1999/2000. The Millennium Edition* (Kluwer Law International, 2001).

IV. Case Study: Convergence of Trade and Labour via Treaty Bodies and their Actors

This section examines convergence of trade agreements and fundamental rights via new treaty bodies and their actors. The case study explored here is the joint Civil Society Forum created under the EU-Canada Comprehensive Economic and Trade Agreement (CETA),[30] which is taken as an instance where convergence between trade and labour rights could be nudged and promoted. The Forum represents an institutionalised mechanism for exchanges between, on the one hand, the EU Commission and Canadian government officials, and on the other hand, civil society representatives of both Parties[31] and the so-called Domestic Advisory Groups (DAGs). Whilst under CETA it is the Parties that are in charge of reviewing, monitoring and assessing the impact on sustainable development as a result of the implementation of CETA,[32] the Forum provides an additional platform for dialogue and exchanges on the sustainable development aspects of CETA, together with a plethora of other actors beyond the Parties themselves.

In addition to civil society actors, the DAGs are newly-created entities that take part in the Forum. Composed of economic, social and environmental stakeholders,[33] the DAGs have been envisaged by the new generation of EU free trade agreements (FTAs) to involve civil society, particularly during the implementation phase of the chapters on trade and sustainable development. The DAGs are bodies that the Parties can consult to seek views and advice on labour and environmental issues in relation to trade.[34] On their own initiative they may also 'submit opinions and make recommendations'.[35] Furthermore, since the public can send submissions to the Parties on labour matters, the Parties are expected to inform the DAGs when this occurs.[36] It follows that, while being bodies of trade agreements, the DAGs can be also understood as hubs of information and expertise on a series of matters related to both trade *and* labour. Their involvement in the Civil

[30] Comprehensive Economic and Trade Agreement (CETA) between Canada, of the one part, and the European Union and its Member States of the other part [2017] OJ L11, Art 22.5.

[31] 'Representative employers, unions, labour and business organisations, environmental groups, as well as other relevant civil society organisations as appropriate', see Article 22.5(2) CETA, *ibid.*

[32] Article 22.3(3) CETA (n 30).

[33] See European Economic and Social Committee, 'The EU-Canada Domestic Advisory Group' available at www.eesc.europa.eu/en/sections-other-bodies/other/eu-canada-domestic-advisory-group. For specific members, see www.eesc.europa.eu/en/sections-other-bodies/other/eu-canada-domestic-advisory-group/organisation.

[34] Article 23.8(4) CETA (n 30). See also Article 24.13(5) CETA generally providing for the establishment of advisory groups. In the context of CETA, the EU has created one DAG, for both labour and environmental matters, while Canada has taken a different approach, and created two separate ones.

[35] *Ibid.* The DAGs can also 'submit observations' to the Committee on Trade and Sustainable Development when monitoring the follow-up and recommendations of the Panel of Experts, see Article 23.10(12) CETA (n 30).

[36] Article 23.8(5) CETA (n 30).

Society Forum means that they are enabled to bring their knowledge and views on the implementation of the CETA to the table, and in this sense, potentially contribute to discussions on trade converge with considerations relating to labour rights.

As a whole, the Civil Society Forum has the role of enabling a dialogue on the sustainable development aspects of CETA,[37] reflecting a purpose for its creation that presupposes discussions on linkages between trade and labour issues. The Forum represents an important interlocutor of the main Committee that deals with trade and sustainable development (TSD), and which also monitors the implementation of the relevant provisions: the TSD Committee has to update the Forum on any matter related to the chapter on trade and labour, present the Forum's views directly to the Parties and report annually on the follow-up to those communications.[38] The meetings of the Civil Society Forum are followed by, and are intended to inform, the meetings of the Committee on TSD and the representatives of the Parties the following day. The Civil Society Forum also has a role in the consultation process for matters arising under the chapter on trade and labour: it can 'submit observations' to the TSD Committee when monitoring the follow-up and recommendations of the Panel of Experts.[39] The second and latest meeting of the Civil Society Forum under CETA took place in November 2019.[40] It has witnessed participation of a wide array of actors and enabled exchanges with EU officials and the representatives of the Government of Canada, with sessions on the review of the TSD chapters, as well as 'any other' TSD issue worthy of discussion.[41] The Forum could thus represent a platform to bring the relevance of fundamental rights into trade discourses.

On the other hand, it is probably too early to judge the role of the joint Civil Society Forum to the convergence of trade and labour rights, in the sense of enabling discussions on their mutual impact and linkages – discussions that could be taken into consideration not only in the context of the implementation of CETA, but also in future trade law-making endeavours. At the same time, it could be expected that exchanges between civil society actors, also across constituencies, can expose different perspectives on matters related to labour rights and trade. On this, liberal theories of civil society would emphasise the possibility for diffuse interests to find in the Forum an arena for their expression and discussion.[42] The Civil Society Forum could work as a 'transmission belt' between citizens and global

[37] Article 22.5(1) CETA (n 30).

[38] Article 22.4 CETA (n 30).

[39] Article 23.10(12) CETA (n 30).

[40] See European Commission, 'EU-Canada (CETA) Civil Society Forum' at https://trade.ec.europa.eu/doclib/events/index.cfm?id=2063.

[41] *Ibid.*

[42] Francesca Bignami, 'Theories of Civil Society and Global Administrative Law: The Case of the World Bank and International Development' in Sabino Cassese (ed), *Research Handbook on Global Administrative Law* (Edward Elgar, 2016) 327.

governance arrangements,[43] through which citizens could find an outlet for their interests and thereby a possibility to influence the decisions of global governance bodies in a way that takes into consideration fundamental rights concerns.[44]

In a context where global governance is often the object of criticism for lacking social legitimacy, a large body of literature has focused on the intermediary function of civil society actors between the local and the global.[45] This would be particularly relevant for local understandings of fundamental rights; for targeting and addressing specific fundamental rights problems in a particular societal, geographical and cultural context, so that fundamental rights could be effectively implemented and applied to local circumstances.[46] If standards were discussed and eventually set in the global fora, civil society actors could act as translators of concepts adopted globally into local terms.[47] Furthermore, it has been observed how civil society actors can have on-the-ground and contextualised knowledge to review certain policies, making them good candidates for continuous monitoring and feedback:[48] not only could they shed light on the main shortcomings, they could also advance solutions and provide perspectives that would otherwise be lacking in official circles.[49] It remains to be seen whether their involvement in the Civil Society Forum can indeed provide such new perspectives, for trade and labour to concomitantly join a common agenda. The framework of convergence is still arguably limited in understanding the means through which this could be achieved.

It is posited here that the lenses of convergence remain short-sighted in understanding the ways in which the Civil Society Forum could be designed in order to truly enhance discourses of labour rights in the context of trade agreements. As a methodological device, convergence can lead one to focus and dig deeper into analytical dimensions where trade and labour could meet, as part of a broader search of convergence of regimes. However, from a normative perspective, convergence would not help with designing the functioning of such process to achieve convergence, in the sense of providing guidance on what such a process should look like in order for trade and labour to convergence. Hence, it would not provide

[43] Jens Steffek and Patrizia Nanz, 'Emergent Patterns of Civil Society Participation in Global and European Governance' in Jens Steffek, Claudia Kissling, and Patrizia Nanz (eds), *Civil Society Participation in European and Global Governance: A Cure for the Democratic Deficit?* (Palgrave Macmillan, 2007).

[44] Robert O'Brien and others (eds), *Contesting Global Governance: Multilateral Economic Institutions and Global Social Movements* (Cambridge University Press, 2000).

[45] See, eg, Steffek and Nanz (n 43); Koen De Feyter, Stephan Parmentier, Christiane Timmerman and George Ulrich (eds), *The Local Relevance of Human Rights* (Cambridge University Press, 2011).

[46] De Feyter, *ibid*.

[47] Sally Engle Merry, 'Transnational Human Rights and Local Activism: Mapping the Middle' in René Provost and Colleen Sheppard (eds), *Dialogues on Human Rights and Legal Pluralism* (Springer, 2012).

[48] Gráinne De Búrca, Robert O Keohane and Charles Sabel, 'Global Experimentalist Governance' (2014) 44 *British Journal of Political Science* 477, 478.

[49] Jan Aart Scholte, 'Civil Society and Democratically Accountable Global Governance' (2004) 39 *Government and Opposition* 211.

a normative picture of deepness of fundamental rights in the analytical dimension of 'actors'. Methodologically, convergence would only point at those *processes* that could nudge convergence. This same limitation would still hold true for analyses of *factual* cases of convergence of trade agreements and labour, such as specific *standards* for labour rights included in trade agreements: in this instance, a methodological framework of convergence would not be helpful in terms of indicating what the relevant standard for labour rights should be (for instance, European Union standards as opposed to international standards); or whether having labour standards in trade agreements equates with 'deepness' of fundamental rights, in the sense of ensuring that the trade agreement in its entirety does not undermine or exacerbate downward pressure on the enjoyment of labour rights.

V. Conclusion

As a methodological device, convergence is posited to prove useful from an analytical and descriptive perspective, yet it emerges that it is arguably less so for the development of a normative perspective, which in this case would consist of a meta-level normative understanding of what convergence of trade and fundamental rights would look like, or what it should imply. Applied to the study of 'deepness' of fundamental rights in the context of 'deep' trade agreements, convergence will only help to pinpoint elements that can nudge convergence of trade and fundamental rights regimes via specific spaces and dimensions of this new generation of EU trade agreements. Convergence can certainly help to *explore* deepness: it provides a roadmap to navigate across actors and objects of EU trade, seeking meeting points of deepening trade and fundamental rights therein; it justifies the targeting of certain analytical elements as opposed to others, namely elements that account for a meeting point, a coming together of two objects. Yet where the meeting point does not necessarily represent the normative meeting point; where it lies is independent from the justification and elements that were used for exploring it. In other words, convergence as a methodological device can provide the framework to guide the researcher in selecting elements for analysing phenomena underpinned by a narrative of convergence, yet it remains for the researcher to develop a normative understanding of the object of observation.

INDEX

www.ingramcontent.com/pod-product-compliance
Ingram Content Group UK Ltd.
Pitfield, Milton Keynes, MK11 3LW, UK
UKHW020239290926
15470UKWH00002B/622